The Civilization of the American Indian Series

THE IOWAY INDIANS

THE IOWAY INDIANS

BY MARTHA ROYCE BLAINE

University of Oklahoma Press: Norman

By Martha Royce Blaine

The Pawnees: A Critical Bibliography (Bloomington, Indiana
    University Press, forthcoming)
The Ioway Indians (Norman, 1979)

Blaine, Martha Royce, 1923-
    The Ioway Indians.

(The Civilization of the American Indian series; 151)
Bibliography: p.
Includes index.
1. Iowa Indians. I. Title. II. Series.
E99.I6B52   970'.004'97   78-21385

*To the Ioway People
and to Morris Siegel*

Contents

Illustrations

Maps

Acknowledgments

T HERE IS A LONG, long path, reaching back many centuries, made by those who wrote by their lives the words of this book. Some, but not many, are here now. Others lie at rest near the Upper Iowa, the Chariton, the Grand, the Des Moines, the Little Platte, the Great Nemaha, and the Deep Fork rivers.

One for whom I have had the greatest admiration and respect is Blaine N. Kent, who spent hours in talking and singing about his people's past. My regret is that he did not live to see the results of his contributions to this book. I thank, too, other Ioways in Oklahoma who accepted me. Thoughts turn also to summer days spent in Kansas and Nebraska when the great-great-granddaughter of the first known White Cloud took me over country roads near the Great Nemaha River to the gray frame shell of her grandfather's allotment house and told me of the problems of the few Ioways who know the past. I remember with sadness, for times do not change much for many peoples.

Many others assisted me greatly in producing this book, and I express my gratitude to the Oklahoma State University Education and Research Foundation for funding three years' research efforts; Mildred Mott Wedel; Dr. Angie Debo; Dr. James Brown; Dr. Robert Hall; Dr. Robert Ritzenthaler; Nicolas Conover English; Mrs. Winona Wettengel; and the staffs of the Federal Records Center in Kansas City, the National Archives, the Public Museum of the City and County of Milwaukee, the Illinois Historical Society, and the Missouri Historical Society for the kindnesses and assistance they gave me.

To Rella Looney, former Indian Archivist of the Oklahoma Historical Society, a special word is due. She helped me, as she has helped so many others over the years, to bring an idea to flower. Her great

knowledge of the history of the numerous Indian peoples now residing in Oklahoma and her patience in leading the unknowing tactfully
to their goals were encouraging. Many books and articles on American
Indians would never have been written without her unfailing interest
and assistance.

A special debt is due Mildred Mott Wedel, who can never be repaid
for her inspiration, advice, and assistance. Her translations of French
passages from archival as well as published sources have added
information to this volume which would have been omitted otherwise and which is essential to understanding eighteenth-century
Ioway history.

THE IOWAY INDIANS

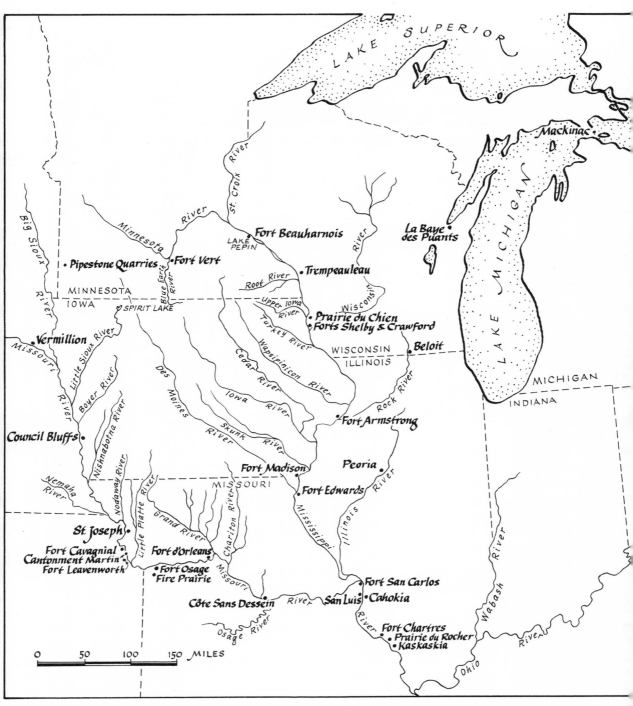

Map 1. A map of the original Ioway homeland showing French, Spanish, and early American locations of the seventeenth, eighteenth, and nineteenth centuries.

Prologue:
The Old People Say

THE OLD PEOPLE SAY that our first home was *Mokashudje,* the place of the Red Earth or the Red Hill. It was to the east, a long way off just below where the sun rises. Here was a village that we made and surrounded with palisades. Some say that our home was on the shore of a great water, perhaps Green Bay. Others say there was an island in a large body of water, and from it all the tribes came swimming or in skin canoes, and the Ioway came too.[1]

Others told that our first home was far to the northeast, and that we came down around the Great Lakes and were one tribe with the Winnebagos. The time came when the Winnebagos, our Fathers, wished to stay by the great water to fish, but we went towards the southwest until we came to a river, the Mississippi with its sandbars where we camped. The wind blew fine sand over us, then others seeing us called us Pa-ho-ja, which some say means Dusty Noses.[2] Some say this river may have been the Missouri and not the Mississippi.

Our brothers, the Otoes, say we are called Ba-ho-ja because, when once they saw us, it was winter and our dwellings were gray with fire-smoked snow, and that our name thus means "gray snow covered." We have called ourselves Pa-ho-dje, which we say means "gray snow," and Ioway, now, which is from the name that the French called us. This name they heard from Algonkian-speaking people such as the people in present-day Illinois and Wisconsin. This name has to do with bone marrow, some say.*[3]

Paxoche (normalized phonetic spelling) is the name by which the Ioways identified themselves when they first met the Europeans. Variants of this appear in different source documents in subsequent years. Translation for the term varies. The Ioway missionaries William Hamilton and Samuel Irvin said the term meant

Another one of our old people said, in about 1850, that long before then we lived on a river which runs from a lake to the Mississippi from the west, on the east side of the great river, and that we lived there a long time. According to our grandfather this would be before 1700. This is the time when we say we first saw white men on the lakes and got guns, axes, kettles, and blankets.[4] Watchemonie in 1840 said that he was the tenth generation to learn about the Winnebagoes being our fathers and living on a great lake.[5]

It is also said that at one time we traveled over two beautiful mountains. This would be on the Chattanooga Lookout Mountain mocassin trail on the Tennessee River. When we heard some of the Cherokee songs in Indian Territory we found them like some of our songs, some words we knew. The Ioways have traveled much since the beginning.[6]

The Dakotas have a tradition saying that, when they first saw the Ioways, they were living near the Falls of St. Anthony on the Minnesota River.[7] A Ponca legend says at one time the Poncas, Omahas, and Ioways were together near the mouth of the White River in South Dakota. Later the tribes descended the Missouri River to the mouth of the Niobrara. Here they separated, and the Ioways went to the vicinity of Dixon County in Nebraska for awhile.[8]

In 1848 Grandfather Wawnonqueskoona was asked to draw a map of the Ioway homes as far back as the tribe could remember. Later, the map was redrawn fitting it to known rivers and other landmarks. The earliest numbered site is on the east side of the Mississippi River near the Rock River area in Illinois, perhaps the place where the Otoe claim they saw the gray, snow-covered dwellings of the Ioway in winter. (See Map 2).[9]

"dusty noses" in their *Grammar, illustrating the Principles of the Language used by the Ioway, Otoe, and Missouri Indians* (Iowa and Sac Mission Press, 1848). Stephen H. Long in his 1819-1820 journey recorded that the Ioway name meant "gray snow." In 1926 Alanson Skinner was told that their name meant "snow-covered." Other translations are known. Mildred Mott Wedel discusses and analyses the various names in "A Synonomy of Names for the Ioway Indians," *Journal of the Iowa Archeological Society*, Vol. 25 (1978), 49-77.

Map 2. Original map drawn by Wawnonqueskoona, an Ioway, in the 1840's for missionaries Irvin and Hamilton and redrawn by Capt. S. Eastman, United States Army. Ioway villages are indicated by small groups of tipis. Some eighteenth-century village sites that were beyond memory in Wawnonqueskoona's time are not shown. The numbers indicate the sites described in H. R. Schoolcraft, *Information Respecting the History, Condition and Prospects of the Indian Tribes of the United States*, Vol. 3 (1853), 361.

4

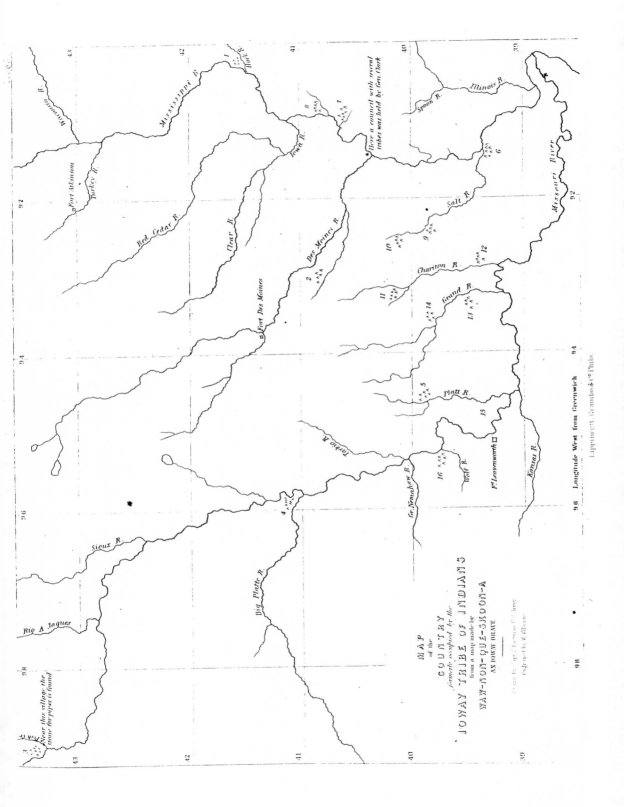

MAP
of the
COUNTRY
formerly occupied by the
IOWAY TRIBE OF INDIANS
from a map made by
WAW-NON-QUE-SKOON-A
AN IOWAY BRAVE

Lippincott, Grambo & Co. Phila

Longitude West from Greenwich

Missouri R.
Raccoon R.
Fort Atkinson
Turkey R.
Red Cedar R.
Clear R.
Mississippi R.
Rock R.
Iowa R.
Des Moines R.
Fort Des Moines
Here a council with several tribes was held by Gen. Clark
Spoon R.
Illinois R.
Salt R.
Missouri River
Chariton R.
Grand R.
Platt R.
Nishna R.
Gr. Nemahaw R.
Wolf R.
Ft. Leavenworth
Kansas R.
Big Platte R.
Sioux R.
Rio A Jaquer
Near this village the stone for pipes is found

1. The Early Ioways of Iowa

OUT WHERE THE TALL CORN GROWS...." is an old refrain from a popular song about Iowa and could well have referred to that area for the last ten centuries. During that time its prehistoric horticultural people would have included the Ayouais — the Ioways — after which the state was named.

Archaeologists had long thought that Ioway Indians had inhabited the state at some time in the past; in the 1920's and 1930's the earliest times were suggested by a series of discoveries in northeastern Iowa by Ellison Orr and Charles R. Keyes. Careful research by Mildred Mott also indicated that certain areas inhabited by people called Ioways by early European explorers and map makers lay within archaeological site areas in northeastern Iowa and adjacent localities.[1]

These people lived in small communities on bluffs along rivers and used the river terraces for growing corn, beans, and squashes. Their dead were interred in cemeteries or in nearby mounds constructed by earlier residents. They were part of a group of tribes or communities that participated in the development of what archaeologists call the Oneota culture, after an Indian name for the Upper Iowa River.[2]

It is generally agreed that the Oneota people, including the protohistoric Ioways, lived in culturally similar communities scattered over a contiguous area in the Mississippi and Missouri river valleys and including the present states of Iowa, Wisconsin, Minnesota, Missouri, Kansas, and Nebraska. All these village communities shared similar material traits and cultural behavior in terms of subsistence patterns and, perhaps, religious activities and kinship types.

Among their present descendants are the Ioway, Otoe,* Missouri, Winnebago, Osage, Kansas, and Quapaw Indians.

Allamakee and Winneshiek Counties are in the extreme northeastern corner of Iowa. Here what are very possibly the earliest known Ioway village sites may be found. Mildred Mott Wedel described the area:

> The Upper Iowa River meanders . . . in successive oxbows through an extremely fertile flat valley bottom from which steep bluffs rise two hundred and fifty to four hundred feet high on either side. . . . . In the oxbows are broad terraces lying sixty to seventy feet above the flood plains that were originally clothed with a lush prairie flora.
>
> In the environment of the Upper Iowa River the Indians found tempting village sites. Nearby were the deep fertile flood plains for gardens. The river itself provided mollusks, turtles, and fish, including channel catfish, bass, pike, perch, sunfish, buffalo fish and crappies.
>
> The hills for some distance back from the river, particularly on their south slopes, were well forested with burr oak, sugar maple, basswood, box elder, elm, ash, and poplar, as well as trees and shrubs bearing edible nuts including hickory of several varieties, hazelnut, butternut, and walnut. Some red cedar (juniper) and balsam fir could be easily found as well as stands of white pine. Wild fruits were abundant; plums, blackberries, raspberries, wild cherries, and crab apples. The woods sheltered the white-tailed deer, black bear, raccoon, porcupine, woodchuck, wolf, rabbit, squirrel, wild turkey, and ruffled grouse. On the higher divides away from the streams where the forest dwindled to prairie were elk, sometimes bison, and prairie chicken.[3]

For approximately fifty miles up the Upper Iowa River there was evidence of what is called Oneota culture, Orr Focus occupation.†

---

* The tribal spelling Otoe is used in this book, because it is the way that present-day Otoes spell it; much of the nineteenth-century government correspondence, as well as various writers, including Berlin B. Chapman (*The Otoes and Missourias,* 1965), used this spelling. It is in current use in other than certain scholarly writings, which prefer Oto. Although Sauk is now considered more correct historically and linguistically, both Sac and Sauk appear throughout this text according to their appearance in quotations and references. In the case of Sioux, modern usage prefers Dakota for the people or tribal name, and the former for language-classification usage. Both forms used as the tribal designation will appear in this text, particularly because Sioux was used for both tribe and language in older sources.

† The term *Orr Focus* is used by Mildred Mott Wedel and this book to indicate the body of archaeological material presently considered to be the cultural remains of the Ioways. This includes the Orr Focus components on the Upper Iowa River and its tributaries and on Riceford Creek, tributary of the Root River in southeastern Minnesota, and the Orr Focus components on the upper Little Sioux River in western Iowa (M. M. Wedel, personal communication, March 1, 1976).

Dale Henning uses the term *Orr Phase* to indicate the type sites along the Upper Iowa River. He also used the term for sites in nearby Houston and Fillmore Counties in southeastern Minnesota. These include the sites referred to by Wedel as Orr Focus on the Riceford Creek. He mentions the McKinney site, near Toolesboro in

The Oneota culture was not the only one present at the different village sites. Sometimes its artifacts were superimposed on earlier Woodland remains. The Oneota occupations date as late as the European contact in the late 1600's and early 1700's, but the earliest dates have not yet been determined.*

---

southeastern Iowa, as Orr Phase with some artifacts similar to those found along the Upper Iowa River. The Midway Village site in La Crosse County, Wisconsin, holds Orr Phase ceramic material, but Wedel is not certain of the identity of these prehistoric people or how they were related to the Orr Focus site inhabitants whose identity as Ioway is documented (ibid., March 1, 1976).

In northwestern Iowa Henning suggests that some components of the Blood Run site on the Big Sioux River are Orr Phase material. The Harriman and Gillette Grove sites on the Little Sioux River are similarly identified. In Illinois the Oak Forest and Anker sites near Chicago manifest certain Orr Phase artifact similarities. Henning states that the Orr Phase sites along the Upper Iowa River appear to be definitely related to the Ioway people, as Wedel maintains, and possibly also to the Otoes in other localities. Orr Phase origins have not yet been determined [Dale R. Henning, "Development and Interrelations of Oneota Culture in the Lower Missouri River Valley," *Missouri Archaeologist*, Vol. 32 (1970), 9-10, 148-51].

* According to M. M. Wedel (personal communication, May, 1974), "There are no radiocarbon dates based on material excavated in the 1930s at seven Orr Phase sites on the Upper Iowa River under the direction of Dr. Charles R. Keyes, then director of the Iowa State Archaeological Survey. At three of them, however, European trade objects were found in association with Indian-made pottery vessels, chipped and ground stone tools, and other native cultural remains [M. M. Wedel, "Oneota Sites on the Upper Iowa River," *Missouri Archaeologist*, Vol. 21, Nos. 2-4 (1959), 66, 73, 77]. The Flynn cemetery, reported upon by Bray (1961:15-25) also produced glass beads and possibly brass. The quantity of the trade objects is more than mere presence, which could be accounted for by intertribal trade, but small enough to suggest the period of earliest primary contact with French traders, that is, the second half of the 17th century, probably the last quarter of it. The nature of the material — iron knives, glass beads, brass wire used to make ear coils — confirms this supposition since it accords with documented records of the easily portable trade good dispensed at this time. And the fact that the amount of native-made artifacts far outnumbers the European objects is a definite corroboration of the time period. Since some of the sites are reported to have shown no trade goods, these Upper Iowa River villages must have been inhabited at least from the proto-historic period into the historic. The length of residency before white contact is open to question. McKusick's (1971:10) too-few radiocarbon dates from the Hartley Fort and Lane Enclosure, which he would associate with the Allamakee trailed pottery characteristics of the Orr Focus, range from A.D. 1460 ± 85 (GX-1993) to 1740 ± 160 (GX-1991), with two in the 17th century (GX-1992, 1990). These dates are provocative, but there are so many possibilities for errors in radiocarbon dating, especially in this time period, that many more examples are required for significant results. One questionable feature of a more than 250-year span of occupation would be the unchanging pottery type. Some archeologists consider this phenomenon unlikely. Obviously many more dates on material excavated with care will be required in order to make an acceptable determination of the length of Orr Focus occupation in the area." Robert T. Bray, "The Flynn Cemetery: An Orr Focus Oneota Burial Site in Allamakee County," *Journal of the Iowa Archaeological Society*, Vol. 10, No. 4 (April, 1961), 15-25; and Marshall McKusick, *The Grant Oneota Village*, Report 4, Office of State Archeologist, University of Iowa, Iowa City, 1971.

The agricultural villages stood on terraces above the river's flood-plain to avoid their being flooded, to permit the fullest use of the rich river-bottom soils for planting crops, and in order to be in a position to observe the movement of life on the prairies about them. The upland forests that followed the streams provided material for building, heating, and cooking. The size of the settlements varied from a few to approximately one hundred acres at the Hartley Lane site.[4] Evidence of house types was completely destroyed by plowing and other disturbances in historical times. It has been surmised that Oneota houses were constructed of wooden pole frameworks and bark or mat roofs and walls, which were sometimes caulked with wet earth.[5]

To survive long, cold winters, villagers prepared and dried their surplus corn, beans, pumpkins, and other items gathered from their fields and forests and then placed them in safe, dry pits near their dwellings. The bowl-shaped or cylindrical pits were two to five feet deep and two to seven feet wide at the greatest diameter. Debris was found in some pits, and the layered contents showed archaelogists bits and pieces of food types; pottery; chips of flint, chert, and other stone implement-making materials; broken arrow points; parts of broken stone tools; bits of bone in the form of food remains; tools; and broken ornaments. Unused fire ashes were also dumped into the pits. Bone and shell remains indicate that the villagers fished and gathered clams and mussels.

Several fire pits were discovered and described. One contained the remains of forgotten roasting ears left to char one summer day centuries ago. Here the roasting pits were grouped together and suggested that this was a communal working area, where corn was prepared for storage. Stone implements used to grind foods have been found among the village remains.[6]

The early Ioway Indians used clay mixed with pounded mussel shells to make round bowls and jars. Decorative details placed on the vessels consisted of lines and dots in repeated designs carefully added to the smooth surface of the moist clay with a stick, a finger-nail, or an implement shaped for the purpose.[7] The Ioways continued to make pottery into historic times, when trade goods replaced it with metal "trade" kettles, iron vessels, and factory-made ceramics (see Figure 1).

> The Black Bear People came out of the ground and taught the people how to farm.
>
> — Ioway legend

Orr Focus agricultural patterns must be inferred from oral tradition and from archaeological remains. Evidence includes corn, beans, and other plants from storage and fire pits and remnants of an animal scapula bone hoe. An agricultural kit also included digging sticks, used to make holes to plant seeds, and woven containers or baskets used to carry the harvest from the fields. The Otoes, allied in history

Figure 1. An Oneota Aspect, Orr Phase ceramic vessel from the O'Regan site in Allamakee County, Iowa. It was found in a woodchuck hole in 1916 by an Iowa schoolboy. Shoulder diameter is 23 by 24 centimeters, height 17.5 centimeters. Courtesy of Iowa State Historical Society and Milwaukee Public Museum.

with the Ioways, called April the "stick-used" month, or the time they dig the earth; the Ioways called this month the "cultivation moon."

The people cleared the land of brush and weed overgrowth by burning it off in late winter or early spring. Burning also flushed small game from the fields at a time when the storage pits were almost empty and food supplies were low. How the villagers divided the chores of farming between men and women is not known. Men probably did the heavy work of field preparation such as tree removal. In later years certain men chosen for the rite performed special ceremonies before planting, women planted and tended the crop, and older children helped harvest the crops and bring them home. Following or contemporaneous with all stages of crop culture was the gathering of roots, berries, and other plants in season. Spring or summer plants such as lamb's-quarters *(Chenopodium),* sunflower seeds, Jerusalem artichokes, nuts, and berries were consumed at the time or were prepared and stored for winter use by villagers of this region.[8]

> . . . and my Grandfather was out hunting and he found Old Coyote digging his hole, and he stopped and talked to him over near Deep Fork.
> — An Ioway account, 1965

For thousands of years before agriculture was developed, hunting was the predominant subsistence activity for North American Indians. The male Ioway ancestors were hunters, and the women aided in the preparation of meat and hides for food and clothing. Down through the ages some animals were assigned supernatural aspects and as such became part of the religious system. They were to be hunted and used, but they were also to be considered sacred. In many ways they were coequals in the scheme of all things created by God and could be talked to like Old Coyote. They were part of Ioway tribal origin stories and were associated with clan ancestors as progenitors and wise spirits, the bringers of great ideas, such as the Bear people, who brought the idea of farming to the Ioways.

The Oneota ancestors of the Ioway Indians hunted animals in the forests and prairies and showed great skill in making fine hunting points and other implements (see Figure 2). Backs were bent as women used stone scrapers for cleaning and smoothing animal hides to be fashioned into clothing and containers. Stone or bone tools, worked to pointed ends, resembling awls or punches, were used to perforate the skins so that cut sections could be laced together or fastened in some manner. Other objects related to hunting were stone knives; sandstone abraders used to smooth arrow shafts; and bone sections, each with a hole in one end through which an arrow shaft was drawn to straighten it into an effective and true projectile.

The question when and how the early Iowas hunted cannot be answered definitely. Hunting may have been an almost daily activity with men, who left the village in small groups or individually, depending on the distance to be traveled and the kind of game sought. For various reasons it may have been unwise for large groups to have been away from the village for long periods of time. An arrow point was found lodged in the sternum of a skeleton in a Burke site burial.[9] Speculation about the hunting pattern includes the possibility that longer hunts occurred in which a large group of men or a major portion of the village traveled to the prairies of southeastern Minnesota and western Iowa to spend as long as two or three months hunting bison and preparing hides and drying meat. After the beginning of trade with the French late in the seventeenth century, the winter beaver hunt became part of the annual pattern.

As illustrated by Wawnonqueskoona's map, the Ioways moved to many different hunting camps and village sites throughout their history. Such camps and later winter village locations changed from

Figure 2. Chipped stone artifacts of the Oneota Aspect, Orr Phase: *a-c,* ellipsoid knives; *d-e,* gravers. Courtesy of *Missouri Archaeologist.*

time to time in documented history, adding to the number of homes that the Ioways recalled in the ninteenth and twentieth centuries.

Streams and rivers were fished by the Oneota people. They could descend from the village by paths leading to the fields and then follow paths to the stream or river. While the women probably worked in the fields, other family members gathered mussels and clams, which supplied not only food but also material for spoons, ladles, scrapers, and beautiful personal ornaments.

Besides furnishing fish, clams, and turtles, the rivers grew reeds and rushes used to make woven mats and containers. The river margins, hillsides, and fields also supplied medicinal plants and roots. The pharmacopoeia of the Oneota people is unknown, but it is probable that various useful plants were gathered in season and stored for future use. Tobacco often accompanied maize, or corn, horticulture in aboriginal times. Mixed with other materials, such as sumac leaves and the inner bark of dogwood trees, it was smoked in catlinite and other pipes found in Orr Focus burial sites in northeastern Iowa.[10]

> And a person's name should only be mentioned at certain times after his death. . . . If you mention the name before the four years is up, then . . . it's not anything in bad ways, or wishing them back luck, but. . . .
> We believe that after a person dies from the first day they say through the ceremonies and teaching that their spirit is still going back over their trail, regardless of where they have been . . . and for four days the family should not leave home.
> — An Ioway account, 1965

Consideration and preparation for the afterlife has occupied the thoughts of human beings for at least 100,000 years. In the earliest Indian occupation of North America there is little evidence of formalized burial, but undoubtedly the consideration of death and afterlife was present, and last rites were performed. In the last thousand years evidence has survived to indicate the presence of formalized burial practices. Individual or group burials have been discovered in pits often lined and covered with stones. Structures as pretentious as the great mounds of the Mississippi River valley regions were also used for interment, and later Oneota people sometimes buried their dead in them.

As many as one hundred burials have been reported in cemeteries of the Orr Focus period along the Upper Iowa River. The graves were placed on ridges near villages above rivers and streams and were sometimes lined with stone slabs.[11] There apparently was no consistent directional orientation of the bodies as in later periods. One burial was of an individual, perhaps of high social or ceremonial rank, in a seated position with a remnant of a cedar staff nearby. Woven mats had been placed under the body, and ornaments included earrings, bracelets, bone and shell beads, and pendants. In other burials finely made shell spoons and pottery bowls were often placed nearby. Stone balls, pipes, mullers, longitudinally grooved abrading stones, bone perforators, bone hoes, whistles, hematite "counters," copper objects, and other items were often included. At the Burke site several burials contained unusually pretty stones and fossil rocks that may have had religious, curative, or other significance for the owner.[12]

The artifacts found at ancient Ioway village sites tell us many things, but they can never say as much as we wish they could about the inhabitants who owned and used them. The most intriguingly human, interesting things — the thoughts, the predictions, the arguments, the humor in the day-to-day social interaction — we can only surmise. We can infer that ceremonial events certainly took place in the villages, because most societies at this technological level utilized ritual as part of planning for survival and in considering life following death. Orr Focus sites point to some form of ceremony around death in the careful preparation of burials. Effigy figures, such as bird carvings, snakelike copper forms, ceremonial stone maces, wands, whistles, pipes, small catlinite or pipestone tablets, fossils, and small beautiful rocks, appear to have had no daily or utilitarian use and may indicate ceremonial usage. Death ritual is evident, but the ceremonial practices associated with other major life events, such as birth, marriage, and status acquisition, are not hinted at in the present evidence.

The Orr Phase culture continued into the seventeenth century and contact with the French, as evidenced by the presence of such trade items as glass beads and fragments of iron and brass objects. By that time the ancestors of previously mentioned tribes, such as the Otoes, shared similar patterns of life with one another. Their village fires' smoke rose along the Mississippi, the Missouri, the Minnesota, the Wisconsin, the Big Sioux, the Little Sioux, the Des Moines, and other streams and rivers.

At the time of recorded Indian history the Ioways were good farmers and hunters who utilized rivers, prairies, plains, and forests. They and their Siouan-speaking neighbors were excellent craftsmen who worked in stone, clay, bone, copper, hide, pigments, and weaving materials. They erected dwellings from materials at hand: saplings, reeds, bark, thatch grasses, and earth. They were probably living mainly in peaceful coteries with established river and land trade routes to connect their lives. Archaeological records indicate that pottery, copper, stone, and other objects found their way from one group to another. Similar languages and similar beliefs may have formed other links not recorded in the days before white men came up their rivers in canoes, waved their hands and banners, and invited friendship.

2. "Aiaoua, Aiauway, Aiaouese, Aouas, Ayoës..."

IT MAY NEVER BE KNOWN when the first words describing the light-eyed men reached the Ioways. Beginning in the sixteenth century, Spanish and later French expeditions began to explore the Lower Mississippi valley and southern Plains and to view the lands and villages of the indigenous inhabitants of present-day Texas, Oklahoma, Arkansas, and Kansas. Whether or not the Ioways were ever heard of in those early days cannot be said, and it was not until the seventeenth and eighteenth centuries that contacts and records were made.

From the Indian viewpoint, news of strange mounted beasts may have moved rapidly to the north, carried by word of mouth by hunting and trading parties moving on foot across prairies and up rivers. Indeed the Pawnees claim that they saw Spanish men mounted on horses for the first time in the sixteenth century. They believed that the man and the horse were one. The flashing of the sun on the Spaniards' swords and the sight of the dust of their trail first caught the eyes of scouts, who ran back to the village or camp to report the strangest of all sights.[1] This Pawnee tale and others may have been carried across the miles to the more distant Otoes, Sioux, Ioways, and their neighbors.

Surely the description of the horses, the clothing, and the sun-reflecting metal surfaces of the strange man-beasts received hours of analysis and feelings of wonder in the villages and camps to which the news traveled, decades before the people ever saw white men for themselves. The Ioways claim to have first seen them "on the lakes" in the early eighteenth century.[2] It is known that French exploration in the seventeenth century included parts of the upper Mississippi River valley, west of the Great Lakes and along the western margins

16

of the Mississippi River, and that the Ioways saw white men there earlier than their legend indicates.

In French documents several events of the seventeenth century indicate the earliest mention of the Ioways. In the 1650's the Ottawas explored the western side of the Mississippi River in their flight from the aggressive Iroquois, who

> held in nominal subjugation all the principal Indian nations occupying the territories now embraced in the states of New York, Delaware, Maryland, New Jersey, Pennsylvania, the northern and western parts of Virginia, Ohio, Kentucky, northern Tennessee, Illinois, Indiana, Michigan and portions of the New England states, and the principal parts of Upper Canada.[3]

While they sought refuge from their pursuers, the Ottawas "ascended that river to a place about twelve leagues from the Ouisconshing [Wisconsin], where they came to another river, which is named for the Ayoës. They followed this stream to its source, and there encountered peoples who received them cordially."[4] In analyzing this description, Mildred Mott stated that the identification of this river would point to the present Yellow or Upper Iowa River. She chose the latter as more probable because "the Yellow River, south of the Upper Iowa, is a small river which, at its narrowed mouth, does not give much promise of continuing far inland. The Upper Iowa is larger, longer, and would have appeared to extend westward a good distance."[5]

Two decades later, on April 20, 1676, the first known detailed report in which the name "Aiaoua" appears was written by Father Louis André from St. Francis de Xavier Mission on La Baye des Puants (La Baye), or Green Bay. The report, based on information of his Indian visitors, says:

> This year we have among the Puants [Winnebago] seven or eight families from a nation who are neutral Between our Savages and the nadoessi who are at war. They are called aiaoua or nadoessi mascouteins. Their village, which lies 200 leagues from here Toward the west, is very large, but poor; for their greatest wealth consists of ox-hides and of Red Calumets. They speak the language of the Puants. I preached Jesus Christ to them. They say that they live at a great distance of 12 days' journey beyond the great River called Mississippi; but they assert that they have seen Savages who say that they have beheld a great lake very far Toward the Setting sun. The Water whereof is very bad.[6]

This report affirms a legendary relationship between the Winnebagos and the Ioways. By the time of Father André the Winnebagos had lost much of their former power. They were described as those "who have always lived here as in their own country, and who have reduced to nothing from their very flourishing and populous state in the past, having been exterminated by the Illinois, their enemies."[7]

In Father André's report the distance of the Ioway home from

Green Bay is given as two hundred leagues. This perhaps was an estimate based on information from his visitors, who may have been measuring distance in *journées* — a day's travel — and cannot be used accurately to locate their home. The products that they brought with them, buffalo hides and catlinite pipes, suggest a bison-hunting economy and perhaps, if the pipes were not trade items, access to a pipestone quarry. This area in present-day western Minnesota or eastern South Dakota was marked as an ancestral site on Wawnonqueskoona's map, and Orr Phase shards have been located at the Pipestone quarry area in Minnesota.[8] The Ioways who visited Father André may have carried the bison hides and pipes for personal use, as gifts for the Winnebagos, or as items for trade.

News of the Ioway visit to La Baye apparently reached Robert Cavelier, Sieur de La Salle, who was interested in the expansion of the fur trade and French interests. He was prohibited from involving himself in the beaver trade, but the Ioways had brought bison hides, and possibly other kinds not mentioned, to La Baye. He sent Michel Accault to find the Ioways, and Accault lived with them for two winters and a summer, apparently between 1677 and 1679.[9] He may have been the trader who provided the Ioway villages along the Upper Iowa River with the trade goods found in the Orr Focus sites, such as O'Regan.

The Ioways' contact with Accault and their long journey to La Baye in 1676 indicated early Indian recognition of the trader's and the trading post's importance. Each supplied them with readily useful articles, such as metal kettles, beads, knives, and cloth. Later the fusil, a light flintlock musket, was available to some and was important for hunting and warfare. The latter use may have dominated the former and may have been the most immediate need in the minds of those tribes subjected to the hostilities of those who already possessed them.

In 1669 the Jesuits chose the La Baye site for the establishment of a mission in conjunction with a trading post. Father Allouez constructed St. Francis de Xavier for members of the Winnebago, Menominee, Sac, Fox, Miami, and Kickapoo tribes, many of whom had been displaced by the Iroquois from homes farther east and south. However, the Fox were not exactly overjoyed when Father Allouez made contact with them. They claimed that they had been cheated by French traders at an earlier encounter. Father Allouez wrote:

> They have a poor opinion of the French ever since two traders in Beaver-skins appeared among them; if these men had behaved as they ought, I would have less trouble in giving these poor people other ideas of the whole French nation, which they are beginning to esteem, since I explained to them the principal and only motive that brought me to their country.[10]

Before the establishment of St. Francis de Xavier in 1669, peace had been achieved through the intervention of the French between the Iroquois and their enemies to the west. Before that, however, tribes pushed westward came in conflict with the Illinois nations. On August 22, 1681, La Salle related that the Miamis, persecuted by the Illinois, took flight across the Mississippi "toward the setting sun to the Otos [Otoutante] and the Ioways [Paote, Maskoutens Nadouessiou] who had been obliged to receive them, for four years."[11]

The decade of the 1680's and those leading into the new century were critical for tribes in the middle and upper Mississippi Valley. The impact of European expansion began to take greater effect with the inroads of French missionaries and traders, the indirect influence of the English, and the attempts of the Iroquois to maintain their position by an invasion of the Illinois valley.

In 1682 the Illinois trading center, established by La Salle at Fort St. Louis on the Illinois River, flourished, and tribes, however distant, were urged to settle there and trade. Even the Wichitas and Osages visited the bustling post. Living around the fort in dwellings characteristic of their individual tribes were the Abnakis, the Mohegans, the Shawnees, and the Miamis, all exiles from the Ohio River valley and farther east. Dutch and English trading interests, as well as French officials jealous of La Salle's success, now urged Iroquois to take up arms and march against the Illinois settlement, but the concentration and confederation of tribes around Fort St. Louis thwarted their attempts.[12]

In 1683, Antoine Lefebre de la Barre, governor general of Canada, sent Nicolas Perrot, a man of great experience among the western Indians, to settle the differences that had developed among certain tribes in the Great Lakes area.[13] He was known as one who could stand the rigors of frontier life; he had explored the wilderness on foot and by canoe, had constructed rude edifices for posts and missions, and had acquired during these efforts the trust of the Indians and a knowledge of their language and their ways.

Many years of service, loyalty, and responsibility in various assignments among the Indians determined Perrot's selection and appointment as commandant of La Baye des Puants and the neighboring regions.[14] His first task was to establish peace among the Foxes, the Chippewas, the Dakotas, and the Ottawas.[15] Late in 1685 he was sent to explore rivers that led toward the Dakota country. He traveled with his companions and was accompanied for part of the way by a party of Winnebagos. The latter group crossed the Mississippi, while Perrot and his men ascended it until they reached a place "where there was timber, which served them for building a fort, and they took up their quarters at the foot of a mountain, behind which was a great prairie, abounding in wild beasts."[16] This post, near Trempealeau, was the site of Perrot's first encounter with the Ioways. Bacqueville de la Potherie, who wrote of Perrot's adventures and knew him in

"Aiaoua,
Aiauway,
Aiaouese..."

19

Canada, based his writings on Perrot's journals and described the event as follows: "About eleven days after this signal [a Winnebago fire] some deputies came in behalf of the Ayoës, who gave notice that the people of their village were approaching, with the intention of settling near the French."[17] After the proper ceremonial greetings, accompanied by the usual ritual weeping over their hosts, the newcomers were given knives and awls. Verbal communication was impossible, because no one in Perrot's party understood the Ioway language. The envoys left, and in a few days four others returned, one of whom spoke "Islinois," an Algonkian language with which Perrot was familiar. He learned that the Ioway village stood on the bank of a river nine leagues (twenty to twenty-five miles) distant. Soon after, the French sought to visit it. "At their arrival the women fled; some gained the hills, and others rushed into the woods which extended along the river, weeping and raising their hands toward the sun. Twenty prominent men presented the calumet to Perrot, and carried him upon a buffalo-skin into the cabin of the chief, who walked at the head of the procession." Here the chief wept over Perrot's head,

> ... bathing it with his tears. These tears ended, the calumet was again presented to him; and the chief caused a great earthen pot, which was filled with tongues of buffaloes, to be placed over the fire. These were taken out as soon as they began to boil, and were cut into small pieces, of which the chief took one and placed it in his guest's mouth; Perrot tried to take one for himself, but the chief refused until he had given it to him, for it is their custom to place the morsels in the guest's mouth, when he is a captain, until the third time, before they offer the dish. He could not forbear spitting out this morsel, which was still all bloody (those same tongues were cooked that night in an iron pot); immediately some men, in great surprise, took their calumet, and perfumed them with tobacco-smoke. Never in the world were seen greater weepers than those peoples; their approach is accompanied with tears, and their adieu is the same. They have a very artless manner, also broad chests and deep voices. They are extremely courageous and good-hearted. They often kill cattle and deer while running after them. They are howlers; they eat meat raw, or only warm it over the fire. They are never satiated, for when they have any food they eat night and day; but when they have none they fast very tranquilly. They are very hospitable, and are never more delighted than when they are entertaining strangers.
>
> Their eagerness to obtain French merchandise induced them to go away to hunt beaver during the winter; and for this purpose they penetrated far inland. After they had ended their hunt forty Ayoës came to trade at the French fort; and Perrot returned with them to their village, where he was hospitably received. The chief asked him if he were willing to accept the calumet, which they wished to sing for him; to this he consented. This is an honor which is granted only to those whom they regard as great captains. He sat down on a handsome buffalo-skin, and three Ayoës stood behind him who held his body; meanwhile other persons sang, holding calumets in their hands, and keeping these in

motion to the cadence of their songs. The man who held Perrot in his arms also performed in the same manner, and they spent a great part of the night in singing the calumet. They also told him that they were going to pass the rest of the winter in hunting beaver, hoping to go in the spring to visit him at his fort; and at the same time they chose him, by the calumet which they left with him, for the chief of all the tribe.[18]

The Ioway village, which the Frenchmen now left to return to their fort, was estimated to be nine leagues, or a little less than twenty-five miles, from Trempealeau. This suggests either the Root River or the Upper Iowa River, which may be more probable from cartographic and archaeological evidence. Perrot at another point suggests that another village or camping site existed farther west in the statement: "The Illinois and their neighbors have no lack of wood for drying their meat, but the Ayoës and Panys [Pawnees] generally use only the well dried dung of the buffaloes, as wood is extremely scarce."[19] Father Jules Tailhan, editing Perrot's manuscript, positioned a village at forty-three degrees north latitude, a considerable distance from the Mississippi.[20] This would probably be in prairie country, west along the headwaters of the Des Moines or Blue Earth rivers or on the prairie toward the Little Sioux and the drainage between that river and the Des Moines. The latter location would give additional evidence of the dual subsistence pattern of horticulture and cyclical hunts toward the west in the area described above. Upper Iowa River Orr Focus sites yield many artifacts made from bison bones.[21] This may indicate the antiquity of bison hunting and possibly the use of hunting localities in the area described by Father Tailhan.

The narrative continued, saying that, after Perrot returned to his fort, he found a Mascoutin and a Kickapoo there, who sought permission for their people to dwell in some nearby location that Perrot should designate. He set off once again, traveling to a place eighteen leagues above the post. There at the visitors' camp the Mascoutin chief, Kikirinous, greeted him warmly and prepared a feast consisting of, among other foods, a bear that the chief had ordered cooked whole. He asked Perrot for possession of a certain river area and sought his commitment that the Dakotas "might be kept from annoying them." In addition, the chief asked permission to bring a large village of Islinois, who would do no harm, he insisted, if they, too, were allowed to settle nearby:

Perrot hardly dared to rely upon their promise, because he knew that most of them were man-eaters, who loved the flesh of men better than that of animals. He told them that he did not like to have those people for neighbors; that he was sure that they were asking to settle near him with the intention of making some raids on the Ayoës, when the latter were least expecting it; and that he could not, moreover, make up his mind to hinder the Nadoüaissioux from annoying his present visitors. They told him that they were surprised that he should doubt his own children; that he was their father, and the Ayoës their younger brothers, and therefore the latter could not strike them without striking him also, since he laid them in his bosom.[22]

The Mascoutin also asked for guns and ammunition. Perrot did not answer this but said that he would soon go to the Sioux and try to prevent their hostility. He said that the Mascoutins must obey his orders if he was not to become their enemy. To this they agreed and went on a hunt to provide their families with food for the winter.[23]

Some time later the Ayoës:

> came to the fort of the French [i.e., Perrot's], on their return from hunting beaver, and, not finding the commandant, who had gone to the Nadoüaissioux, they sent a chief to entreat him to go to the fort. Four Islinois met him on the way, who (although they were enemies of the Ayoës) came to ask him to send back four of their children, whom some Frenchmen held captive. The Ayoës had the peculiar trait that, far from doing ill to their enemies, they entertained them, and, weeping over them, entreated the Islinois to let them enjoy the advantages which they could look for from the French, without being molested by their tribesmen; and these Islinois were sent back to the Frenchmen, who were expecting the Nadoüaissioux. When the latter, who also were at war with the Islinois, perceived these envoys, they tried to fling themselves on the Islinois canoes in order to seize them; but the Frenchmen who were conducting them kept at a distance from the shore of the river, so as to avoid such a blunder. The other Frenchmen who were there for trade hastened toward their comrades; the affair was, however, settled, and four Nadoüaissioux took the Islinois upon their shoulders and carried them to land, informing them that they spared them out of consideration for the Frenchmen, to whom they were indebted for life.[24]

When the Sioux and the Ioways established trading agreements with the French at the Mississippi posts, the Mascoutins and their Algonkian-speaking allies threatened and attacked. The Dakotas and the Ioways were in alliance at this time (after 1685), and La Potherie wrote that the latter and the Winnebagos made a village in the lands of the Nadoüaissioux. The Mascoutins, who were considered by the French to be their allies, went into the Ioway village and carried off some of its inhabitants.[25] They also turned against Perrot, saying that . . . "they intended to sacrifice him to the shades of many of their men who had been killed in various fights for which he was the cause." Through apparent connivance with a group who did not sanction his death, he was allowed to escape.[26]

In 1695, Perrot was requested to bring to Montreal the Miami chief, as well as the Sac, Fox, Menominee, and Potawatomi leaders to urge them to make war against the Iroquois.[27] While the Miamis were giving proof of their fidelity to Governor General Louis Buade, comte de Frontenac, the Mascoutins had openly declared hostilities against the Ioways and had cut their main village to pieces.[28] Either at this or at a subsequent time the aggressive tribe raided the Ioway village and carried away prisoners, a woman and three children, whom they seated before Perrot and said:

*"Aiaoua,
Aiauway,
Aiaouese..."*

"We have borrowed thy guns; they have thundered upon a village, which they have made us eat. See the effect which they produced, and which we bring to thee," at the same time displaying these slaves. They placed forty beaver robes before him, and continued their speech thus: "We have taken from thee a garment to dazzle the sight of our enemies and make ourselves feared by them, and we pay thee for it by this beaver; we do not pay thee for thy guns and merchandise. If thou art willing to receive us with forgiveness, we know where are some beavers, for we saw them on our road [to this place]. If we live a few years, thou shalt be satisfied; for we did not intend to plunder thee, and we have only placed thy merchandise to thy credit."[29]

Perrot told them that to make amends for their behavior they must destroy a village of Iroquois, who once again were threatening French and Indian alliances on the west. He continued that they must not attack people who had not made war on them and who were dear children of the French (such as the Ioways, it is inferred). But the situation did not improve measurably. At another time, "Twelve hundred Nadoüaissioux, Sauteurs [Chippewas], Ayoës, and even some Outaouaks [Ottawas] were then on the march against the Outagamis [Fox] and the Maskoutechs [Mascoutens], and likewise were not to spare the Miamis. They had resolved to take revenge on the French if they did not encounter their enemies."[30]

Eventually Perrot's life was threatened and his entire collection of pelts destroyed by fire. His life in the West was soon to end. In May, 1696 a royal ordinance revoked all trading licenses, prohibited the carrying of trade goods to the West, and evacuated forts and posts of all but missionaries.[31] Perrot returned to his land grant and family at Bécancour in Canada to settle permanently. He had done much in his years in the West to bring the tribes of that area into relationship with the French and to foster trade with them. Apparently he and Accault were among the first to trade with the Ioways. He died on August 13, 1717, at the age of seventy-four.

By the end of the eighteenth century the Iroquois had abandoned their ideas of controlling the western fur trade. Their fighting strength had decreased, and they had made peace with the French and had agreed to stay neutral in any state of conflict with the English. "This new turn held out a frightening prospect for the northern English colonies that had relied on the Iroquois for their defense."[32] Far to the west the Foxes and their allies were aligned against the Dakotas and their alliance partners. The Foxes wished to control the waterways of Wisconsin and prevent French trade with the Dakotas. Adding to intertribal hostilities was the decrease of fur-bearing animals in the older trading areas. Antoine Le Mothe de la Cadillac, in describing hunting in the northern Michigan peninsula, told that in 1694 the beaver in the regions south of Lake Superior had become very scarce and that the Ottawas and the Hurons had to travel two hundred leagues to the west to find enough peltries to maintain the supply needed in their trade with the French. Between October and November the average catch for a good hunter would be between fifty and seventy skins. The animal population was not able to maintain itself as a result of this yearly attrition, and tribes were often forced to move into territory hunted by others, who reacted with hostility, as might be expected.[33]

While they searched for new beaver sources, the Ojibways (Chippewas) moved south and west from their homes south of Lake Superior, exerting pressure on the Dakotas who claimed that area as their homeland. That in turn eventually caused their movement into the hunting grounds of others, among them the Ioways. Into this time and place came Pierre-Charles Le Sueur, who was born in Artois, France, in 1657 and went to Canada as a young man. The adventure and economic advancement to be found in the pine-forested Indian country called him to seek his way for a time as a *coureur de bois*. Pursuit of the fur trade without a license was illegal, and he was sentenced and imprisoned for a short time. After his release in 1680 he made various government-sanctioned expeditions with others into the Green Bay and the Mississippi river areas. He reported that after 1683 he lived in the Sioux and surrounding country from time to time for seven years altogether. During that time he learned the languages, attitudes, and customs of the Indians. In May, 1689, he was present at Fort St. Antoine on Lake Pepin, when Nicholas Perrot claimed the region for the king of France. In the next year he married Marguerite Messier, a cousin of Pierre Le Moyne d'Iberville, a noted Canadian naval officer and later governor general of Louisiana.[34]

Life in the West called LeSueur from his home, and he returned there in 1691 and in 1692. Governor General Frontenac ordered him to establish a post at Chequamegon Bay on Lake Superior. There as commandant he assisted in establishing peace between the Dakotas and the Ojibways, thus keeping open the way for French traders to reach the remote area. He built several posts or forts on the Mississippi River in subsequent years. It is believed that the third was situated on Prairie Island in the river.[35] In 1697 he proposed construction of a post among the Dakotas, supposedly to mine copper, but his idea was seen by some as a pretext not to mine but to tap another lode, the fur trade of the region, although that activity had been declared illegal since 1696. His request was denied. Using the influence gained from his family relationship to d'Iberville, he was able to obtain a fur-trading license in 1698, which was revoked on May 27, 1699, ostensibly because of Fox hostility toward French trade among the Dakotas. However, d'Iberville, who also had economic interests to advance, was instrumental in obtaining permission for Le Sueur to organize an expedition to the Dakota region from Louisiana as a starting point. The purpose was to mine for copper and other precious metals, if they should be found. He was allowed also to trade for deer, bison, and furs other than beaver.[36] In the new Company of the Sioux, Le Sueur, d'Iberville, and Alexander L'Huillier, farmer general of Canada, were members. Hoping to be successful in his venture, Le Sueur made his way up the Mississippi toward the Dakota country in the spring of 1700. He was accompanied by eight *engagés,* two volunteers, and his valet.[37]

While he was ascending the Mississippi, he was joined by some Canadians with experience in the region toward which he traveled. The voyage northward was not uneventful, and various encounters were made with the inhabitants of the lands through which the expedition traveled. In late summer he came to the St. Peters River (the Minnesota), where he turned westward on September 9, 1700, and moved through southern Minnesota forests and prairie lands, until he came to the mouth of the Blue Earth River, so named for the blue-green earth on its banks. Here he disembarked, hopeful that reward lay in his discovering mineral deposits there.

Soon nine "Sioux of the East" came to visit him. Their lands were near the Mille Lacs area. They told him that this river was the country of the "Sioux of the West, of the Ayavois [Ioways] and the Otoctatas [Otoes]," that it was not their custom to hunt on the grounds of others without being invited by those to whom the land belonged and that, if they should wish to come to the fort, they would be exposed to danger. If he wished to take pity on them, he should settle on the Mississippi farther east at the mouth of the St. Peters River, where they and others could reach him safely.[38] This request placed Le Sueur in a delicate position, for he knew they were a powerful nation. He observed that they were "the masters of all the other Sioux and the Ioways and the Otos because they are the first with whom we traded and to whom we gave arms so that they are rather well armed."[39] At the time he told them that he wished that he could acquiesce to their request, but that the season was too far advanced for him to return, and that his principal purpose was not to trade but to explore the region for minerals.

LeSueur and his men completed Fort Vert on October 14. It consisted of cabins and picketed stockade walls. On the nearby prairie the men hunted and killed a good supply of bison, which were prepared and placed on a scaffold to freeze and to be protected from predators. André-Joseph Pénigaut, the carpenter, recalled that they got along very well without vegetables and other customary foods during the winter.[40]

Le Sueur expected that the Ioways and the Otoes would be in an adjacent area, where he either had known them to be during his previous visits or had been told they would be. On October 22 he sent two men to find and invite them to make a village nearby, because they were "very industrious and accustomed to cultivating the land." He hoped that they would make gardens and provide food for those who would work the mines, according to one source,[41] or would do this and also work the mines.[42] On October 24 the men returned saying that they could not find the road to the Ioway and Otoe village. One of the searchers had been to the village some time before but he could not "get his bearing" in the trackless prairie where no trail had been made recently. Le Sueur noted that it was a wise decision to return to the fort, since it was difficult to find a lake on a prairie twenty to thirty leagues in diameter, especially when there was no compass at hand. Later the men were sent again to find the village. This time three men found the location, but from all signs no one had occupied the dwellings all season. On November 16 the French "learned that the Ioways [Ayavois] and the Otos [Otoctatas] had gone toward the Missouri River to settle near the Omahas [Mahas], a nation which lives in that region."[43]

Mildred Mott Wedel writes of Le Sueur's location of the Ioway village "as being on a lake 30 leagues (c. 80 miles) inland from Fort Vert. From the French post, the site was approached by crossing the headwaters of the Des Moines River and skirting some little lakes until the 'large lake' was reached. This lake was described as draining into several smaller lakes and thence into a river which entered the Missouri. Such a description definitely suggests Spirit Lake in Dickson County, Iowa, the Lakes Okaboji to its south, and the Little Sioux River." (See Map 3).[44]

Affirming this location is the northern section of Baptiste Louis Franquelin's 1697 map, which carries a notation that the "Aiaouez Nation that was formerly on the Mississippi at the place where the river enters which carries its name [as indicated on the map, the present Upper Iowa River] and which withdrew here 10 or 12 years ago having made peace with the Sioux." This note was placed in the present-day Spirit-Okaboji Lakes area of Iowa.[45]

One explanation for the Ioway removal from an area not too far distant from Le Sueur's fort to the Missouri River region may be found in a letter written to Le Sueur by Father Gabriel Marest on July 10, 1700, from the Kaskaskia Mission on the Illinois River, saying that the Piankashaws had been defeated by the Sioux and the Ioways. The Piankashaws had allied themselves with the Kickapoo, Mascoutin, Fox, and Metesigami tribes, not to attack "the Sioux of whom they are too much afraid, but on the Ayavois, or else on the Paotees, or rather on the Osage, for these last suspect nothing and the others are on guard."[46] This would seem to indicate that at some time before July, 1700, the Ioways were in a region accessible by foot to the tribes mentioned, who lived on the eastern side of the Mississippi. The harassment by these tribes may have decided their movement westward toward the Missouri-Little Sioux rivers region, along which Oneota cultural sites have been found.

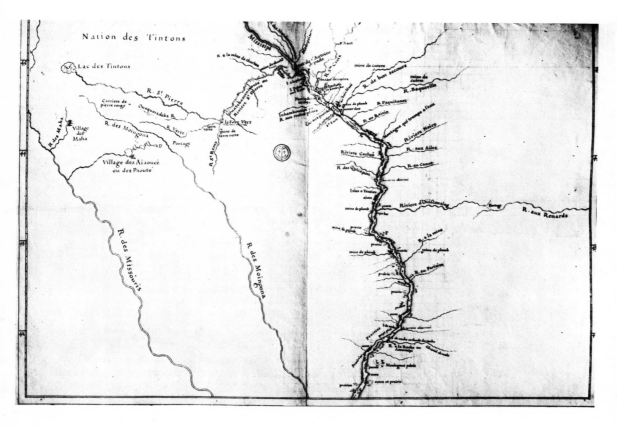

Map 3.   A section of a larger map by Guillaume Delisle dated 1702 and
called "Carte de la Rivière de Mississippi." It shows Fort Vert (established
by Le Sueur) and an Ioway village (Aiaouéz ou des Paouté) on the river
leading into the Missouri from a series of lakes. The Mississippi and its
tributaries have the French names of the period. M. M. Wedel describes the
map in *Iowa Journal of History and Politics,* Vol. 36 (1938), No. 3, p. 307.
Courtesy of the Library of Congress.

The Dakota-Ioway alliance in other hostilities was mentioned by
Le Sueur. He noted that around 1695 or 1696 the Sioux and the
Ioways had forcefully attacked the Miamis living east of the Mississippi and had caused their withdrawal from their homes toward
Canada.[47] Such hostilities with the tribes across the Mississippi may
have finally determined the Ioway decision to take up residence away
from that area. Lending credence to a more westerly Ioway location
at this time is Le Sueur's reported remark that "le Français qui avait
épousé une Aiaouesse et était allé au village des Aiaouez, en passant
par la rivière Moingona avait été faire la guerre aux Panis, etablis

tout le long de la rivière des Missouri" ("The Frenchman who had espoused an Ioway and has gone to the Ioway village, passing by way of the Des Moines River, has gone to make war against the Pawnees living along the Missouri River").[48] He was a *coureur de bois,* an explorer or trader. He and other "trafiquants, avaient du parcourir la valle basse du Missouri avant l' année 1700" ("traders must have traveled through the lower Missouri Valley before 1700").[49] Le Sueur was also told that the Ioways did not live directly on the Missouri but on a river entering it above the Oto River: "On the right, I know of only one river where the Paoute and the Ioway are, a numerous people and allies of the Sioux, whom they are near. This is all, Monsieur, I have been able to learn of these two rivers, but I have not been there yet, nor has any Frenchman. Thus, I have learned only from Savages who do not know the latitudes and are unable to state exactly the distance between villages."[50]

The Ioways' memory of their residence and travels between the Mississippi and Missouri rivers could be heard in words given in claims made by the Ioway 140 years later:

> Although once the most powerful and warlike Indians on the Mississippi and Missouri Rivers, they have been cut off and reduced to nothing, a mere handful of that Nation that was once master of the Land. No Indian of any other Tribe dare build his fire or make a moccasin track between the Missouri and Mississippi Rivers, from the mouth of the Missouri as high north as the head branch of the Calumet [Big Sioux], Upper Iowa and Des Moines Rivers, without first having obtained the consent of the Ioway Nation of Indians. In fact this country was all theirs, and has been for hundreds of years.[51]

Le Sueur had no better luck finding the Ioways near Fort Vert than he had finding mineral riches in the area. In spring, when the river ice melted, he began his exploration. The colors in the banks of the Blue Earth River suggested the possibility of a profitable mineral source. This was not to be true, although 4,000 pounds of clay were taken from there to France. While there, Le Sueur gained additional government support and permission to return to America. But unfortunately he died en route in 1704.

The early years of the eighteenth century were marked by continual competition between the French and the English in the New World. It involved Indians on the west in intertribal strife, as well as those farther east in the Ohio River valley. The Treaty of Utrecht in 1712 ended a long period of French and English hostility and, among other provisions, placed the Iroquois under British rule. The English now presumed certain rights over their lands and continued exploration toward the west and the establishment of Indian trade relationships. However, the absence of clearly defined boundaries between the French and English territories led to continual disagreement. The Indians, most of whom had never heard of the 1712 treaty, undoubtedly considered the lands divided by the Europeans as their own and continued life unaware of the long-term results. They tended, with some exceptions, to support that power that could give them the greatest advantage in their individual situations. The Ioways were not exceptions, as events were to show in the coming century.

"Aiaoua, Aiauway, Aiaouese . . ."

In the area between the Great Lakes and the Mississippi River the Foxes, who had for the most part shown anti-French sentiments throughout the years, continued their aggressive behavior and continued to take the offensive against many of their neighbors, who showed inclinations toward European alliance. They made special expeditions to attack French posts and those tribes that used their facilities as trading stations. So effective were the Foxes in their efforts to disrupt the French trading system and to control the rivers and area themselves that historians describe the period from 1701 to 1716 as the First Fox War and the period from 1727 to 1738 as the Second Fox War.[52]

In 1714 the French government decided to send the Miami and the Illinois Indians against the Fox. It was believed that the Dakotas might sympathize or ally themselves with the Foxes. Therefore, an envoy was sent to the Dakotas to avert their participation in any hostility against French-allied tribes and to ask them not to offer the Foxes sanctuary should they seek it.[53] Marchand de Lignery, as emissary, wrote in June, 1714, that he feared that the Foxes would take refuge among the Ioways three hundred leagues from the place where the Foxes were settled and, after placing their families in security among that nation, return again to carry on the war.[54] Apparently the Ioways did not give sanctuary to the Foxes, who reached eastward and made an alliance with the Iroquois, who were now being urged by the English to march once again toward the west to make war on French-allied tribes in order to weaken French control in that region.

In 1718 the important decision was made to unite the young province of Louisiana with the older province of Illinois, until this time a part of Canada. Illinois relations, commercial and otherwise, had been historically oriented toward Montreal, and the new position brought resentment to Canadian officials and others. This was particularly so when the boundary was determined. The Louisianans claimed the region as far north as the Wisconsin River valley, but the Canadians protested that that was too far, that the boundary should be between the Wisconsin and Illinois rivers, where the Mascouten and Kickapoo lands belonged to Canada.[55] Louisiana officials planned to construct Fort Chartres on the Mississippi in Illinois near the settlement of Kaskaskia and to send Charles Juchereau, Bénard de la Harpe, Claude Charles Dutisne, and Étienne Véniard de Bourgmont to explore various rivers and adjacent lands west of the

Mississippi in order to claim new territory and to establish tribal relationships in Louisiana Province.

The Spaniards now became aroused and alarmed at the interest of the French in what they claimed to be their territories in present-day Texas, New Mexico, and Oklahoma and as far north as Kansas and Missouri. In 1720, Don Pedro de Villasur headed an expedition to establish a fort at Jicarilla and then to march northeastward and reconnoiter in the Platte River area in order to seek out French traders who were supposedly there.[56] The expedition left Santa Fe in June and marched sixty-three days to the northeast, coming to the Platte River in the lands of the Pawnees. This tribe did not deign to counsel with the Spaniards and instead "attacked them with guns and arrows and wrought the havoc that is known," that is, the destruction of the expeditionary force. Some escaped to relate the tale, but the attempts to thwart French intrusion into what the Spanish claimed as their lands failed.[57]

Pierre Francois Xavier de Charlevoix gave a version of that skirmish to account for Spanish objects that he found in the hands of the Winnebagos. He visited that tribe around 1722 and reported:

> On the next day, the Chiefs of the two nations [the Winnebago and Sac] paid me a visit, and Ot-cha-gra the Winnebago, showed me a Catalan Pistol, a pair of Spanish shoes, and some kind of Drug, which seemed to me like a sort of Ointment. All of these he had obtained from an Aiouez, and now I will tell you by what opportunity these articles fell into the hands of the latter. About two years ago, some Spaniards, who had come, it was said, from New Mexico, intending to penetrate as far as the Illinois, and drive out thence the French, whom they saw with extreme jealousy advancing so far as the Missouri.[58]

Charlevoix then gave an inaccurate description of the battle, which is presumed to be the Villasur incident. Although it appears from most accounts that the Pawnees were the principal antagonists of the Spaniards in this event, the Ioways may have obtained some of the booty from the Otoes. Alonso Rael de Aguilar, who was present, later recalled that he knew that "the twelve fleeing ones, who were able to escape from the encounter, retreated with the bulk of the horseherd, having left in camp all their equipage and provisions,"[59] and it is possible that various items were shared, traded, and given by one tribe to another. This encounter might have been the one alluded to by a Missouri chief, who spoke on November 19, 1724, before members of that tribe and others who were taken to Europe to visit the French monarch, saying, "We love the French people and naturally hate the Spaniards and the Englishman. We proved it three winters ago. The Otoptata [Otoes], Panimaha and ourselves completely defeated a large party of Spaniards who came to settle down among us."[60]

As the Spaniards were well aware, the French for some time had envisioned the establishment of posts on the interior rivers west of the Mississippi. Bourgmont explored the Missouri River in 1714 and 1717 and described its route, direction, and tributaries and Indian nations that dwelled near it.[61] In his "Exact Description of Louisiana" he wrote that the Otoes were allies of the French, lived on the Saline River on the west side of the Missouri, and traded in furs. The Pawnees who lived nearby were a strong, alert people and good horsemen. "The French know them and see them sometimes, and they all use arrows" (a few years later, at the time of the Villasur incident, they apparently had acquired guns). Approximately twenty leagues beyond the Otoes on the Missouri lived the Omahas, who traded with the Spaniards, as did the Padoucas, who lived nearby.* Continuing, he wrote that one hundred leagues farther up and to the left,† in ascending, was a nation named by their neighbors and the French, "Ayowest or Rakode, whose commerce is in furs."[62] *Rakode* was an attempt to render an Ioway Chiwere Siouan name, *Pa-ho-ja*, or a similar name that the Ioway called themselves. In a later description Bourgmont said that the nation lived between the Big Sioux and Little Sioux rivers, approximately halfway between and opposite the Platte and Niobrara rivers.[63]

Several years later the French, fearing attempts by the Spaniards to establish themselves on the Missouri, again sent Bourgmont to establish France's claim and to negotiate with the Indian nations there. In 1723 he built Fort d'Orleans on the river near its junction with the Wakanda (or, some say, at the Grand), among the Missouris whom he had known for many years.[64] On January 11, 1724, he reported in a letter to the Commissioners of the Colonies:

I was very surprised to learn that the Otos and the Ioways had begun a strong alliance with the Sioux and the Fox, our enemies. These two nations [the two first ones] wanted to sing the calumet to me, to which I did not want to agree, because they had not given me satisfaction. I reproached them firmly, even threatening them. I came just in time to break up this league. Inevitably, if these two nations had turned away from us, the Mahas and the Panismahas would have joined with them, and it would have been impossible to make any establishment on this river. I doubt even if M. de Boisbriant could have maintained his post [Ft. Chartres at the Illinois].

* Padoucas are thought to have been either the Plains Apaches or the Comanches at this time. Waldo R. Wedel (*Introduction to Kansas Archaeology*, BAE Bull. No. 174, 77-78) suggests that until 1750 the term Padouca probably applied to the former tribe and after that date, approximately, to the Comanche. Dolores Gunnerson, in *The Jicarilla Apache* (pps. 223-24), identifies the Padoucas with the Cuartelejo Apaches.

† The location of the Ioways on the "left" side of the Missouri is thought to possibly be a copyist's error or a hasty entry by Bourgmont in his original manuscript. (Mildred Mott Wedel, personal communication, October 1, 1973).

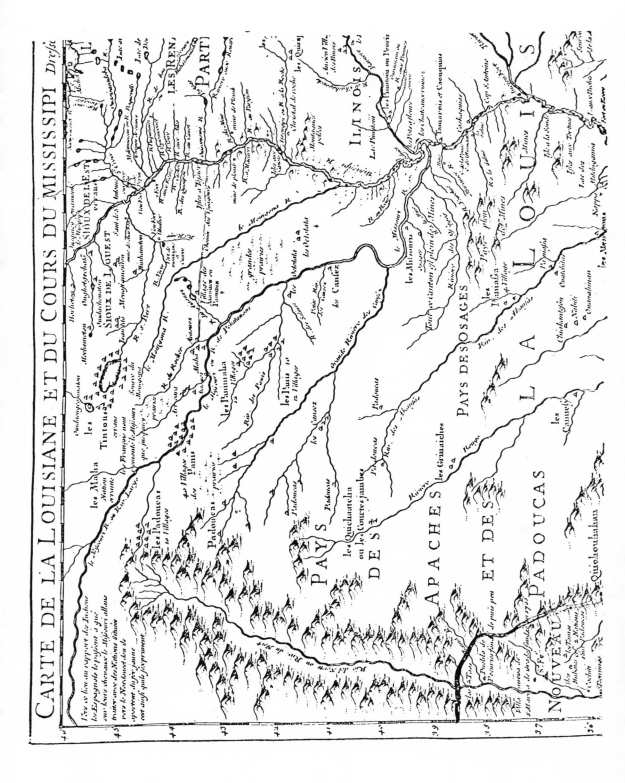

I think that extreme poverty and lack of merchandise brought them into this alliance, their not having seen in the five years since I left here for France, but one Frenchman at their villages.[65]

Later on February 18 he declared, "I caused the alliance to be broken which the Oto and the Ioway had made with the Fox, and they should even bring me some [Fox] scalps at the first opportunity. . . ."[66]

It is possible that the Bourgmont, Otoe, and Ioway confrontation and later council could have occurred at Fort d'Orleans or at another nearby point. The Ioways may have been visiting the Otoe village, or they were on a hunt on lands later claimed by them along the Missouri, Grand, and Chariton rivers or farther west. It is also possible that they had moved their villages from locations in present northwestern Iowa farther downstream, although Bourgmont's 1717 description placed the villages opposite the Platte and Niobrara Rivers. The Delisle map of 1718, based on information from Le Sueur, shows three Ioway village areas (See Map 4):

1. the "Village des Aiaouez ou Paoutez" (two terms for the Ioways) south of the chain of lakes joined by a river, thought to be the Little Sioux

2. a village higher on the Missouri on a river flowing into it where the trade road showing on the map ended (this possibly could be the Blood Run site in Lynn County on the Big Sioux River or some other undesignated site)

3. a village farther up the Missouri near the mouth of a river leading to the Arikara country (Oneota material has been found near the mouth of the Vermillion River)

Bourgmont's instructions from the Company of the Indies for establishing French influence on the Missouri included the statement: "He also knows of what importance it is to induce the Padoucas to make peace with all the Savage nations who are allied to the French. He will neglect nothing in order to succeed, because it is one of the principal objects of his voyage."[67]

Having established contact with the Osages, the Missouris, the Otoes, and the Ioways, Bourgmont now laid plans for the expedition

---

Map 4. "Carte de la Louisiane et Du Cours du Mississipi Dressée sur un grand nombre de Memoires entrautres sur ceux de Mr le Maire." A section of the June, 1718, map of Guillaume Delisle showing the trade road (Chemin des Voyageurs) as two parallel lines that begin at the Mississippi River opposite the Wisconsin River mouth. The road runs westward on the map, crossing the Des Moines River at the Ioway village near Spirit and Okobojie lakes and proceeding to another Ioway village near the Missouri River on the Rock River (which is believed to be the Big Sioux River). Courtesy of the Library of Congress.

westward to the remote Padoucas. On June 25, 1724, commanding an entourage of 25 Frenchmen and approximately 165 Missouri and Osage Indians, he left the post, bearing with him a sufficient amount of gifts and French goodwill to be distributed among those he would encounter.[68] Unfortunately Bourgmont became ill and was forced to return to Fort d'Orleans, but he sent a subordinate, Gaillard, with two Padouca slaves belonging to the Kansa Indians to the distant Padouca village to inform it that he was coming on a friendly visit but was detained by illness. On September 20, 1724, after receiving news that Gaillard had survived the visit to the Padoucas, he set off with a small party to complete his mission. He journeyed to the principal village of the Kansa Indians, where he was pleased to find Padouca chiefs and subordinates that Gaillard had persuaded to return with him. The Padoucas had participated with the Spaniards in the Villasur expedition. Now that the Spaniards were routed, they evidently wished to explore French motivations and offers. They invited him to visit their village.

Other regional tribal representatives began to arrive at the Kansa village. On October 5, at 6 o'clock in the morning, six Ioway chiefs arrived, carrying their large peace pipes.

> M. de Bourgmont received them courteously, and afterwards he had a large fire built in a suitable place in the front of his tents, at the head of his camp. He assembled the Chiefs whom I named here; he seated himself at the door of his tent, facing the fire. He seated the Padouca chief on his right, next to the Great Chief of the Missourys and the chiefs of the Othos, and, following, the chiefs of the Ayoois and the chiefs of the Canzés, all around the fire, with several warriors of all these nations, with M. de Saint-Ange and the Sr. Renaudière on his left. After everyone was seated, M. de Bourgmont stood and commenced to speak to all these nations in this way: "My friends, I am happy today to see you all assembled here in order to tell you of my intention. I announce to you that I have come here on behalf of the Great Chief of all the nations, who is on the other side of the Great Lake, and in behalf of the Great Chief who is at the sea [the Gulf in Louisiana] to bring you his word and to give you their sentiments. He has given me full power to make peace with the Padoucas, and so, because they are with us, I wish presently that we make altogether an alliance with them and that you remain in good accord, and that you trade one with the other, as you do with us, and the Othos, the Osages, the Ayoois, the Canz..s, the Panimahas, the Missourys, and the Illinois."
>
> All these chiefs stood and began to reply in a loud manner: "We want it, and we have already promised you, and thus we have no other wish than yours." Then all chiefs of all the nations began to pass from one to the other their valuable pipes to smoke, and to perform courtesies, according to their custom, and they appeared very contented.[69]

After this the Padouca chief arose and invited Bourgmont to visit his village, promising him various gifts, including some of his many horses and turquoise stones. That evening the Padoucas danced before the Missouris, the Otoes, the Ioways, the Kansas, and others, and the pipe was smoked among them. The journal continues:

"Aiaoua, Aiauway, Aiaouese..."

Today, October 6, 1724, M. de Bourgmont prepared the trade goods and had them divided into three portions, one for the Othos, one for the Ayoois and the other for the Panimahas. He has put in these allotments some powder, some balls, some vermillion, some large and small knives, some glass beads, some hatchets and picks, some awls, wad extractors, gun flints, and other merchandise suitable for their needs.[70]

By October 7 preparation had been made to visit the Padoucas, and before departure, the Kansa chief invited the participants to visit his tipi for a feast. He invited the Frenchmen, the five Padoucas, the Ayoois, the Othos, the Missourys and the Panimahas. It was then decided who should accompany Bourgmont on the visit to the Padouca village. The next day the retinue began at nine in the morning "with arms and baggage, and the French flag flying ... with five Padoucas, seven Missouris, the Great Chief of the Canzes with four warriors of his nation, four chiefs of the Othos and three of the Ayoois." It is not known whether the Ioways completed the journey; they are not included in the list of participants at the Padouca village council.

When it was his turn to speak, Bourgmont once again expounded on the virtues of the French and told of the Great Chief, the King of France, beyond the sea, and how he held the interests of the Indians close to his heart. Later gifts were distributed to the hosts, including fusils, swords, hatchets, kettles, bullets, red and blue woolen cloth, hand mirrors, shirts, awls, needles, scissors, bells, beads, vermillion for paint, and other items that, it was hoped, would brighten the Indian eye and the prospects of the French for Indian alliances, trade advantages, and territorial acquisition.

Fox aggressions against French-allied tribes continued, and the solutions to the Fox problem varied from the extreme one of extinction to the suggestion that conditions which led to their continued hostility might be ameliorated. The rivalry for the furs and friendship of the upper Mississippi tribes between Louisiana and Canadian commercial interests had increased, and the Fox and Sioux war effort had been aided by Louisiana traders, who supplied arms and ammunition with the permission of the Louisiana officials. In response to this, the Governor-General of Canada expressed fear that its upper Mississippi commerce would fall into the hands of Louisiana traders and merchants. He added that the Company of the Indies had no sanctions to enter the colony of Canada at all.[71]

In order to offset the Louisiana influence over the tribes of the region, particularly the Dakotas, permission was granted in 1727 to build Fort Beauharnois on Lake Pepin. The need to dissolve the Sioux-Fox alliance also motivated its construction. Governor General

Charles de la Boishe, Marquis de Beauharnois, brought with him from France in 1726 the order authorizing it.[72]

The Foxes continued to follow their own grand scheme in spite of a severe setback in 1728 at a battle near the tip of Lake Michigan, in which many of them were killed. They continued their raids against the Kickapoos, the Chippewas, and the Illinois. The Dakotas, now benefiting from trade at Fort Beauharnois, refused them sanctuary when they requested it in 1729, and the "Quicapoux had sent to the Ayowets to request them not to give shelter to the Renards in their territory," according to Governor General Beauharnois on May 16, 1729.[73]

In 1733 at their fortified village at Marameg in present-day southern Wisconsin the Fox were again attacked. Now much weakened by their years of battle, they asked sanctuary from the Sacs, and their plea was answered. A short time later at the Sac village fort a French officer, Nicolas Coulonde Villiers, who had come to ask the Foxes to give themselves up, was killed by a young Sac.[74] Fearing reprisal for such a deed the Sac and the Fox remnant left at night, pursued by the French. After a fierce battle at Little Butte des Morts, they eventually reached the Mississippi and crossed it into old Ioway lands. They built two forts near the mouth of the Wapsipinicon River and a few miles upstream. A report of 1734 reads: "Since the blow struck by the Sacs and Renards at La Baye the 16th of September, 1733, and their flight they have wandered about for some time, asking in vain for refuge among the Sioux and the Ayouais who refused it to them."[75]

While they were in Iowa, they were attacked by a force of Kickapoos, Potawatomis, and Iroquois led by Nicholas Joseph de Noyelle. They withstood the attack but were later attacked by the Kansas and the Missouris. In 1735, Beauharnois reported, "As to the *Renards,* it is not known what decision They have taken nor the place they have selected for their retreat. It is certain that they can find no asylum among any nation either in the Mississippi country or this. The *Ayowais* to whom They looked for help have taken a scalp from them."[76] In time they left the Ioway area and returned to their former lands across the Mississippi.

Before the 1720's, Bourgmont had placed the Ioway location near the Big Sioux or Little Sioux river. Some time later the tribe, all or part of it, moved to the present-day Council Bluffs, Iowa, area to establish a village near the Missouri River. The exact time when they left the upriver northern villages and moved to the Council Bluffs location, some 150 to 200 miles to the south, has not yet been definitely determined.[77] Later observers, among them Lewis and Clark, noted the site, and Auguste Chouteau said that around 1765 he had urged the tribe to move east to the Des Moines River area.

Horses had now become important to the Missouri River valley villagers. The Council Bluffs area was a good place for dealing with tribes that had horses to trade. After the Bourgmont councils the

Ioways and Pawnees may have had a friendly understanding, and it is possible that they were trading with each other and the Otoes for horses. The Otoes lived at this time near the mouth of the Platte, which led to the Pawnee country.

Although there was more than one factor contributing to Ioway migration southward, the increasing aggressiveness of the Sioux may have been the most important factor in determining the decision. The need for hunting grounds free from continual harassment by the Teton or Yanktonai Sioux was imperative not only for trading purposes but for survival. On the south the Otoes may have permitted the Ioways to accompany them, or they may have hunted independently on lands east and north of the Missouri along the Grand and Chariton rivers, which they used in later years.[78] Some scholars, however, believe that the Ioways continued to live to the north in the Iowa lake area and along the rivers flowing into the Missouri, such as the Big Sioux and the Little Sioux, until the 1740's and 1750's.[79]

In 1744, Governor General Beauharnois commented on the Sioux aggressiveness and the general hostility maintained among many tribes in the upper Mississippi and adjacent areas:

> Whatever precautions and care may be taken to restrain those savages, it is rather difficult to Prevent the hatred they have borne one another for a great many years from manifesting itself occasionally by slight acts of Treachery which they commit amongst themselves and which happens at the very moment they are supposed to be reconciled.... We cannot Entirely congratulate ourselves on maintaining a very lasting peace among those Nations, nor on Completely Removing from their minds, the hatred they have of one another, especially the western Nations, who cannot forget a former act of treachery whereof the Sioux were guilty against them, and the memory whereof they have promised one another to retain forever.[80]

In the 1740's an intensive British effort began to erode Indian loyalty to the French. The pawn status of the Indian nations became more obvious as the colonial governments attempted to maneuver them into hostilities against each other. It is certain that an increasing number of tribal leaders realized that it was impossible to remain isolated from the eccentricities and requirements of the colonial powers that shared their lands. They had become part of a total pattern of competition and aggression, in which their own power or defenselessness was dependent on the intruders' whims and on their own astuteness in choosing the path of greatest advantage and least destruction.

In the 1750's and 1760's the French and Indian War was a continuation in the series of European struggles that involved the colonial empires of Britain, France, and eventually Spain. Among other goals, Britain desired to acquire American French possessions and sent men and supplies to undertake the task. The Ohio River valley became an area of stress as British colonists moved beyond the Alleghenies into territory claimed by France. In this same period, far to the west, the Ioways killed two Frenchmen, according to Governor Pierre F. Rigaud de Cavagnial, marquis de Vaudreuil in a letter to the French minister dated July 20, 1757:

"Previous to my arrival in this colony the Ayoouois killed two Frenchmen in the Missouri country. I at once hastened to give my orders to the commandants of the post whither that nation might come, that the first officer to whose post they came was to compel them to bring me the murderers."[81] The post commandant at La Baye was the first to see the Ioways and, according to Governor Vaudreuil's directions, told them that the French knew of their deed and that they must surrender the murderers to the governor. That summer they journeyed to Montreal and delivered the men to Vaudreuil, who described the scene as follows: "They presented them to me in the name of their nation with great submission and resignation that I might have their heads broken if such was my intention. They nevertheless earnestly begged me to pardon them and assured me that they themselves would avenge the death of the two Frenchmen and would compensate me for their loss by the blows they would strike against the English."[82]

In this regard the French had worked earnestly to solicit military aid from the Canadian mission and the western Indians in their struggle against the English. The fall of the British Fort Oswego, Ontario, convinced many nations that the French would win the war, and the Indians continued to support them, traveling in significant numbers to Montreal to join expeditionary forces under officers Montcalm, Rigaud, and Langlade. So it was that the town was filled with Indians of various nations when the Ioways arrived.

Vaudreuil described the reaction to the Ioway plea for pardon:

All our nations of the upper countries and our domiciled savages who were in this town, to the number of from 1,700 to 1,800, joined those Ayoouois and gave me the most touching words to induce me to pardon them. I did not deem it advisable to refuse them because all those nations were about to start to join my expedition against fort George and circumstances required that I should give proofs of kindness to all those nations.

Nevertheless, I made them very anxious to obtain that favor and granted it only after repeated solicitations.

That favor will contribute more to restrain the savage nations than if I had had the two murderers' heads broken, because all the nations that interested themselves in their fate are, at the same time, obliged to punish them if they dip their hands in French blood in future.[83]

General Montcalm (Marquis Louis Joseph de Montcalm de Saint-Véran) wrote of the occasion that there were in attendance eight hundred Menominees and three hundred Winnebagos, Sacs, Foxes, and Ioways, adding that they had "never appeared before at Montreal": "There occurred here, yesterday, the grand ceremony of pardoning two Iowas who had killed two Frenchmen, two years ago. They smoked the peace calumet; the murderers were brought out, bound, with the emblem of a slave [prisoner] in their hands, singing their death song as if they were to be burned. Saint-Luc and Marin fulfilled the functions of the chevalier de Dreux and Monsieur Desgranges."[84] It would have been rather difficult for the French to refuse pardon under these circumstances in view of their need for Indian manpower in the coming campaign against the English in New York.

"Aiaoua,
Aiauway,
Aiaouese..."

Before they launched the expedition, the French held a celebration, and gaiety prevailed on the Plain du Sablon. Montcalm wrote, on that occasion, among the other tribesmen, "the Ioways, heads shaved, wore bells that sounded in beat with their leg movements. They jumped high in the air and sang 'Hi, Hi' among other words."[85]

Later the French and Indian forces moved southward for the planned attacks in British colonal New York. Fort William Henry, established in 1755 at the head of Lake George, was a primary target. It was attacked twice, first by Rigaud and then by Langlade. Finally its garrison surrendered to General Montcalm. In the lists of Indian participants is read "Ioways of the Western Sea — 10."[86]

For the first time Indians from the Great Lakes, Mississippi River, and Missouri River areas saw at first hand the strengths and determination of the two great European powers. What thoughts crossed their minds and occupied their discussions as they realized what the battles were really about? It was an accident, in some respects, that the Ioways were participants in those events so far from their Missouri River lands, which would continue to affect their lives from that time on. In 1758, Forts Duquesne and Frontenac were lost to the English. With the loss of these two major points in the protective line of posts established to prevent English expansion westward, the French posts farther west were more vulnerable.

During these years of conflict it was difficult to obtain trade items; frontier posts were abandoned or not restocked. Fort Beauharnois was abandoned in 1756, and its garrison sent to fight in the war. In such cases the tribes who were accustomed to trading there stopped using European articles, or sent trading parties to more distant posts in search of goods, or perhaps moved their villages to more advantageous positions. For the Ioways available posts may have been Fort Cavagnial on the Missouri River, Fort Chartres, or La Baye, where they had been informed of the charges against them. By this date the tribe possessed horses to enable them to travel farther to visit, hunt, trade, or form more mobile war parties.

In the 1757 "Memoire" of Louis Bougainville, the following report on Fort Cavagnial is found among others describing French posts and the Indians who used their facilities:

and including that distance on the East side thereof to a point opposite the beginning.

The Tribes of Missouri, Otes (or Olaclatos) Iowas & Winnebagoes formed one nation under the name of Missouris the Missouri Tribe, built a village on the left bank of the Missouri river, and occupied it under the protection of fort Orleans (built in 1723 by Mr Bourgmont) But when the French evacuated that Fort and erected another near the village of the Kansez, the Missouris crossed the Missouri river and with the consent of the Grand Ozages built another village on their lands six miles above the village of the Little Ozages, where they afterwards resided.

The Country of the Missouris was bounded as follows to wit: on the North by the dividing ridge that separates the waters of the Missouri & Mississippi river, East by the country of the Little Ozages, South by the Missouri river, and west by the Country of the Kansez.

The Country of the Otos is bounded as follows, to wit: beginning at the mouth of the Nishibatone, thence binding on the line of the Kansez to the dividing ridge that separates the waters of des Moins & Grand river, thence westwardly with said ridge about fifty miles, thence southwardly to the mouth of the river Platt, thence up said river about ninety miles, thence by a direct line to the Sources of Big Nimahas about one hundred & eighty miles, thence down said river to the Missouris and up the latter to the beginning. The Iowas formerly had their village on the right bank of the Missouri about eighteen miles above the river Platt on the lands of the Mahas, they however pretended to claim that small tract of land on which necessity had compelled them to settle, but their country was bounded on the North by the dividing ridge that separates the waters of the Grand & des Moins rivers, East by the Otos, South by the Missouri river which separated them from the Mahas, & west by the sioux their most inveterate enemies.

Afraid to hunt on their own lands lest they might be attacked by the Sioux, and constantly threatened by the Mahas & Otos who wished to drive them from small tract of country on which they had establis

Kanses — In ascending the river [Missouri] eighty leagues farther a village of the Kanses is found; we have a garrison with a commandant furnished like those of Pimiteoui [Peoria] and fort Chartres by New Orleans. There comes from this post a hundred packages largely of beaver, but badly dressed, the other peltries are the same as those of the preceding post, eighty packages of deer and bear skins. Fifty leagues above are found the *Otoks* and *Ayoues*, two hundred men furnish eighty packages, of the same peltries as those of the Kanses.[87]

"Aiaoua, Aiauway, Aiaouese..."

Fort Cavagnial, chartered in 1744, was built overlooking the Kansa village on the Missouri River in present-day Kansas, and it seems likely that it was available and convenient for the Ioways to visit from any of their postulated village sites of the time. Auguste Chouteau wrote of the Ioways that they "formerly had their village on the right bank of the Missouri River about eighteen miles above the Platte River on the lands of the Mahas [Omahas]. They, however, pretended to claim that Small Tract of land on which necessity had compelled them to settle but: their country was bounded on the East by the dividing ridge that Separates the waters of the Grand and des Moins rivers, East by the Otoe, south by the Missouri River which Separated them from the Mahas, and West by the Sioux their most inveterate enemies" (See Figure 3 and Map 5). On Chouteau's map the Missouri River flows from west to east, hence the erroneous directions for the tribes' locations. In actuality, the Otoes were to the west, the Missouri River was more on the west, and the Sioux were to the north. Chouteau's statement about Ioway territorial claims cannot be verified as the Ioways' own views are unknown.

Figure 3. A page from the 1816 Notes of Auguste Chouteau describing the lands of the northern Louisiana tribes shown in Map 5, including the Ioways. Courtesy of the National Archives (Ancient and Misc. Surveys, Vol. 4, No. 26, 251-65).

41

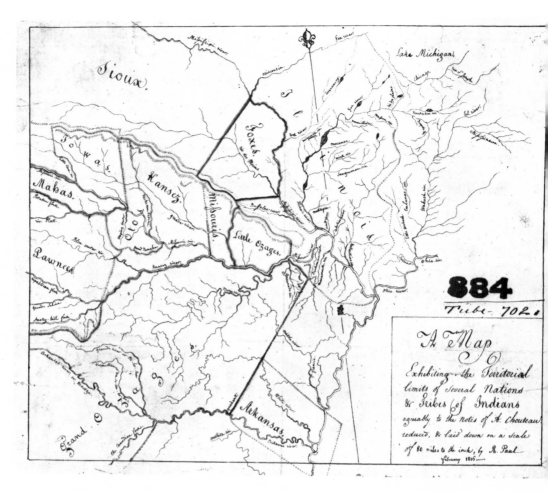

Map 5. "A Map Exhibiting the Territorial limits of Several Nations & Tribes of Indians agreeably to the Notes of A. Chouteau reduced, & laid down on a scale of 80 miles to the inch, by R. Paul february 1816." Courtesy of the National Archives Cartographic Division (number 884, tube 702).

3. Changing Colonial Powers

IOWAY WARRIORS OBSERVED four different flags flying over forts and posts along their Mississippi and Missouri valley waterways in the last four decades of the eighteenth century. In 1718 the Illinois region was part of Louisiana Province, and three years later Fort Chartres was built to be a departure point for French exploration and expansion into areas west of the Mississippi and to protect the nearby French settlements of Kaskaskia, Cahokia, and Prairie du Rocher. In addition, it would serve as a guardian of French fur-trade interests, now threatened by the English advancement and the establishment of English posts in areas north of the Ohio River. In 1721 Louisiana Province became nine districts, one of which, the Illinois, extended east and west of the Mississippi between the Arkansas on the south and the fortieth parallel north, including the lands of the Ioways.[1] At the end of the French and Indian War the French lost the Illinois country east of the Mississippi to the English, and they transferred the western section to the Spanish on November 2, 1762, to fulfill a secret agreement and to prevent Britain from acquiring it in the peace negotiations.

Even before the end of the war the French did not have complete control of the Illinois region's fur trade. In June, 1760, Vaudreuil wrote, "The English being vigilant profit by our scarcity of goods. They have invited the Illinois nations to go to trade at the Rock."[2] This post was the site of La Salle's establishment near the old Illinois village on the Illinois River, near present-day La Salle, some ninety miles southwest of Chicago. Western entrenchment by the English was aided by the abandonment of French post garrisons as the war drew to an end. As the French lost control of the Ohio River, the

English advance became more rapid. In addition, the land in the Mississippi and Missouri valley systems, although nominally under French jurisdiction, did not belong to Frenchmen except in limited ways. In 1765, the British Captain Stirling wrote to General Thomas Gage from occupied Fort Chartres: "I have not been able to find that the French King had any possessions in this country except the ground the fort stands on, as no lands were ever bought from the Indians who claim the whole as their property."[3]

The British sought to change this status, and in the next year, in his "Reasons for Establishing a British Colony at the Illinois," Sir William Johnson noted:

> It has been the mistaken Policy of the French to aim at establishing Military, instead of Commercial Colonies.... Had the French contented themselves with Settling and improving the Country they actually possessed, they would have rivaled the English in their most valuable American commodities....
> Let the Crown purchase of the Indians all their Right to that Tract of Country lying on the East Side of the River Mississippi, between the Illinois River and the River Ohio, and fifty miles back from the Said River Mississippi.... They have a greater Quantity of fine Hunting Country than they can ever have any use for. This would be a sufficient Tract to begin a Colony upon, and having a natural Boundary would be the most preferable.[4]

Other differences existed in the English and French attitudes toward the Indians and their land. When they acquired and maintained positive relationships, French officials and traders accepted the Indian culture as they found it for the most part (except for attempts at religious conversion). They understood the gift-giving ceremony, a valued part of the Indian way of life, and participated in it at the proper times. Gifts were presented when one tribe visited another and were reciprocal in the future. Early in the Indian relationship the British tended not always to understand this custom for what it was, an expression of friendship and a continuing bond. General Jeffrey Amherst said in 1763, "No bribes [gifts], if they don't behave, they are to be punished."[5]

Indian misgivings about the British increased. This was particularly true of Pontiac, principal chief of the Ottawas. His fears of British westward movement grew and crystallized as the French and Indian War drew to a close, and his great influence among the tribes inflamed their anti-British feeling. To announce his purpose of driving out the British in 1762, he sent wampum belts of shell beads, colored red and black for war, to forty-seven different tribes and subtribes as far as the lower Mississippi River valley. In a great council held near Detroit in April he reviewed all the wrongs suffered by the Indians at the hands of the British, stated his belief that someday the French would return, and presented his plan to overcome the British-held forts and drive out the intruders. In May the assaults

began. Eight forts were captured, and several English expeditions
were prevented from reaching their assigned posts.

The post at La Baye was not approached by Pontiac's supporters because of the regard that tribes in the area had for its commander, Lt. James Gorrell, who had been sent to the West to occupy French posts in 1760. At La Baye (or Green Bay, as it was now to be called) he kept a journal that gives the particulars of his new assignment.[6] He wrote that, when his contingent came to the post, they found only one family in the nearby Indian village. All the others had gone on the winter hunt and were expected to be gone until spring. In order to establish relationships with the tribes in a proper and diplomatic manner at a later time, Gorrell discovered that the exchange of belts of wampum would be expected. He proceeded to assemble the belts by trading and buying in order to be ready for the coming talks. During the winter the men repaired the fort, and a few Indians stopped by and were treated well. This surprised them, since they said the French had assured them that this would not be the case. The first small group asked for ammunition and flour for the old men who were ill.

The winter hunt passed, and the area tribes — the Menominees, Winnebagos, Sacs, and Foxes — began to return to their villages. With the chiefs present, it was possible for formal diplomatic exchanges to occur. Promises were made, the newly acquired belts were presented, and equanimity appeared to be established between these tribes and the new colonial representative.[7]

As part of his duties Lieutenant Gorrell tallied the number of Indian tribesmen under his jurisdiction. He said the figure was 39,100 warriors besides women and children who were dependent on Green Bay's post for their supplies.[8] His figures are listed below. His estimates gathered from various informants cannot be proved and, in the case of the Ioways, seem to be extravagantly high.

Tribe	Number of warriors	Location
Taways [Ottawas], etc.	100	Little Detroit and Milwacky
Folles Avoines [Menominees]	150	La Baye in Two Towns
Puans [Winnebagos]	150	End of Puans Lake and near Louistonstant
Sacks	350	Above Louistonstant, in the Government of La. [Louisiana]
Reynards [Foxes]	350	On the River Reynard
Avoys [Ioways]	8,000	On each Side of the Mississippi
Sous [Sioux]	30,000	On [the] West Side [of the] Mississippi Near 300 Leagues off

In 1764 Colonel Bouquet estimated the Missouri River Ioway population at 1,100. See H. R. Schoolcraft, *HCPIT*, Vol. 3 (1868), 258. The exact locations of the Ioway villages known to Gorrell were not discovered. It is possible that some, or all, of the Ioways, were residing on the Des Moines, as Auguste Chouteau suggested. They were near enough to find it advantageous to visit La Baye in 1762 and to be known by the officials at Fort Chartres.

In August, 1762, Lieutenant Gorrell wrote that three Winnebago chiefs and four ambassadors from the Avoy nation came on their first visit. The Winnebagos gave him a belt and proclaimed their continued friendship. The Ioways said that they had come very far, and they had brought no belts because, as Gorrell described it, "they had come to see if I would shake their hands and forgive them, as I had done the rest. I gave them belts and strings of wampum for the return of prisoners. They said their king would come in the Spring and visit me."[9] The winter hunts began again, and Gorrell's journal reports lessened post and tribal interaction. On March 1, 1763, twelve Sioux visited, and Gorrell estimated that in the tribe "not over two thousand were armed with firearms, the rest depending on bow and arrow." The Sioux were forthright, saying, "all Indians were their slaves or dogs," which may have been a pose or may have been an indication of their increasing power and confidence.

The four Ioway ambassadors had promised to bring their king or chief in the spring, and on June 14, 1763, they appeared. The journal says, "The traders came down from the Sack country and confirmed the news of Landsing and his son being killed by the French. There came with the traders some Puans [Winnebagos] and four young men with one Chief of the Avoy nation, to demand traders to go amongst them. They promised four hundred and fifty other men would be down in August to trade. I gave them presents."[10] The promise of visitation by 450 men would point to an entire village unit perhaps accompanied by women and children. If this was the case, the group may have planned a visit to the Winnebagos in the late summer. After a summer's visit they would settle for the winter farther south in their traditional lands along the Mississippi, somewhere in present-day Iowa, or in Illinois, where it was later reported that they may have been located.

Pontiac's attempt to rouse the tribes against the British had its affect on La Baye. Soon after the above encounter with the Ioways, the fort was abandoned. Lieutenant Gorrell had established amicable relations with the area Indians, and, rather than attack him as urged by Pontiac, they escorted him to safety when it became necessary to attack the fort in late June, 1763. The traders left with him but later returned. At "Mishamakinac" the inhabitants were not so fortunate as Lieutenant Gorrell. The fort was on Mackinac Island, at the straits between Lake Huron and Lake Michigan, and had been a prominent Indian trade post from the time of the earliest French contact with the Indians of the region. On June 4 the fort was taken by surprise by the Chippewas, and many of the English were killed.[11]

The Indians in the Illinois region continued to have a negative attitude toward the British. Between 1762 and 1763 the British government, somewhat surprised by the continued resistance and urged by their Indian colonial officials, had endeavored to find a better Indian policy. Throughout the summer and fall of 1763 peaceful solutions were sought. It was proposed that lands be reserved west of the Alleghenies for the Indians and fair trade regulations established. At a conference held in August at Montreal General Gage and those assembled heard one of the Indian spokesmen from the friendly tribes around Green Bay, or La Baye:

> Brothers, I am desired to speak to you in Behalf of the Nations about La Bay, who also are very uneasy, and Concerned about what Happened at Michillimacinac. The following Nations take a fast Hold of your Hand, and declare themselves your firm Friends and Allies — vis. — the Folsavoine, Puans, Saks, Renards, Ayoways, Fiox, and la Prairie, or Illenois. — All which Nations you may regard as one Mind, and one Body, who are Resolved to remain always in your Interest, and Die with you, and they by this Belt of Wampum Implore you to grant them a Supply of their Necessaries of Life by Establishing a Trade with them, and not, on the Account of One Nation, whom they look upon as Strangers, and Disturbers of the publick Peace, and Tranquility, to make all the Rest unhappy.[12]

New British policies came too late. Pontiac's reprisals against the forts began in the spring with major successes. The revolt became more widespread, as Ohio River Valley tribes stopped British attempts to reach the western areas near the Mississippi and Great Lakes. In November, 1763, General Gage decided to send a force up the river from New Orleans. The river was open to British traffic in agreement with the Treaty of Paris. All went smoothly upriver for approximately two hundred forty miles. Then a force of Choctaws, Ofogoulas, Tunicas, and Avoyelles attacked the expedition forcing it to retreat down river. The British were unaware that Pontiac's war belts had reached the southern tribes.

In the Illinois country, at British request, St. Ange de Bellerive, veteran of French colonial service, took command at Fort Chartres in June, 1764. During this summer the Ioways had promised that they would bring the large trading party to Green Bay. Whether they returned or not is unknown. It is possible that trade was carried on with the French traders from New Orleans in the Illinois area, where Ioways were reported by St. Ange from Fort Chartres, August 12, 1764:

> A certain Mitaminque, chief *a Mevaille* [?] of the Potawatomi nation of St. Joseph, arrived here the thirtieth of the past month [July]. He re-

asserted his attachment to the French and assured me of the fidelity of his people. He informed me of a measure he had taken with the Peoria [Indians] at the camp of a band of Iowa, which is established on the bank of the Mississippi, on the occasion of the insults which they had offered to the French inhabitants of Peoria and the thefts of horses and slaves which they had committed. He assured me that if this nation continued this brigandage it would draw upon itself the hatred of those who are attached to the French. The conduct of this chief was confirmed by a man named Detailly.

PS. Since writing the present the Iowa concerning whom I have had the honor of writing you, have wounded a Frenchman who was hunting on the Mississippi thirty five leagues above this fort. It appears, sir, that the threats that the one named Metimigue made to them have made no impression. This fact has caused me to oppose the departure of the traders who were preparing to go into this region until I should be able to inform the Sauk and Foxes of the conduct of these knavish savages.[13]

The letter indicates that a band of Ioways were camping or living on the Mississippi River that summer and that the Peorias were with them, either in a mutual hunting effort or paying a socially prescribed visit, approximately one hundred miles upriver from Fort Chartres. Camping indicates hunting rather than agricultural pursuits. During the summer tribes within the prairie woodlands area traveled from a settled horticultural village to hunting grounds usually far enough from the village to necessitate a campsite, rather than a daily return to the village. If this were true in the case of the Ioways, it is possible that some of the tribe had already moved to the Des Moines River, where Chouteau reported them to be in the 1765-68 period, after the Missouri River villagers requested French traders and offered to establish themselves on the Des Moines. It is also possible that this particular band was visiting temporarily in the Illinois area, possibly from the Council-Bluffs-area villages.

By 1764 Pontiac had become disheartened. He had learned that the Spanish had true possession of the French lands west of the Mississippi, and he faced the reality that the French would never again be reestablished in the lands lost to England and Spain. When he learned that his former allies on the Ohio River had made peace with his enemy, he agreed to meet with George Croghan, who was sent by Sir William Johnson, the superintendent of Indian affairs, when Croghan arrived in Illinois. In July and August he and Pontiac met and agreed to establish peace. This paved the way for British possession and final occupation of the land to the Mississippi. In all, nine attempts were made by the British to claim the territory completely.

In October, 1765, the British flag was raised over Fort Chartres, and St. Ange took leave of the post, moving across the river to the new small village of San Luis in Spanish Louisiana, where he established a government post in agreement with the Spaniards. He and others from the villages of Cahokia and Kaskaskia left their homes and gardens to reside in San Luis, a community of fifty families. Ferries that crossed from one side of the river to the other carried settlers and their household goods, tools, and livestock.[14]

Pierre Laclede had established San Luis in 1764. Young Auguste René Chouteau was the son of his common-law wife and assisted Leclede in his expanding trade business. In 1816 Chouteau recalled that in 1764 the Ioways resided in a village eighteen miles above the Platte River in the lands of the Omahas. The Sioux were their inveterate enemies, and the Ioways had grown fearful of hunting on their own land because of Sioux attacks, as well as threats from the Otoes and Omahas, who, it was said, considered the Ioways intruders. Apparently hard pressed, they had sent a deputation to Laclede to ask for traders to be sent to the Des Moines River area, where a village would be established according to Chouteau. It was agreed, and LaBacasse and Boudria resided among them with "merchandise to supply their wants."[15]

Spain became involved in the Louisiana territory when it agreed to help France in its struggle against the British in the final stages of the Seven Years', or French and Indian, War. For this assistance Spain was promised possession of Louisiana on January 2, 1762, and became the official owner on November 23 of that year. On October 23, 1763, the land east of the Mississippi was formally transferred by ceremony from France to England. In May France had sent notification to Spain, requesting it to assume possession of the western territory, which constituted Louisiana. By the end of the year Spain had made several steps to accomplish this and had informed France that it was prepared to conclude the official act of transferral. But in January, 1764, France had not yet drawn the necessary papers. During the previous year Spain had sought information about the new possession by interviewing past residents who had returned to Europe, and Spanish officials had become knowledgeable about Indian relations. They had collected lists of posts, officers, and their duties and statistics on demographic, economic, governmental, ecclesiastical, and social conditions.[16] In April, 1764, papers of possession where drawn by France. In June, Spain began to purchase the necessary Indian trade articles and gifts. At this point a lack of available Spanish troops slowed the process of conversion from French to Spanish administration. It was estimated that 1,800 troops would be needed to garrison the entire Louisiana territory. France offered to allow its troops, already present, to serve under the Spanish flag until replacements could be sent.[17] This was agreed on, and Don Antonio de Ulloa, a Spanish colonial official from Peru, was named governor of Louisiana. In 1766 he conducted an inspection tour of the vast colony and set reports back to Spain in which he indicated various needs and requested approval for necessary changes. Three expeditions were sent, one of which was under

Captain Francisco de Rui. He established a post north of San Luis near the junction of the Missouri and Mississippi rivers and named it San Carlos el Principe. Its purpose was to guard the entrance of the Missouri and to observe the traffic thereon.

On the eastern British side of the Mississippi, the loyalty of the Illinois Indians to the French and their suspicion of British motives caused them increasingly to move their trade across the river to San Luis. At the same time augmented British trading activity occurred near the Great Lakes and on across the Mississippi into Spanish territory. Competition between the Spanish-French and English traders grew, and both sides sent agents into each other's lands. Issuance of decrees to prohibit such trespassing made little difference to the profit-seeking traders. The Ioways and other Indians enjoyed an advantageous bargaining position and could exhibit partiality toward any trader they preferred. It was possible to visit each government's representative to renew friendship, to receive gifts, and to observe foreign behavior. While this competition lasted, the Indians possessed some advantage in commerce, although in the long run it happened that the rate of exchange was unfair, and traders' and merchants' profits excessive. The Ioways and other Indians of the Mississippi and Missouri valleys from north to south had by now accepted and needed the guns, ammunition, and various other articles that tied them to the foreign culture. In order to possess these articles, intensive trapping and hunting in the upper Great Lakes area had by now reduced the game in some areas to the point that periods of famine existed in tribes that relied on hunting as their main subsistence and economic activity. When a tribe could not produce the going price in peltry for guns, brandy, and other items in demand, and when expansion into new hunting areas already claimed by other tribes became more difficult, hunger and increased intertribal warfare resulted.

The French influence continued in Spanish Illinois even after Spanish officers arrived to assume command of the posts and government. The veteran St. Ange, with his great knowledge of Indians, compiled in March, 1769, a list of the tribes "accustomed to receive presents in this district" for Francisco Rui, the commandant of the Illinois. It included all the tribes of the Upper Mississippi district:

Indian tribes: Report of the various tribes, who, according to my knowledge, are accustomed to receive presents in this district of Yllinneses. To wit:

1. Kaskaskias	5. Saks
2. Kaokias [Cahokias]	6. Renards [Fox]
3. Ayooua [Ioways]	7. Sauteux [Chippewas]
4. Sioux	8. Kikapu [Kickapoos]

50

I certify that the tribes here above expressed are the same one who are accustomed to come here to get presents. San Luis, May 2, 1769.

SAINTE ANGE.[18]

Pedro Piernas, commandant at Fort San Carlos from March to May, 1769, reported:

In the short time of my residence in that post, there came to hold discussions the tribes of the Osages, Ayoua, Kikapu, Masaten, Pou, Putatami, Utoa, Putchicagu, Renard, and others of the vicinity attracted both by the novelty of the arrival of a new commandant in order to receive their presents which it is necessary by established custom to give them for that reason, and those with which the traders impose on them, being assured that they are indispensable to them, and in order to benefit the habitants of the settlements with the goods and products of the hunt.[19]

Piernas explained that the Indian visits were held at the post rather than at San Luis, because the latter place was conducive to extended visits, which were costly to the king. For a visit to the remote area of San Carlos "their stay would be but in passing, and consequently, there would be a great saving of food, whose consumption has hitherto been considerable, and therefore costly."[20]

He also described certain aspects of Indian life. He related that in May and June the tribesmen came down the rivers to the fort with their traders to declare the furs acquired in the winter hunt. The king provided bread and corn; the Indians provided their own meat. The exchange of furs for brandy was noted as important to some: "Most tribes of the Misoury are accustomed to the use of brandy, and prefer a small portion of it to any other present of merchandise even of four times its value."

The presence of the tribes' traders should be noted. They usually spoke the tribal language and had a certain advantage in interpreting and translating according to their own bias and benefit. They eventually gained great influence in many tribes, and many records in later decades indicate how instrumental they became in forming tribal opinion and decisions. As will be seen, some traders intermarried with Ioways and exerted their influence through kinship ties.

The Spanish commandant's role dictated that he must always endeavor to be attentive to the Indians who visited him, to listen to them with patience and resolve differences and discord among the various tribes. Sometimes he had to make rulings and mediate with persuasion and sometimes with firmness. He must present gifts at the proper times and supply certain foods as described above.[21]

Following the above dicta, the Spaniards were largely successful in their Indian relationships. Older French traders continued under Spanish licenses, and a lenient and fair set of trade regulations made for peaceful conditions, except for English traders, who here and there continued to disrupt the Spanish-Indian relationship by endeavoring to convince the Indians that Spanish officials and traders were exploiting them.

Traders and trade increased as a natural result of augmented demand among the increasing number of tribes who were in contact with Europeans. Trade products gathered by the Indians of this area included peltries of beaver, bear, deer, bison, swan, cat, wolf, fox, and lynx; tallow, oil, and grease of animal extraction; and beaver tails and deer tongues. These items were traded for iron spoons, gunpowder, spears, chisels, scissors, knives, nose and ear-rings, blankets, silver-plated crosses, lockets, bracelets, bones to decorate girdles, copper jars with lids, and brass kettles.[22] Eight thousand pounds of European goods were carried up the Missouri in 1767. Trade returned a 200-percent profit, it was claimed.

Pontiac was murdered while visiting San Luis (Saint Louis),* but this did not put an end to the hostility and dissidence among some tribes who had supported or opposed his cause against the British. Self-motivated, or by French or Spanish instigation, anti-British feeling increased until in the spring of 1769 several tribes became actively hostile in the Fort Chartres area. The Kickapoos and Sacs were among them. The British accused the French and their trade interests of fomenting the trouble.[23]

Regardless of the intrigues and the skirmishes, December, 1769, found the Ioways and other regional tribes on their winter hunts to gather food for their own storage and sustenance and furs for trading in the spring. At San Luis merchants such as Laclede, Chouteau, and Jean Gabriel Cerre contemplated their future profits and ordered their wares to be ready when the Indians should return.

* The date of Pontiac's death varies. It is given as 1768 in *WHC*, 18:367; as 1769 in Paul C. Phillips and J. W. Smurr, *The Fur Trade*, 1:560; as 1767 in F. G. Hough, *The Diary of the Seige of Detroit;* and 1769 by Cyrus Thomas, *Handbook of North American Indians*, 2:280.

4. The 1770's

THE 1770'S WERE A tumultuous period in the region peopled by the Ioways and the other tribes of the central and northern Mississippi River system. During this decade four powers were involved in the economic and political affairs of the Native Americans. The French, the English, and the Spanish were already well known. The new nation that reached its explorative fingers westward was the nascent republic of America, whose citizéns were called the "Long Knives" by the Indians. Each country endeavored to maintain or to gain control of some larger portion of the midcontinent and the Indian populations residing there.

France

French influence after 1765 moved from the east to the west side of the Mississippi River. Early in its administration the Spanish crown had relied on French officials and others to assist in governing the territory and in establishing its relationships with the Indians. One hundred years' experience had given the French knowledge of Indian languages, customs, and values, which on the whole had resulted in successful relations. France used the early years of Spanish territorial ownership to entrench itself, although it functioned outwardly under the Spanish flag. Laclede, Chouteau, and other merchants of San Luis reached the Indian nations of present-day Missouri, Iowa, Kansas, and Nebraska by sending traders far up the various rivers with goods brought from New Orleans, where the aristocratic French owners of warehouses, stores, and shipping facilities continued to control much of the commerce of the New

World via the Mississippi and the Gulf Coast. Gradually French domination lessened as Spain became more involved and replaced French authority, curtailing French commercial activities.

During the 1770's France allied itself with Spain to repress and repel British New-World interests. France was fully aware of the economic potential of its former possessions and resented England's recent exploitation of them. During the American Revolution both Spain and France decided to aid the ambitious American colonies as another way of limiting England's future in America. By aiding the revolutionists directly and indirectly, France furthered its own ambitions. In the final years of the decade French interests secretly considered means of regaining the colony of Louisiana.

England

After 1763, England's possession of Canada and the formerly French territory east of the Mississippi River gave it a foothold for expansion into rich fur-producing areas with numerous new trade markets among the resident tribes. However, British traders had to compete with long-standing French-Indian relationships and the Indians' loyalty to the French king. Certain tribes such as the Fox, Sac, Winnebago, Menominee, and Ioway were more interested in English offers than they were in maintaining any remnant of French alliance.

Spain's influence began to be felt early in the decade as it sought to devise trade regulations to develop and control its newly acquired lands in upper and lower Louisiana. One concern was the English attempt to invade Spanish territory in order to entice the Indians to trade. It was decreed that such entry was forbidden, but enormous difficulties made it impossible to control the English traffic completely. Occasionally the Spanish were fortunate enough to apprehend a licensed English trader.[1] One Spanish inventory of seized cargo discloses the variety of items offered for trade: blankets, mirrors, beads, alum, spun wool, scissors, razors, knives, woolen tape, sail sewing needles, awls, vermillion, porcelain vessels, thimbles, woven materials such as cotton flannel, iron spears, chisels, spades, pewter cups, silver-plated lockets, crosses, bracelets, nostril rings, finger rings, copper jars with lids, brass kettles, iron spoons, gunpowder, used muskets, salt, earrings, and other items.

Spain

Spain's problems with its new possession increased in the 1770's. The colony's government and economic development, Indian relations, and the intrigues and demands of the French, British, and Americans broadened administrative difficulties. The Spanish gov-

ernment had relied heavily on the French governmental and com- *The 1770's*
mercial system already in operation in the previous decade. But with
the New Orleans citizen revolt in 1768 and the potential future
problems that such French influence might bring, the crown decided
to reorganize the colony's affairs giving greater emphasis to Spanish
control. Changes included the creation of new provincial districts
with a corps of administrative, military, and judicial personnel. One
such district was Ylinneses, or Spanish Illinois, inhabited by the
Ioways. A lieutenant governor stationed at San Luis would manage
its affairs subject to the approval of the governor general.[2] To make
Spanish rule more attractive to the native population the new policy
stressed creation of alliances, establishment of favorable trade regulations, and abolition of Indian slavery.[3] Although in other parts of
their American empire the Spanish were often more callous in their
treament of Indian subjects, using methods that often decimated
portions of the population, English successes in the Indian trade
made more humane treatment necessary in Louisiana. Indians were
to be treated fairly in all trade relationships. Prices were to be set
and moderate, and traders were to be licensed. Intoxicating liquor
could not be used as a medium of exchange nor given to the Indians
as a gift. This was not to protect Indian morality. It was apparent
that, from the Spanish point of view, dissipation was economically
unrewarding. Policy also included the distribution of gifts, Spanish
flags, medals and titles, pledges, and the description of the English
as aggressive, hostile, and covetous of Indian land.

The Otoes accepted the Spanish traders and trade regulations in
1773. A passport issued by Pedro Piernas, lieutenant governor at
San Luis, describes the conditions of trade:

Passport Given to Traders of the Oto Nation
September 11, 1773

DON PEDRO PIERNAS, lieutenant governor of the settlements and
dependencies of the Illinois:

The Sieurs Chauvin and Lajoye are permitted to go to trade with the
Hotos nation with Pierre Lange, Nicholas Saint Pierre, Joseph Cadien,
Jean Lamontagne, and Baptiste Mary, their employees. They shall do it
peaceably, without giving cause to the savages to complain of their
methods. In order to forestall any complaint on their part, the Indians
shall agree upon and establish a price with the traders for each kind of
merchandise which will be destined for their nation. This price must be
equitable, and applied without cheating or dissimulation.

The traders are forbidden to sell, loan, give, or intrust to any of the
Frenchmen who have remained and are at the present time in the
nations, any kind of trading merchandise or goods, no matter of what
nature, for trading purposes, and not even for their own personal use.
On the contrary, they are commanded to force these Frenchmen, in our
name, and by virtue of this deprivation, to return with them. They are

55

expressly commanded to return to this post with all their employees without exception in the month of July the next year, 1774, at the latest, whether they have finished their trading or not. They shall not leave any kind of goods either in this nation or in any others, or on the way, or still less in the hands of any Frenchmen under any pretext whatever, under pain of being severely punished according to the circumstances and necessities of the case.

They shall not trade with any other nation except the one with which they are licensed to trade, and they shall not take any goods over and above the quantity which is allotted to them. They shall watch over the conduct of their employees, and if any one of the men happens to fail in his conduct and causes trouble in the nation, and also if they should hear of any statements made by the savages which would be to our disadvantage, they shall give us a full account of it upon their return. They are granted eight or ten jugs of brandy which are solely meant for the indispensable needs of their crew and not at all for trading purposes. They shall pass by Fort Missouri to have this passport viséed.

Given at ST. LOUIS on the *11th of September, 1773.*

PEDRO PIERNAS[4]

The final attempts to eliminate French influence and control of economic activities among the Indians, wherever possible, are reflected in this document. The strict control of the licensed trader and the prohibition against liquor dispensing is clearly stated.

During this period the Spanish explored far and wide, up and down the tributaries of the Mississippi and Missouri river systems, their appetites whetted by profitable trade possibilities. Their activities were not confined solely to the western side of the Mississippi. Their vessels also explored the Ohio, Illinois, and Wisconsin rivers in an attempt to bring those tribes whom they could reach into relationship with themselves. Certain of these nations and their traders began to bring their furs to San Luis, which soon became the trading center of a widespread area.[5]

This activity was not without competition from a smaller but active British community up the river at Prairie du Chien, established earlier by the French at the site of an older Indian trading rendezvous. From here, opposite the old Ioway Orr Focus sites, British-sponsored traders fanned out into Spanish territory, entering Ioway country via the Turkey, Iowa and Des Moines rivers.[6] Here they contacted the Ioways and continued the trade relationship that possibly had its roots in the visit to Lieutenant Gorrell at Green Bay in 1762.

Charles Gayerré summarized the situation at the middle of the decade as follows:

"In this indirect way, the English having monopolized the trade of Louisiana, this colony had in a commercial point of view become for its owner an entirely worthless possession."[7] Although 600,000 pesos of commerce resulted, only 15,000 of this amount went through legitimate channels to Spain; the balance accrued to England.[8]

The American colonists' rebellion against England was the next event to affect Spanish administration of its colony. Although the lands west of the Mississippi were remote from the battle scenes, the war affected all of continental North America. Eventually all resident powers became involved in some manner, especially in the peace settlements of the next decade. At this time American pioneers had already reached the Mississippi shore as settlers, traders, and adventurers. The prospect of American movement into this far western region was not a serious concern to the Spanish, who were still interested in attracting settlers to the colony. England was the greatest threat to Spain's economic and military position. Spain saw an opportunity to break the English commercial monopoly and to hinder further gains, and the crown decided to assist the American cause by financial and material means. An American merchant residing in New Orleans, Oliver Pollack, became the chief negotiator in obtaining Spanish assistance.

A 1777 Spanish report of the Yllinneses nations described their locations, economic pursuits, and population numbers, among other details. Ten tribes considered to be under Spanish rule were listed: the Big Osages, the Little Osages, the Missouris, the Kansas, "La Republica Pawnee," the "Pawnee of the Platte," the Otoes, the Omahas, the Ioways, and the Sioux. Each tribe's location was given as the river closest to its villages. The total estimated number of warriors was given but not the total population for each tribe. On the basis of warrior numbers the Osages were the largest tribe, and the Otoes were the smallest. These figures gave the Spanish important information on the relative strength of each nation in terms of how many men each could muster against its enemies, whether they were Spanish, English, French, or Indian. The strength of coalitions of tribes could also be ascertained. The Spanish had ideas of sending certain tribes against the nonconforming Osages to control them, and had already encouraged the Sacs to go on the war trail against them in 1772.

Descriptions of tribal economic activity noted whether the tribes were hunters and/or agriculturists. The farming nations included the Missouris, the Kansas, the Pawnees, the Omahas, and the Ioways. Except for certain Siouan groups, tribes not mentioned in this list undoubtedly practiced some horticulture and raised corn, squashes, and beans.

The report stated that the Ioways traded only with the English. Their fur trade was carried on continuously "with the traders who enter the Des Moines River from the English District." At this time the Ioways' location is specifically stated to be eighty leagues from San Luis, near present-day Iowaville in Van Buren County.[10] This village or villages near the Mississippi permitted access of traders from Prairie du Chien. It was impossible for the Spaniards to control this illegal trade without stationing troops in the villages, an act that would have been both impractical and impolitic. It is certain

The Ioway
Indians

from the English point of view that this nearby tribe was worthy of their efforts to maintain and to further their interests on the western side of the Mississippi River. Other pro-British tribes listed were the Big and Little Osages, the Sioux, the Fox, the Sacs, and the Winnebagos. The latter four resided in the English district, although at this time parts of the Sac and Sioux nations were on the western side of the river. The Sioux, who lived 230 leagues northwest of San Luis, were directly in contact with the British traders from La Baye, Prairie du Chien, and other posts. In 1775 a Sioux delegation had arrived at San Luis and requested a trader and goods, which were later supplied.[11] Nevertheless, the majority of this large tribe apparently was considered more interested in English than in Spanish relationships.

The report also described one aspect of intertribal relations. Each tribe had one or more enemies. The Osages were at war or hostile with all the tribes on the Mississippi, as well as the Kansas, the Pawnees, the Wichitas, and the Otoes. The Otoes apparently had the Osages and the Kansas for enemies. The Omahas had only animosity toward the Kansas. The Ioway enemies were tribes in the lower Missouri River area, including the Little Osages, the Missouris, and the Kansas. How active this enmity was is not described for any of the tribes. Nor is it known how much of it was inspired by Spanish, French, and British intervention. The report, speaking of the Ioways, gave the name of the chief as El Ladron, or the Thief. Whether this was his name translated into Spanish or whether it was another tribe's appellation for him is not known.

"Tribes which Generally come from the English district to receive presents from this post" are listed as the Menominees, Foxes, Sacs, Winnebagos, Kickapoos, Potawatomis, Mascoutins, Ottawas, Chippewas, Peorias, and Kaskaskias. The Ottawas were noted as dissatisfied with the English and were planning to move to the Spanish district. Presents were also given to the distant Pawnees and Omahas who lived near the Missouri River. From San Luis, then, the Spanish endeavored to influence and attract Indian trade within a radius of three hundred miles by gift giving and by persuasion of the benefits of Spanish allegiance.[12]

In 1778 two American colonial officers, James Willing and George Rogers Clark, moved with their small forces into the upper and lower Mississippi valley areas. Willing attacked British posts in the South, and Clark concentrated his efforts along the Ohio and in the British Illinois regions. Soon after Clark seized Kaskaskia, Fernando de Leyba, then lieutenant governor at San Luis, followed Spanish policy and established contact with him. He wrote two letters, one to Joseph Bowman stationed at Cahokia and the other to Clark at Kaskaskia. He informed Clark that he had spoken favorably to the Indians about the Americans and promised to visit if it were possible. He also invited Clark to visit him.[13]

58

Soon after De Leyba arrived, Indian delegations from tribes on both sides of the Missouri and Mississippi had come to pay their official regards. In a letter to Governor Bernado de Gálvez written in the summer he described the situation:

ST. LOUIS, *July 21, 1778*

Señor Governor General.

MY VERY DEAR AND MOST ESTEEMED SIR: The following Indian nations have come to welcome me: the Kickapoos, Sacs, Mahas, Mascutens, Missouris, Great and Little Osages. According to reports I have received, about a dozen more are still to come. Some nations have sent me word that they will leave their dogs to guard their villages, that is, that they will come with their wives and children. The Missouri nation has done this and has been here for two weeks, eating us out of house and home. There are only two ways of treating these people, either run them out with guns or feed them. For the former they give no cause, nor have we the forces to do so. I am following the latter, although I have found in the archives a regulation or statement drawn up by Don Pedro Piernas of January 4, '71, concerning the rations of bread which are to be given to the Indians during the year. However, those times were very different from the present. The war with the English is causing a great number of Indian tribes to go from one side to the other without knowing which side to take; or, more certainly, terrified by the Bostoneses, and in order to escape their anxieties for a few days, they come to this post under the pretext of asking for advice on their troubles, and consume many rations of bread. These were not distributed in the year '71 because of the absence of any such reason. Since my arrival here, the fewest that have been distributed in one day is fifty rations, and there have been days when it was two hundred. Each nation which arrives, even though a foreign one, must be given not only bread but also a present. We are using for these, (and they are not sufficient) goods which were intended for some tribes which did not come to get them. I advise Your Lordship of this matter so that you may tell me whether my certificate for the total of the rations which have been distributed to the Indians will be honored by your treasury in favor of the purveyor or only the number specified in the above-mentioned order of '71 that is, 1,072 rations.

I remain with all respect at the orders of Your Lordship and pray God to preserve your life for many years.

My very dear Sir, your most affectionate servant kisses your hand.

FERNANDO DE LEYBA (Rubric)[14]

These occasions, although they taxed the treasury, augumented De Leyba's influence on the Indian visitors. He could assume the role of wise father and — while speaking well of the Americans, as he assured Clark he had done — he also used these visits to promote Spanish interests. On November 16, 1778, De Leyba, now well established in his office, sent Gálvez a report of his district. He stated that the most loyal Indians lived on the Missouri and its tributaries, but if their loyalty was to be assured, the fort at San

Carlos should be moved to another site. Trees obscured its view of the river, and English trade boats entering the Missouri en route to these tribes could not be seen and stopped. He suggested that another fort be built at the mouth of the "Mua" (Des Moines), 8 leagues distant, in order to stop the English trade going to the Ioways, from whose village goods were transported to the Missouri River. This was "a matter, which, if totally accomplished as they did part of last year would reduce this settlement of St. Louis to the greatest misery."[15]

It is probable that at this time the Ioways had two villages on the eastern side of the Mississippi in British Illinois. The Thomas Hutchins map of 1778 shows two towns on that side of the river; they may have been near the mouth of the Des Moines and Iowa Rivers.* Settlements at these or other strategic sites on the British side would have lessened Spanish interference and would have given the Ioways some control over the traders who entered their territory on the western side of the Mississippi.

The Des Moines River was important, because it transected the area from the southeast to the northwest for over two hundred miles with portages of from twenty to thirty miles to Missouri River tributaries. Thus the Ioways were in a very advantageous position for promoting their economic gain.

No only did De Leyba have difficulty with the Ioways and other tribes who traded with the British, but the local population of San Luis decided that trading with the Indians was more profitable than most any other endeavor, such as raising their own foodstuffs. He complained to Gálvez that certain numbers should be ordered to grow food in order to sustain the population. Added to the difficulty was the loss of wheat, which had annually been imported from across the Mississippi and which could no longer be obtained because of the unsettled conditions in Illinois.[16]

De Leyba's request for construction of a fort at the mouth of the Des Moines was rejected by Gálvez, who said that there were no instructions from Spain for such a facility, and even if there were, he could not spare men from the New Orleans garrison to man it. In response to another urgent request for the fort, he replied, "I would suggest to you that you endeavor to prevent the entrance of the English into the aforesaid rivers, and see that they do not win our Indians."[17] This helpful response must have gladdened De Leyba's conscientious heart considerably.

Meanwhile in Europe Spain had attempted and failed to keep peace between France and England. In June Spain broke off relations

---

* This map, along with others referred to in this book, is one of a valuable collection of maps that are quite useful to the student of this period. See Sara Jones Tucker, "Indian Villages of the Illinois Country," *Scientific Papers*, Vol. 2, Pt. 1, Springfield, Ill., Illinois State Museum, 1942, Pl. XXIX.

with England and, on July 8, 1779, instructed the Spanish-American colonies to be in a state of war with the British and to aid its ally, France, with whom Spain had made a treaty in April.[18]

The American Colonies

The American colonies became the fourth and last European-derived power to influence, alter, and eventually control the lives of the American Indians. The colonies, too, wanted loyalty, trade, and land. In order to settle the coastal regions their ancestors had had to deal with indigenous Indians in one manner or another. But the prevailing policy was to assume the right of dominion of land and people by virtue of discovery and possession. In all contests between European nations regarding claims to territory in the New World, the rights of native inhabitants rarely were allowed to intervene.

The recent British suppression of American colonists' rights perhaps gave the first Indian policy statements of the Continental Congress a just, humane, and sympathetic ring. It was as if the fledgling government wished to advertise its belief in the rights of all mankind, including the Indians. However, in practice, the so-called Indian rights were rarely observed, except as they served the purpose of the colonist farmer, trader, merchant, or soldier. Genuine spokesmen for the eighteenth-century Indians' views were few.

In July 1775 in Philadelphia the Second Continental Congress had set in motion processes by which Indian lives became entwined with the American government, a relationship that, no matter how well intentioned, eventually removed from the Indians the very freedoms that the colonies espoused so fervently in the Declaration of Independence exactly one year later.

After the Continental Congress created a Department of Indian Affairs to deal with the Indian nations, it provided means to make the relationship more formal and binding through treaty conferences. On May 6, 1776, it passed a resolution: "That treaties be held with the Indians in the different Departments, as soon as practical; and the sum of ten thousand Dollars be paid out of the Treasury to the Commission of each respective Department, for presents to the Indians, and the expenses of such Treaties."[19] In the subsequent treaty conferences the department attempted to follow Indian protocol by use of gifts, wampum-belt presentation, formalized modes of address, and styles of language. Indian and white speeches were couched in alliterative phrases, using parables from life and nature to make basic points. Also included were evasion, veiled and direct threats, and dramatic contrasts that made the speeches given by all parties an intriguing part of American historical literature. No white man involved in such proceedings ever downgraded the Indian powers of persuasion and logic. As the years passed, the protagonists became more desperate and more aggressive; and the tone changed. In 1776, one commissioner, in council with the Delawares, the Wyandots, the Mingos, and others, said that, if the British lost, the Americans would be "incensed against the Indian who fought against them, that they would march an army into their country, destroy them and take their lands from them."[20]

Such American retaliation, when it did occur, often cloaked more than one motive. Frontier deaths from Indian attacks were used as excuses to invade and to defeat Indian villages. In subsequent peace councils certain privileges to use Indian land were requested and gained. In later years the technique became more refined, and the treaty usually contained reparation clauses by which large tracts of land were relinquished.

The colonial government tried several schemes in order to gain a greater share of the fur trade. One was to establish traders under the supervision of agents. Another plan was to seize the southern and western posts that controlled the British fur trade at its sources along the Ohio and Mississippi Rivers. It was hoped that Spain would lend aid in capturing Baton Rouge, Natchez, and posts in Illinois.[21] But, all in all, the efforts to control the interior trade were not successful. The Virginia Colony decided to act directly to effect certain political, economic, and military goals. By its Charter of 1609 Virginia claimed an area that included land within present-day Illinois, Indiana, Ohio, and Kentucky. In order to gain the greatest advantage from this vast territory, certain sections of which were also claimed by Connecticut and Massachusetts, it was necessary to curtail Indian depredations and hinder the British, and thus control the fur trade. At this time George Rogers Clark began to make plans that would further Virginia's aspiration. He had served in 1774 as captain of militia in Lord Dunmore's War, and he had long been interested in the Indian lands north of the Ohio. In 1776 he represented Kentucky in the Virginia legislature, and with his assistance it was established as a separate Virginia county in 1777. During these years he had worked on plans to invade the country north of the Ohio, now claimed by England. Afraid of publicizing the scheme by presenting it to the Virginia governing body, Gov. Patrick Henry, Thomas Jefferson, George Mason, and George Wythe listened and agreed to lend it their support. As an inducement to recruit men for the expedition each volunteer would be granted three hundred acres of conquered land.

In January, 1778, Clark, now a lieutenant colonel, began plans for the actual capture of Kaskaskia, sixty miles south of San Luis. All went well, and on the night of July 4 he entered the village with his small army and captured it. In February France had entered the war against Britain, and he counted on French inhabitants to adhere to the American cause. This they did, swearing allegiance, as did the villages of Cahokia, St. Phillipe, Prairie du Rocher, and Vincennes on the Wabash River, when Clark requested it.

Clark realized that the next step to consolidate his military position entailed his convincing the area's Indian nations to accept the American presence and reject the British authority. In August under the title, "George Rogers Clark, Esq., Colonel and Commandant of the Eastern Illinois and Its Dependencies, etc., etc., etc.,[22] he prepared and sent speeches inviting various tribes to counsel with him:

> I sent letters and speeches by Capt Helms to the Chief of the Kickebues & Peankeshaws residing at Post St Vincents desireing them to lay down their Tomahawk, and if they did not chuse it to behave like Men and fight for the English as they had done; but they would see their great father as they called him given to the Dogs to eat (gave Harsh language to supply the want of Men; well knowing that it was a mistaken notion in many that soft speeches was best for Indians) But if they thought of giving their hands to the Big knives to give their Hearts also, and that I did not doubt but after being acquainted, that they would find that the Big knives of better Principals than what the bad Birds the English had taught them to believe. [23]

In later reflection on his Indian policy he declared:

> Excell them if possible, in their own policy, treat them with indifference, make war on them, prosecute it with all the vigor and devastation possible, mention nothing of peace to them, and you would soon have them suing for mercy. Turn the scale upon them and oblige them to give up a part of their country to pay for the expenses of war. [24]

Clark may have assumed that his Indian policy and oratorical style were responsible for various Indian nations' declarations that they would no longer fight for and be loyal to the English. In reality other factors were responsible, one of which was France's entering the conflict on the American side. This had the greatest impact on their decision and in the minds of some rekindled the hope of French return.

Cohos, or Cahokia, was soon filled with visiting tribesmen. Clark indicated that many traveled five hundred miles "to treat for peace and hear what the big knives had to say." Delegations of Chippewas, Ottawas, Kaskaskias, Potawatomis, Winnebagos, Ioways, Sacs, Foxes, Miamis, and Osages arrived, plus "others all living east of the Mississippi, and many of them at war with us."

The presence of the Ioways at this initial Clark council in August, 1778, can perhaps be explained. Spanish reports of this year indicate the pro-British sentiments of the Ioways and their dependency on and involvement in the British fur trade. At this time there was a shortage of trade goods partially as a result of the Canadian government's restriction of Great Lakes cargo transportation. In view of this, and especially because the Ioways apparently served in some capacity as middlemen in trade with the Missouri River tribes, it is possible that economic motives sent them to the council to see what the Americans had to offer. They came perhaps from the villages on the eastern bank of the Mississippi.

Both the English and the Americans had agents in the Mississippi River area to propagandize the Indians. Charles Gautier served British interests, particularly in lands west of Lake Michigan, among the Sioux, Winnebago, Menominee, and Chippewa tribes. In the winter of 1777-78 he traveled to Rock River and sent a runner with a war belt for the Ioways to induce them to maintain their British relationship. In April he went to Prairie du Chien. In his journal he described the situation: "... I expected the nations and prepared to receive them. I bought food, drink, and some merchandise that I thought necessary, Indians arrived every moment from winter quarters. The Agovoin [Ioway] took the lead and left their comrades preparing to come." Later he again sent another belt to the Ioway chief to induce him to join the British. On June 4 he wrote:

> Sr. de Linctot the Younger arrived from the Village of the Agosoin and in giving the account of his mission, he said to Sr. de Langlade his friend, that the Spaniard had sent word to the Agosoin not to heed the Venimous and empoisoned mouths which should come or which had already spoken to them that those bad men had no other end in view than to destroy them by the Bostonniens, that they were braver men, than any nation, and they were upheld by the Spaniards (among whom the Agosoin go very often and indeed are neighbors).[25]

Gautier was able to recruit seven Ioways and their families in spite of the Spanish message to them not to fight and be destroyed by the Americans. Sioux, Foxes, Sacs, and Winnebagos also joined his recruits. Among the Ioways was their chief, Le Voleur, to whom Frederick Haldimand, captain general and governor in chief of the British provinces, awarded a medal of King George III. The presentation certificate was dated August 17, 1778, and read:

> In consideration of the fidelity, zeal, and attachment testified by Le Voleur, Grand Chief of the Zaivovois, to the King's Government, and by virtue of the power and authority in me vested, I do hereby confirm the said Le Voleur, Grand Chief, and all officers and others in his Majesty's service to treat him accordingly.[26]

Thus a portion of the Ioway nation actively affirmed its pro-British position in the American Revolution. Whether the entire tribal leadership was thus committed cannot be said. However, in October, 1778, Joseph Bowman, stationed at Cahokia, reported to Clark on the events of the post, including a visit from some Indian warriors:

> Their has been Some Indians of the sack Nation here, which I dispatcht a few days ago with them caime one cheif and another of the Iwaya Nation which had never been in, their complyance has not satisfyed me with a Regard to peace, as they confessd to me that their principal cheifs

whear gone to Montreall to fight against the big Knife, I sent them off and gave A Kag of Rum and told them to go and hold a counsel with their Nation, and give them choice which side to Join, with Drinking their Health with the Rum.[27]

The Ioway visit to Bowman may have been to investigate the American strength and position with little intention to ask for peace or to pledge allegiance. Some of the Sacs took Bowman's advice. On November 16 Governor Henry wrote to the Virginia delegation in Congress that the Winnebagos, the Sacs, the Foxes, and others "have submitted to our arms all their English presents, and bound themselves by treaties and promises to be peaceable in the future."

On December 9, 1778, when Virginia reached its goal of placating the regional Indian nations and outwardly gaining their allegiance, it created a county from the land north of the Ohio to the Mississippi and called it Illinois.

During this decade the Ioways, who seemed to have resided on both sides of the Mississsippi, visited and counseled with Spanish, English, and American officials. They visited San Luis, they conferred with George Rogers Clark, and they accepted Gautier's proposal to continue the relationship that the English traders had initiated some years before. They conceived of their relationship with the English as important enough that some went to distant Montreal to take up arms and to give their loyalty to the British crown.

5. Freedom in the Spanish Years

ON JANUARY 29, 1780, Thomas Jefferson advised George Rogers Clark:

> endeavour that those who are in friendship with us live in peace also with one another, against those who are our Enemies let loose the friendly tribes. The Kickapoos should be encouraged against the hostile tribes of the Chickasaws and Choctaws and the others gainst the Shawanese. . . . Ammunition should be furnished gratis to those warriors who go actually on expeditions against the hostile tribes.[1]

This warlike message contained one important aspect of the emerging nation's procedure for subjugation of its Indian population: divide and conquer. It was not an innovation. Since the days of Cortez in Mexico, who with the aid of the Tlaxcalans had defeated the Aztecs at Tenochtitlán, the procedure had worked well. It continued to be employed on the North American continent as late as the 1870's, when the United States recruited the Pawnee Scouts under Maj. F. North to subdue their ancient enemies, the Sioux and the Cheyennes. Both had attacked and destroyed the Pawnees for many years, and from their point of view, the United States Army served to help them end the aggression and even the score. The American officials, like the French, the Spanish, and the British, soon learned who the Indians' enemies were and utilized these enmities to further their own goals.

The British continued their plans to gain a greater share of the fur trade in Spanish Louisiana. Partial justification for military and economic expansion into Spanish territory resulted from Spain's declaration of war the previous year. In 1780 they decided to capture

San Luis in order to gain control of that vital trading center and entryway to the west. To gather Indian allies for such an endeavor emissaries were sent to various tribes, including the Ioways, the Sacs, and the Foxes. To do this in a proper diplomatic manner war belts for nine tribes were readied and sent by Lt. Gov. Patrick Sinclair at Mackinac, who said, "I have prepared them and placed two figures with joined hands and raised axes — it serves to please them." Emmanuel Hesse, a trader and former British soldier, was commissioned a captain and was instructed to assemble the Menominees, the Winnebagos, the Sacs, and the Foxes at the portage of the Wisconsin and Fox Rivers to await other tribesmen of the area, including the Sioux and the Ioways.[2] From this rallying point the expedition would then move secretly down the Mississippi to "Pencour," as the British called San Luis. Meanwhile, another group composed of tribes who lived near southern Lake Michigan would travel down the Illinois River toward Peoria and on to the villages held by the Americans on the Mississippi.

These secret plans had been known by the Spaniards since March, and after bolstering their forces and strengthening their defenses around the fort and village, they met with the Americans across the river to plan their strategy against the British. A series of signals was devised to alert each side of the attack. On May 26, 1780, the attack on both the Spanish and American settlements came. San Luis was attacked by Captain Hesse with his forces of Winnebagos, Sioux, Ottawas, Chippewas, Ioways, Foxes, Sacs, and other Indians.[3] The Spanish were able to repulse the onslaught, not because of their numbers, which were certainly fewer, but because, the British later accused, the Sacs and some others did not really attack but deliberately held back. This group was led by two traders, Joseph Calvé and Jean Marie Ducharme, who acted treacherously, Sinclair declared. Both men were said to have profited handsomely by the trade in fur and lead in Spanish territory, and an attack on the Spaniards would have interfered with their commercial prospects.[4] It had been planned that G. R. Clark would come to the aid of San Luis, but a wayward wind blew the sound of the signals in another direction. However, with five hundred men he later pursued the attackers of the American settlements and sent them fleeing.

Indians from both sides of the Mississippi continued to visit St. Louis. The following excerpt from a 1780 Kickapoo chief's speech to Francisco Cruzat, now lieutenant governor after De Leyba's death, gives insight into the confusion of the times as the tribes found themselves caught up in the affairs of the three warring nations:

> My French, Spanish, and American father: I cannot prove a greater fidelity to you, my French, Spanish, and American father except by recalling the life of our old chiefs who took up arms against their relatives, the Renards, for the sake of their father the Frenchmen, who is still in our hearts. That is why, my father, we are begging you to help

67

us. In the past our hands have not been dipped in the blood of the French. They are all in a position to render us this justice. Our old chiefs have always told us never to let go of the Frenchman's hand, and that they would take pity on us. I am not speaking to you with sugared words. The Master of Life hears us, and we wish never to fail in our duty towards him. This is all that I have to say to you, my French, Spanish, and American father.[5]

In their strategic position on the Des Moines River the Ioways continued to give Cruzat concern as he reported in a December, 1780, letter to Gov. Gálvez:

> I have just learned that a band of the Aioas [Iowa], doubtless excited by the enemy, has corrupted the Hotos [Oto] tribe which is located on the upper Misury and has promised them to join the other tribes opposed to us in order to show as great hostility as possible toward us. I do not doubt the truth of this, for I know the Indians, and I know by experience that the appearance of gain does not excite them to take action, but the reality of the presents does. Since the English make so many of these to all tribes of whom they wish to make use, they always obtain from them whatever they desire, unless, by the same methods, we destroy their hopes by deceiving the barbarians as they are doing.... [6]

The Spanish administration under Cruzat became more aggressive against the British. In the summer Auguste Chouteau, now a commissioned officer, traveled northward from New Orleans with a consignment of Indian gifts, stopped and participated in an attack on the British post opposite the Spanish Arkansas post, and continued on upstream with the important cargo.

It was the custom at this time to present each Indian chief who visited San Luis a group of gifts which included the following articles: one axe, one hatchet, one mattock, one gun, four pounds of gunpowder, eight pounds of bullets, one pair of trousers, one fine trimmed shirt, one pair of knitted stockings, one pair of shoes, one pair of buckles of cannon metal, one-half pound of vermillion, six large, heavy knives, one pound of beads, and one bundle of tobacco.[7] This was the type of cargo that Chouteau brought to San Luis.

For the most part such gifts and supplies were never in adequate supply, and Cruzat was forced to purchase on the open market. Even so, the British were winning this aspect of the struggle, as in the case of the Ioways, by superior amounts of gifts and promises of more.[8] The Sacs and the Foxes, although they still leaned toward the Spaniards, asked Cruzat if they could trade with the English for much-needed articles that Spain did not have to offer. Cruzat gave his permission, for he had little choice. A. P. Nasatir noted that, "In a sense, this may be taken as a beginning of the end of effective control of the Upper Missouri-Mississippi Valley region. For now the British traders were allowed to trade with the Indians as the Spaniards had no goods...."[9]

In spite of this, Cruzat reported in March, 1782, that 132 tribal delegations who lived in the territory bounded by the Mississippi and Ohio rivers had visited St. Louis to ask for protection and peace. If accurate, this was a remarkable number in view of the efforts of the British and Americans at this time to woo the nations to their cause. But considering the awareness of the Indians that their territories were coveted by the intruders, whose politics of conquest were fully revealed, it is not surprising. The migration of Indian tribal fragments across the Mississippi increased from this time, as did the problems for the nations already living there.

When the Revolutionary War ended, there was little immediate change in the lives of the Indians of the Spanish territory. In the peace negotiations that involved four nations, Spain did not gain the goals that it sought. It had hoped that the boundary between itself and the new nation would lie far to the east of the Mississippi River along the western slopes of the Appalachians. Instead the Mississippi became the boundary.

On all accounts the final British terms of September, 1783, were generous. The United Colonies gained a tremendous territory, most of it in the hands of its indigenous inhabitants. Many tribes had never trusted the Long Knives and now viewed the future with apprehension. Without the competition of the colonies and Britain for their favor and alliance they would be forced to deal with a people who, on the whole, had not indicated a wholehearted dedication to the principles of "liberty and justice for all" as far as the Indian was concerned.

Evidence of the Indian feeling is revealed in the speech made to Cruzat in August, 1784. At that time two hundred Iroquois, Cherokees, Shawnees, Chickasaws, Choctaws, and Loups visited him at San Luis. One said:

> The Americans, a great deal more ambitious and numerous than the English, put us out of our lands, forming therein great settlements, extending themselves like a plague of locusts in the territories of the Ohio River which we inhabit. They treat us as their cruelest enemies are treated, so that today hunger and the impetuous torrent of war which they impose upon us with other terrible calamities, have brought our villages to a struggle with death.[10]

The Indians offered loyalty to the Spaniards, but Cruzat, while making a noble reply, could offer them little for the moment. In spite of their desire for Indian allies against any future American thrust, the Spanish could not encourage wholesale migration. There were insufficient supplies and food, and their presence would be more burden than boon.

In December, 1785, Estevan Miró, intendant and governor of Louisiana, submitted a list and locations of the tribes to whom annual presents were given under his jurisdiction in Upper Louisiana.

They were the Sioux, Big Osages, Ioways, Kansas, Pawnees, Omahas, Sacs, Otoes, Little Osages, Missouris, Foxes, and Kaskaskias. The report noted that:

> The Otos live 15 leagues up the Chato River [Platte] in the center of a prairie, and they have about 900 men capable of bearing arms. The Otos are the only nation on the Missouri who have no necessity for trade or commerce with Ylinoa [Spanish] because they are on the most friendly terms with the Iowas who live on the upper Des Moines River. This river may cause much injury to the upper Missouri and still greater to the inhabitants of New Mexico if the traders from the American district or the English continue to open up trails and commerce with the Otos by means of the Iowas. It is therefore well to know the Oto hunt on Grand River, two days march from the Missouri and that from the Grand River up to the large island which is in the Des Moines River eighty leagues from its mouth, takes only two days journey. The traders from the other district, would have only 2-3 days travel to get to Oto lands. In this case the traffic would be even more troublesome than on the upper Missouri because it would be easy to attract the PaniMahas nation, and the traders could more easily trade with the Iowas. Whenever the Otos are at war with the Sioux they prefer to trade with the Ylinoa and it is always to be feared that the English will enter into the villages of the Pawnees and Otos as they did in 1773 and 1777.[11]

From the Louisiana government's point of view, fear of the new American trader and the old British Canadian trader and their aspirations to reach New Mexico continued. It would also seem that the Ioways, although outwardly friendly toward the Spaniards, were allowing English traders to use their lands and themselves as contacts and participants in the trade.

The 1790's brought Spanish Illinois to its most difficult times in the eighteenth century. In thirty years the accumulated problems had grown large and insoluble, even though colonial officials did what they could to mitigate them under most circumstances. In Europe Spain became involved in wars with France and England, and the New-World colony did not receive the attention, direction, and resources that it might have received otherwise. Unofficial British control of northern Spanish boundary areas and resident tribes continued to be one of the major problems. Several trading posts and tribal relationships had been established in Spanish territory by Canadian traders, who had penetrated the villages of the tribes of the upper Missouri River.

On December 4, 1790, Lt. Gov. Manuel Perez at San Luis wrote to Miró:

> From the Ottawa tribe I have learned that the English have actually talked with them as well as with the Iowa and Puz [Potawatomis] telling them to be ready to come down with them to the Big Town, meaning this one. . . . I shall not be surprized if they cast their eyes upon the

Ylinueses, even for no other reason than to get to the Missouri which they have desired for a long time.[12]

The Otoes, who resided near the Missouri on the Platte, continued their old relationship with the Ioways and the British. In spring, 1791, one group traveled east through Ioway lands to visit the English traders on the Mississippi. The traders, with Ioway permission, traveled westward to visit and to trade with the Otos.[13]

The Spaniards had not seized the initiative in dealing with the tribes in these areas because of the usual lack of men, capital, and goods. Perez notified Miró on April 5, 1791:

> Other persons who likewise have come down from the Mississippi have assured me that some Englishmen had gone to trade with the Omahas and Pawnees. Notwithstanding the fact that I have given to their party the orders necessary for the traders of these two nations to arrest any English trader who may present himself in their district, I greatly fear that it cannot be done, because the contraband traders will, in all probability, have savages from other nations accompanying them who will not permit our traders to arrest them or do them any harm.[14]

Those Indians who accompanied the Canadians could well have been Ioways because much of this trade passed through Prairie du Chien and moved up rivers and along trade roads in Ioway lands. To prevent this movement, Perez, as had commandants and lieutenant governors before him, requested that forts be built and manned at the mouths of the St. Peters (Minnesota) and Des Moines Rivers to prevent not only foreign trade entry but any attempts that any nation should have in mind to reach the "Kingdom of Mexico." By 1793 as many as thirty English boats were counted on the St. Peters, and horse caravans traveled through the Ioway Des Moines River valley areas.[15]

South of San Luis the Osages continued to pose problems not only in their own area but in others. On August 6, 1790, Perez wrote to Miró:

> I take note from your Lordship's letter, dated May 10 that the hunters of the Arkansas have again requested that they be given ammunition, so that they with the aid of the Arkansas tribe they may go to attack the Great Osage... I think that nothing is more advisable than for the Arkansas to make war on them, as I believe that this is the only tribe the Osage fear. At the same time the Sac, Foxes, and Iowas are determined to do so themselves this autumn, as they have promised me; and I shall give them what assistance I can without exposing these inhabitants.[16]

Although the Ioways leaned strongly toward the British in matters of trade, it is obvious in this statement that they maintained diplomatic ties with the Spanish, particularly when it served their purpose, as is the nature of such relationships. In this case the Spanish supplied them with ammunition and supplies in order to make war on a tribe who interfered with both their interests.

In summer, 1793, complaints against the Osage continued undiminished. Gov. F. H. Baron de Carondelet ordered all trade stopped to them and permitted any Spanish subject the right to kill them. This included the Sacs, the Foxes, and the Ioways of the Des Moines River, who were at war with them. Although the Spanish were pleased with the Ioway efforts to harass the Osages, they were not so pleased with the tribe's raid on the settlement and post at San Carlos earlier in the summer. Here they had boldly driven off thirty-eight horses, possibly for use in the war expedition against the Osages. According to the owners' complaints, these were the only horses that the inhabitants had to work the fields, and few crops would result from the Ioways' brash deed. Carondolet was informed of the act and wrote to Lt. Gov. Don Zenon Trudeau, who had replaced Perez at San Luis: "You must see if the Ioways are a nation from whom the stolen horses may be reclaimed. Propose to me any means that may seem feasible."[17] Trudeau responded:

> I have received the most complete satisfaction from the chiefs of the Indian nation for the theft of the horses which the men of the same had committed at the Post of San Carlos and even though they did not return the same horses, they completed the number with the exception of one which they paid for. They came right away to see me. Because of the fine way in which they acted and because I need them to guard the River of *Des Moins*, I received them and feasted them well, giving them a full barrel of *aguardiente*, fourteen guns, and the rest proportionately, which is the best I have been able to do. But with all that, they still were not happy.
>
> All these nations who trade with the English and go to receive gifts at Michilimaquinac are very given to drink and accustomed to receive the best of large gifts. They refused and mocked at the ones received from us, showing us what they have received in said Michilimaquinac in silverware, fine material, coats bordered with silver and gold, etc.
>
> This Ayoa nation is at war with the Kansas, having entered this spring a camp of the said Kansas to buy horses from them. The latter went out to hunt in order to feed them and while they were gone, they killed, and took prisoner forty-eight women and children, and carried off all the horses. This is the reason why they do not dare send ambassadors to ask for peace and they have come to bring me five boy prisoners in order for me to make peace. I am keeping them in order to return them to the nation as soon as the occasion presents itself for that, and I will attempt to make peace if possible.[18]

On September 25, Carondolet notified Trudeau of his satisfaction with the outcome of the affair:

> In your official letter No. 91 informing me of the complete satisfaction given by the Ayoas Indians for the robbery of horses, which the young men [*mozos*] of the same nation made in the *Pueblo* de San Carlos,

animals which were all returned with the exception of one that they paid for, you tell me of the present which you gave them and which I approve of; likewise the step that you are thinking of taking to make peace between the said Indians and the Cances with the five boy prisoners which the former took from the latter.

With this motive in mind, I can do no less than recommend to you that under no circumstances should your inhabitants take Indian slaves, because it is forbidden by our laws under the severest punishment, and I find myself forced to maintain with the greatest rigor the observance of such laws, so just and comfortable to humanity.[19]

The early 1790's were a period of Ioway militancy, economic involvement with English trade interests, maintenance of diplomatic contacts with the Spanish government at San Luis, and existence as an autonomous tribal government with freedom of action.

The Jay Treaty of 1794 between England and the United States gave Spanish Louisiana new hope. Article I asserted that the King would "withdraw all His Troops and Garrisons from all Posts and Places within the Boundary lines assigned by the Treaty of Peace [1783] to the United States. This evacuation shall take place on or before the first Day of June one thousand seven hundred and ninety-six."[20]

Carondolet saw an opportunity in this treaty to recoup some trade advantage over the British. Andrew Todd, who now resided in New Orleans, was the nephew of an important British merchant, Isaac Todd, at Michilimackinac (later Mackinac). Todd had been supplying merchandise to the Spanish Company of Discoveries for their Missouri River ventures. He was also a primary supplier for the British traders at Prairie du Chien, from which these individuals had now to withdraw their interests. The Jay Treaty necessitated that he make a choice, if he wished to continue his profitable commercial interests with the Spanish, inasmuch as Michilimackinac and Prairie du Chien would no longer be in British hands. Jacques Clamorgan of the Company of Discoveries soon approached Governor Carondolet with a proposition that he be allowed to build a post or fort near the mouth of the Des Moines to stop incursions of foreign merchants or traders into that area. It was requested that Clamorgan's company be given exclusive trading rights to that river and the Indian trade there, including those Indians living near the Skunk and Ioway rivers. It was known that Todd was the instigator of the plan. The Chouteaus and others who had dealt with British merchants via Cahokia, Kaskaskia, Prairie du Chien, and Mackinac since the Revolutionary War also had interests to preserve in maintaining a chain to the British supply houses in Canada and London.

On December 18, 1795, Todd sent Carondolet a letter in which he illustrated the realities of the situation as far as Spanish and Todd interests were concerned.[21] It was pointed out that the business and profit that the Spanish did enjoy from British suppliers would fall to the Americans after the posts were taken over by them. He mentioned that certain Indian chiefs had advised him to apply for Spanish government permission to trade. In so doing, he belived that he could gain Indian loyalty for the Spanish crown. Furthermore, such alliances might well serve Spanish interests in any future hostilities with the aggressive Americans. If this were not accomplished, the Indians, who must procure their supplies somewhere, would be forced to turn to the Americans. His request was accepted by Carondolet and Francisco Rendon, the intendant, on December 21, 1795, and later by the Spanish council of state. He immediately began to implement his agreement, ordering and receiving goods at New Orleans in August, 1796.

In September Trudeau dispatched a corporal and two soldiers to protect Todd's new interest at the Des Moines River. They were to order any English or American traders to leave and to seize their goods if they would not.However, the English traders who came only laughed at the three-man military force and went about their business. At the end of two months the soldiers return to St. Louis. Todd's employees who remained at the post requested protection because the Ioways, under the influence of the English traders who had not vacated the area, were becoming increasingly hostile — so much so that Todd's men finally abandoned the post.

To accelerate further the ruin of Louisiana's plans to abate the long-standing frustrations on their northern border, Todd succumbed to yellow fever in December. Although trading and explorative expeditions continued and sporadic attempts were made to oust the British by minor military efforts in 1797, 1799, and 1800, none was successful.[22] British trading posts were established in Ioway country in 1800.

In the last decade of the century Spanish-Indian relationships tended to deteriorate. It was a time of attempts to develop good relationships that were never lastingly successful. In 1795 Lt. Gov. Trudeau reported that the Ioways were now actively hostile:

> Two *voitures* [carts] of our traders coming from the Kansas Nation, were stopped by 164 Ioway Indians who were going in war against the same nation. The said traders were pillaged by them and soundly thrashed with blows of sticks.[23]

On the other side of the Mississippi in the United States Indian territorial autonomy was becoming history. The Ordinance of 1787 designated a Territory of the United States Northwest of the Ohio, called for eventual survey and division of it into six-mile-square townships composed of 36 sections of 320 acres each, allowed for individual purchase, and provided for statehood when the population for a given area reached sixty thousand. All of this assumed the extinguishment of the Indian title to the area. Congress soon transferred large sections of land at bargain prices to the Ohio and Sciota

Land Companies for development. A few small settlements were created near and north of the Ohio, but Indian resistance made this difficult. In 1786, Congress had conceived the Indian reserve, which would set aside sections of land for Indians who were removed from their original homes. The reasons that were given for this were to protect the Indians from destruction and to avoid bloody battles over territorial rights, and, perhaps most particularly, to set in motion a scheme for "complete control of the Indians by restricting them to a certain area."[24]

The Indians' hostile resistance to the white intrusion into their lands and the wars on the Indian nations north of the Ohio were two reasons for the land cessions that were part of the peace treaties that followed. In late August, 1794, Gen. Anthony Wayne fought a battle against an estimated one thousand Indians and Canadians near the English fort on the Miami River in Ohio, near Lake Erie. The Indians were defeated, and Wayne destroyed many acres of Indian corn and burned the villages. The Spanish governor was informed "It is not worth the misfortune they are suffering and their annihilation sooner or later if they persevere in opposing the Americans."[25] Nevertheless, the Indians would continue far into the next century to struggle to keep their homes and the graves of their ancestors in all parts of the expanding nation.

At the end of the eighteenth century the Ioways were still far from the struggle of the Indians east of the Mississippi. They lived in the Spanish sphere of influence without being dominated and continued a successful and profitable economic relationship with the English traders. They sent their warriors to seek revenge and chastise their enemies and were able to maintain their tribal sovereignty. It was a time of success for the Ioway people.

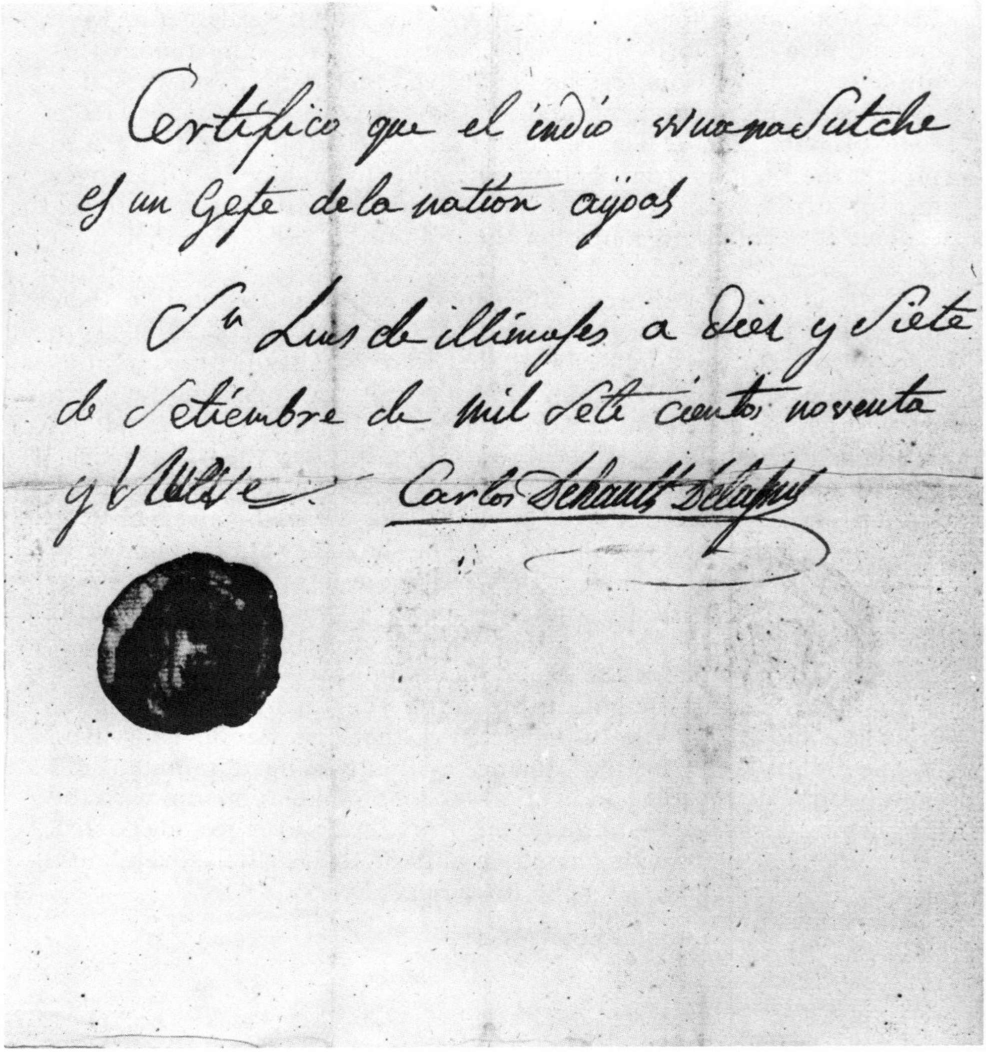

Certifico que el indio wuonaesutche
es un Gefe de la nation aijoas

S.n Luis de illinoses a Diez y Siete
de Setiembre de mil Sete cientos noventa
y Nueve ____ Carlos Dehault Delassus

Figure 4. A certificate given to Wuonaesutche on September 17, 1799, by Lt. Gov. Carlos Dehault de Lassus at San Luis, proclaiming him a chief of the Ioways. Actual size, before folding, is 26 inches by 16 inches. Courtesy of the Indian Archives Division, Oklahoma Historical Society, Section X — Iowa Indians.

6. Grandfather Has Spoken

It is a leading object of our present government to guarantee the Indians in their present possessions and to protect their persons with the same fidelity which is extended to its own citizens.
— Thomas Jefferson, 1791

When they withdraw themselves to the culture of a small piece of land, they will perceive how useless to them are their extensive forests, and will be willing to pare them off from time to time in exchange for the necessaries for their farms and families.
— Thomas Jefferson, 1803

ON OCTOBER 1, 1800, Napoleon Bonaparte's determination to regain Louisiana was successful. The Spanish crown agreed to retrocession of the province, and Napoleon promised to build the colony into a strong barrier between the ambitious United States and Spanish Mexico.

Presidential and congressional reaction to the disclosure was one of apprehension. A quiescent Spain was far less to be feared than the Napoleonic power that might soon occupy a territory that had long caught the American eye. Napoleon soon sent General Le Clerc, his brother-in-law, with more than ten thousand troops to occupy Santo Domingo to begin the domination of the New World empire he wished to create and to fulfill his commitment to Spain. On October 18 Don Juan Ventura Morales, Intendant at New Orleans, closed the port to Americans for the deposit of goods. When those Americans who were involved in commerce learned of the proclamation, their indignation was complete. Proposals to retake the port by force, petitions, and memorials from various sources descended on the President and Congress. The American point of view was enunciated as follows: "The Mississippi is ours by the law of nature; it belongs to us by our numbers, and by the labor which we have bestowed on those spots which, before our arrival, were desert and barren."[1]

President Jefferson appointed James Monroe as special envoy to France with powers "to enter into a treaty or convention with the First Consul of France for the purpose of enlarging and more effectively securing our rights and interests in the river Mississippi and in the territories eastward thereof . . . and, as the possession of these provinces is still in Spain," to approach that country in a similar manner.[2] Napoleon, faced with war in Europe, possible loss of Louisiana to England, unforeseen failure of the Santo Domingo expedition (because of mass illness and the strong resistance of Toussiant L'Ouverture), and other considerations, decided to sell not only the port of New Orleans but the entire colony. Monroe and Robert Livingston were happy to complete the agreement on April 30, 1803. The Lousiana Purchase almost doubled the size of the United States and included the lands of the Ioways, the Pawnees, the Sioux, the Osages, and many other nations yet unknown to the United States.

At this time the Ioways resided along the Des Moines and Iowa rivers and hunted south and west to the Missouri. Apparently relations had continued with the Spanish government, as evidenced by a red-sealed certificate issued at San Luis, September 17, 1799, saying that "El indio Wua-na-sut-che es un jefe de la nacion ayoas" (See Figure 4).[3] The signature was that of Carlos dehault de Lassus, who had succeeded Trudeau on August 29 as lieutenant governor of Upper Louisiana. Customarily new heads of government invited Indian leaders to council with them, and this certificate was probably presented on such an occasion after De Lassus took office.

The Spaniards had established a trader, L. Taisont Honoré, at the Des Moines rapids, who had contact with the Ioways and could observe English trading operations and report what he learned to San Luis. On August 18, 1799, he informed De Lassus that another trader, Pierre Dorion, "will descend the Illinois River to San Luis to obtain permission to trade on the Des Moines." He warned that Dorion was actually employed by a Mackinac merchant and carried goods for trading with the Sioux, "as soon as he has received your permission." Taisont had also heard that he planned to meet with "Crofeurte [Crawford] who for several years has done his worst to prevent expansion of [Spanish] trade on the Des Moines," and that Dorion and Crawford also planned to send three goods-laden canoes up the Iowa River. Taisont could not descend the river at that time to prevent their intrusion because of "fear the Iowas give us because of the difficulties in getting the murderer who did everything on the Missouri, so it will be necessary for me to remain here until I can leave my house in safety."[4]

In September, 1799, he saw Dorion on the Des Moines and reported that "he has been coming and going there for two months." Soon thereafter a group of Ioways stopped to visit Taisont and informed him that they had recently journeyed to see De Lassus. They said, he later wrote De Lassus, "that you had put one in irons."[5] They held a council concerning the prisoner, Quillon, and Taisont said he was "as humiliated as pained by their unhappiness, they beg us as well as the French here to ask for their good graces and mine in particular." Taisont asked De Lassus to release the prisoner and begged him to consider his position in the situation. Understandably, his trade would suffer if the Spanish carcer in St. Louis held an Ioway.[6] Receiving no response, he wrote again for an answer to his previous request for "... the next year's exclusive trading rights on the whole of the River Des Moines." He hastened to inform the governor that Dorion was in fact Crawford's clerk and had two sons who had entered the Des Moines "with two large canoes of wood loaded with merchandise to trade with the Ioways."[7]

A year earlier the North West Company sent twenty-five-year-old Jean Baptiste Faribault to trade with the Potawatomis at a post on the Kankakee River in Illinois. He did so well that the next year Mr. Gillespie, the company agent, assigned him a post named Redwood on the Des Moines two hundred miles upstream, in country hunted by the Sioux, the Ioways, the Sacs, and the Foxes. He traded there for four years, the term on which he had agreed.[8]

Thomas G. Anderson, employed by a Green Bay merchant, carried a cargo of trade goods up the Des Moines to the Ioway village past the "great Turn" in the winter of 1801-02. His opinion of the nation was that they were a "vile set," a view that he did not gain so much at this visit as in incidents recalled in later years. At the same time, Julien, a Frenchman, also arrived in the area to trade with the Ioways, who were on their winter hunt ninety miles away near the Missouri. Instead of going to the expense of traveling to these winter camps the two traders decided to wait for the Indians to return with their catch in the spring. Each took up separate quarters, and Anderson spent the winter whittling paddles and other objects. Sometime later Julien and his interpreter quarreled and separated. The latter went to Anderson and confided that Julien intended to go to the winter camps of the Ioways in spite of the agreement. Anderson's own words reveal the outcome:

This was a thunder-clap to me. An immediate explanation from Mr. Julien was demanded. I was furious, and showered all the abuse I could muster on his cringing head. My mind as to what was best to do under the circumstances, was soon made up. I called my interpreter into council, and said, "Now, boy, you know how Mr. Julien has deceived me; are you willing and ready to carry a load on your back across to the house near the Missouri, which Mr. Julien has treacherously put there, with the intention of stealing all the credits I made to those Indians last fall." All were willing. "Tit for tat," said I; "he wanted to *ruin* me, I will only *injure* him. Some of you ask his interpreter to go with us, and carry a load." He accepted the invitation. Then my party, including myself, became nine strong.

I left my own interpreter in charge of the Des Moines trading-post, and started the next day with seven loaded men, taking provisions for one day only, depending on game for our supply. The little islands of wood, scattered over the boundless plains, were swarming with wild turkeys, so that we had plenty of poultry. At the end of six days we reached our destination safe and sound, taking Mr. Julian's two *engagés* by surprise. My party soon fitted up a temporary shop. Not long after, the Indians came in, made a splendid season's trade, managed for the transportation of my packs of fur by leaving a man to help Mr. Julien's two *engagés* down with their boat. Thus I completed my winter, and Mr. Julien found his trickery more costly than he anticipated.[9]

During the short retrocession period, Francois M. Perrin du Lac, a Frenchman, had traveled in Louisiana and had described the Indian commercial potential by listing the fur packs that each nation produced. "The Oyoas on the Iowas River and the Sac and Fox bartered several hundred packs of fur each year" to the English, and the trade could well belong to the French, he asserted. The tribes now were peaceful, he added, and no danger existed for those who would trade with them.[10]

Others were interested in the Indians west of the Mississippi. Thomas Jefferson had been interested in the trans-Mississippi West since he had been in the Continental Congress — many years before the Louisiana Purchase. Even while Louisiana was a Spanish possession, he had envisioned an expedition of a scientific nature to gather information on waterways, minerals, and agricultural potential; ascertain the military and economic progress of the British on the upper Missouri; and make observations on the indigenous populations. This effort would have to wait until Spain and France relinquished their claims. On December 30, 1803, Marqués De Caso Calvo and Juan Manuel de Salcedo, the Spanish commissioners, informed Lt. Gov. De Lassus that Louisiana Province had been delivered to the French Commission. On January 12, 1804, a letter informed him that Capt. Amos Stoddard would soon receive military and civilian possession of Upper Louisiana in the name of the United States. On March 9 Stoddard, Capt. Meriwether Lewis, and their troops left Cahokia, crossed the Mississippi, and proceeded to the government house in Saint Louis. De Lassus received them and spoke to the assembled Spanish government officials, prominent citizens, and other inhabitants, informing them of Spain's withdrawal from ownership and authority and its replacement by the United States. A Spanish salute fired from the fort announced the final step. American troops then took possession of the fort and raised the flag.[11]

The province's Indian nations had to be informed. Stoddard saw the wisdom of having De Lassus explain the American presence, and he requested that this be done. De Lassus addressed the Delawares, the Abnakis, the Sacs, and other area tribes that were present, saying, "For several days past we have fired off cannon-shots to announce to all the nations that your Father the Spaniard is going, his heart happy to know that you will be protected and sustained by your new father, and that the smoke of the powder may ascend to the Master of Life, praying him to shower on you all a happy destiny and prosperity in always living in good union with the whites."[12] The Osages heard of the cession some time later and "committed the paper to the flames." The Indians would not believe that the Americans were the owners of the country.[13]

On June 3, 1803, Captain Stoddard informed Secretary of War Henry Dearborn that, prior to departure with William Clark on May 21, Meriwether Lewis had instructed the trader Crawford to deliver a speech or "parole" to the "Ayowais and Sioux who dwell on the banks of Des Moines" and are at peace.[14] Stoddard soon traveled up the Mississippi to gather data on the geography, resources, and people. He noted that the Des Moines River area had great potential for internal commerce. It flowed from the northwest and paralleled the Mississippi, and, in its estimated 450-mile length, "its size remained about the same with few branches." Some Ioways lived on the river; they were neighbors of the Sacs and Foxes who lived near the western bank of the Mississippi.[15]

Stoddard reported that the original Ioway population of two hundred warriors and their families had been reduced recently by a smallpox epidemic. Their population before the epidemic had been relatively small. The survivors confronted the problem of survival on their land, which was now being used both by other Indians and by whites. To be considered was the decision of alliance or resistance to the powerful Sioux and the Sac and Fox tribes, which now hunted and dwelt on Ioway land. The Ioways could not drive out the more numerous eastern and nothern intruders, who had been and were being forced westward or southward by pressure from the westward movement of whites and displaced Indian nations. In response to the Sacs and Foxes at this time the Ioways played mainly a role of accommodation rather than co-operation. The relationship existed from some time before the middle of the previous century, when the Sacs and the Foxes took temporary refuge from the French and their Indian allies on Ioway soil. As early as 1712 the Sacs had been removed by French persuasion from the Detroit to the Lake Winnebago area. Later they had settled near the Rock River in Illinois. The Foxes had lived in various locations in Wisconsin. Therefore, both tribes were comparative newcomers to the western side of the Mississippi. Sometime in the late eighteenth century a Sac-Ioway relationship began, which allowed them to participate in several events, such as the 1778 visit to Clark and Bowman, the 1780 attack on St. Louis, and the raids on the Osages, from time to time in the 1790's. In the nineteenth century the Sac role in Ioway affairs increased. Hunting needs brought the Sacs across the Mississippi into Ioway lands as their own territories became depleted of game and white settlers intruded. In exchange for use of hunting land, the Sacs helped the Ioways to maintain their territorial integrity by driving out parties of Sioux, Kansas, Missouris, and Osages, who came chiefly to hunt and to contact the English traders in the Des Moines River area. The use of Ioway rivers and lands as access routes to more distant tribes gave the Ioways — and the Sacs, who saw a good thing — a certain power position, both tribes co-operated with English traders who dealt with tribes near the Missouri.

The boundaries of the lands in which the Ioways maintained an original interest and which, it might be said, they possessed at this time can be given only imprecisely. It is possible to reconstruct boundaries only through the words of cession-treaty commissioners' interpretations of the Indian description and through the surmises and experiences of explorers, traders, and others. Indian claims were confounded by the continual movement in the eighteenth century of tribes onto each other's lands, whether by agreement or aggression. The claimed territory may have been land that was occupied only yesterday, so to speak, at the expense of a weaker neighbor who could not dispute it. The closest approximation of Ioway territory at the beginning of the nineteenth century would include lands that lay west of the Mississippi in present-day Iowa, somewhere south of the northern boundary of the state beyond the Ioway River watershed to the Des Moines River at forty-three degrees latitude. This area then extended to the Spirit Lake locality, which was occupied at the beginning of the previous century, down the Little Sioux River to the Missouri, and then down that river to the Grand and Gasconade Rivers area. It possibly included the land between the Chariton and the Mississippi and south of the Jeffreon River. These lands included all those ceded by the Ioways to the United States during the nineteenth century.[16] The peripheries of those areas were claimed by, contested by, or shared with the Otos, the Missouris, the Kansas, the Osages, the Sacs, the Foxes, the Omahas, and the Yanktonai Sioux during different periods of Ioway history.

After the Louisiana Purchase, the expedition envisoned by Jefferson was finally undertaken. The great venture that would span the continent west of the Mississippi began on May 14, 1804, under the leadership of Meriwether Lewis and William Clark. It started at present-day Wood River, Illinois and ended more than two years and eight thousand miles later. Detailed descriptions were made, and each day's journal entry brought new information about the people, geology, flora, and fauna of the scenes that passed before the explorers. Occasionally the Ioways were mentioned: "We passed Deer Creek, and at the distance of five miles, the two rivers called by the French the two Charatons . . . enter the Missouri together. They are both navigable for boats; the country through which they pass is broken, rich, and thickly covered with timber. The Ayauway nation consisting of three hundred men, have a village near its headwaters on the River Des Moines."[17]

At a point west of the Chariton River at the mouth of Moreau Creek the travelers observed the river crossing used by the "Sauk, Ayauways, and Sioux in their excursions against the Osage." The area was well provided with deer, elk, and bear in the woods and on the prairies. On June 26, parroquets were observed farther upriver.[18] The feathers of these beautiful, now extinct, birds were used by the Ioways in portions of a particular sacred bundle.

The Kansas lived in two villages twenty leagues apart near the mouth of the Kansas River. It was reported that, "they once lived 24 leagues higher than the Kansas (River), on the south bank of the Missouri, and were more numerous, but they have been reduced and banished by the Sauks and Ayauways, who being better supplied with arms have an advantage over the Kansas, though the latter are no less or warlike than themselves."

On July 28, near Indian Knob Creek, the journal continued:

At one mile, this morning we reached a bluff, on the north, being the first highlands, which approach the river on that side, since we left the Nodawa [Nodaway River]. Above this, is an island and a creek, about fifteen yards wide, which, as it has no name, we called Indian Knob creek, from a number of round knobs bare of timber, on the highlands, to the north. A little below the bluff, on the north, is the spot where the Ayauway Indians formerly lived. They were a branch of the Ottoes, and emigrated from this place to the river Desmoines. [19]

As the expedition ascended the Missouri River, another significant event occurred, which also affected the lives of Indians west of the Mississippi. In June, 1804, in St. Louis, Governor Harrison met in council with a delegation of five Sac and Fox chiefs who resided in a village on the western side of the Mississippi, apart from the main tribal group in its principal village on the Rock River in Illinois.

The history of this council can be traced in the words of President Jefferson. On January 18, 1803, in an address to Congress he declared, "The Indian tribes residing within the limits of the United States have for a considerable time been growing more and more uneasy at the constant diminution of the territory they occupy, although effected by their own voluntary sales, and the policy has long been gaining strength with them of refusing absolutely all further sale on any conditions...."[20]

This Indian attitude produced government concern over Indian removal. It was hoped that the newly acquired land of Louisiana would ameliorate the situation. If the eastern Indians could be induced to trade or sell their lands for those west of the Mississippi, and if the tribes west of the Mississippi could be persuaded to sell or cede some of their lands for this purpose, then Indian problems east of the Mississippi would be greatly reduced.[21]

Map 6.   A map of a section of the Mississippi River drawn by Nicholas King from Anthony Nau's notes for Lt. Zebulon Pike, who arrived at the Des Moines River on August 20, 1805. The trading posts, or forts, used by the

In order to do this it was necessary to initiate diplomatic relations with the western tribes, and Jefferson said that he deemed it necessary to "open conferences for the purpose of establishing a good understanding and neighborly relations between us. . . . By pursuing a uniform course of justice toward them, by aiding them in all the improvements which may better their condition, and especially by establishing a commerce on terms which shall be advantageous to

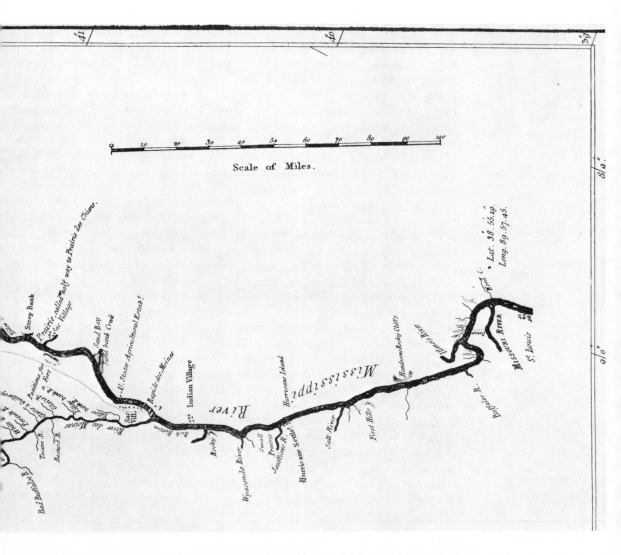

Scale of Miles.

Ioways are located along the river. Reproduced from *The Journals of Zebulon Montgomery Pike, With Letters and Related Documents*, ed. Donald Jackson (Norman, University of Oklahoma Press, 1966), Vol. 1, 69.

them . . . we may render ourselves so necessary to their comfort and prosperity that the protection of our citizens from their disorderly members will become their interest and their voluntary care."[22]

Jefferson chose the more subtle course of planning to place trading posts, or factories as they would be called, in strategic places in order to create the economic dependency that he mentioned. This was to be preferred to the military persuasion that had become part of many Indian relationships with the government in the eastern half of the continent. However, military posts would also be necessary to protect the Indian and white population. They could serve as bases of federal authority to control any civil disorder that might occur. Land was necessary for the factories and also for the establishment of Indian agencies, agency farms, schools, and churches as a means of changing by peaceful means the Indian value system in all areas of social, economic, and political affairs. It was planned that these installations and institutions would "civilize" the Indians and would bring them into the scheme of things as white men saw it.

Thus the council held in June, 1804, in St. Louis was important. The first tribes from west of the Mississippi to meet there were the Sacs and the Foxes. The outcome of the first treaty was the acquisition of a wedge of land and the establishment of a commercial relationship which, it was hoped, would lead to the economic dependency necessary for peaceful coexistence. The amount of land ceded included all the Sac land east of the Mississippi in present-day Illinois and Wisconsin and a portion of land north of the Missouri, along the Mississippi, north to the Jeffreon River and west to present-day Shelbyville. The boundary then turned to the southeast and followed a straight line to the mouth of the Gasconade, which the Sacs claimed but which they had used only in comparatively recent times. The ceded land totaled approximately 15,000,000 acres.

The treaty was signed by only five chiefs who were not representative of the entire tribe. As a result enmity existed within the Sac tribe for many years. The Sac chiefs who lived on the eastern side of the Mississippi had not been present and had not signed the document. Consequently they were determined not to be bound by terms that alienated their lands forever. The grief and anger of one division of the tribe led by Black Hawk, who were embittered by the treaty and for other reasons, culminated some years later in the Black Hawk War.

In order to establish a position for the treaty-stipulated fort and factory the St. Louis military commander was instructed to send a military party to search for suitable sites and to plot the course of the Mississippi to its headwaters. Lt. Zebulon M. Pike, chosen to lead the expedition, left St. Louis in August, 1805. His journal, portions of which were written by Lt. Henry R. Graham, described bluffs, hills, streams, prairies, and other features along the river.[23]

Although the original journal, maps, and descriptions offer no direct evidence that Pike inspected the Des Moines River to any great distance, the completed, redrawn map by Anthony Nau indicated extensive features of that river, including eighteen subsidiary streams along a distance of approximately 240 miles to the Redwood Post used by Faribault just prior to this time. Scattered along the river were Crawford, Fort St. Louis, Fort Crawford, Fort Gelaspy, and another Fort Crawford. These trading posts, called forts, had been established by Lewis (Louis) Crawford, Redford, and Crawford and Gillespie of the North West Trading Company of Mackinac. They indicate how intensive was the use of the river and Ioway lands by English traders in the years prior to this time (see Map 6).

Opposite Fort Gelaspy, on the eastern side of the Des Moines River and eighty miles from its mouth, stood an Ioway village. One can imagine its appearance with its small fields of corn, beans, and pumpkins that surrounded the bark houses of its inhabitants. A dwelling was probably bowl shaped, perhaps elongated, built of interwoven and tied saplings to make a frame that was covered with large slabs of rectangular cut bark or thick reed mats. Over this layer another frame of tied saplings held the mats and bark in place. The houses of the Ioways, the Winnebagos, the Osages, the Sacs, and the Foxes, were similar to one another; the Winnebago and Ioway lodges had the greatest similarity (see Figure 5).[24] A lodge might have featured an arbor in front of the main entrance to the house. This arbor was constructed of three- to five-inch diameter poles set in the ground and had a roof of poles, branches, and mats laid across their tops. Under this open arbor, still a feature of Indian life in the twentieth century, the family ate, talked, slept, and received visitors.

In an Ioway winter village or encampment along the Missouri in 1848 three types of residence were observed: the movable skin tipi; the lodge, "constructed of osier twigs or withes, and covered with rush mats"; and a third type "constructed with pieces of bark with a roof of the same material, that is strips of bark laid across the top."[25]

The fields lay in fertile places near the summer villages. Here the women and children planted corn, squash, pumpkins, and beans. During the harvest the women and children left the village and camped in the fields, according to missionary Samuel Irvin, in 1837.[26] It is presumed that only slight modifications in house type or agricultural technique had occurred since the beginning of the century.

On August 20, 1805, Pike's party passed the mouth of the Des Moines and approached the difficult rapids, near which Taisont had had his trading house. They were met there by the Sac Indian agent, William Ewing, and nineteen chiefs and warriors of the Sac village on the western side of the Mississippi. On August 24 the party reached the mouth of the Iowa, sixty miles up river from the Des Moines, and camped. The original map sketch indicates an Ioway village a few miles up the Iowa River. If the number of drawn tipis is indicative of comparative size, it was smaller than the Des Moines River village. The distance between the two villages could indicate separation of the tribe into two groups at this time, unless reference is made to an older unoccupied village site.

From information gathered at first hand, from others encountered on his route, and from later sources, Pike complied a chart that listed the tribes that he had met or knew to live along the Mississippi.[27] For each tribe he recorded information under a number of headings.

Figure 5. *Top,* an Ioway dwelling and, *below,* a Winnebago wigwam showing the great similarity between the dwellings of the two tribes. Courtesy of National Anthropology Archives, Smithsonian Institution.

Map 7. A map of the Des Moines River area showing the fur trading posts and the Ioway village two-thirds of the way up the Des Moines. Reproduced from *The Journals of Zebulon Montgomery Pike, With Letters and Related Documents,* ed. Donald Jackson (Norman, University of Oklahoma Press, 1966), Vol. 1, 52.

Red wood

F.T. Crawford

Otter River

Fort St Louis Fort Crawford

Glaize River

Little turn

St Cloud River

Prairie River

THIS Sketch of the River des Moines extends for 240 miles, which is supposed to be half its length, having its source in Spirit lake, it is bordered by a narrow strip of wood land, in the rear of which are vast prairies, extending on the W side to the Missouri.

Big buffalo or horn river

Ayouwa Village

Village River

Fort Belsfroy

Grand River

Fort Crawford

Great rock

The two Rivers

White rock river

Perault river

Paul river

Great turn

Glaize a Guilleroy

Bad buffalo River

Tecane River

Glaize River

Bastard River

Three Islands River

Clay Hill

Yellow banks

Prairie

DES MOINES Prairie

THE RAPIDS FROM

ROAD FROM THE RAPIDS

Prairie

Red cedar

Iowa village

Iowa River

Sand bank

Prairie

Yellow banks

Steep bank

Prairie called half way to Prairie des chiens

Bald shore Hilly

Sandy Prairie Two Rivers

St Position for a Fort

Sauk village

Prairie

Sand bay

Sand bank creek

L° 91° 13´ W Lat.

U.S. Establishment for Promotion of Agriculture.

PRAIRIE DES MOINES

Yellow Iowa River

Prairie

Sauk Village

Rapids des Moines

Port of the Rapids

River 2 miles wide

Rich

Comparison of the Sac and Fox and the Ioway tribes indicates that the Ioways numbered approximately 300 warriors and 400 women with a total population of 1,400 in two villages. It was also noted they possessed 250 firearms. The Sac and Fox warriors numbered 1,100 with a total population of 4,600 in six villages on both sides of the river. Traders came from Michilimackinac, St. Louis, and Prairie du Chien to the Sacs and the Foxes, but only from Michilimackinac to the Ioways. According to Pike the Sac and Fox nation consumed $23,500 worth of merchandise and the Ioway nation $10,000. In annual exchange for this amount of trade items, the Ioways produced 300 peltry packs of deer, bear, otter, beaver, mink, raccoon, gray fox, and muskrat. In addition to hunting, the Ioways cultivated some corn but not as much as did the Sacs and Foxes, Pike said. At this time all three tribes were at war with the Chippewas and were at peace with the Winnebagos, the Sioux, the Osages, the Potawatomis, the Menominees, and all other Indians of the Missouri.

Pike made an important point: "the Sacs, Reynard, and Iowas, since the treaty of the two former with the United States, claim the land from the entrance of the Jauflioni [Jeffrion, probably the North Two Rivers in Marion County, Missouri] on the W. side of the Mississippi, up the latter river to the Des Iowa, above the Prairie Des Chiens and westward to the Missouri; but the limits between themselves are undefined. All the land formerly claimed by those nations E. of the Mississippi, is now ceded to the United States; but they reserved to themselves the privilege of hunting and residing on it as usual." According to Pike the Ioways lived on small streams "in the rear of the Mississippi." They lived "out of the high road of commerce," which renders them less civilized.[28] Because there had been at least five trading posts scattered along the Des Moines, it appears that commercial relations could have been quite active. If Pike's figures for population and for consumption expenditures are used, per capita expenditures, disallowing barter differences, were $5 for the Sac and Fox villagers and $7 for the Ioway villagers.

No final arrangements for posts and factories were made by Pike, but tentative sites were selected at the present-day site of Burlington, Iowa, and further north near present-day McGregor, Iowa, opposite Prairie du Chien. Posts where Indians could trade would not only foster their need for American goods but would induce a situation by which greater political control could be exerted through the relationships between Indian and traders.

The Ioways' turn to deal with the United States came soon. From 1775 government policy had been to invite Indian chiefs and leaders to the seat of government to counsel. The purpose of these visits was to persuade Indian leaders to accept some particular set of premises; for example, warfare was disadvantageous, traffic with foreign powers was not permitted, excess land holding was wasteful, and the need for the white man's protection and acceptance of white

Figure 6. A wooden mortar and pestle used by Ioway women of the last century to grind corn on the Great Nemaha Reservation. Courtesy of St. Joseph's Museum, St. Joseph, Missouri.

civilization were inevitable. In 1805, plans were made to bring together at St. Louis certain chiefs of the "Sacques, Iayowas, Renards, Ricaras, Ottos, Missouris and Scioux," to make peace with the Great and Little Osages. Gov. J. Wilkinson, one of the commissioners, informed the secretary of war on September 22, "I have said before I believe, and I beg to repeat that an indispensable preliminary to the transfer of the Southern Nations, to the West of the Mississippi is a solid peace between those nations and the Osages particularly, and a general Peace among the whole. . . ."[29]

The nations' leaders gathered in October and, after much discussion, placed their marks on a treaty dated October 18, 1805. It was brief and contained two articles: Article 1 stated that the tribes agreed to cease all hostilities among themselves, and that "a good understanding and friendly intercourse shall exist between them through all Succeeding generations"; Article 2 noted that no private revenge shall be conducted, that instead negotiation shall take place, and if, from this, desired results do not occur, that the Superintendent of Indian Affairs shall "interpose his influence and Authority to effect a reconciliation. For the Ioway, Voi-Ri-Gran placed his mark above that of White Hair of the Great Osage Nation and below He-ha-vois-the-qua, of the Scious Nation of the River Demoin. Chiefs of the Delaware, Miami, Pottawatomi, Kickapoo, Sacque, Fox and Little Osage Nation also testified with an "X" to their agreement."[30] The treaty framers had in mind the previously stressed necessity for peaceful and stable conditions among these tribes. The treaty interjected a subtle new element, the use of a non-Indian third party for the settlement of disputes. This intervention would become in time a means of tribal control and loss of independence. Gone would be the traditional conciliation and alliance-making procedures.

Although the friendship alliance was signed by chiefs of the nations listed in the treaty, Governors Wilkinson and William H. Harrison wrote the next day to the secretary of war that they were "induced to believe that the Indians of the Mississippi are inimically disposed to the United States." An "Ayoua chief who was with the Pawnee on a mission of peace, and who is to be relied upon," related that the Grand Pawnees had killed two white men and had declared that they would not "hold intercourse with any persons from this quarter." It was said that Spaniards had excited them and other nations against the United States.[31]

In December Wilkinson reported that the Ioways and the Sacs and the Foxes were "certainly disposed for war and beyond all doubt are excited by their traders from Canada." As a solution Wilkinson voiced the opinion that a method for "humbling those refractory nations" would be to stop all trade next season except for "certain scanty supplies which may be allowed to such nations as implore our protection."[32]

In Jefferson's fifth annual message to Congress in December, 1805, he announced that various Mississippi and Missouri River

Figure 7. Ioway household objects; *left,* grinding stones, the larger of which is 6 inches in diameter; *right,* a wooden ladle, 8⅞ inches long, and wooden bowl, 7⅜ inches in diameter; *center,* an elk-horn scraper or hide flesher from the Great Nemaha Reservation area, about 12 inches in length. All the objects were made by the Ioways and were collected in 1922 and 1923 by Alanson Skinner. Courtesy of Milwaukee Public Museum.

chiefs were on their way to Washington, and they would come "charged with assurance of their satisfaction with the new relations in which they are placed with us."[33] The Osage, Missouri, Kansas, Otoe, Pawnee, Sioux, and Ioway delegations arrived in January, 1806. On January 4, the following message was delivered to the assemblage by the President:

My Friends and Children, Chiefs of the Osages, Missouris, Kansas, Otos, Panis, Ayoways, and Sioux, I take you by the hand of friendship, and give you a hearty welcome to the seat of government of the United States. The journey you have undertaken to visit your Father on this side of our island is a long one and you having undertaken it is a proof that you desire to become acquainted with us. I thank the Great Spirit that he has protected you through the journey, and brought you safely to the residence of your friends. And I hope he will have you constantly in his safe keeping and return you in good health to your Nation and Friends.

My Friends and Children, we are descended from the Old Nations which are beyond the Great Water, but we and our forefathers have been so long here that we like you seem to have grown out of this land. We consider ourselves no longer as of the Old Nations beyond the Great Water, but as united as one family with our Red Brothers here. The French, the English, the Spanish have now agreed with us to retire from all the country which you and we hold between Canada and Mexico, and never more to return to it. And remember the words I now speak to you, My Children, they are never to return again. We are become as numerous as the leaves of the trees, and thus do not fear any nation. We are now your Fathers, and you shall not lose by the change. As soon as Spain had agreed to withdraw from all the waters of the Missouri and the Mississippi, I had the desire of becoming acquainted with all of my Red Children beyond the Mississippi, and uniting them with us as we have done those on this side of that river in the bonds of peace and friendship. I wished to learn what we could do to benefit them by furnishing them with the necessaries they want in exchange for furs and peltries. I therefore sent our beloved man, Capt. Lewis, one of my family, to go up the Missouri River to get acquainted with all the Indian nations in this neighborhood, to take them by the hand, delivering my talks to them, and to tell us in what way we could be useful to them. Some of you who have seen him and heard his words. You have taken him by the hand and been friendly to him.

My Children, I thank you for the services you rendered him, and your attention to his words. When he returns he will tell us where we should establish factories to be convenient to you all, and what we may send to them. In establishing trade with you we desire to make no profit. We shall ask from you only what everything costs us and give you for your furs and peltries whatever we can get for them again. Be assured you will find your advantage in this change of your friend. It will take us some time to be in readiness to supply your wants, but in the meanwhile, and until Capt. Lewis returns, the traders who heretofore have furnished you will continue to do so.

My Friends and Children, I have now an important advice to give you. I have already told you that you are all my children and I wish you to live in peace and friendship with one another as brethren of the family ought to do. How much better it is for neighbors to help than to hurt one another. How much happiness it makes them. If you will cease to make war on one another, if you will live in friendship with all mankind, you can employ all your time in providing food and clothing for yourselves and your family; your men will not be destroyed in war, and your women and children will lie down to sleep in their cabins, without fear of being surprized by their enemies and killed or carried away. Your numbers will be increased instead of diminishing and you will live in plenty and in quiet.

My Children, I have given this advice to all your Red Brethren on this side of the Mississippi. They are following it, they are increasing in their numbers and learning to clothe and provide for their families as we do. And you see the proofs of it in such of them as you happen to find here.

My Children, we are strong, we are as numerous as the stars in the heavens, and we are all strong men. Yet we live in peace with all nations, and all nations respect and honor us because we are peaceable and just. Be you then peaceable and just also. Take each other by the hand and hold it fast. If ever bad men among your neighbors should do you wrong, and their nations refuse you justice, apply to the beloved man whom we shall place with you. He will go to the offending nation and endeavour to obtain right and preserve peace. If ever bad men among yourselves injure you, injure your neighbor, be always ready to do justice. It is always honorable in those who have done wrong to acknowledge and make amends for it. And it is the only way that peace can be maintained among men. Remember my advice, My Children, taking it home to your people and telling them from this day we become father to them all. We wish as a true father should do that we may all live together as one household, and that before they strike one another they should come to their father and let him endeavor to make up the quarrel.

My Children, you are come from the other side of our great island, from where the sun sets to see your new friends at the sun rising. You have arrived where the waters are continually rising and falling everyday, but you are still distant from the sea. I very much wish that you should not stop here, but go on and see your brethren as far as the edge of the Great Water. I am persuaded you have so far seen that every man by the way has received you as his brothers and has been ready to do you all the kindness in his power. You will see the same thing quite to the sea-shore; and I wish you therefore to go and visit our great cities in that quarter, and see how many friends and brothers you have there. You will then have traveled a long time from west to east, and if you had time to go from north to south, from Canada to Florida, you would find it as long in that direction, and all the people as sincerely your friends. I wish you, my Children, to see all you can, and to tell your people all you see; because I am sure the more they know of us, the more they will want to be our hearty friends. I invite you, therefore, to pay a visit to Baltimore, Philadelphia, New York, and that if you should be willing to go further, we will provide carriages to convey you, and a person to go with you to see that you have want for nothing. By the time you come back the snows will be melted in the mountains, the ice in the rivers broken up, and you will be wishing to set out on your return home.

My Children, I have long desired to see you. I have now opened my heart to you. Let my words sink into your hearts and never be forgotten. If ever lying people or bad spirits should raise some kind of clouds between us, call to mind what I have said, and what you have seen yourself. Let us come together as friends and explain to each other what is misrepresented or misunderstood. The clouds will fly away like the morning fog, and the sun of friendship appear and shine forever bright and clear between us.

My Children, it may happen when you are here occasions may arise to talk about many things which I do not now particularly mention. The Secretary of War will always be ready to talk with you, and you are to consider whatever he says, as said by myself. He will also take care of you and see that you are furnished with all comforts here. [34]

What the Ioways thought of all of this was never recorded, but the point that the English, the French, and the Spaniards were gone, "never to return," and that a "father" would come to live among them to oversee them, to whom they should take their quarrels with other tribes, undoubtedly raised the flag of apprehension in their minds. What the Ioways said about the proposed tour of the great cities is also unknown, but it was planned to awe them and the other chiefs from the West, and it undoubtedly did so.

On April 10, 1806, their first "father," Nicolas Boilvin, was appointed assistant Indian agent. His instructions told him that he should live near the Sac village north of the mouth of the Des Moines and that he should occasionally visit the "Iawa towns on the LeMoin, the other Sacque towns, and the Prairie du Chien." In his dealings with the Indians he was to encourage peace and friendship; to prevent acts of hostility among red and white people; to bring about proper punishment of individuals who committed aggression; to prevent use of ardent spirits, not allowing any trader to sell or dispose of any; and to teach by example the arts of agriculture and domestic manufactures by planting his own vegetable garden and orchard.[35]

Boilvin's instructions were based on various acts and regulations of Congress, including the Ordinances for Regulation of Indian Affairs in 1786 and 1787; the Indian Acts of July 22, 1790 and March 1, 1793; and the Intercourse Acts and Amendments of 1793, 1795, 1796, 1799, and 1802. All attempted to define and to set Indian policy and to provide for its administration and execution. Briefly they covered the following points:

(1) Trade was regulated by the licensing of traders; abuses in selling and buying were prevented; and a factory system controlled by the government was established.

(2) An attempt was made to prevent white settlers from utilizing Indian land. Over this issue arose constant confrontations between the settlers and the Indian agent, the military, and the Indians themselves. The frontiersman's view and the federal view of Indian land use and possession were basically similar, but the latter was more insinuative and long ranged, while the former was immediate and to the point. Gov. John Sevier of Tennessee said, "By the laws of nations, it is agreed that no people shall be entitled to more land that they can cultivate. Of course, no people will sit and starve for want of land to work, when a neighboring nation has more than they can make use of."

(3) Steps were taken for the prevention and the control of crime and aggression between Indian and Indian and between Indian and white. Provisions were made for apprehension, detention, and court procedures for Indian criminals.

(4) To sell or to give whiskey to an Indian was illegal.

(5) Provision was made for administrative apparatus at the tribal level to carry out acts of Contress that related to the above points.

The Indian agent was under the supervision of the territorial governor at first and later was subordinate to the superintendent of Indian affairs in a given area. He was under the protection of the nearest military post. In later years in some instances the agent and the military representatives often worked at crossed purposes, when objectives in Indian affairs were dissimilar.

The appointment of Boilvin can be considered a point of importance in Ioway history. The agent brought the presence of the United States more directly into Ioway life in a form that would endeavor over the coming decades to persuade, dissuade, and coerce them to change their lives. The process was gradual at first, the goals cloaked in idealistic pronouncement, but the purpose was always the same: conversion, conformity, and control. In August, 1806, Boilvin, while attempting to keep peace as a third party, reported that the Sacs and the Ioways were hostile, but that he would attempt to reduce the tension between them. This hostility might have stemmed quite naturally from increasing Sac use of and movement onto territory claimed by the Ioways. Or it might have arisen from an unrecorded act of aggression.

Regardless of Boilvin's presence the Ioways continued to trade with the British. Meriwether Lewis had reported that the "Ayaways who have been known in several instances to capture boats on the Missouri, in their descent to St. Louis, and compelled the crews to load themselves with heavy burdens of their best furs and cross the country to their towns, where they disposed of them to the British merchants. In those cases they always destroyed the pirogues and such of the peltries and furs as they could not carry off."[36] They also traded with Julien Dubuque, who had settled on the western side of the Mississippi many years before the Louisiana Purchase. He reported unrest among the tribes in the region.[37]

On July 22, 1807, the commander of Fort Bellefontaine, the United States headquarters for the Army west of the Mississippi, established at the site of San Carlos, reported that "a powerful association of all the Indians between the Lakes and the Missouri was formed for commencing a war on the frontiers of the United States." Tribes within this area continued trade with Canadian traders, and their influence was not diminished by Presidential speeches, treaties, or claims on Indian loyalty to the United States. The communiqué continued: "The Ioways, only we are told withhold themselves from this threatening combination. The others are ready to strike as soon as their corn is harvested, so they will be provisioned for the contest."[38]

A partial explanation of the Ioway position may be contained in the September lists of trader licenses issued at St. Louis. One was issued to Denis Julien to trade with the Sioux and the Ioways. Another document from Frederick Bates, secretary of the territory, attests that "that draft is at five days sight in favor of Messers. Falconer and Comegys, St. Louis, on orders, I will cover some small disbursement, which in the absence of Gen'l Clark, I have been oblidged to make to the Iowas."[39] In November Bates notified Meriwether Lewis, now governor of the territory, that a Mr. Dickson was licensed to trade with the Sioux of the Des Moines and would be relied on to relay what passed among them and the Ioways of that river. It would appear that for the moment, some or all of the Ioways had retreated from their pro-British sentiments, and that they were partially or totally dependent on American-licensed traders. For this and possibly for other reasons they did not wish to ally themselves with the aforementioned coalition.

In 1808 the United States sought more Indian land west of the Mississippi. Jefferson in his January 15 message to the Senate declared:

> although it is deemed very desirable that the United States should obtain from the native proprietors the whole left bank of the Mississippi to a certain breadth, yet to obliterate from the Indian mind an impression deeply made in it that we are constantly forming designs on their lands I have thought it best where urged by no peculiar necessity to leave to themselves and the pressure of their own convenience only to come forward with offers of sale....[40]

Such statements were not sufficient to obliterate the knowledge of increasing land cessions. Indian nations west of the Mississippi and in the Great Lakes area were not ignorant of the vast land cessions made by their neighbors and more distant southern and eastern nations. Indian discontent was powerfully expressed through the Shawnee Prophet, Tenskwatawa, and his brother, Tecumseh. Rancor lay deep in their hearts; their people had been driven out and had lost their lands in Kentucky before the turn of the century. Their original homelands had extended into Tennessee, South Carolina, and Pennsylvania, but in the early 1800's they lived along the Tippecanoe and White Rivers in Indiana Territory and eastward into Ohio.

In times of stress among minority populations, strong individuals may arise to relieve the unrelenting pressure on themselves and their people. By superimposing their own beliefs and revelations on traditional values they seek to return their society to an earlier state by removal of the source of the oppression destroying their culture's autonomy and life-styles. To do this the individual must unify his people by charismatic oratory and forceful actions. The followers must become so imbrued by his presence and desires that they will overcome states of reluctance, irresponsiveness, and anomie to perform those acts that will bring about the leader's goals for them.

Tenskwatawa assumed this role in the early 1800's by calling his people and their allies around him at Wapakoneta in present-day Ohio. He had had a series of visions from God in which he was directed to change and to reform the lives of the people. He denounced the use of liquor and stated that all property must be owned in common, the old should be respected by the young, Indian women must cease relationships with white men, the white man's dress should be discarded, and every tool and practice brought by the white people should be eliminated. The Indian should return to his own culture and live as he had before he encountered the white man.

At first his message had no military implications. People were excited and responded to the ideas he espoused. Later he called councils of more distant tribes in order to bind greater numbers to the purpose of driving out the whites, by aggressive means where necessary.

In March, 1808, the Prophet set out for the Wabash River for a council to which he had invited the Sacs, the Foxes, the Menominees, the Winnebagos, and the Ioways. The purpose was "to put the tomahawk in their Hands and direct them to Strike the white people — as well as those Indians that will not listen to them," reported Agent William Wells at Fort Wayne.[41] *2/77/6*

During the next month Agent Wells reported that Indians of his area were exhorted by the British to war against the United States. Those Indians who had attended the councils of the Prophet during the previous summer were in a state of starvation, and it was feared that they would give the British a ready ear. To avert this, articles had been taken out of the factory at Fort Wayne and were delivered in liberal quantities to Mar-pak, the war chief of the Potawatomis, who had great influence among the Indians, and who could persuade the Sacs, the Foxes, the Ioways, the Menominees and the Winnebagos to be peaceful instead of following the Prophet's path. An arrangement was rumored "about to take place among the Indians of this country for them to determine never to sell any more of their lands to the United States or anyone else, and make it a crime, punishable by death to any Indian to put his name on paper for the purpose of parting with any of their lands."[42]

At this time all was not well between the Ioways and the Sacs. They were in disagreement, and their Agent Boilvin said that, if hostilities should occur between these two small nations, it would tend to render the navigation of the Mississippi dangerous. The cause of the disagreement is not given, but it is evident that the alliance or relationship had become weakened by any number of events which caused one or both tribes to feel constrained in their rights. During the year before, it will be recalled, the Ioways had refused to become party to the decisions or plans of the coalition of the Sacs and other tribes. Governor Lewis reported that, in late winter or early spring of 1808, the Sacs had killed several families of Des Moines Sioux and several Ioways.

For some time the Sacs had been moving and extending the area that they claimed as theirs southward and westward from their main locus on Rock River. The Ioways at this time, or sometime before, may have been antagonized by their increasing intrusions and high-handedness. The situation may have reached the point in 1808 where the Ioways refused to concede or share any more of their territory for hunting or settlement. The insolence of the Sacs in killing Ioway tribal members could not be forgiven, although there is no proof that the killing was not in retribution for some act by the Ioways. The words of the agent attest that disagreement existed and could indicate an underlying resentment of some duration which was only then observed and recorded.

On May 14, Governor Lewis wrote to Boilvin and outlined several points for him to consider in dealing with the Ioways and the Sacs. Lewis stated that spending money to keep intertribal peace had proved futile. It became a continuous process that tribes could use to gain reward, and it was against policy to pay "for disobedience to our will." Also, "paying to cover the dead," as it was called, to compensate an injured nation's pride, was only practiced at those earliest times when the traders among the Indians were defenseless and had used that means to protect themselves. Boilvin was to replace this custom by persuasion and reason, the governor admonished. If tribes did not maintain peace, "no traders can be permitted to bring them merchandise, and thus they will be deprived of means of making war or defending themselves."[43]

As a result of foreign traders' agitation, or the Prophet's influence, or because of other tribal motives, Indians west of the Mississippi in several instances harassed and killed the traders among them. In 1808, the Omahas robbed their traders and killed their *engagés*. The Kansas plundered their traders. In June two other murders took place on the Missouri near the Grand River. "The nation is not known, but the Ioways are suspected," Governor Lewis reported to Secretary of War Dearborn on July 1. Regardless of his uncertainty, he had issued a proclamation on June 22 that offered a reward of $600 for the apprehension and delivery of "Mera Naute" and "Mashkakahi," two Ioways warriors charged with the murder of Joseph Tebeau, an old French trader who headquartered at Beloit in present-day Wisconsin.[44] Events moved swiftly. On July 23, the two Ioways were tried in St. Louis for Tebeau's murder. Other Ioways arrived in St. Louis, and the streets teemed "with Indian warriors who remittantly beseeched and harassed Lewis and General Clark to pardon their tribesmen." Notwithstanding, the two were convicted. They were granted a new trial to be held on August 3, but again they were found guilty. They were placed in jail until the advice of the President could be obtained.[45]

The robbery and murder of traders, with subsequent Indian trials and sentencing, did little to enhance indigenous attitudes toward the United States. The establishment of interior trading posts or factories became more imperative. If this were done, the influence of the Spanish and the British would diminish, and trade abuses practiced on the Indian by licensed and unlicensed traders would decrease. It was hoped that if the posts were strategically located, those tribes

100

who had been enemies would of necessity become less hostile as they shared the same trading house.[46]

On June 25, General Clark had set off from St. Louis to locate a site suitable for a trading post. He decided on the location called Fire Prairie on the western side of the Missouri some miles above the mouth of the Osage River. The post would be available to the Osages, the Ioways (whose hunting lands lay across the river along the Grand and Chariton rivers), the Sacs, the Missouris, and the Kansas villages some miles upstream. However, dissension arose among the Osages. One group had given notice that they did not accept the authority of the United States. Threats of removing their traders did not bring a positive response. The Osages had been through all of this before with the French, the Spanish, and now the Americans. But White Hair, chief of the Little Osages, remained loyal to the United States and was asked to take his band safely away from the dissident group to Fire Prairie. Then Lewis informed the Shawnees, the Delawares, the Kickapoos, the Ioways, and the Sacs that the other Osages were no longer under the protection of the United States, "and they were at liberty to wage war against them, if they thought proper, under this restriction only, that they should attack in a body sufficiently large enough to cut them off completely or drive them from their country." Other nations east of the Mississippi were adroitly advised of the new open season on the Osages. The Shawnee chief later informed Lewis that about twelve hundred warriors from various tribes would converge at the Missouri River near the Gasconade to attack them. One might question why the Indian nations would attack one of their own at the suggestion of the United States government for whom they had little love or great respect. The answer may be found in at least sixty to seventy years of Osage harassment, which left many of these tribes victims of past Osage attacks.

Concurrently with locating a site for Fort Osage, plans were made to place a post at the mouth of the Des Moines or higher up the Mississippi. Governor Lewis complained that the North West Company representatives "mar our best arrangements for the happiness of the Indians" and the tranquility of the frontier. He conceived a plan by which "Old Dorion," the respected trader among the Ioways, would be the instrument for withdrawing not only the Ioways, but also the Sacs, the Foxes, and the Yanktonai Sioux from the British. Two of Dorion's sons and Maurice Blondeau, a clerk in the Mackinac Company, had been working for the British company. They would now be induced to work for the United States and to use their influence on these tribes to sway them toward the Americans. If, however, this is not successful, and these tribes continue trading with the Canadians, Lewis threatened, then a military force will guard both the entrance to the Illinois and Wisconsin rivers to prevent British trader access to the Mississippi.[47]

President Jefferson responded to Lewis by restating firmly that war as a means of coercion was an unending process, and that as soon as the factories were operative they would have a greater effect than "so many armies." The British traders' factories within the United States limits would be broken up to make the former more necessary and utilized by the Indians.[48]

During this period when concern over establishing posts prevailed, the Ioway prisoners were still in prison. On August 24, Jefferson wrote to Lewis about the Ioway trial, which he just had time to consider:

> ... that four Iowas had been delivered up to you as guilty of the murder which had been charged to the Sacs and Foxes, and that you supposed three of them would be hung. It is this latter matter which induces me to write again. As there was but one white murdered by them, I should be adverse to the execution of a second, and nothing beyond that. Besides their ideas that justice allows only a man for a man, that all beyond that is new aggression, which must be expiated by a new sacrifice of an equivalent number of our people, it is our great object to impress them with a firm persuasion that all our dispositions towards them are fatherly. ... [49]

The Ioways, whether guilty or not of the attack and murder on the Missouri, continued their antagonism. Faribault, while en route to his old post, Redwood, on the Des Moines, was encountered by a party of Ioways, who requested that he stay with them, since they were without a trader as a result of Lewis's order.* When he refused to go with them, it was said that they threatened to kill him and to steal his goods. A contingent of Yanktonai Sioux with whom he planned to trade appeared and escorted him safely to his post.[50]

Plans were accelerated to establish a factory for the Sacs and the Ioways. On September 26, 1808, a site was selected thirty miles above the Des Moines on the Mississippi.[51] Work began immediately on the post and the factory. The post was constructed of hewn lumber from the nearby forest and consisted of a surrounding stockade, one-story barracks, storehouses, a trading store, and other buildings. The stockade had a front gate that faced the river, and a rear gate that faced the forest. Outside the front gate and on either side were a sutler's building and the factory. A sentry posted outside the stockade could see what was happening at both places. The 1804

---

*On September 26, 1809, Frederick Bates noted that Governor Lewis had suspended trade with the Ioways, but he could find no mention of it in the office papers. Governor Lewis had retired this year and had returned to Tennessee. Bates commented that "the Measure is not supported by any principle of Law, Justice or Policy." See Frederick Bates, *Life and Papers*, Vol. 1, 86.

schism in the Sac tribe showed itself by the hostile and silent observation of the fort's building by Black Hawk's warriors from the eastern side of the river.[52]

John Johnston was appointed factor and arrived at the beginning of September to initiate business with the neighboring tribes. His instructions stated that he was to charge for articles only enough to cover their costs and give a minimal profit. He was also to assist the Indians in small ways in order to encourage their friendship. This Johnston and his assistants did by repairing broken articles such as traps, axes, kettles, and guns.[53] He was also to extend credit to the chiefs, for as Jefferson had said: "To promote this disposition to exchange lands which they have to spare and we want, for necessaries which we have to spare and they want, we shall push our trading-houses, and be glad to see the good and influential individuals among them in debt; because we observe that when these debts get beyond what the individuals can pay, they become willing to lop them off by a cession of lands."[54]

By November John Mason, superintendent of Indian trade, congratulated Johnston on his good work, saying that he had brought peace between the Sacs, the Foxes, the Ioways, and the Sioux — a rather immediate and superficial observation, as it turned out.

In 1808 the Osages made a treaty with the United States by which they ceded lands east of a line that ran south of Fort Clark (Fort Osage) to the Arkansas River and included all Osage-claimed lands west of the Missouri River. The entire area encompassed present-day Missouri and the northern part of Arkansas. The land north of the Missouri River was not considered to be Osage by the Ioways or the Sacs, who also claimed it. Neither tribe contested the cession at the time, but it soon became the source of strife among all three tribes, as well as the settlers who moved into the area almost immediately.

President Madison took office in 1809, and Fort Belle Vue near the Des Moines became Fort Madison in his honor. The factory there was successful in turning a fair profit, in contrast to others that operated at a loss. In February a young Ioway visited the post sutler, who had "befriended him at Detroit" (Indians of many tribes visited the factory at Detroit and the British post, Malden, across the river in Canada to trade, counsel, and receive presents). The Indian confided that the Sacs planned to seize the fort by deception and raid the settlements nearby. British agents had spent the winter at Saukenak instigating and planning the attack with the Black Hawk faction.[55] In the spring the young Ioway returned to the fort and reported that the Sacs planned to carry out their ruse the next day. They were on their way to their summer village to plant crops and would stop to trade in furs and to settle their debts. With that done they would ask to perform a dance inside the stockade for the garrison. When all were present, they would begin, but at a certain point they would draw their weapons and put every man to death.

The Sacs arrived, paid their debts, traded, and as predicted, requested that the young men be allowed to perform a dance for the garrison. Led by Black Hawk, they appeared at the gate but were astounded to be faced with a loaded 6-pounder and a soldier with a lighted port. Their plans were quickly laid aside for the time.[56]

In the *Missouri Gazette* of June 14, 1809, the following brief notice appeared: "Some straggling Ioway Indians, infesting the country on the other side, between Cahokia and Wood River for several weeks, stealing pigs, et., crawling on all fours, and imitating the notes of the mud lark. One poor devil more successful than the rest in his imitations, and being obscured by the bushes, was fired on and killed. This has put a stop for the present to their depredations." From this it would appear that a small hunting party was probably camped near the settlement and intended to catch not only wild game but perhaps a pig or two to supplement their larder if game were scarce in this area, where they might have hunted since the 1770's.

During the summer the President presented papers and a medal to Hard Heart, a leading Ioway, which confirmed his position as chief. Hard Heart had come to the attention of Horatio Stark, commandant at Fort Madison, in August in a heated discussion over the two Ioways, who had recently escaped from prison at St. Louis. Bates wrote to Stark on September 26:

"The Iowa Fugitives the subject of your misunderstanding with Hard Heart" were tried by our courts last year... they could not be punished by our laws, and it ever appeared to me that their escape was fortunate for themselves and for us. Hard Heart has acted with too much hate and passion, and I believe him to be a man of native viciousness of temper. Yet we know that Indian manners are generally different from our own... Hard Heart has been made Chief by the President himself, and I doubt our power to degrade him.[57]

The Ioway escape rankled Governor Lewis, and he had written to Jefferson that he disagreed with the Ioways' counsel at their first trial, who had declared that the Ioways had no treaty with the United States and could not be tried, and that the indictment did not state in what county, riding, or district the offense was committed, nor in what part of the body the mortal wound was given; above all, the offense was committed outside the jurisdiction of the court. In the subsequent trial in August, 1808, the judge had acted under a special commission created by Governor Lewis (under the Intercourse Act of March 30, 1802) and extended to Louisiana Territory on March 26, 1804. The judge ruled, "Offenses committed on Indian lands, by Indians, upon white People or their property, are not punishable in this Court under that act... that the offense was committed out of and beyond the boundary line of the United States as established by Treaty with the Sac and Foxes on the 3rd of November, 1804, and committed too by Ioways, a tribe or nation

104

not in Treaty with the United States." Judge Shrader and Judge Lucas had differed in the final opinion, and Governor Lewis believed that, on that basis, pleas should have been overruled on a division of the court.[58] In spite of the decision, the Ioways were held illegally until their escape in 1809.

One of the escaped prisoners was "Mashkakahi," or Mahaska (White Cloud). He was the son of the chief of the same name. At the time of the trial he was about twenty-five years old. Years later he visited Washington and related his side of the incident. He said that during his life he had led many war parties against the Osages, with whom the Ioways were in frequent conflict. At this particular time in 1808, he arrived at the bank of the Missouri and, seeing a canoe with three Frenchmen in it, called out to them to assist him in crossing the river. The men refused, fired on his party, and wounded one of them. The fire was returned, and one man was killed. According to White Cloud, "he called for his gun, saying that he would kill another one of the rascals to keep the first company to the House of the Black Spirit." The whites along the frontier raised a clamor, and an armed party was sent to find him. He and his party were captured and thrust into prison where he stayed many months, he said.[59] After his escape in 1809 he made his way safely to his village. There he married four sisters whose protector had died. It was the custom of the tribe when brothers or husbands fell in battle for a brave to adopt their wives. Later it was said that only chiefs and nobles, the distinguished warriors, could have multiple wives.[60]

White Cloud's story continued. After his marriage he settled into village life and to its responsibilities. When it became necessary for him to reaffirm his status, he planned a war party against the Osages, the old enemy. He selected ten men to accompany him to the Little Osage plains, south of the Missouri River, approximately two hundred fifty miles upriver from St. Louis. He said that on this expedition he took three scalps, but during the fray he was wounded in the ankle. He retreated and submerged himself in a stream beneath a large log until nightfall, when he cautiously crawled out. He found a loose horse and rode it to the Missouri, where he dismounted and swam across the river, while he held the horse's reins in his hands. Eventually he made his way back to his village on the Des Moines.[61] There he "paraded his trophies and ordered the scalp dance." Since he was wounded and could not dance, he placed the scalps in the hands of Big Ax, who, as first brave of his band, was entitled to the distinction.[62]

Among Indian nations the total sequence of war-party events was highly structured. In order to be a member of such an expedition, the Ioway leader first went to the war-bundle owner in his clan and presented his petition with an appropriate offering, requesting approval for his proposal. If the request were approved, the war-bundle owner issued invitations to those individuals suggested by the leader, "who consider themselves men enough to face the enemy." Those leaders capable of issuing invitations through the religious figure of the sacred bundle keeper were chiefs, chief's sons, and noble braves, as the term was translated; they represented two of the three stratified classes in Ioway society: royalty, nobility, and commoners[63]

When the sacred rituals and practical preparations were completed, the party left the village after dusk or before daylight. Three or four men served as scouts and rode ahead. The leader carried the clan's war bundle (see Figure 8). Accompanying him were one or two nephews familiar with the bundle ritual. A noncombatant member of the group, called the Prophet, would predict triumph or warn of impending disaster that could terminate a party. Also expected to accompany the group was the Buffalo Bundle Doctor, who performed rituals and provided medicine that would heal wounds and cause impurities to drain away.[64]

When the scouts found the enemy tracks or observed them directly, they returned to the main body and sang a sacred song composed for this purpose. This signaled the ritualistic act of opening the war bundle and removing from it the paraphernalia used in battle preparation: the paints for the body, small sacred amulets to wear, and herbs to be rubbed on the body for protection against bullets and arrows. Except for the bundle owner, who stayed at the camp to sing songs of protection and victory, the group then imbued with induced supernatural aura, advanced and attacked. If it were successful, the party showed the scalps, horses, and other trophies to the bundle owner, who sang the sacred clan song for each victor. If a warrior requested, the bundle owner would change his name to honor his valor in battle. A name change indicated a positive status gain for the Ioway warrior. The significance and number of names held by a man at the end of his days indicated much of the success of his life. This is not to say that battle was the only means of recognition. The good hunter also was respected, as was the wise civil leader.

The party then returned to the village. If they had not been successful, they entered quietly and ashamed. But if they had been triumphant, they paused at a great distance from the village, shouted, or fired off their guns to announce their presence. When they heard these sounds, the kingroup members were elated, since they would gain importance by the success of their warrior relatives. They left whatever they were doing and went to the road that led from the village, and waited. When the party arrived, each man went to his sister or nearest female relative, recounted his participation in the venture, and said his name for all to hear.

Then the war post was prepared. A white oak about two feet in circumference was peeled and sharpened to a point and was placed upright in the ground at one of the four corners of the village. The

Figure 8. Ioway ceremonial objects. *Top left:* a Thunder clan war bundle that once belonged to Raining All Day; among its sacred items is the scalp of an ivory-headed woodpecker. *Top right:* a Black Bear clan tatooing bundle that belonged to Chief David Tohee; the outer wrapping is an Ioway woven mat, and the length of the bundle is about 20 inches. *Bottom:* an otter-hide medicine bag with metal tinklers and bells, quill and beadwork decoration, and feathers attached; length, 34 inches. Courtesy of Milwaukee Public Museum (Accession Nos. 31501, 31552, and 30541).

surface was first painted red, and on this the party's exploits were depicted in charcoal. The scalps were represented as spread on netted hoops and suspended from stick handles. Headless figures indicated the victims. Following the preparation of the war post, the scalp dance was given. The scalps, stretched on netted hoops with handles, were carried by designated individuals. Details of ritual — movement, song, or dance — as it was performed at that time are unknown.

One event of the performance called for the nephews, uncles, sisters, and brothers of each warrior to give away horses or other gifts to certain participants and onlookers. This affirmed the givers' status and maintained the links of social and sacred reciprocity of tribal members.

Declarations of coups attained during the war expedition followed. In deciding a contested coup, the Oath Bundle was brought forth, on which the individuals would be asked to swear the truth of their assertions. The gaining of a coup was absolutely necessary in order to attain rank within the system. Each designated coup held a special value according to the valor that was needed to perform the act. In order to rise in the Ioway hierarchy and acquire titles as a warrior the following deeds were described:

1. *Watcle,* "successful partisan," the greatest title a man could possibly receive, given only to bundle owners who had conducted victorious war parties; a hunt leader *(gixrowatogera)* who was attacked and whose men fought off the foe was entitled to great honor also.

2. *Wabothage,* "foe killer," the term applied to a man who actually killed a foe. This is next in rank to the preceding.

3. The following honors are all third rate and all belong to the same group, being of equal value:

    (a) *Ushkaon,* "coup striker," a term applied to the first two men to strike a foe, living or dead.

    (b) *Paruthe,* "head cutter." Galloping up to the body of a fallen enemy a man would make the motions of cutting off the head or nose, or if he had time he would actually do so. For this he received this title.

    (c) *Axodulte,* "scalper" given the man who secured an enemy's scalp. In scalping, the bowstring was tied around the top of the victim's head, a knife cut made under its guidance, and the scalp ripped off.

    (d) *Nanthudilte,* "lock taker," was awarded to the warrior who succeeded in cutting a lock of hair, other than the scalplock, from a fallen foe.[65]

The Big Ax in White Cloud's account was chosen to carry the scalps in White Cloud's place, because he was titled "successful partisan." His importance in the village and tribe is attested to by his signature on an Ioway treaty in 1815.

After the coups were claimed, and titles awarded, the ceremonies ended at the leader's signal. Ideally, he would raise three additional war parties. With the accomplishment of the fourth with its ceremonies, he would have placed war posts at each corner of the village. This was the greatest accomplishment of all. Honor descended on this man and his family, and songs were composed that told of his deeds and bravery.

After the ceremonies the war post gained added sacred qualities. No one was supposed to go near it, but from time to time the grass

would be cleared away from it in a circular area. If the warrior's
relatives saw the villagers doing this, they were obligated to give
gifts to them.[66]

The White Cloud war party was not the last against the Osages.
Both tribes continued to send men against each other in 1810 and
1811.[67] But war with the Osages was not the only military involvement considered by the Ioways. In July, 1810, the Shawnee Prophet
sent messages to the Ioways, the Sacs, and the Foxes, to strike the
whites whenever the call was sent. Only the Foxes seriously considered the action. In the same month a party of four settlers, while
they pursued horses stolen from them were attacked and some
killed. Gen. William Clark, in seeking to ascertain the attackers'
identity, was visited by parties of Ioways, Sacs, and Kickapoos, who
disclaimed any involvement. The Potawatomis in Illinois were suspected, but they denied any knowledge of the act, saying that it might
have been committed by some group under the Prophet's influence.
But not all existence in the new territory was so troubled, and there
were those who did not dance for war. The *Missouri Gazette* reported
that on Monday evening, September 24, a public dinner was given
by the citizens of St. Louis for Governor Howard, and "in the evening
the Assembly Room was thrown open to a crowded assemblage of
beauty and fashion, where the lovers of the mazy dance enjoyed
themselves until morning."

Lead mining claimed the position of being the first mining industry
in Upper Louisiana. The French had first discovered the deposits,
and the Spanish had given grants to a few individuals to work them.
Julien Dubuque's grant in northeastern Iowa embraced 169,344
arpents, whose mines yielded 84 to 92 pounds of pure lead per
hundredweight.[68]

In 1811, Agent Boilvin advocated the building of a factory at
Prairie du Chien for the numerous tribesmen of the area, including
the Iowa River Ioways' village of 400 warriors. He reported that at
this time the Ioways, the Sacs, and the Foxes had turned their
attention to lead mining and spent less time in hunting, except to
furnish themselves food. The mines were 60 miles below Prairie du
Chien and had produced 4,000 pounds of ore in the previous season.
Boilvin believed that with specialized tools and a blacksmith for
repairing them the mines' income would substitute for the precari-
ousness of the chase. He envisioned that mining among these tribes
would serve as a means to reduce the influence of Canadian traders,
for they would not take lead in trade.[69]

Boilvin related that each year the different tribes met in council
at Dog's Prairie (Prairie du Chien) to settle their affairs, to determine
on peace and war, and so forth. The Sioux, the most numerous with
six thousand members, were able to dominate the Menominees, the
Winnebagos, the Foxes from Fox River, the Sacs and the Ioways. "If

the Sioux goodwill is maintained, there is little to fear from the others."[70] Boilvin heard that at the recent council complaints had been voiced that the Americans were stopping all the rivers so that few English traders could reach the Indians, who still preferred well-made British products to American ones, which were shoddy, and broke easily, and were laughed at by the Indians. "The traps were good for nothing; the blankets were small and thin, weighing but half the weight of an English trader's blanket, and the calico would not from age hold together, it would seem that all the old goods of our cities were bought up as good enough for the Indian."[71] Boilvin ominously informed the secretary of war that the council had been told that soon the English father would declare war against the Americans and again take under his protection his beloved children, that if they sided with him they would have everything in abundance.[72]

British agents succeeded in maintaining Indian hopes and alliances throughout the year. Tecumseh and his brother gained strength among many tribes and counted on British support if the day should arrive when they could drive out the Americans. Indian anxiety and resentment increased as Gov. William H. Harrison continued to urge and to push them toward land cessions. Tecumseh and the Prophet called on all nations not to cede another inch of their land. Harrison, in his plans for aggrandizing his career, saw the possibilities in fulminating an Indian war to further his national reputation. He gathered his forces and marched to the village of the Prophet and Tecumseh, who was absent at the time. The village of twelve hundred was located near the junction of the Wabash and Tippecanoe rivers. The Indians, learning of the maneuver, attacked him by surprise on November 7 with 400 warriors. With superior numbers he succeeded in beating off the attack, advanced to the village, and burned it to the ground. His career was launched. Newspapers carried the story, and he was hailed as the hero of the Northwest, especially by young so-called War Hawks in Congress, who cited this as an indirect strike against England through her Indian allies.

Six months later, on June 12, 1812, President Madison signed a proclamation of war with Great Britain. The nation's long years of harassment and frustration on the seas and the frontiers culminated in this action. The Indians of the Northwest particularly were hostilely inclined, and although the British agents and traders played a large role in fanning their discontent, they were only catalysts, not the basic reagents that precipitated the next reactions. The territorial governors, the Indian agents, the fort officers, and the traders now all turned their ears and eyes toward the tribes surrounding them for rumors and reports of incidents that might indicate the underlying currents of alliance and attack.

John Johnston, the factor at Fort Madison who seemed to have had the trust of several Indians, planned to use Mellesello, a young

Sac, as a spy for the American cause. Mellesello agreed and soon reported that on June 26 a nine-nation council had taken place at the large Rock River Sac village, and it had been attended by ten Winnebagos, six Kickapoos, four Potawatomis, three Shawnees, two Miamis, one Menominee from Green Bay, one Sioux from the Des Moines, and Ioways, Otoes, and Foxes. Five of the nations represented the Prophet. A Kickapoo chief spoke for him and the five nations, each of which presented a wampum belt tied with red. The sacred pipe was smoked. Words spoken after this must be true. It was told that the Prophet entreated each tribe to join him at his village, where the corn was made, "so we can all agree there when and where to strike the Americans." Messages had been sent as far as the Missouri River nations to come in the fall. He argued that the Americans "will take your lands and you will become poor. You can see by my dress that I am not. When I need clothing my British father will clothe me again." His appeal met with resistance. The Sac war chief, Non-wait, refused the invitation by saying that the Americans had furnished the Sacs with everything they wanted. "We are their children and must listen to their Counsel," and with this he refused the pipe.

The Ioways responded when their turn came: "There are no chiefs here with you belonging to our nation. We are a nigh neighbor to the Sacs. We have no wish to be at war with them. Our American Father gives us good counsel. Whatever the Sacs agree to, we shall."[73]

The Sac and Ioway refusal to attend the Prophet's fall council does not indicate their disagreement with his beliefs and purposes. Certainly the Sac war leader did not reflect the viewpoint of Black Hawk, an emerging power figure, whose anti-American sentiments were well known. The Ioways' response may have been influenced by their proximity to American laws and their experience with American justice; by the need and desire for American goods, which were improving in quality and quantity; by the coercion and persuasion of the American traders and Indian agents among them; and by the news of the recent disaster at Tippecanoe.

Regardless of their stated reluctance to extend their military effort to aid the Prophet, the Ioways, the Sacs, and the Winnebagos continued to harass and attack the Osages near Fort Osage. Their continuing raids had been so successful that since April, 1812, the Osages had not used that post for trade but had moved to their old villages farther to the east. A disastrous encounter with the Ioways and the Sacs near the post had resulted in great loss of Osage life, animals, and belongings.[74]

The evidences of war increased near the Mississippi. On July 21 Ninian Edwards in Illinois wrote to the secretary of war that Indian depredations were frequent. The Kickapoo head chief had gone to Canada to see his Great Father, and the Winnebagos who had lost heavily at Tippecanoe, were said to be ready to go to war against the Americans.[75] Fort Madison had stood in constant state of alert since spring, 1812. Parties of hostile Indians moved through the area. In September Black Hawk with two hundred Winnebagoes and Sacs attacked the fort. For three days they unsuccessfully beseiged the fort, attempting to set fire to it by hurling burning wood onto its interior roofs.

In February, 1813, the secretary of war was notified of rumors that certain tribes, among them the Ioways and the Sacs, had joined a large force of twelve hundred to three thousand Indians at Green Bay. Warriors also came from the Winnebago, Ottawa, Chippewa, Sioux, Potawatomi, Kickapoo, Miami, Delaware, Shawnee, and Piankashaw tribes and other tribes of the region. They had been called to meet a British vessel that would contain military supplies and a force of four hundred Canadian recruits. The ammunition and arms were to supply them "with every necessary" to drive the Americans from the Mississippi and Great Lakes lands.

That internal disruption among the Ioways existed was confirmed by French traders acting as spies for the United States, who reported that they had met three Sacs who told them the Sacs, the Foxes, and the Ioways were divided, part for war and part for peace.[76] The nonaggressive bands had been informed by the others that they would be treated like Americans if they did not join their British-aligned brothers. The real depth and extent of the differences between the Ioways over this matter are unknown. Hard Heart, it is suspected, led the pro-American advocates, but how large his following was, or who his opponents were among the other chiefs, is not known. It is probable that the two main Ioway villages, one on the Des Moines River and the other on the Iowa River, represented opposing points of view. The latter may have contained pro-British proponents because of its accessibility to Prairie du Chien and the British agents there, as well as its nearness to the Sac village and to Black Hawk's influence. The warriors who had gone to Green Bay probably originated in this village.

Governor Howard, utilizing the same device that General Clark had attempted several years before to control the Osages, gave Pierre Chouteau, their agent, permission to allow this nation to attack their pro-British enemies, that is, the Kickapoos, the Potawatomis, the Winnebagos, and the Prophet's group on the Wabash. Those tribes who were enemies of the Osages, but were at peace with the United States — the Ioways and the Sioux of the Des Moines — were not to be attacked.[77]

In April, 1813, Hard Heart's son went to Fort Madison and asked Captain Stark for aid and permission to go against the pro-British Sacs and Foxes. No sooner had he requested this than a small Sac party came to the fort. Captain Stark reported: "This circumstance was applied so as to intimidate the one and not encourage the other, but this state of things cannot last long. The Ioways deserve every assistance and I hope will receive it. It is a just war on their part, and I am inclined to believe it is unavoidable."[78] Hard Heart's son asked for a medal, which he had sought in the previous autumn. He also needed a rifle. Frederick Bates, acting governor, had given one to him but someone at the salt works on the Missouri had taken it from him "in an improper manner through the agency of Louis Dorion, the trader," Stark added.

The turmoil of this area at this time was perhaps greater than at any time in its previous history. Tribal movements, voluntary or induced by the Americans or the British; disruptions of cyclical hunting and agricultural systems and the consequent reduction of food resources; internal divisions and political factionalism; fear of the future; aggravating and intensifying of old tribal enmities; depopulation by foreign disease; breakdown in moral codes by the use of alcohol with the resultant associated behaviors; and the use and frequent abandonment of Indian women by white men all began to tear apart the bindings of formerly well-regulated societies.

For example, the Ioways on the Des Moines were uprooted in the late summer of 1813. William Clark, who replaced Governor Howard, reported that "the Greater part of Sacs, Foxes, and Ioways nations still profess friendship; those tribes are formidable in numbers, and have for some time past been in a state of poverty, and if suffered to continue, I believe they would be obliged to join our enemies." Clark had induced some of the Sacs and the Foxes to settle on the Missouri, and "I have sent also to the Ioways directing them to pass across to the Missouri where a trader will be situated to trade with them." He estimated that "this maneuver will keep nearly one thousand warriors from aiding the British."[79]

Not all Ioways, however, responded to Clark's inducements and removed to the Grand River. Col. R. Dickson, who professed British allegiance, said in a report in May that the Sioux, the Ioways, the Winnebagos, and the Rock River Saukies were for war.[80] In July, another British officer, Col. William McKay, reported an incident that he said was one of the "most brilliant actions fought by Indians since the commencement of the war." The Americans had sent six barges up the Mississippi, three of which were armed. On the night of July 21 they stopped near some rapids. Early the next morning the Sacs, the Foxes, the Ioways, and the Kickapoos attacked and killed one hundred persons, burned one barge, and captured five cannons. Women participated by jumping on board with their hoes, "breaking heads and casks." An Ioway who had come from Michilimackinac with McKay leaped on deck, cut a hole in the bottom of the barge, fired into the American soldiers, and then plunged into the river and swam ashore.[81]

During the war and the years preceding it time had not stopped for the fur traders on the interior rivers west of the Mississippi. In 1807 the *Missouri Gazette* announced that in the spring Manuel Lisa and

George Drouillard, who had been with Lewis and Clark on their expedition, embarked on the upper Missouri to trade; they carried a cargo estimated to be worth $16,000. By 1808 Lisa had established Manuel's Fort at the mouth of the Big Horn River. After several years of successful trading the St. Louis Fur Company was organized. William Clark was named president and Lisa general manager and commandant. Each contributed $10,000 to it. In May, 1812, the company sent out an expedition which established Fort Lisa above present-day Omaha. It was to serve as headquarters for the new expansion, but the war began to interfere with the enterprise's hoped-for profits. In 1814, when Clark became governor of the territory as well as Superintendent of Indian Affairs, he appointed Lisa Subagent for the tribes of the Missouri above the Kansas River. He soon left St. Louis to continue his old business as fur trader and to begin a new endeavor, that of representing the United States interests among the Indians. When he arrived at his headquarters near Council Bluffs, he invited leaders of Sioux bands to counsel with him at the spring rendezvous on the James River. Clark and Lisa planned to turn the Sioux of that area against the anti-American Ioways, Sacs, Foxes, and Santee Sioux. Lisa's success among the Indians was assisted by the fact that he had married an Omaha woman and had thus gained great influence with the nation. By giving certain gifts and using his kinship affiliations he was able to persuade the Omahas to raise a war party against the Ioways. While they were en route to the Des Moines area, they encountered an Ioway party that was on its way to attack Fort Hunt, the trading post near Council Bluffs. In the ensuing battle the Omahas claimed to have annihilated the Ioways; as proof they presented Lisa with two scalps. Not content with this, Lisa tried to convince the Otoes to attack the Ioways. They refused to do so at that time and vaguely mentioned that sometime in the future would be more favorable. Lisa was more successful with the Poncas, who promised to send a war party against the Ioways in the spring.[82]

The Ioways were quite vulnerable to these attacks. Their lands lay adjacent to the lands of those tribes, and the tribe itself was divided in its loyalty, which reduced its effective fighting power. In the 1815 spring council with the various Sioux leaders, Lisa again actively promoted the advantages and virtues of the American cause. The Sioux accepted his arguments and agreed, according to their protocol, to visit Governor Clark at St. Louis. They assembled a party of 742 men and 92 women whose auxiliary purpose would be to war against any British-inclined tribes whom they should encounter on the way. In June they came upon twenty-six Ioways and killed all but two, whom they delivered to Lisa. They also destroyed the Ioway crops in fields along the Chariton River. It will be recalled that this group of Ioways two years before had stated their American loyalty and had voluntarily moved their villages from the Des Moines River

114

area. If Lisa sent the Omahas, the Poncas, and the Sioux against them or the Ioway River villages, it indicated that enough anti-American acts had occurred since 1813 to convince Clark that such forceful measures were necessary. One incident was an attack in conjunction with the Sacs on the village of Côte sans Dessein, which lay opposite the mouth of the Osage River on the Missouri. In this attack several villagers were killed, and, according to an Indian source, fourteen Ioways and Sacs met death.[83]

The war ended, and Lisa resigned as subagent in 1817. In his resignation letter he proclaimed his role in keeping the Missouri tribes on the American side and his success in striking the Ioways, allies of the British.[84] But with the war's end the strained relationships between the Indian and the United States did not cease. The tribes who had openly supported Britain were more fearful than ever of the retribution that would come. It came subtly, as the United States increased efforts to establish peace and friendship treaties and called councils to ask for land cessions and sites to build forts farther inland. It culminated in the surveying and platting of the ceded lands for settlements and the subsequent movement of settlers onto Indian land, sometimes before it was either ceded or surveyed. In September, 1815, Treaty Commissioners William Clark, Ninian Edwards, and Auguste Chouteau were hard at work but not with the facility that they may have wished. They reported, "A considerable backwardness, if not positive reluctance on the part of several tribes, has been manifest in accepting the overtures of peace which we were authorized to offer them. . . ." The Sacs of Rock River had refused outright to deal with them and had firmly stated their opposition to forts on their lands. The Ioways reacted in another manner. The recent Lisa-inspired attacks apparently had some effect on the Ioway decision to treat with the commissioners and seek United States protection. Led by Hard Heart (Wy-in-wah-hu) and seventeen other leaders, the nation signed a treaty of peace and friendship at Portage des Sioux on September 16, 1815. It was a simple treaty of four articles and granted mutual forgiveness for acts of hostility and injury, established perpetual peace between the Ioways and the citizens of the United States, returned all prisoners regardless of reason for capture, and stated that any previous treaties, agreements, or contracts between them should be recognized and reestablished.[85]

On October 15, 1815, the commissioners reported, "the Ioways are very desirous of coming more closely under the protection of the United States and for this purpose wish to cede a part of their lands in order to obtain annuities like the rest of the neighboring Indian tribes. This is a spontaneous offer on their part, and as the land would be a valuable acquisition on many counts, particularly so in the event of future hostilities, it might be very advisable to accept the proposition."[86] If the "spontaneous" offer of cession were true, the Ioways must have been under pressure of some type to make it.

One questions the spontaneity, since the tribe was already short of good hunting land after the earlier Sac and Osage cession of Ioway-claimed lands and the continuing intrusion of the Sacs into the land the Ioway claimed along the Missouri and between the Mississippi and Des Moines rivers. But if the Ioways appeared to be losing control of the land, they might have seen in cession some benefit in the form of annuity payments and other guarantees.

It is possible that only one segment of the tribe was represented in the treaty-making councils. A list of traders' licenses issued in 1816 at St. Louis included Denis Julien (with the Sacs, the Foxes, and the Ioways of the Mississippi), and John P. Cabanne (with the same tribes on the Missouri).[87] It is possible that part of the Ioways settled in Illinois after the war. An 1817 report states that the Ioway, Kickapoo, Chippewa, Potawatomi, Menominee, and Shawnee tribes had held a council, the object of which was to form a confederation to prevent settlement of lands that had been ceded to the United States in Illinois Territory.[88] Although the Ioways never ceded any land there, they had lived and had hunted there near the Mississippi River for some time.

The interest of British Canadian traders in the upper Mississippi and upper Missouri River tribes did not diminish with the end of the war. In order to end their interference, Congress passed new regulations, which forbade foreign nationals from carrying on trade but did allow them to act as interpreters, boatmen, and clerks for American fur traders. In order to establish firm control of the area, Fort Crawford was established at Prairie du Chien to supersede Fort Shelby, which had been built there in 1813 and had been captured and damaged by the British. Fort Armstrong at Rock Island and Fort Snelling near the Falls of St. Anthony also carried out the policy of moving the frontier westward by overseeing the peace and maintaining vigilance over the Indian nations. The factory system continued to expand in conjunction with the forts. Thomas L. McKenney, appointed Superintendent of the United States Indian Trade by President Madison sought to organize and to better the system. He decided in 1817 that a factory at Fort Edwards at the mouth of the Des Moines would serve the Sacs, the Foxes, the Ioways, and the Kickapoos, who were dependent on private traders, whose practices were often an anathema to the government.[89]

The establishment of forts and factories along the Mississippi and the Missouri hastened the arrival of settlers. Isolated farms and small settlements sprang up in present-day Callaway, Boone, Howard, Carroll, and Chariton counties in Missouri on lands that had been ceded by the Osages or the Sacs but that the Ioways continued to claim and to use for hunting.[90] Depredations such as horse stealing served to increase hostility between Indians and whites. In 1814 General Clark noted that 400 families were settled along the Missouri River on lands that were claimed by the Sacs and the Ioways but that had previously been ceded by the Osages. The conflict between the Ioways and the Missouri Valley settlers may have precipitated the Ioways' return to their Des Moines River villages in 1817: Maj. Stephen H. Long, who ascended the Mississippi in that year, reported that the majority of the tribe of 1,200 people had settled there. In July, 1818, Thomas Forsyth, an Indian agent, recorded that the "Ihowai" Indians were at their old village, 120 miles up the Des Moines.

Various strains on the Sac social organization were developing. The length of time spent away from the village in order to reach distant hunting grounds and the pressure from the Americans undoubtedly motivated the chiefs' decision to move at least one village across the Mississippi River to a site sixty to eighty miles upstream on the Iowa River.[91] The decision to settle on this river indicated either their assurance of welcome by the Ioways or a disregard for the latter's territorial rights. It well could have been the latter, for in July the Ioway interpreter, Julien, reported that the "Sac chiefs at the principal village on Rock River await the arrival of the Ioway chiefs to settle differences between them." He added that all of the Ioways were living again in their old village on the Des Moines, which may indicate that the so-called Mississippi group of Ioways had joined the others in anticipation of the Sac removal across the river. On July 24, the council between the Ioway, Sac, and Fox chiefs was held. Forsythe reported that the differences between them appeared to be solved.

As the close of 1818, President Monroe again reviewed for Congress the year's treaties, including those made with the Quapaws, the Osages, the Chickasaws, and others in Indiana, Ohio, and Michigan. The continuing westward expansion of the fort system was confirmed in the statement: "With a view to the security of our interior frontiers, it has been thought expedient to establish strong posts at the mouth of the Yellowstone River, at the Mandan village on the Missouri, and at the mouth of the St. Peters," and "It can hardly be presumed while such posts are maintained in the rear of the Indian tribes that they will venture to attack our peaceable inhabitants. Experience has long demonstrated that independent savage communities cannot long exist within the limits of a civilized population. To civilize them, and even prevent their extinction, it seems to be indispensable that their independence as communities should cease, and that the control of the United States over them should be complete and undisputed."[92]

In February, 1819, the Ioway chiefs, Hard Heart and The Crane, presented themselves to George Sibley, agent at Fort Osage.[93] Their visit concerned a desire to notify the United States government of their claim to lands to the north and east of the Missouri that had been previously ceded by the Osages. They asked for an impartial investigation and a just compensation.

As long as the Ioways could drive the Osages and others from these hunting lands, the fact that the Osages had ceded them probably did not concern them. At that time the land seemed remote from white settlers, and the Indians considered the cession, if they knew of it at all, an illegal act by which they would not abide. However, after the exigencies of the war, with the increasing reach of settlers into the area — the last of their good beaver-hunting territories along the Missouri, Grand, and Chariton rivers — and with the appearances of surveyors, the nation was sufficiently alarmed to confront the United States agent near their winter villages across the Missouri.

Sibley asked them to refrain from interfering with the surveyors in the disputed area and to deliver all horses stolen from the whites, if they wished him to intercede on their behalf with the government. Hard Heart's reply was reported as follows:

> [He] can only promise to use his utmost exertion to do what I desire. His People are so foolish and so ignorant and so poor that 'tis impossible to make them act as they ought.... They are surrounded he says on every side by enemies, who are continually making war upon them; which compels them to be always on the watch, sleeping with one eye open, and one hand upon their Guns; so that they have but little time to hunt for the subsistence of their families.... He says that his people are truly objects of compassion; and most feelingly and urgently begs that the Government will allow them an Annual Stipend, either as an act of justice for their Lands, or as an act of Charity.[94]

He added that the Ioway claim seemed justified, since the Osages had told him that they never claimed lands on the northern and eastern sides of the Missouri, nor did they sell any to the United States. "The Missouris once claimed there, but they have long since abandoned the country and left the Iowa in possession of it," he added.[95] Sibley suggests that the nation would probably be satisfied with an annual annuity of five hundred dollars for their claim.

From the remarks reputedly made by Hard Heart, it is apparent that the Ioways had lost another portion of their autonomy as a nation. Not only is the principal chief put in the position of appealing to a lesser United States official, but he is compelled to plea for consideration of a serious wrong that he suspects will not be righted.

When summer returned, Major Forsyth, the Sac agent, commented that some of the Sacs and the Ioways had planted corn near Fort Edwards, "where they reside." Occasionally they went to the settlements, brought back whiskey, got drunk, and acted disorderly, insulting those living in the fort. Forsyth suggested that a few soldiers stationed there could keep them in awe and prevent their obstreperous behavior. Fort Edwards served as a factory competing with the outlawed Canadian traders and with John Jacob Astor's

American Fur Company. This company's agents often used whiskey as a medium of exchange. None was sold at the government factories, and for that reason various Indians preferred to trade with private companies. Robert B. Belt, the factor at Fort Edwards, had been placed there by Thomas McKenney to compete with the fur traders for the Sac and the Ioway trade. The American Fur Company wanted no such competition here or elsewhere and began to use its influence in Congress, particularly with Sen. Thomas Hart Benton, to do away with the system. Its efforts were successful in 1822.[96]

When a society or a group within a society is reduced to fewer options in the direction of its cultural life — that is, in following traditional religious, economic, and political patterns — various re-actions to the constraints may result. At times efforts to agree and to conform may be made or behavior can be reshaped so as to avoid conflict or punishment. Another possible course of action is to react aggressively to change the situation and overcome the dictates of the restrictive force. Ideas for changing the Indians' lives were in most cases completely alien and increasingly destructive to Indian society. Older Indian leaders often tried to lead their people within the new structure; the younger men often were opposed to this method and chose the option of aggression, not only as a vent for their frustrations but also as a genuine attempt to throw off the restrictions that constrained their people. In May, 1819, several young Ioways attacked a United States officer and two riflemen somewhere between Cantonment Martin and the Fort Osage trading post, robbing and abusing them. Later, at the Council Bluffs trading post, a visiting party of Ioways "insulted the Trader and boasted of their outrages upon the Americans." The officer there "confined and punished the principal offenders," and it was said that "their chiefs express great satisfaction that those offenders were thus punished, stating that it will have a tendency to deter many of their thoughtless young men, whom they can't themselves well restrain from repeating such outrages."[97] The erosion of tribal authority is evident here, and it forecast the next stage in the Indians' reaction to the constraints on their life-style, that of demoralization, expressed by more wanton acts and the wider use of alcohol.

Added to the problems of the Ioway nation was a disagreement with the Sacs, which flared anew in the summer of 1819. It reached the point that the Ioways moved from their Des Moines River villages to the lands of the Otos, where they were reported to be living in the fall. At this time Maj. Stephen H. Long established winter quarters near Lisa's Fort at Council Bluffs. He was a Dartmouth graduate who had entered the United States Engineering Corps in 1814. He had been appointed to conduct land surveys and to hold Indian councils in the trans-Mississippian area.

In September, 1819, Indian Agent Benjamin O'Fallon summoned

various tribes to come to Lisa's Fort to counsel. A group of one hundred Otos and Ioways appeared on October 3. The chiefs came first leading their people. When all were seated, an Otoe, Shongatonga (The Great Horse), acted as spokesman. He formally requested permission to perform an appropriate dance and ceremony for the visitors. Major O'Fallon responded properly, and the dance began. The singers were accompanied by a drum made from a keg with skin-covered ends and by a stick of hard wood notched like a saw over which another stick was pulled back and forth. After the introductory passages, three dancers sitting among the others on the ground leaped into the circle, danced the prescribed steps, and returned to their places when the music stopped. As they sat down again, they patted their mouths and emitted sounds like the short barks of a dog. This sequence was performed by various sets of dancers. In the intervals between the singing and dancing, a warrior would arise and, striking a pole that had been set there, declaim his exploits of bravery. He struck the pole with his whip, stick, or weapon to accent his accomplishments. No exaggeration was made in these declamations, since any member of the assemblage could rise to condemn a speaker who did not relate precisely the events of a particular episode.[98]

This day, Miaketa, a renowned Otoe warrior, described his coups against the Osages, the Kansas, the Pawnees, the Poncas, the Omahas, the Sioux, the Comanches, the Sacs, the Foxes, and the Ioways.

The whites who first saw the dance performed called it the Beggars Dance," for the proper response was to offer small bits of tobacco, whiskey, or trinkets to the participants. The Otoe version was performed on this occasion. It may have been similar to the Ioway Braves Dance, or Welcome Dance, given for strangers who were welcomed to the village or out of respect to any persons to whom welcome was to be expressed. The Ioway War and Scalp Dance also contained intervals for the expression of exploits by warriors.[99]

After the event whiskey was served to the participants. The principal chiefs and representatives of other tribes had not taken part in the ceremonies except as observers. At the end they requested that their people leave and return to their camps. All left except a few Ioways, "Who appeared to be determined to keep their places notwithstanding their chief's command." At this Ietan, an Otoe chief, sprang toward the Ioways, and, if the other Otoe chiefs had not intervened, violence might have resulted.

This event indicated a strong negative reaction to the Ioway chief's authority on the part of certain members of the tribe, who may have been chiefs from among the Mississippi Ioways. Both Hard Heart and White Cloud were present at the meeting. Both were chiefs, so it is not clear who was defied in this instance.

The next morning the council began. The Indian principals arrived and shook hands with the visitors as they entered the area. Present were one hundred Otoes, seventy Missourias, and fifty or sixty Ioways. A few howitzer rounds signaled the meeting's beginning. Major O'Fallon spoke; the chiefs responded with "extravagant gesticulation" and speeches.[100] Following the talks, which in the usual fashion spoke of peace and friendship, blankets, guns, tobacco, kettles, and ammunition were presented. Some time later Hard Heart visited the quarters of Maj. Long. Long described Hard Heart as follows: "He is a very intelligent Indian, with a solemn dignity of deportment, and would not deign to enter our houses or even approach them until invited. He is said to have a more intimate knowledge of the manners of the whites, than any other Indian on the Missouri, and to be acquainted with many of the words of our language, but will not willingly make use of them, fearing to express himself improperly, or not trusting to his pronunciation."[101]

Hard Heart acted as an observer at the meetings and listened and watched with keen interest the movements, glances, and words of the whites. He remained near the fort for some time after his nation went to the Boyer River on the winter beaver hunt. With him were three of his wives, one a young girl of nine or ten, it was estimated, who was thought at first to be his daughter. This girl may have been the younger sister of one or all of Hard Heart's wives. The kinship term *wife* applied to her although she was not yet of marriageable age. It was customary for a man to marry sisters as they came of age, but the term *wife* could apply before that time.

Hard Heart had been among the Otoes for some time. James explained that during the recent war he had "turned his back on his own nation when they acted against the United States." He crossed the Missouri and "lived among the Oto, who received him and treated him with distinguished respect." In the autumn of 1819 his tribe rejoined him and submitted to his authority, except perhaps for those members at the ceremony who had refused to depart.[102] The incident with the Sacs had precipitated their movement from the Des Moines. The Ioway move may have been more one of escape than of real desire to realign themselves with Hard Heart.

At this time the Ioways were organized into two divisions, each made up of clans or gens as they were formerly called. In the early years of their history before the Europeans came and the culture was disrupted, they traveled between villages and hunting grounds, went on trading jaunts, or visited other tribes in prescribed order, where they camped in two half circles composed of related clan groups. Each day's march was under the direction of a chief, chosen the evening before as the chiefs gathered to discuss the day's events. During the day, the designated leader was responsible for choosing and following the route, for protecting the people by the dispersal of scouts and other means, and for selecting the next camp site. All the tipis were erected in a circle or semi circle behind his tipi, and no one dared pitch a tipi beyond it. The principal chief camped in the center of the circle.[103]

The first division's chiefs and organizations planned and controlled the winter hunt and other tribal affairs of winter and early spring. The other division controlled the agricultural activities of late spring, summer, and early fall and the decisions and events of that period. The leading clan of the first division was that of the Black Bear.[104] The clan was divided into four subclans: Large Black Bear with a White Spot on Its Chest; Black Bear with a Red Nose; Young Black Bear and Small Reddish Black Motherless Bear Who Runs Swiftly. The other clan members of the group were the Wolf, the Eagle and Thunder, the Elk, and the Beaver, which were similarly subdivided into subclans. Each of those clans had an origin story that explained its name and its history. In the second division were the Pigeon, Buffalo, Snake, and Owl clans. Lewis Henry Morgan, who visited the Ioways in the middle of the nineteenth century, gave the clan names as Wolf, Bear, Cow Buffalo, Elk, Eagle, Pigeon, Snake, and Owl.[105] Alanson Skinner was told by the Ioways in the early twentieth century that the following clan and subclan groupings existed in addition to four that were extinct long before:

Bear	Four Together, Comes with Him, Strong Mind, Good Tracks
Buffalo	Village Maker, Clear Day, Road Maker, Mired in Mud
Pigeon	"Mister" Pigeon, Old Pigeon, Up Wing, Big Raccoon
Elk	Elk Bend, Big Elk, White Elk, Bull Elk
Eagle and Thunder	Storm and Hail or Thunder, Lightning Struck, Always Raining (Walking Rain?), Soaring Eagle
Wolf	Black Wolf, Big Wolf, Half Coyote (Gray Wolf?), Coyote

The four extinct clans were:

Red Earth	A band who, according to tradition, first moved westward from a mythical home in the east where the sunrise reddens the land by the ocean. No subclans are remembered.
Snake	Yellow Snake, Rattlesnake, Real Snake (named after a species of rattlesnake), Small or Young-like-the-Copperhead Snake, Gray Snake (a long snake which the Omahas call swift blue snake).
Beaver	No subclans are remembered.
Owl [106]	

Each clan's origin story told a sacred and marvelous tale of the mythological clan progenitor. The Ioways related the Wolf origin myth as follows:

Originally, back in Moka-Shutze [Red Earth, the mythical point of origin of the Ioways, thought by them to have been in Wisconsin on the shore of Lake Michigan], there were no people, only animals. Finally a wolf came out of the water. He had great power over all the other fourfooted creatures, and he became a man, the first Wolf gens ancestor. As he came out of the water he walked away from there, hence comes the name, Manyihu and Manyihumi or, Walks From the Creation On in the gens [clan]. Moreover when the wolf became a human being he was then master of himself, hence in the Wolf gens are the names, "Master of Himself," and Mistress of Herself." Other names come to us from his weapons and the way in which he conducted himself. The pipe came from above, as is related in other myths.[107]

J. O. Dorsey recorded the stories of the Bear, Wolf, Eagle, and Pigeon clans, as they were related in 1848:

The Black Bear people came out of the ground, and taught the people how to farm. Some say that they brought the canoe, others, that they brought the pipe, but that is claimed by most of the families (*i. e.,* gentes). When the Bear people first met the Eagle and Pigeon people, they lived under the ground in the form of bears. The Eagle and Pigeon people saw the trail of the bears and followed it till they came to a den. When they struck the ground with their war-clubs, out came a bear, saying, "My elder brothers, it is I. I am your younger brother." Another tradition is that the Wolf and Bear people used to fight and eat one another. But meeting one day, they said, "We are both black," — it was the black wolf that spoke, — "we have teeth, eyes, and ears alike. So we must be brothers. Let us not fight any more." So they made peace, and ever lived in friendship. But they preyed upon the Buffalo people, who were greatly worried. So one day the Buffalo said to them, "Here is some corn. Eat it. It is good." They ate it; but as it was raw and hard, it made their mouths bleed, and the blood stained the corn red. That is the reason why so much of the Indian corn is red. Afterwards the Eagle people called them into the large skin tent, where they . . . killed about a thousand men. Then the Eagle, who brought the fire, said, "You have killed one another to your satisfaction. Let there be an end to this." And he made a feast, and cooked the corn in the fire, which made it very pleasant to eat. From that time they lived in peace.

The Bear, Wolf, and Elk gentes came from the island where the Eagle and Pigeon gentes alighted on coming down to earth.

The Wolf people came out of the earth, bringing bows and arrows. They taught the people how to hunt. Because they brought the arrows they are the cause of men's wounding one another. After the two Bird gentes had met the Black Bears, they travelled on till they saw the track of a wolf coming out of an island. This they followed until they came to another hole in the ground. Striking on the ground with the war-clubs, they made another wolf come out. Said he, "My brothers, it is I. I am your brother." The Wolf people spoke different languages, according to the different divisions of the gens. Some think that the Wolf people brought the tobacco, as in that gens there are many (personal) names derived from that plant. The other gentes asked the Wolf people to kill the Buffaloes for them, while they sang:

I am your brother.
I am of the Wolf gens.
I am invited to a buffalo chase.
I am your younger brother.
Staggering, it is about to die;
The tail trembles.

When the Eagle people lived above, they had a great sacred house in the shape of a skin tent. In this house resided the members of the Eagle and Pigeon gentes; and when there, they held a council to consider whither they should go. They were all brothers. They concluded to come down to earth, and to speak the Winnebago language, as that nation was the first to make any discoveries about Wakanta, the Great Mysterious One. When they left the sacred house in the upper world, they saw a blue cloud in the west. One of the party said that he could make a blue cloud appear in the sky; and he did so. This is why they paint their faces blue. When they first came to earth, they ate people, and so they hunted them for that purpose. The Bird gentes considered themselves superior to the other gentes, but they finally became friendly, and then they ate animals. When the Eagle people came down, they had bodies with wings. They said to the others, "Cut off our wings, or we will kill you." So they cut them off. When they got down to earth, the leader said, "My younger brothers, what shall we eat?" Then he sent the young men to hunt game. They killed a deer, and cooked it by a fire, turning the body around on a stick held in the hands. They made fire by rubbing two sticks together. After they had eaten, they continued their journey, and they scared away many demons by the aid of a war-club made in the shape of the butt-end of a gunstock. Little demons kept running across the road till they drove them away with the war-club. These Eagle and Pigeon people came to earth in the form of birds, alighting on an island where there was a lake near a mountain. As they alighted, they sang,

On what tree have I alighted?
To what land have I come?

It was there they proposed to hunt men. In their travels they met the Bear and Wolf people. After leaving them, they journeyed until they reached a certain place, where they made a village. They surrounded this with palisades, calling the settlement . . . [Man-cu-che], Hill or Bank of Red Earth. All the Indians lived there at that time. It was while these first gentes dwelt there, that the others came and asked to be admitted to their village. They pitied them and allowed them to come in.

The members of the Elk gens are generally waiters on the chiefs. They act in that capacity because when they first came they sang,

Who is that?
I am of the Elk gens.
Brother, I think that man is a chief.
No, I am of the Elk gens. I am a soldier.
He fears me because I have this club.

The Elk people must have been allies of the Bear and Wolf people, because they travelled together after they left the island.

Some say that the Buffalo gens came from above, as it is related to
the Pigeon gens. The Owl people came out of a hollow tree, near the
Red Bank. The Snake people came out of the bank (of the island?) near
the water. The Beaver people came out from a little stream on the island.
The Bear and Wolf gentes have led during the fall hunt. They used to
do all the talking and planning for starting on the hunt, etc., till the
season when the Elk whistles. The Pigeon and Buffalo gentes used to
lead the tribe when frogs were heard again in the spring: then they made
the village. The members of the Snake gens laid off the ground for the
village. [108]

The principal chief of the Ioways was chosen from the royal Bear
clans in winter and from the royal Buffalo clans in summer. All
chiefs of clans and other leadership positions were hereditary.[109] The
hereditary principal chief could not be arbitrary in all decisions. In
many tribal societies opinions heard in council usually directed the
chief's final decision, particularly in the ever-changing area of foreign
affairs that involved other tribes and European and American governments. No chief's decision was final if it was challenged by a group
of dissident chiefs. Evidently this situation developed as a result of
Hard Heart's actions. During the War of 1812 he had had to choose
between the newly arrived Americans, whose President had proclaimed him chief of the Ioways, and the older English allies. Some
of the Ioways did not agree with his choice of the American side
and continued to cooperate with the British and to harass the
Americans. It is interesting to speculate that a system of tribal
government may have existed in which the Bear clan chiefs dominated decision making in the summer and the Buffalo clan chiefs in
the winter. Hard Heart, although he was recognized as principal
chief by the United States government, might have made his decision
in the season when traditionally he was not in authority. That the
alternate chiefs of the Buffalo clan would then have overruled him
might have caused Hard Heart's decision to leave the tribe.

The intrusion of European governments into Ioway affairs, as well
as changing residence patterns, subsistence activities, and traditional
intertribal relationships, brought changes to Iowa government in the
eighteenth century and culminated in the nineteenth century with the
United States's recognition and appointment of one principal chief.
Power struggles to maintain older forms of government may have
accounted for frequent divisions of the tribe, as the leadership
structure underwent change and chiefs vied for power. Hard Heart,
thus challenged, chose to leave his tribe rather than to go against
the commitment that he had made to the United States. He undoubtedly felt the wind of the future and had decided that his
position was correct and in the long run would benefit his people.
His position and attitude toward the United States and its representatives were not those of total acquiescense, however. In one
instance after a former army officer had supposedly insulted him
grossly, Hard Heart, in the manner of the whites, challenged him to

125

a duel and requested that the officer choose whatever weapons he wished. He also spoke strongly to the Fort Madison commandant in 1809 and had recently voiced complaints to George Sibley at Fort Osage.

Ioway tribal factionalism seems to have carried over into their relationships with other tribes. In the winter of 1819 two Otoes reported that some Ioways had stolen their horses while they were hunting beaver near the camps of the Kansas, and they added, "They are still fools, as they always have proved themselves to be."[110] Within the same period James heard that a party of five Ioways had fired on three Omahas on the east side of the nearby Missouri. As was the custom, the members of the aggressive party called out their names as they fired. Two Omahas were wounded. The others set out to pursue the Ioways but returned after they lost sight of them after a fifteen-mile chase. The Ioway-Omaha hostility dated at least from the War of 1812, when Lisa had sent the Omahas against the pro-British faction.

In early January another group of Omahas, who were returning from a war party, visited the expedition's camp. They originally had been in pursuit of the Sacs, but, having not found them, they resolved to strike at the Ioway instead. They followed the Nishnabotna River south to the Missouri, but again success eluded them: the Ioways were not in the area. When they were asked if they had not made peace with the Ioways some time before, they replied affirmatively but added that the Ioway were bad men: "We do not like them, the whites do not like them." But, as if to justify their pursuit, they said that it might have been not the Sacs, but the Ioways, who stole their horses in the first place.

James's opinion of the Ioways seemed to have been mixed; he noted that the Omahas, the Otoes, and the Ioways were "excessively attached" to the use of whiskey. Then he praised Hard Heart's character and ability. Later he stated that as a whole the Ioway were "a faithless people." They had obtained a large amount of credit for trade in the fall from the Missouri Fur Company, but, instead of discharging their debts by returning with their catch, they had gone down river to the United States factory at Fort Osage, where they could trade more equitably. It should be noted that they would not obtain whiskey at Fort Osage, so perhaps James's estimation of their use of it was exaggerated.

Another observer of the Ioways in 1820 was David Meriwether, who later served as governor of New Mexico Territory. He was a young trader and became acquainted with the nation at the October council. He reported that Major O'Fallon had asked the chiefs of the Omahas, the Otoes, the Pawnees, the Ioways, and the Missouris to respond to his requests for peace.[111] The Pawnee and the Omaha chiefs responded. When the Ioways were asked to speak, White Cloud arose. When O'Fallon saw him, the major turned away. White

Cloud immediately asked the interpreter for an explanation of this behavior. O'Fallon said that he had come to hear the chiefs and not boys speak. The young chief replied, "How am I to know that the Major has been appointed by his nation to hold this council with the Indians?" Major O'Fallon retorted that the cockade that he wore on his hat indicated his official rank and office. White Cloud, said he already knew this, and asked if the major had known that his red feather was his rank of office. He added, "No one has a right to doubt my appointment by my tribe to deliver their answer," and, if "my Brother does not receive their answer through me, he will get no answer at all." The major listened.

> My brothers call me a boy. It is true I have not seen as many days as my brother, but the Indians do not count their age by the number of times they have seen the snow fall in the winter or the grass grow in the spring. They measure their age by the number of scalps of the enemy they can show [at the same time pulling from his pouch two or three scalps which he displayed] and by the number of scars they can show on their bodies, the wounds which have been inflicted by their enemies [at the same time pulling aside his blanket and showing a large scar on his side]. Now, . . . measure my age in this way, and long before my brother was born I saw the sun rise and set in my native trees. . . . My brother said he would force us to make peace with the Pawnees. Now, this is a question between Redmen and in which the white man has no right to interfere, but I will say to you that my tribe will not consent to make peace with the Pawnees. The Great Spirit has placed this broad river [pointing to the Missouri] between us, and woe to the Pawnees who cross it. I know that we are not able to cope with the whites. I have seen some of your soldiers and know that they have better guns than we have, and I am told they are numerous as the sands on the riverbank or the great herds of buffalo on the prairies, but if the whites compel us to make peace with the Pawnees, we will, if we can do no better, scratch you with our toe and finger nails and gnaw you with our teeth. Now my brother has our answer. [112]

He then stalked off in a majestic manner and was followed by the other Ioways.

The assertion by White Cloud that he was the Ioway chief and spokesman (thus inferring that Hard Heart was not) may indicate that he was the one who refused to leave after the opening ceremonies, and that I-e-tan, the Otoe, was defending Hard Heart's authority.

Later, it was said, the major, admiring White Cloud's frankness, invited him to his tent, "where they conversed for hours."[113] As a footnote to this occasion, Meriwether added, "I have listened to Mr. Clay at the height of his fame as an orator and to Tom Marshall and other eloquent speakers in Kentucky, but I think White Cloud was the greatest natural orator I ever listened to."[114]

Meriwether had another opportunity to know White Cloud. In January, 1821, the troops at Council Bluffs were seriously ill, and medical supplies were exhausted according to the surgeon, Dr. John Gale (who in 1821 or 1822 married Necomi, an Ioway). Meriwether volunteered to go to Cantonment Martin to procure the medical supplies and other items.[115] They could not be brought up the frozen river. At the Platte they met White Cloud and a party of Ioways. The chief hesitantly agreed to lead the party across the wintry countryside. He explained that the route crossed the Otoes' land, and they were his enemies. This might indicate that White Cloud and Hard Heart were leaders of opposing Ioway factions, since Hard Heart had been living in peace and respect among the Otoes for some time.

Meriwether promised that the troops would protect him, and he agreed to accompany them. Meriwether's eye was caught by White Cloud's snowshoes. They were ingeniously made "of a light hoop of wood, about two and a half feet long and eight or ten inches wide, across which narrow leather thongs were woven. The foot being placed in the middle of this loop, and being attached to it from the instep, the shoes would sustain a person on the surface of the snow; and by bearing one's weight on the middle, the hoop would slightly contract, and on relieving the shoes weight the hoop would spring apart again, which assisted very much in walking." He asked White Cloud if he could have a pair like his, and the next morning they were brought to the camp. White Cloud led the 270-mile march through the deep snow on foot. Each day they kept to the ridges, and each evening they went down to the river to chop through the ice to get water. Meriwether or White Cloud would start a fire with flint and steel, using dry vines they found entangled in the bushes. They would then hunt separately for supper and breakfast meat. After supper the horses were fed and footgear dried before the men turned in for sleep. Watch was kept during the night, and each bitter chilling day was much like the one before. Finally they reached Martin Cantonment, where the medical and other supplies were packed. When the party was ready to leave, White Cloud advised Meriwether that they should now travel up the west side of the river to avoid the Otoes. A few days before the end of the journey, White Cloud reported that he had seen signs of the Otoes while he was out hunting and asked Meriwether if he could finish the journey without his direction. Meriwether suggested that White Cloud might want to return to Council Bluffs to be paid for guiding the party. White Cloud replied that the Otoes had some horses, and that this was a good opportunity for him to capture some. If he had not returned in the morning, he asked that the party leave without him. When camp broke the next day, he had not returned, so Meriwether continued without him. Some time later a party of Otoes rode up and inquired about some horses that they had lost. Needless to say, Meriwether replied that he knew nothing about them.[116]

Pacification attempts, such as those made by Major O'Fallon in the council at Council Bluffs in 1819 were a part of the United

128

States policy to make possible the planning and building of forts. In January, 1820, Col. Henry Atkinson, while commanding the Ninth Military Department, reported to Secretary of War Calhoun that a road along the Missouri had been planned from Council Bluffs to Chariton. It would cross the Grand River near its mouth and would pass through a country frequented by "no other Indians but the Ioways, a small band of not more than one hundred and fifty warriors." It would become a good wagon road, he continued, over which supplies could be carried with little trouble. He also asked for permission to plan a road to be built the following summer, from Council Bluffs to the mouth of the St. Peters. He believed that it would be necessary to station four or five hundred men at Council Bluffs and said, "This point holds in check a greater body of Indians than any other on the rivers." At the great bend two hundred men would be garrisoned, and, eventually, at the Mandan village far up the Missouri five hundred men would be able to guard the frontier and control the Indians and "cover our frontier from insult or depredation."[117] Thus, with forts and roads joining them, the United States quietly and gradually extended its control into western Indian territory.

Far to the east another long-reaching project developed. Rev. Jedidiah Morse of Connecticut had interested himself in the Indians and their future in the United States. His was part of a new citizen interest and involvement in Indian welfare, which began after the War of 1812 and developed chiefly under the influence of church organizations, which were interested in the religious and secular education of Indian youth. Reverend Morse made many inquiries concerning different tribes and their living conditions. In September, 1819, the government responded to public pressure and distributed a circular that told of the philanthropic work already in progress among the Indians under the aegis of the government. Replies came from many sources with offers of assistance to further the "Civilization of the Indian," as the project came to be called. What had been done and what would be done to the Indians in the name of progress called for some humane response, as their degradation and losses became more and more visible to thoughtful persons. In this year Congress established the Civilization Fund with $10,000; this was soon enlarged with private donations. Reverend Morse's travel and study resulted in his 1822 *Report to the Secretary of War of the United States on Indian Affairs.*

In answer to Morse's query about the Ioways, Agent George Sibley wrote:

The Ioway visit Fort Osage occasionally. Lately they were much divided among themselves, and it was hard to say where they all were located. One half the tribe had previously joined the Otoe near Council Bluffs, and the others were in two villages, one on the Des Moines, and one on the Grand River. They hunted between the Mississippi and the Missouri, north of the latter, from the headwaters of the two Charitons up to the Nodaway and sometimes farther up. [118]

Ioway hostilities in 1820 were directed at the Otos, the Omahas, the Sacs, and the Sioux. Sac Agent Forsyth reported that the Ioways sent a deputation to the Sioux to ask for peace. Instead of granting this the Sioux killed all of them and continued to harass them for the next several years.[119] The Ioways sent another delegation to a council with the Sacs over the difficulty that had arisen when a Sac killed an Ioway in 1819. So angered were the Ioways by this Sac perfidy that they joined the Sioux in hostility against the Sacs for a short time.

Sac chiefs Black Hawk and Pashepaho many years later described an event, which may have been the one mentioned above or a smiliar instance of the continuing difficulties between the Ioways and the Sacs. On the first day of May, they said, the Ioways had returned from their winter hunt to the Des Moines River village. The hunt had been successful, and the ceremonies and dances of thanksgiving, games, and horse racing were in progress. The Sacs under the leadership of Black Hawk and Pashepaho silently surrounded the village and at a signal attacked the unarmed warriors. Pashepaho directed his attack against the race track area, while Black Hawk entered the village, which lay at the lower end of a prairie four miles long and two miles wide. According to the chronicler the hand-to-hand battle lasted the entire day. At sunset only a bare handful of the villagers were alive. Black Hawk is said to have offered to adopt them into his tribe in the customary manner.[120] In 1828 the graves of the slain were still visible.[121] This event, of catastrophic dimensions to a small tribe, could cause them to move to a safer area. If the event was as reported, the tribal population diminished greatly. The Sacs' purpose was to drive the Ioways away from the Mississippi area, to punish them for some undescribed reason, or simply to gain honor for their young men and leaders. Morse said that the tribe's population was static or diminishing during this time.

A new chord in Indian policy was heard in the 1820's, in this decade, and that was the chorused advice that promoted severalty, or the allotment of land to individual Indians. In 1817 President Monroe had indicated to Gov. Lewis Cass that each Indian who wished to own land could do so, and those who did not wish this could exchange their lands for others. Some Indians in the Great Lakes area did choose to take land in this manner and were given a fee simple title.[122] Other Indian nations refused flatly to participate in such a scheme. Sibley, in the Morse Report, suggested severalty for that area. Speaking of the Osages, the Kansas, and the Ioways he said, "Whenever an Indian evinced a serious disposition to settle himself permanently, and to pursue civilized habits, a portion of this land, from 160 to 640 acres, as might be proper, should be allotted to him, patented to him by the Government, and secured to him and to his family forever."[123] In January 1821 Thomas Hart Benton and David Barton of the Congressional Committee of Indian Affairs suggested that agents were needed for tribes along Missouri's border, including the Kickapoos, the Ioways, the Sacs, and the Foxes, and roving Sioux bands. Growing dissension between Indians and nearby white settlements had caused bloodshed and called for government representatives who could intervene.[124] Not only were the whites and Indians involved in hostile acts; the Indians themselves increasingly warred on each other. Thomas McKenney suggested that "the frequent causes of collision between tribes which are so common" could be prevented, perhaps, if a trading factory were reestablished at Ft. Osage to serve the Osage and Cherokee now settled there, and the Ioway and Kansas.[125]

McKenney's suggestion was adopted. Maj. Daniel Ketchum and his troops would man Fort Osage, and David Meriwether would serve as post sutler and trader at a salary of $500 a year.[126] Meriwether and his party loaded their keelboat with supplies and trade goods. At the mouth of the Platte they glimpsed a group of Indians in "bark canoes." They feared hostile intentions and moved as quickly as they could; but the party caught up with them. Meriwether's interpreter recognized the war party leader, an Ioway, who drew alongside and stepped aboard. He said that they were returning from an unsuccessful raid on the Omahas. The interpreter warned that Indians in such a state were dangerous and that all precautions should be taken. That night the Ioways again came alongside and asked why they did not land and camp. Meriwether said that they could cook and sleep on the boat and it was not necessary to leave it. Guard was posted all night, but no incident occurred. At daybreak the keelboat left the Indians sleeping on the shore. Later a strong wind impelled them to tie up to a snag, and the Ioways overtook them. The leader told Meriwether that the Indians had no food and intended to hunt. Just downriver, he said, the river made a short bend, and there they would land. They planned to cross the small point of land and drive the game toward the river, where some of them would shoot the animals. He invited Meriwether to participate. The apprehensive interpreter warned him not to do so, but Meriwether confidently agreed. He probably realized that these men were his future customers. The next morning after the hunt the keelboat left and never saw the Ioway party again.

At Fort Osage Meriwether was given a building, the only one outside the fort, in which to set up his store. When he was prepared to do business, he sent his interpreter to the Osage village to inform them that he was ready to trade. The interpreter returned with the principal chief, Sans Oreille or Walks-in-the-Rain, who examined the goods carefully, seemed satisfied with their quality and the rate of exchange, and promised to bring his people with their peltries to trade.

Eleven Ioways soon arrived at the fort. They told Meriwether that they came to hunt, because game was scarce on their side of the Missouri. They visited and hunted all day, and left during the following morning. A few days later Meriwether found a wounded Ioway at his store. Dr. Nichols, the fort surgeon, found that the wound was not dangerous, but the Indian was weak from the exertion of returning to the fort. Meriwether persuaded him to stay to recuperate. He said that after the party left the store, it had traveled and had camped near a white settlement. The next morning, before daylight, they had been fired on, and he believed that everyone but himself had been killed.

Shortly after dinner three armed men came to the fort and asked Meriwether if he had seen a wounded Indian. He replied that the Indian was resting. Palmer, the white man, said, "Yes, damn him, I intend to kill him." Meriwether protested, but the man drew his gun. Meriwether slammed the door, and Palmer shot through it. The sergeant of the guard appeared, because firing within the fort area was prohibited. Meriwether called, "Tell Major Ketchum to come here."

When he arrived, Meriwether opened the door. Palmer became more tractable and told his version of the story. An Indian party had stolen some horses, and when they returned (it was said to steal more), the whites attacked them. Meriwether asked him exactly which night the horses had been stolen. When Palmer told him, Meriwether protested that the horses could not have been stolen by the Ioways because they were at the fort that night. Palmer called Meriwether a liar, and Major Ketchum told Palmer to leave and never to come back. He refused, and Ketchum ordered the guard to march the three men down to their boats, "which was promptly done."

Meriwether tried to explain to the frightened Ioway that he should go inside the fort to recover. A night or so later the interpreter came to Meriwether and said that the Ioway was crazy and could not be managed. When the trader arrived, the Ioway called, "Men-pa-wa-ra," the name that White Cloud had given to Meriwether the year before. He explained that a spirit had come to tell him that he was to be killed and burned by the white people, and he was preparing to die by singing his death songs. Meriwether assured him that he was only feverish and his fears were unfounded. After this he made a point of visiting the Indian several times a day as he slowly recovered. Three or four weeks later he tied his blankets together and lowered himself to the ground to escape.

According to Meriwether's memoirs the story did not end there. Dr. Nichols was ordered to transfer to Council Bluffs, 300 miles away. He decided to travel overland. One morning the doctor awoke and noticed that his horses and mule were gone and his camp surrounded by Indians. The recovered Ioway recognized him and came forward. He was glad to see Dr. Nichols and told his companions how Dr. Nichols had taken care of him. They accompanied Dr.

Nichols to Fort Osage, where he bought tobacco for the Ioways. He then decided to wait for spring and to travel upstream by water.

Some time later Dr. Craig, who had replaced Dr. Nichols, received a message that a white man was very ill at Palmer's settlement. There he found that the sick man was one who had been involved in the Ioway shooting. He gave his version of the incident: A wounded Ioway had run into an empty house and had locked the door. When the house was surrounded, he opened the window and made signs of friendship to those outside. Palmer ignored this gesture and shot and killed him. When the doctor returned to the fort, he told Agent George Sibley, who relayed the story to General Clark at St. Louis. After investigation Clark had Palmer arrested and tried for murder. As was often the case, the white man was acquitted. According to Meriwether Clark's action caused deep resentment and widespread accusation that he was a friend of the Indians and not of the whites. When he ran for governor of the state some time after, he was defeated; Meriwether assumed that this was the reason.[127]

That summer Thomas Forsyth, who acted as agent for the Ioways in the Mississippi area, notified Clark that he would send the expenditures for the "Ihowais" during the next quarter, because he had already sent the last quarter's accounts. He was also preparing a speech that would direct the Ioway nation to be peaceable together, and to plant their corn at their old village 40 leagues up the Des Moines. The Sacs, he added, appeared to be more sympathetic than ever toward the Americans and were endeavoring to make peace with the Sioux, the Omahas, and the Otoes.[128] At the same time he wrote to the secretary of war that the Ioways resided in three or four villages, and that they never visited Fort Armstrong (near present-day Davenport, Iowa) because of its distance from them. For that reason he was not able to be of much assistance to them. He suggested that a subagent and an interpreter be stationed at Fort Edwards for their convenience, so that they could have someone to give them advice and perhaps to persuade them to all live in one village, where their chiefs would be able to exercise greater control over the young men.[129]

In January, 1822 Clark wrote a lengthy report of the Sac land claims west of the Mississippi. He declared that they tended to claim "much higher up the Mississippi than they have a just title to, and lower down that river than many believe they should claim." A specific area under discussion was the strip that had been ceded in 1804, an area north and west of St. Louis. Clark stated that the Osages and the Ioways could also lay claim to it, as well as the Sioux and others who from time to time could assert right by use or conquest. "In late years, the Sac, Fox and Ioway, and some others of the Mississippi tribes had hunted there, but that alone could not give them any right, for if it could, the French have been the first occupant after the Illinois tribes," he commented.[130] In answering Agent Forsyth's and Clark's letters about Sac and Ioway land claims,

Secretary of War Calhoun replied that the Sacs and the Foxes have "a very questionable title to the lands below the River Des Moines, whatever they may have to those above it."[131]

The animosity between the Sacs and the Ioways surfaced once again in the spring when a Sac party killed an Ioway chief. The nation appealed to a subagent, Duff Green, who described them as destitute and starving when they appeared. He gave them cornmeal, meat, powder, and lead. He recalled that during the previous summer the tribe had stolen some horses, and, when the chiefs had returned them to him, a young chief spoke as follows:

> My, Brother, You say we have had a bad name we never deserved it — look around you and you see the white man cover *our* plains — we have seen the Spaniard and the French in their power yield to the Americans — and our Fathers who used to hunt the deer and the Buffalos *here* have dwindled before you. You are rich and we are poor, we have no Father [Agent] we have no *trade* no powder and lead — and must depend on your charity — I am too proud to beg but we have given our country to the Americans — we love you as friends — yet other Indians around have their Father, they have presents they have powder, lead and Whiskey; We can get none, — why is it so? Our Father the Red Head told us otherwise, you have told us otherwise why is it so?

Agent Green noted that the tribe had been promised a blacksmith as a reward for good conduct, but that that promise had not been kept. If that could be done and small presents given to them from time to time, "I will take on myself the distribution gratuitiously until the Government thinks proper to authorize an agent for that purpose."[132] The young chief's address presents a picture of increasing Ioway difficulty in maintaining their society. Decreasing hunting territory, disturbed agricultural patterns as they moved from one place to another, tribal division into three or four groups for strategic purposes or as a result of factionalism, decreasing manpower, increasing contention with surrounding tribes, white encroachment, and a request for an agent to provide them with power, lead, and whiskey — all suggest difficulties of increasing magnitude.

With the abolition of the factory system by Congress in 1822, private interests rejoiced and sent traders into Indian country. Five traders were licensed to trade with the Sacs, the Foxes, and the Ioways in the area between the Mississippi and the Missouri. Vance Murry Campbell was licensed on July 20 to trade at the Ioway villages and camps on the Little Platte and Grand rivers. In August John Campbell was licensed to trade with them at their town on the Des Moines. In the same month Joshua Palon and Maurice Blondeau, representing the American Fur Company, were at the same place, and William Downey was to trade with the "Sacks, Foxes and Iowais" at Fort Armstrong.[133] During the following winter some of the tribe had decided to settle at the mouth of the Nodaway.[134]

The British were not entirely out of the picture. Nicolas Boilvin at Fort Crawford at Prairie du Chien wrote to Lewis Cass in July, 1822, that he had informed the nations of the area that their Great Father, the President, would be displeased if they visited the British at Malden, Drummond Island in Lake Huron, or other Canadian settlements. Nevertheless, he added, a few Sacs, Foxes, Osages, and Ioways would probably go anyway.[135]

During the winters of 1822 and 1823 the Foxes and the Ioways settled their differences by pledges of friendship and exchanges of gifts and horses. But the Sac and Ioway relationship continued to deteriorate. In May 1821 (or 1823, the record is unclear), the Sacs attacked the Ioway village near present-day Iowaville, Iowa just after their return from the winter hunt. The year may have been 1823, for information taken to Forsyth late that summer indicated that the entire tribe moved to the Grand River to build their villages. Sac motives became more apparent, when Keokuk, the Sac negotiator reviewed to Calhoun in Washington in 1823 the history of the Sacs' migrations to the Mississippi River:

> Then they turned their faces toward the setting sun. They met the Ioways whom they took under their wing, as you my Father have the French of our country. Their interests were one, they made war against the Osage and Missouri, who then were hunting in the tract of Country [the ceded land near St. Louis and westward] which we now claim. They were driven across the troubled water, our Fathers remained in peaceable possession of the Country, up to the time that the Osages disposed of their right to the United States, we do not want the land, but we are not willing that the Osages should receive pay for that, which by right is ours.... My Father that Country which we were driven from on the Fox River we do not claim because our fathers were conquered and were not then in possession. [136]

Although Keokuk did not wish to believe it, the Sacs and the Foxes were comparative newcomers to the land that they now said was theirs. In 1735 the two tribes had taken refuge on Ioway lands near two forts that they had built on the Wapsipinicon River, but they had later returned to the eastern side of the Mississippi and their own village areas. In 1805 and 1806 Zebulon Pike had observed that the Foxes lived in villages on the western side of the Mississippi, and the Sacs lived in four villages, two on the eastern and two on the western side of the river. While it is true that the Ioways rode in war parties with the Sacs and the Foxes against the Osages, the Kansas, and other tribes, they did not believe that the land on the western side of the river belonged to either the Sacs or the Foxes. They were living there only as intruders to which the Ioways more or less accommodated themselves.

The significance of Keokuk's last sentence above cannot be overlooked. If the copyist accurately reflected his attitudes concerning land acquisition by conquest, then the harassment and attacks on the Ioways in the preceding decade were attempts to drive them from their Iowa River and Des Moines River villages in order to lay claim to the land. Keokuk and others knew that the days of Sac residence east of the Mississippi were numbered, since that land had already been ceded. But by making vast claims he perhaps justified the movement of his people across the Mississippi onto Ioway lands in the past and also in the future.

When the United States obtained the Louisiana Territory and crossed the Mississippi, the independence that the Ioways apparently had had under Spanish rule diminished rapidly in the two decades that followed. They lost control of the Des Moines waterway and trail system to the Missouri that had enhanced their economic position as they did business with the English trading companies who crossed lands under their control. After the American intrusion they were forced to deal more and more with United States traders and factories, and they had to settle for goods whose quality fell far below the standards maintained by the British.

The Ioways first encountered United States treaty commissioners in 1805 when they promised to live in peace and friendship with their former enemies, the Osages. Then in 1815 there was a postwar flurry of treaty making with tribes in the middle Mississippi and Missouri river valleys, including the Sacs, the Foxes, and the Ioways. According to the commissioners who dealt with the Ioways, the chiefs implied that they might wish to cede some of their land to the United States in return for annuity payments. Just how universal this idea was among the general Ioway population is not known.

Conflict with the United States legal and judicial system arose in 1808 and 1809, when White Cloud and another Ioway warrior were accused of and arrested for the murder of French traders. A long incarceration period and trial did not enhance their regard for or relationship with the new government. The pro-British attitude of some Ioways during the War of 1812 led them to serve on that side in military engagements. Others, led by Hard Heart, declared their loyalty to the United States and consented to be moved away from the Mississippi to the Missouri River area. This division of the tribe into separate villages along traditional lines had existed for some time, but the antagonism that is evidenced by this type of split is not indicated in earlier records.

The Ioways, whose population probably never exceeded 1,500 during the 1800's, lived at various locations in the first two decades of the century. Some sites were undoubtedly summer agricultural villages; other were winter hunting camps. The factionalism that developed during the War of 1812 and traditional tribal village separation account for other sites. Movement of the Sac and Fox and the Sioux nations uprooted the Ioways from their old village sites

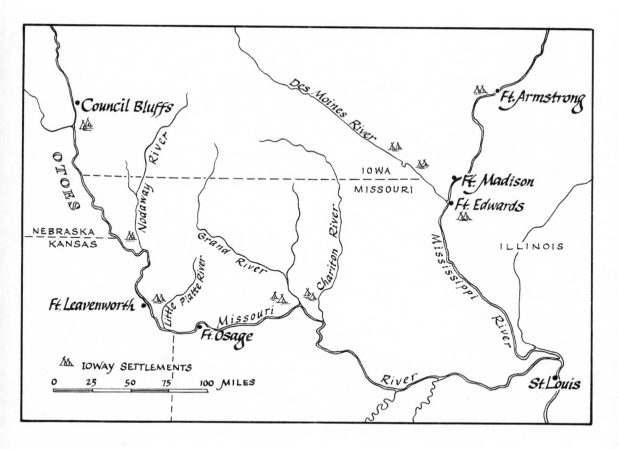

Map 8. Ioway locations from 1821 to 1823 according to the reports of agents, traders, and others:

1821	David Meriwether	On the north side of the Missouri and at Fort Osage.
	George Sibley	One-half of the tribe with the Otoes at Council Bluffs. One village on the Des Moines River at present-day Iowaville, Iowa. One village on the Grand River.
	Thomas Forsyth	A village forty leagues up the Des Moines and three or four villages in the Fort Edwards region.
1822	Thomas Forsyth	Some Ioways with the Otoes.
	William Clark	Licenses issued for trade with Ioway villages and camps on the Little Platte and Grand River. A village on the Des Moines and another at Fort Armstrong.
	Duff Green	At the mouth of the Nodaway River.
1823	Thomas Forsyth	A new village on the Grand River, removed from the Des Moines River village.

(In 1820 the Ioways were hunting and camping along the Grand and Chariton rivers.)

and hunting areas on the Des Moines and from other sites between that river and the Mississippi. They moved west and south toward their winter hunting grounds along the rivers that flowed into the Missouri. The entry of whites into lands that they claimed along the Missouri (which had been ceded by the Osages in 1808), hastened their withdrawal and provoked the comment by White Cloud that they were surrounded by their enemies (see Map 8).

7. The Treaty Period

AFTER 1820 OPINION CRYSTALLIZED among white citizens that the Indian was an unwanted neighbor in the development of civilization west of the Mississippi. In late 1822 General Duff Green at St. Charles wrote to Secretary of War Calhoun regarding the removal of Indians from Missouri, where friction, such as that experienced in the so-called Palmer settlement, caused concern. In the same letter he mentioned that "I am informed that a band of the Ioway have determined to locate themselves at the mouth of the Nodaway.[1] This river flowed into the Missouri River in the upper northwest corner of present-day Missouri and was at this time used as hunting grounds by the Otoes and the Missouris, whose villages were on the western side of the Missouri.[2] However, the group referred to by Green may well have moved there recently. In 1824 he said:

> The Ioway were in the habit of friendly intercourse with the Otoes and Missouria and are now in their neighborhood, and an entire removal of the Ioway Indians and their location west of our boundary line [Missouri] is important and much desired by the frontier settlements.[3]

Before this the Grand and Chariton river environs had been the usual Ioway winter hunting campsites. Did the hostility of the whites force them to live and hunt far to the west of their usual grounds? Did the continued intrusion of the Sacs push them westward? Part of the answer may lie in a letter by Russell Farnham, Sac trader, in January, 1824. He found 30 Sac lodges on the Missouri, two days' march above the Platte and south of the Nodaway. He received from the tribe 140 packs of peltries.[4] Blondeau, a trader with the American Fur Company, traded with the Sacs on the Grand River for 150 to 160

Figure 9. A pipestem taken to Washington and presented by White Cloud, August, 1824, at the time of the Ioway treaty signing. Courtesy of National Anthropology Archives, Smithsonian Institution.

packs. It appears that the Sacs were hunting farther to the west on Otoe and Ioway lands. But it cannot be said that they, too, had not hunted in the same areas as the other tribes for some time.

Many instances of hostilities between the Sioux, the Sacs, and other tribes of the region finally prompted the federal government to call a treaty council in Washington. In June, 1824, William Clark, superintendent of Indian affairs, informed Secretary of War Calhoun of a deputation of Sacs, Foxes, Piankashaws, and Ioways, led by White Cloud and the Great Walker: "about fifteen in number will leave this place about the 22nd under the care of Captain Kennerly." To outfit them stylishly for the visit, money was requested to purchase elegant coats, arm bands, stockings, powder horns, pairs of pistols, silver buckles, chief's hats trimmed with green, red, and blue plumes, epaulets, swords, and other items. Perhaps it was thought all this finery would make them more amenable to reason when they finally arrived in Washington and heard what would be said.

In Washington the visitors explained their positions. The secretary of war listened politely and expounded on the necessity for the maintenance of peace. However, for the Sacs the issue was not so much peace as it was the status of the claimed lands that the Osages had ceded in 1808. This was the land north of the Missouri River which included part of the present state of Missouri to the Iowa state border. The Ioways then accused the Sac of claiming land that belonged to them, inferring that the ceded lands had never belonged

140

Figure 10. Mahaska, or White Cloud, son of White Cloud and Female Flying Pigeon, or Rantchewaime. This portrait was painted during the winter of 1836-37 in Washington, D.C., where White Cloud "told in his own simple but eloquent style the story of his wrongs and claimed the interposition of the Government for its injustices resulting from the 1825 treaty." Reprinted from Thomas McKenney and James Hall, *The Indian Tribes of North America,* Vol. 1 (Edinburgh, 1933).

to either the Osage or the Sac and Fox nations but belonged to them. To this Keokuk replied:

> It appears to me that you must be surprised that our chiefs hesitated to speak yesterday — It is very true that the business which we carried on yesterday shocked and stunned us from the insults which we received from two individuals (meaning the Ioways) We acknowledge that we were shocked and amazed yesterday — and could not speak, it therefore became necessary that we should retire and collect our ideas, so as to be enabled to give you a correct answer — It is very shameful that such language should come from those men, who, when they were weak we took under our wing, and have ever since protected them, had it been in our village it would have been another thing — but here we could say — nothing you have always recommended to us to have compassion on those who are weaker than ourselves....[5]

To this White Cloud retorted:

> My Father, we the Ioway have been much deceived by the Spaniards and the French — for they had no right to the Country which they sold to the Americans, lying in the forks of the Mississippi and Missouri — The lands lying within the boundary of the lines which we see on that paper, you have possession of, and I shall not again say that it belongs to the Ioways. I came to our great Father fully empowered by my nation to make any arrangement which I might think right. I now relinquish the claim which the Ioways may have to that portion of Country to the American people, and have only to request that your nation will send what they intend giving us, to our villages.[6]

The second chief, Hard Heart, approved and confirmed what White Cloud had agreed to.

At the end of the discussion the suggestion was made that perhaps both the Ioway and the Sac and Fox tribes could sell the land to the United States. To this they agreed and affixed their marks on August 4, 1824. With this act, the first cession of their land, the Ioways stepped into the lengthening line of Indian nations whose backward trail led to the Atlantic, and which in the end would stop at the ocean far beyond the Missouri River.

As full compensation for the ceded land the Ioways were to receive in cash or merchandise $500 initially and an equal amount annually for ten years.[7] In order that they understood that they were indeed to leave the ceded land, officials set 1826 as the day after which the Ioways could not live or hunt there without permission. A blacksmith and a farmer would help them acquire the arts of civilization.

As usual the signers were taken to see the sights of Baltimore, Philadelphia, and New York. Each man wore his new officer's uniform. At a New York circus the equestrians drew their greatest approval.

Circuses and fancy uniforms aside, the Ioways had formally relinquished some of their land. The large section of present-day

Missouri included hunting lands and village sites. But the fact was that whites were already settled in that area along the Missouri. The Ioways could do little to change this, since the white man had accepted the Osage cession as valid extinguishment of title sixteen years before.

A new era began for the Ioways with the signing of this treaty. Now they could be subjected to the processes of civilization that were in the minds of non-Indian reformers. But even before the Ioway chiefs went to Washington they had been interested in education as the white man saw it. St. Regis at Florrisant, near St. Louis, was a Jesuit institution.[8] Father Van Quackenbourne, ardently advocated that the Indian should be prepared for his new future. He was notified in May, 1824, that the Ioway chiefs, who visited St. Louis on their way to Washington, had informed General Clark that some of their sons would be sent to school there. On their journey the Sac tried to intercept them and persuade them not to send their sons, but the Ioways persisted and sent five students with Gabriel Baron Vasques, their assigned agent. Of the original five that had started, two had become ill on the journey and had returned to the village. The three who arrived on June 11 cried and wailed that they did not want to stay there. Vasques warned the priest they they might try to run away, and, in spite of close watching, they did so in the middle of the first night. They were caught 4 miles away and were returned. Thus the first Ioways tried to resist the acculturating forces of Indian schools far from their families and their homes.

The St. Regis buildings were handsome three-story structures of wood and stone. Brick chimneys and encircling porches completed the design. The students were taught carpentry and blacksmithing, as well as agriculture — much to their disgust. When a hoe was first given to them, it was said that some of them cried, ashamed that they were being made to do women's work. In order to overcome this stigma, the fathers worked with them in the gardens. They kept in close association with their charges in order to learn their languages. It was planned that eventually some would go to their pupils' villages and establish Catholic missions.

On April 25, 1825, Father Van Quackenbourne said, "We received here chiefs and twelve warriors of the Hyaway Nation. The boys appeared at St. Louis before these visitors while they had their talk with General Clark. They were well dressed and behaved well. One drove the cart. Amazed, the Indian fathers exclaimed over the changes they saw." One said, according to the priest, "I wish all Indian boys were Catholics." Nevertheless, in 1826, the boys continued to try to go home to their villages, and the prefect had to watch them at night. Their teachers' attempts to learn their languages proved difficult, and enthusiasm for the plans of going to the villages waned with some of the brothers, except for Father Van Quackenbourne, who like "Napoleon wanted to conquer all, white and red."

Two Ioway children are mentioned in the school's records: Maximas, son of an Ioway chief and a good scholar, and Peter, the Great Walker's son whose baptism was recorded on June 5, 1825, at age thirteen. The Great Walker had signed the 1824 treaty with White Cloud and had been painted by Charles Bird King. He had a reputation among his people as an independent individual who often went by himself into the prairie to hunt. He was often said to be of dour disposition but did not lack brilliance, bravery, or skill. It was said that he regretted to the end of his life his mark on the treaty, and he had blackened his face as a sign of mourning for "selling the bones of my fathers." Later in the decade he was involved in conflict with white settlers on land that he thought was his own.[9]

Inadequate funding forced St. Regis to close in 1831, and Father Van Quackenbourne said sadly, "I am convinced that the youth of the aborigine stand in need of as much perhaps more assistance after they have left the school, than when they actually enjoy its advantages."[10] This was one of the first admissions that the white man's Indian school did not or could not equip the Indian for life in his own environment, and that for many persons of imagination, creativity, and an intellectual turn of mind there was something beyond the manual labor and agricultural skills that later Indian schools still considered adequate education.

In September, 1824, the Ioways arrived in St. Louis to receive the treaty payment that had been promised to them the month before in Washington. They had ceded their land according to the wishes of the Great Father, some of their children were in school to learn the ways of the white man, and the "civilization and preservation" of their nation could officially begin. But the hoped-for results of the August council agreements were not all manifested. Differences between signatory nations erupted in continual war parties and village attacks. In December, Clark suggested that another treaty council was necessary to settle the deep-seated differences. There was another purpose also: Pressure to remove tribes from the tier of states north of the Ohio had increased. It was necessary, therefore, to determine what each of the tribes adjacent to the Mississippi and Missouri rivers considered its territory. As long as tribal remnants from the east, who had long been present by Spanish permission, and older resident tribes struggled to retain or gain village sites and hunting grounds, there could be no settled boundaries. It behooved the United States government to terminate in one manner or another the shifting claims and the warfare that constantly acerbated the situation and thus ease the way to additional land cessions west of the Mississippi, which were needed for the settlement of eastern tribes.

In January, 1825, in a letter to the Illinois governor, Clark noted his difficulties with resident tribes who resisted moving off their ceded lands. Clark asked, "What propriety and possibility is there

that the legislature can act to prevent them from planting corn and
refusing them access to traders?"[11] A Shawnee chief who had already
consented to leave his lands said:

> For several years you have asked us to exchange our lands, with pain we
> have consented to, and upon your word we have left them . . . since we
> have left we are more than poor, we are miserable, we are all dispersed
> like turkeys. Had you not assisted with corn, several of us would have
> died with hunger. We have started to go see our grandfather. We believe
> him to be just. We hope he will give us what we asked him for four years
> ago in exchange for our land, and that he will pay us for the property
> taken from us by his white brothers. [12]

At the same time Clark heard the Indians accuse the United States of
treaty breaking and learned of increasing intertribal hostilities, he
reorganized his superintendency, including the establishment of various subagencies and their facilities. In March, Thomas McKenney
informed Clark of the appointment of Martin Palmer as subagent to
the Ioways, who would "repair to the Ioway Towns and begin his
duties there." Vasques, the interpreter and acting subagent, became
the Kansa agent. Colonel Palmer, however, did not last long. In September Clark reported that he "has run off to Texas and there is no
chance of recovering anything of the property left in this state. I expect
to borrow the money to pay the Ioway annuity."

Soon Clark was notified that the President had approved of the
requested treaty council to be held August 2-20 at Prairie du Chien.
He calculated the cost for an estimated 39,250 rations, gifts, and
agents' travel expenses. On July 6, Clark and his party, including
Thomas Biddle, acting secretary of the proceedings, left St. Louis in
a keelboat. When they reached Fort Edwards, Clark was surprised
to find White Cloud and his chiefs there. White Cloud said that the
agent had told them to wait at that place for the Red Head chief,
as Clark was called. Clark, annoyed at his subordinate for this
suggestion, bowed to circumstances, paid for the beef that they had
consumed, and bought the group a barrel of pork and another of
biscuits. He also presented White Cloud with a rifle and powder and
borrowed a canoe to transport his party upriver to the meeting place.
The next day he stopped at Maurice Blondeau's trading post and
encountered another group of Ioways en route to the council. He gave
them a note for Agent Forsythe that instructed him to give them
provisions."[13]

When Clark arrived at Prairie du Chien on July 30, almost all of
the one thousand participants had arrived from the Winnebago,
Sioux, Chippewa, and other tribes, and they had set up camps all
along the river for a great distance. The opening of the council was
delayed, because the Sac, Fox, and Ioway delegations had not arrived.
According to Biddle's journal, on August 4 a flotilla of seventy
canoes was sighted. The party had stopped on an island downstream

to arrange themselves in their finery. They sang their war songs, while in compact formation, they slipped up the river, passed the village, and with paddles flashing swooped back again. At the landing they were greeted as brothers by the Chippewas, but the Sioux stood apart scowling. "No tribes attracted so intense a degree of interest as the Iowas and the Sacs and Foxes, tribes of radically diverse languages, yet united in a league against the Sioux."[14]

General Clark opened the council. In his speech he declared that the President had not sent him there to ask for anything: "We want nothing, not the smallest piece of your land...." "The President," he said, "thinks that there is no further cause for war, and that all should live in peace." He reminded them to look around and see how the once-powerful nations had been reduced by warfare to a few wandering families. "White people have not been the cause of your decreasing numbers, you yourself have done so by your incessant battles, for tribes who have no contact with the whites have also decreased. Your hostilities have resulted in great measure from your having no defined boundaries, you follow game into lands claimed by others which you think you own. All the warfare will cease when we will establish boundaries together." After he had made his main points, he announced the procedure for the following days, the pipe was passed around, and the meeting adjourned for that day.[15]

When the chiefs finally agreed to speak in council about their individual tribal boundaries, different points of view on land ownership were expressed. Cut Ear, a Chippewa, said, "...I wish to live in peace, but in running marks round our country or in giving it to our enemies, it may make new disturbances and breed new wars."[16]

White Cloud spoke:

My Father, I claim no land in particular. The land I live on is enough to furnish my women and children — I go upon the lands of our friends the Sacs and Foxes — we alternate to go upon each others land — why should we quarrel about lands when we get enough on what we have. My Fathers the Socs, Foxes, Winnebagos, Menominees, Chippewas and Pottawatomies are links of the same people. I speak for them as well as for myself. My Fathers you see people here apparently of different nations, but we are all one. You Socs, Foxes, Winnebagos and Menominees — we are one people — we have but one Council fire and eat out of the same dish. [17]

Pumpkin, an Ioway, stated, "My Fathers, My heart is the right place — I live with my relations the Socs and Foxes — I have no reason to deny my brethren."

Co-ra-mo-nee, a Winnebago chief said:

... The lands I claim are mine and the nations here know it is not only claimed by us but by our Brothers the Socs, Foxes, Menominees, Iowas, Omahas and Sioux, they have used it in common — it would be difficult to divide it — it belongs as much to one as the other. My Fathers I did not know that any of my relations had any particular land — It is true every one owns his own lodge and the grounds he may cultivate — I had thought that the Rivers were the common property of all Red Skins and not used exclusively by any Particular nation. [18]

Toward the end of the council each tribe endeavored to outline the land that they claimed. The Sacs and the Ioways could not agree on their boundary beyond the Des Moines River forks until after a great deal of discussion. The Sacs and the Sioux agreed to a strip of neutral ground between their two claims, but the final decision could not be made until the Yanktonai Sioux (who were not present) had been consulted.

When the council closed, 1,103 Indians had agreed to be peaceable and had indicated imprecisely what they considered to be their lands. This information later became the basis for another round of councils for the purpose of land cession. Clark wrote on September 1, 1825, of what he considered its success:

We concluded and signed a treaty of peace and limits at Prairie du Chien with the Chiefs, representatives and Warriors of the Chippaway, Soc & Fox, Ioway, Sioux, Winnebago, Menomonee, and Illinois Tribes of Indians. . . . The establishment of equitable boundaries among the tribes was the most difficult part of our task. We will not trouble you with the details of it, but merely observe, that a just compromise between former possession and more recent conquests was the basis of the arrangement. All parties were well satisfied, and in fact the boundaries were established by themselves. [19]

In the following year the secretary of war, who had jurisdiction over Indian affairs, requested Clark's view on the civilization of the Indian. His opinions indicate the thinking of those who were responsible for formulating Indian policy. Clark said that before the northwest Indian wars in 1794 and those in the south in 1818:

The tribes nearest our settlements were a formidable and terrible enemy. Since then their power has been broken, their warlike spirit subsided, and themselves sunk into objects of pity and commiseration. While strong and hostile, it had been our obvious duty to weaken them, now they are weak and harmless, and most of their lands fallen into our hands, justice and humanity requires us to cherish and befriend them. . . .

He then continued to advocate a policy of teaching the Indians those aspects of American culture, such as agriculture and educational and mechanical skills, which would enable them to survive in it. To accomplish this, it would be advisable to remove them from their scattered holdings east of the river to some "country beyond those limits where they could rest in peace and enjoy in reality the perpetuity of the land on which their buildings and Improvements could be made." He suggested that the place to which they could be removed lay west of the boundary of the Missouri and Arkansas Territories.

Many of his suggestions concurred with those of others holding similar views, and they became a part of U.S. Indian policy. They were: (1) to employ commissioners to negotiate for Indian removal by convincing the Indian nations that they cannot survive within the "limits of the states and territories"; (2) to delineate suitable sections of the country (reservations) for settlement of different tribes; (3) to assist the Indians in the establishment of an agricultural life by setting aside small parcels of land near their villages, fencing them, and designating each to a family (individual land ownership, or severalty); (4) to establish common schools in the villages with a plan of education and of accountability, the superintendent and agents should be charged with execution, liberal payment to teachers, and regular reports to the government (the system of government Indian reservation and boarding schools); and (5) to inculcate the tribes with the idea of submission to the authority of a civil and not a hereditary government through the agencies and the growth of a federal bureaucratic system to control Indian affairs:

> For this purpose as many of the tribes or of the scattering bands as possible, understanding one language, be collected near each other, over which a competent agent should be placed with full power of conducting the executive part of a Government, to be submitted to and adopted by the Indians subject to each such change as may be recommended by the President. It is believed that the executive agents of this authority will prevent the Indians from killing one another for the Chief place, and keep the inferior officers (who should be Indian) within the bounds of their duty.... Some of the chiefs who wish to be head men themselves might object to this, but the body of the Tribe would approve it, when they understand, and there would be stations enough under the Agent to try the abilities and satisfy the ambitions of the different contending chiefs. A General Government over the whole might be necessary and proper.

and (6) to pay out annuities on a shorter-term, lump-sum basis and invest the money in such items as mills, fences, and mechanics to make ploughs and other objects that would start the Indian on his path to civilization:

> It would free the treasury from what would otherwise remain an everlasting charge upon it, and which in the lapse of a century would amount to an annually increasing amount for the Indian department.... The largest annuity we pay affords but a few dollars per head which divided among a tribe contribute nothing of much importance to the amount of their property, and it is property alone which can keep up pride of an Indian and makes him ashamed of drunkenness, begging, lying and stealing.[20]

With these ideas in mind the government began the control and "civilization" of the Indians west of the Mississippi in earnest, and the Ioways were thrown into the hopper with the others. In the summer of 1826 their subagent was a Captain Ford, who drew a salary of $500 per year. They again were promised the blacksmith, which they did not yet have, and an interpreter to assist the agent in his dealings with them. A trading license was granted to Vance Murry Campbell to trade at the Ioway village on the Grand River. In January, 1827, Captain Ford died and was replaced by Acting Agent Maj. Wharton Rector. Clark hired a married couple in April to serve as farmer to the men and teacher to the women of the tribe. Their instructions for duty said to teach industry, to prove its value by their own examples, and to introduce among the men a taste for agriculture: "Whenever you cultivate your farm it will be suggested that you get some of the Indians to attend to you and see how you cultivate the earth, and instruct all those who attend by getting them to take hold of the plough." The instructions for the farmer's wife said, "Indian women who feel inclined show how to milk the cows, make butter, and also the art of spinning."[21]

To replace temporary subagent Rector, Clark appointed Charles Bent, an "enterprising young man." However, Bent did not arrive at the agency to take his position. He changed his mind and preferred the profits of the fur trade on the upper Missouri. Rector was asked to remain, but he "declined acting," so Jonathan L. Bean, "an active, young and intelligent man," was appointed as the seventh Ioway agent.

But the Ioways' time on their original homelands was over; the two years that they had been granted to stay on their lands had expired. Agent Bean was instructed to remove them to the Little Platte River area, which lay west of their 1824 cession. They packed their belongings, said farewell to the graves of their ancestors, and harvested the crops that were mature. On August 2, 1827, Clark reported that they were 40 miles beyond the Missouri border on the Missouri River. No details of the removal are known, but one group led by The Great Walker, who was also known as Big Neck, declined to go with the others. His regret at signing the 1824 treaty never ceased, and he continued to paint his face black and to roam the northern limits of the cession lands.[22]

In order to make room for the Ioways, the Kansas had ceded part of their land. This careful planning was unusual, though, and many homeless tribal remnants continued to arrive from across the Mississippi. In October, 1826, a large party of destitute Shawnees and Senecas arrived. Clark furnished them with meat and corn and reported, "These people will not be able to kill wild game to support them. It will be necessary to assist them in order to prevent them scattering in search of food."[23]

The summer brought the Ioways another agent to add to their growing list. Agent Bean, who spoke Sioux, and Gen. Andrew Hughes, subagent of the Upper Missouri, wished to exchange posts and were granted the request. The agency for the Ioways now counted five employees and an annual salary budget of $2,200.

Although the Office of Indian Affairs considered itself efficient in handling the affairs of its charges, discontent, resentment, and wrath smoldered and then flamed among the tribes of the Mississippi and Missouri River valleys in the year, 1828. Much of the discontent resulted from the peace and boundary council of 1825. The boundaries of the Sacs and the Sioux still had not been determined, because the Yanktonai Sioux who lived on the headwaters of the Des Moines and St. Peters rivers had been absent from the council. Other tribes contested the boundaries of the area along the eastern side of the Missouri River. As usual the stronger tribes, particularly the Sacs, claimed more than their share, while the smaller tribes such as the Otos and Ioways claimed land on the basis of long-term residence and the location of their ancient villages and the graves of their ancestors. Perhaps they considered reconquest of their lands, but they could not face such large tribes as the Sacs and the Sioux. In February Clark wrote to McKenney that he was attempting to bring peace to the Osages, the Kansas, the Ioways, the Otos, and the Pawnees. The first four tribes historically had hunted north, south and east of the Missouri before cessions and the Treaty of 1825 and were now reaching into Pawnee hunting areas west of the Missouri River where they were challenged by the powerful Pawnee tribe. The Sacs were also intruding in lands west of the Missouri.

In November, 1828, the situation became serious enough for John Dougherty, Indian agent for the Otoes, the Omahas, and other Missouri river area tribes, at Cantonment Leavenworth, to review the events of the summer and fall. He suggested that immediate steps be taken by the government to resolve the numerous conflicts among the tribes. According to his account, the Otoes and the Omahas had not yet decided how to deal with the intruding Sacs. In August Keokuk had crossed the Missouri with between one and two hundred "sackes" to visit the Otoe nation. During the ceremonies several calumet pipes were passed in friendship. Dancing followed, and the Otoes presented a group of seventy horses to their guests. After the Sacs departed, they traveled a short distance to the Elkhorn, a tributary of the Platte. Here they camped and invited the Otoes to visit them for a reciprocal feast. When all the Otoes were assembled and seated, Keokuk spoke:

> My Brothers, I have been down to Saint Louis . . . a few moons since to see our red headed father on the subject of the great treaty held at Prairie du Chien. . . . The red head told me that all the land lying along the left bank of the Missouri, from the mouth of the Nodaway to the mouth of the Big Sioux river, and back to the DesMoines river belonged to the Sackes, and Foxes, and Ioways, and further that if the Otoes or Omahaws continue to hunt upon said land, I should order them off and make them go even were I obliged to kill them in so doing. I am a man, my brothers, who obeys every word my red headed father tells me. Therefore, I advise you to keep to your own side of the Missouri.

150

The Otoe chiefs then informed Keokuk, who seemed to them a "johnny-come-lately," that the bones of their fathers lay on both sides of the Missouri, and that they would cross and recross the Missouri when they needed to visit the graves, "so long as the master of life gives us breath."[24] The Otoes reported this obvious Sac power plan to their agent. Dougherty told them what had actually happened at the treaty council, and they were then convinced that Keokuk was lying in what he had relayed to them as Clark's words.

To keep their threat and to assert their claim to the region, the Sacs scattered in hunting parties along the headwaters of the Nodaway, Nishnabotna, and Boyer rivers in the fall. With Keokuk's threat in mind, the Otoes decided that they would visit the Sac and tell them what Dougherty had reported that Clark had said on the subject of their mutual interest. At this the Sacs retreated from their militant position, and the two tribes agreed to keep peace until Clark had been informed of their differences. Soon after, Dougherty encountered Blondeau, the American Fur Trading Company trader to the Sacs, and was convinced that he had had a hand in influencing the Sacs to try to wrest the area along the Missouri from the Omahas and the Otoes. Dougherty reported that Blondeau understood that this tract of land had been ceded to the Sacs, the Foxes, and the Ioways, and that the Indians themselves thought so. It was conceivable that his economic interest in acquiring peltry would determine his interpretation to the Indians.

In reality Article II of the Prairie Du Chien treaty stated that the Sioux and the Sacs agreed on a boundary that began at the Upper Ioway River and crossed the forks of the Cedar to the second or upper fork of the Des Moines, then followed a straight line to the lower fork of the Calumet River, and went down that river to its juncture with the Missouri River. However, since the Yanktonai Sioux, who were also principals in the decision, were not present, the line from the forks of the Des Moines, to the Calumet, down to the Missouri "is not to be considered settled until the assent of the Yankton shall be given thereto." In Article III the Ioways acceded to the Sac and Sioux arrangement, but it was "agreed between the Ioway and the Sac and the Foxes that the Ioway have a just claim to a portion of the country between the boundary line described in the preceding article, and the Missouri and the Mississippi, and that they shall peaceably occupy the same until some satisfactory arrangement can be made between them for a division of their respective claims to the country." Article IV stated that the Otoes, who were not present, had a just claim to a portion of the country on the Missouri, east and south of the boundary line that divided the Sacs, the Foxes, and the Ioways from the Sioux, and that the claim "shall remain as valid as if this treaty had not been formed."[25] Article XI stated that in 1826 another council would be held to arrange final boundaries. However, when Clark tried to plan it, the War Department informed him there were no funds available.

In 1829, the Sacs continued to pressure the Ioways and others in lands that the Sacs coveted across the Mississippi and toward the Missouri. Keokuk told Agent Forsyth that they might leave the Rock River, Illinois, area and move across the river to live on the Iowa River; that he would do so definitely. The hostile Sioux had made hunting difficult where the Sacs usually hunted, and hence they would hunt on Ioway lands. Keokuk added: "The Ihoway Indians having committed a fault should not interfere with us. . . . However, [that] you have been directed by Genl. Clark to tell all the Indians that they must hunt in their own country and not south of the boundary line is well, and we must do as well as we can, and it is hard to say what our young men will do if they fall in with the Ihoways."[26]

This was not the only problem that Clark and his agents faced in 1828 and 1829. The tribes continued to appeal to the Canadians as old friends, and the Sacs, the Foxes, the Winnebagos, and the Ioways had traveled to Canada to procure goods and advice. They were reported to have said that "they were almost consumed by the Big Knives," and they begged the English to join them and they would be ready "the moment we hear the sound of their war club, which will begin in a short time, to raise ours at the very same moment and crush the Big Knives." On July 12, 1828, an Ottawa named Pishicke arrived at Drummond Island from the neighborhood of Chicago and reported that eight or ten Indian nations were preparing to go to war against the Big Knives. He named the Winnebagos, the Sacs, the Foxes, the Ioways, the Miamis, the Sioux, and others. "All those westward are engaged in the plot, but I do not believe," said he, "that they will carry out their threats." During the following summer, Black Hawk, the Sac chief, visited Canada in hopes of soliciting assistance against the Big Knives, but it was a fruitless endeavor; all that he received were a few presents and no promises of military cooperation.[27]

On March 4, 1829, Andrew Jackson delivered his inaugural address as President. Of the Indians he said, "It will be my sincere and constant desire to observe toward the Indian tribes within our limits a just and liberal policy, and to give that humane and considerate attention to their rights and their wants which is consistent with the habits of our Government and the feelings of the People."[28]

One of the "habits of the government" had been an attempt to uphold the March 30, 1802, Intercourse Act, which in its fifth article, provided the obligations of the government to remove all settlers from any Indian lands with the use of military force if needed to effect the removal. The act had been violated many times, and many times the army had adhered to its duty and removed intruders from Indian lands east of the Mississippi River. Thomas McKenney, head of the Office of Indian Affairs since 1824 and one of the more benevolent figures in American Indian relations, soon observed that

Jackson's reponses were not as one would expect in carrying out the provisions of the Intercourse Act. He commented: "This act passed through all the forms of law, and was approved by T. Jefferson. So far as my experience went, or my knowledge, it was, from its passage till several months after General Jackson's accession to the presidency, regarded as the law of the land, and had been enforced in good faith, by the government as such."[29] He continued:

But this law was destined, at last, though unrepealed, to become a dead letter. The solemn compacts with the Indians, guaranteeing to them "protection" were treated as things obsolete, or regarded as mockeries. In the face, and in violation of the provisions of the one, and of the enactments of the other, surveyors were permitted to penetrate the Indian territory, roam over it, lay it off into counties, and to proceed, in all things, for its settlement, as though no Indians occupied it, and no laws existed demanding the interference of the government to prevent it! In vain did the Indians implore the government to protect them; in vain did they call the attention of the Executive to the provisions of the treaties, and to pledges of the law. It was when these outrages first began to show themselves, and thinking President Jackson could not be aware of their existence, that I called on him, and referred to them, and also to the provisions of laws and treaties that guaranteed to the Indians a freedom from such trespasses. His answer was, "Sir, the sovereignty of the States must be preserved," concluding with a determination so solemn, and the whole thing spoken in a manner so emphatic, as to satisfy me that he had concluded to permit Georgia, and the other States to harass, persecute and force out their Indian population.[30]

Not long after, Jackson removed McKenney from office while he was away from Washington on a trip. On his return Dr. Randolph of the War Department informed him of his removal: "Why sir, everybody knows your qualifications for the place, but General Jackson has been long satisfied that you are not in harmony with him, in his views, in regard to the Indians." "And," continued McKenney, "thus closed my connexion with the government."[31]

And it was true that with the advent of the Jackson administration the harsh, unremitting removal policy accelerated, especially for the large southern nations: the Cherokees, the Chickasaws, the Choctaws, the Creeks, and the Seminoles. The Indians were an annoyance, a thorn in the conscience, and, more importantly, holders of vast, valuable lands. They had to leave. In time the Ioways and others west of the Mississippi would have their own "Trail of Tears," as the results of the removal policy came to be called.

After 1827, the Ioways continued to live in at least two groups. As in records of former times, the structure of the Ioway groupings is unknown, but documents most often referred to villages or bands. A band appeared to be a group that separated from the larger section and camped or lived apart, often migrating from place to place. The group led by Big Neck was called a band. It consisted of several named relatives and other individuals, including young men who left White Cloud's village on the Little Platte and visited or joined the migrants. The difference between Big Neck and White Cloud was indicated by the widely different paths chosen by the two leaders after their signing of the Treaty of 1824. Big Neck, except for the brief period when his son attended St. Regis, spurned association with white men and their ways. White Cloud appeared to accept the inevitable. He moved his village and tribe when the agent directed him to do so, for he had signed and accepted the 1824 treaty that stated that the tribe would leave their lands before January 1, 1826. When the agent and other employees talked about farming and fences, spinning and milking cows, he listened. Regardless of his inner feelings, he accepted and encouraged his people to accept the new ways. He moved into a log house and tried his hand at agriculture. His wife set an example to others by seating herself at a loom and learning how to weave. Some Ioways were so motivated to be "civilized" that on January 18, 1829, Agent Hughes predicted that in five years they could live without any assistance from the government.

In November the agent reported on the year's progress and noted that, except for Big Neck's band, the nation was at peace. The acculturating Ioway group had built three hewn-log houses, fifteen women were taking spinning and weaving instructions, a surplus of corn and other vegetables had been raised, and many Indians were capable of giving instructions to others in the new skills. During the year a committee of citizens had visited the agency to see the civilization program in progress. In his report, Rice B. Davenport of Henderson, Missouri, said that the Ioways appear to be completely civilized. The women were as good weavers as any in the white settlements, and the men had not been reluctant to build houses for their chiefs to occupy. The letter was full of praise for the project and for the government in installing it. And while the praises were fulsome for the Ioways who were observed, this was only a handful of the tribe and probably represented White Cloud's kin group. At the village 10 miles away on the Little Platte River, buffalo hides were used to cover traditional Ioway bark houses, agriculture continued in the indigenous manner, and religious ceremonies and other aspects of life remained much as before.

Agent Hughes's annual report omitted one event, which resulted in more correspondence regarding the Ioways at an official level than had ever been written. The tragic affair and the subsequent arrests, tracking, jailing, and trial continued throughout the rest of the year, 1829 and into 1830. Why a similar amount of official concern, energy, and action could not have been channeled toward more important matters and problems of the Ioways is difficult to understand.

On July 17, members of Big Neck's band killed three white men of Randolph County, Missouri. Everyone agreed on the fact, but the versions of why and how differed. Big Neck's band, according to the agent, resided on the Grand River about 140 miles from the agency on the Little Platte. It consisted of between thirty and forty warriors and their families and thus represented less than one-fourth of the tribe.

A deposition by Nathaniel Richardson and Augustus Gatewood on July 20 stated that a party of Ioway men, women, and children came to a farm near a settlement and ordered them to leave, saying that if "we did not depart, they would send off their women and children and kill us." When they apparently attempted to kill one of the white women, settlers sent a rider to Howard County for help, which arrived after the Indians had departed. A group of approximately thirty men pursued them. When the posse overtook the Ioways, the settlers "tried to pursuade them of our pacific purposes, and get them to lay down their arms. They presented their guns, and one shot James Myers." A Reverend Johnson, who was asked for information on the affair, stated that the whites had been trading whiskey with the Indians. After they became sober, the Indians were dissatisfied with the trade. They believed that the white settlers had invaded Ioway country and ordered them off. On July 24 Hughes called the Ioway chiefs together. They disavowed any connection with the event and proclaimed their loyalty and friendship to the government.[32] Correspondence increased. Clark informed the secretary of war of the event. Hughes assured Governor Miller of Missouri that all necessary steps were being taken. The governor activated one thousand Missouri militiamen to pursue the offenders and be ready for any eventuality. But General Atkinson ordered that the Ioways should not be pursued in this manner. The militia's function was to protect and not to pursue. He did not believe that the Ioways intended to murder but to plunder, and he feared that pursuit would bring Indian retaliation and possibly a frontier war.[33]

An established procedure in Indian-white relations was to hold innocent hostages until those accused turned themselves in to the proper authorities or were captured. Hughes, therefore, took White Cloud, some of his family, and some chiefs of the Missouri Sac and Fox tribes — nineteen individuals — to Gen. Henry Leavenworth, who escorted them downriver to St. Louis to Jefferson Barracks, where they were to remain until they could be delivered to General Clark. Clark at this point asked the secretary of war for "any instruction which you think proper to give on the subject of our Indians."

Meanwhile Hughes and a few agency employees searched for Big Neck to ask him to surrender. On the North Fork of the Grand River, twenty-five miles above the old Ioway village that had been abandoned in 1826, they found another village, which showed no signs of recent occupancy. There they crossed to the Chariton headwaters, where they expected to find Big Neck's village. They crossed a suspicious, divided trail with one branch leading toward the north and one toward the east. Hughes followed the trail to the Des Moines River and then downstream to the Mississippi. He talked to Sacs and Foxes, who indicated that Big Neck had been seen shortly before. Sometime later a report came that the band's deserted camp was found at the Two Rivers headwaters. Later in their flight the band was said to be on the plains between the Flint and Iowa Rivers. By forced march Hughes located them there. Hughes reported that the sixty-five men, women, and children "at first seemed to be very much alarmed as well as very hostile, believing as they did that there was a much larger force coming on behind me. The squaws seemed to be very much enraged. They said they had no men, that all were squaws." Hughes continued, in his report to Clark:

> I told the Big Neck that you, as well as his Great Father's war chiefs had sent me for him and that he must go with me. He expressed a desire to see you, and said that he had often hoped to see you before he died, but that there was a large body of Americans in pursuit of him and that he would never be permitted to meet you before he was alarmed from his purpose, that he was now resolved to make his stand there, and die, in the Prairie. [34]

After continued urging, Big Neck weighed the possibilities of not going and finally consented to accompany Hughes. With him went Pumpkin, a chief in the band, and five of the principal braves. They encountered a company of troops, and the entire party descended by boat to Jefferson Barracks, where the prisoners were delivered to General Leavenworth. Later Clark sent the group to jail in Fayette County to wait for their trial, which "will not be held until next March." [35] Hughes, in his report, made it known that he had swum various rivers and had traveled 2,100 miles to capture Big Neck, and that he had suffered deprivations and difficulties in so doing. [36]

In November, James Birch, a Missouri citizen, argued to Clark that capital punishment should not be used in the Ioway case. He believed that the Ioways thought that they were on their own land at the time of the incident, and that they may have acted under the impulse of self-defense. He suggested that the government provide them with counsel. [37] Clark sent a surveyor to ascertain if the attack had taken place inside or outside the Ioway cession line. He learned that it had occurred 18½ miles within the state, and that Ioways were living in that area. Clark sent instructions to them to leave, or Governor Miller would remove them from state land.

Later, when called on to testify, Chief Walking Cloud, or Pumpkin, told the Ioway account of the incident:

> My father at the time of the difficulty my band was on the River

Desmoines — My father we had planted our corn and were going down to the forks of Chariton, on a hunt — and we met with some Sacs who had been killing some hogs belonging to white men — and when we were returning back we came to five white men's houses — and whilst we were talking with the white men we told them we thought their houses were over the line. It was then that the Sacs passed by with six horses stolen from the whites — One a Black one a Sorrel one a gray and the other three dark bays, all were American horses — after which I thought *that* was the cause of the difficulty — our party consisted of 30 men, including women and children all together sixty souls. We were eating with the white men in friendship. After which we were marking the lines between the whites and the Indians. My son did not like my marking and made a stroke at my hand with his arrow and missed it — after this I was very friendly with the white men and when we left the house one of my young men killed one of the hogs and my son shot some hogs — when I came up I asked the young men what they did it for? and they said they wanted to eat some fat meat — they killed six hogs I did not think much of it — and we traveled very far that day & the next day and got very near our village on the 2nd day I stept out and said here come the Americans and now the Americans are mad at you now — see what the killing of the hogs has brought on you — My son was setting off a little distance I went to shake hands with them and as they were shaking hands with me, the Americans killed my son, and three more, and then my men fired on them and killed three of the Americans. Big Neck and I, tryed to stop it and we did stop our men. If we had not stopped them they would have killed more of the whites, three more of my men were wounded and four women and children ran off and starved to death — My father I shake hands with you & my great father when I met with you, my father, I gave up four horses and the whites took one from me we gave 3 of our own horses and lost nine of our people we ought to be paid instead of paying any thing — there were a great many white men attacked us I thought there might be more than 100. This is all I have to say. I stayed in jail all winter and to save my young men I suffered very much and when I came out I hoped to have peace, they killed my son they broke my heart and I suffered in jail and when I came out I expected to get paid for my losses but instead of getting pay they demand pay of me.

Fort Leavenworth Augt 3rd 1835 [38]

Another version reported by Thomas L. McKenney of the incident stated:

He [Big Neck]... was told the treaty was made and that he and Mahaska had sold the country. He continued to endure the state of things until 1829 when unable to sustain it any longer he determined to go to St. Louis and state his grievances to General Clark. On the way thither he encamped on the borders of the Great Chariton. His party consisting of about sixty persons. While there resting his comrades from the fatigues of their march, a party of whites came up, having with them some kegs of whiskey. It was not long before the Indians were completely besotted, when the whites plundered them of their blankets and horses and whatever else was of value and retired. Recovering from their debauch the Indians felt how dearly they had paid for their whiskey with which the whites had regaled them, and being hungry one of the young men shot a hog. Big Neck rebuked him saying, "that is wrong, it is true we are poor and have been robbed, but the hog is not ours and you ought not to have shot it." It was soon rumored along the border that the Indians were destroying the property of settlers and the dead hog was brought in as evidence to prove the charge. Where upon a company of about sixty white men was raised and marched to the Indian camp. They ordered Big Neck to leave the country instantly, adding that if he delayed they would drive him out with their guns. Big Neck thought it prudent to retire, leaving his encampment he went fifty miles higher up into the country to a point which he believed was beyond the boundary of the state. While there the same party pursuing them arrived, and having seen them coming and not suspecting that it was a quarrel, Big Neck stepped from his lodge unarmed with his pipe in his mouth and his hand extended towards the leader of the party in token of friendship. The pipe is a sacred thing and it is among most of the Indians tribes the emblem of peace. Nor have they ever been known to permit any outrage to be committed upon a man who had advanced toward another with this symbol of peace. . . . As the Indians came out of their lodges to see the calvacade of white men they were fired upon and one child was killed as was the brother of Big Neck. The Indians obtained their arms, Big Neck, supported by Mah-she-mo-nie, Big Flying Hawk, decided to attack. The white man who killed the child was killed and Big Neck shot James Myers, the leader of the party. At the same moment a man named Wynn shot the sister of Big Neck. "Ioway Jim and Major Ketchem," two of the band, then shot Wynn. According to this version, a furious fight ensued and the whites were driven off. [39]

Finally, on March 13, 1830, Big Neck and his chiefs were tried. The jury acquitted them because of evidence presented by their counsel which indicated that the whites had been guilty of provoking the killings. Clark informed Secretary of War Eaton that measures would now be taken against the whites who had been involved in the incident. After six months in prison Big Neck and his bandsmen were released and returned to their families. [40]

Between 1825 and 1830 the tribes that had signed the 1825 treaty at Prairie du Chien had become increasingly warlike, as they hunted and crossed lands that each claimed. The government feared that white lives would be lost, traders' profits disappear, and the rate of tribal removals from the East appreciably slowed by the constant hostilities. Therefore, General Clark requested another peace council at Prairie du Chien, and agents notified all tribes involved within the disputed area. At this time the Ioways lived in two or more localities. One village was seven miles from the mouth of the Little Platte River, while another, described by George Catlin in 1830, was a "snug little village" on the eastern side of the Missouri River near Fort Leavenworth. Big Neck's band continued to live by itself in an undesignated area. In July, 1830, Agent Dougherty informed Clark that the Ioways claimed all land north and west of the Missouri River to the Nodaway, which flowed north and south some miles west of and above the Little Platte, and then from that river east to the Des Moines.

In the eyes of the United States, the most important dispute to be settled was that between the Sacs, the Foxes, various bands of Sioux, the Ioways, the Omahas, and the Otoes, who all claimed portions of land east of the Missouri River from the present Missouri state line northward through Iowa and into Minnesota. This region was considered to be an excellent hunting ground, and the government hoped that the tribes involved might agree to a joint or mutual right to hunt on it. Tribal cessions of the entire disputed region would be even more desirable. If this area were relinquished, the constant problem of ownership would be eliminated, it was believed. In addition, the United States would gain considerable valuable land. Clark suggested an offer of $3,000 to $4,000 per annum for the entire region.[41]

The Indian nations' leaders, treaty commissioners General Clark and Col. Willoughby Morgan, and various agents and interpreters met on July 7, 1830. Colonel Morgan delivered the President's message that noted that the assembled tribes had not kept their promise to maintain a peaceful coexistence. He demanded that they must make peace, and threatened:

> If you continue your wars, he will march into your country, and take side with those who regard his admonitions and chastise those who refuse to regard counsel, and if you hereafter disregard the counsel of your Great Father, the President, and continue or even attempt to continue your wars, it will be my duty . . . to seize your chiefs and principal men and hold them until those who shed blood shall be surrendered to me. All the troops in this country are now placed at my disposal . . . consider how swiftly the steamboat moves through your waters, and the rapidity with which troops and all sorts of supplies are transported from place to place. . . . Let your Great Father but stop your traders and you starve; the white People do not go to war until they have fully deliberated. When they strike, they strike down whole nations. . . .[42]

After further remarks, Morgan praised specifically the Winnebagos, the Omahas, the Ioways, and the Otoes for having lived peacefully. As was customary each leader then spoke. White Cloud expressed his desire to conform to United States demands but his talk revealed his rancor over Ioway harassment from neighboring nations. He said that he had kept the peace, but he did not think that others would do as they had said. He pointed out the fact that he had learned to plough and now could feed himself. Of other tribes he said, "These people eat everything and yet they are lean. They can't get fat even by eating their own words." He was bitter toward the Sacs, the Foxes, and the Sioux, who had perennially attacked his tribe. After continued persuasion the Ioways agreed to cede their claims in the disputed area in present-day western Iowa and north-western Missouri. The Crane, another Ioway chief, then spoke:

> I don't think 'tis fear of us that induces our Great Father to buy our land; but 'tis for our peace and comfort. . . . I hope all the Red Skins here are as well satisfied as I am. My People, we only wish to have an equal portion with the rest. You have given to some of the tribes more than to other of us. That part of the country which my tribe now dispose of is perhaps the only part where there is more than two animals left alive; and that is the reason why I claim more. . . . These people, the Sacs and Foxes are related to me, and I wish to maintain my relationship with them, yet they sometimes kill me. . . . I don't think these relations of ours can say we went into THEIR lands to hunt, but they come into ours, and for this reason we should have a little more than they. . . .[43]

Some of the other nations' chiefs also contended that the price paid for their lands was insufficient. Colonel Morgan answered: "I have deliberated on what you have asked, and will answer you. My Friends, I know your Great Father when he makes a purchase of his Red Children, allows as much as he can, without laying too great a weight upon his white children. . . . I repeat that I wish to be liberal, as your Great Father wished, but can go no farther." On July 15 the proposed treaties with the Sacs, the Foxes, the Sioux (including the "Medawakanton" and "Wappahcoota" bands), the Ioways, the Otoes, the Omahas, and the Missouris were brought forth and signed. (The Yanktonai and Santee Sioux did not sign until October in St. Louis.) During the treaty negotiations the commissioners insisted that the participants would have to make peace with one another. If they did not, the United States would send troops into their lands, seize their chiefs, and remove their traders. Such coercive tones undoubtedly contributed to the treaty signing. The United States planned that careful effort then would be made to gain tribal consent for complete relinquishment of the disputed lands. If all tribes agreed to cession, the land would be held in trust, and they would be able to use it as a common hunting ground. The treaty wording would be such that the President would be allowed to settle other tribes within the area at his discretion. The Ioways, the Sacs, and the Foxes of the Missouri would cede their lands in western Iowa and Missouri; and the Sioux, the Sacs, and the Foxes of the Mississippi would relinquish two twenty-mile-wide strips in north and central Iowa. These would serve as buffers and neutral hunting grounds.[44] No whites would be permitted on any of the ceded land. The treaty was not to affect the claims of the Ioways or other tribes to other of their lands south of the Sioux, Ioway, Sac, and Fox line as determined by the 1825 treaty.[45]

It is believed that the Indians at the treaty proceedings were un-aware that the Indian Removal Act had been adopted earlier, on May 28, 1830, and that the commissioners were aware of this.[46] The act provided for the movement of tribes across the Mississippi by exchange or sale of lands. In addition, the Ioways were not provided with an interpreter and could not be fully cognizant of the proceedings or any implications to be derived from it. Since the United States provided the interpreters, it is obvious that even tribes who had them were at a disadvantage. Without knowing it, as they later claimed, the Ioways ceded all lands that they claimed in western Iowa in Cession 151 (see Map 9). With the Otoes, the Omahas, the Santees, and the Yanktonai Sioux, the government established a tract of land for the tribes' half-breeds, as they were called, on Otoe land west of the Missouri. For this land each tribe agreed to pay a stipulated amount to the Otoes. For the Ioway share of the land east of the Missouri the United States agreed to pay them $2,500 annually for ten years and promised schools, a blacksmith, and agricultural implements.[47]

In the spring of 1834 Agent Hughes informed the Indian commissioner that the Ioway, the Sac, and the Fox tribes of the Missouri desired to sell their lands north of the Missouri state line between the Missouri and the Des Moines River in order to apply the proceeds to the education of their children and the promotion of agriculture. Before this could be considered, however, it was necessary to determine the respective areas claimed by the two tribes.[48] The division promised in the third article of the 1825 treaty had not been undertaken, but Clark believed that the agents and the chiefs could reach agreement. Indian Commissioner Elbert Herring requested that the agent "endeavor to prevail upon the chiefs of those tribes to make a partition of their lands on the Des Moines River."[49]

By this time covetous whites were eying the small triangular area between the Missouri line and the Missouri River to which the Ioway had been moved by their treaty agreement of 1824 but which they relinquished in trust in 1830. Intruders had already settled on the Ioway lands and had planted their crops, built their houses, and raised their animals in spite of Agent Hughes's repeated requests for their expulsion. The Indian Office informed the occupants via circulars signed by the commissioner that they must remove voluntarily or Col. Henry Dodge's troops would assist them. Hughes sent sixty-four notices but said that that would not be sufficient because there are "so many skulking and lurking about, who have no particular residences."[50]

In turn the settlers petitioned that they had not intended to break the law of the land but had been informed — "by our members in Congress" — that the land would soon be annexed to the state of Missouri, and for that reason they had assumed that it was correct to claim the land. Forty-eight men signed the petition and sent it to Clark, who forwarded it to the Indian Office.[51]

On advice from the commissioner, Clark urged Hughes and Dougherty to persuade the Sacs and the Ioways to move to the other side of the Missouri River and accept land there, that the present location

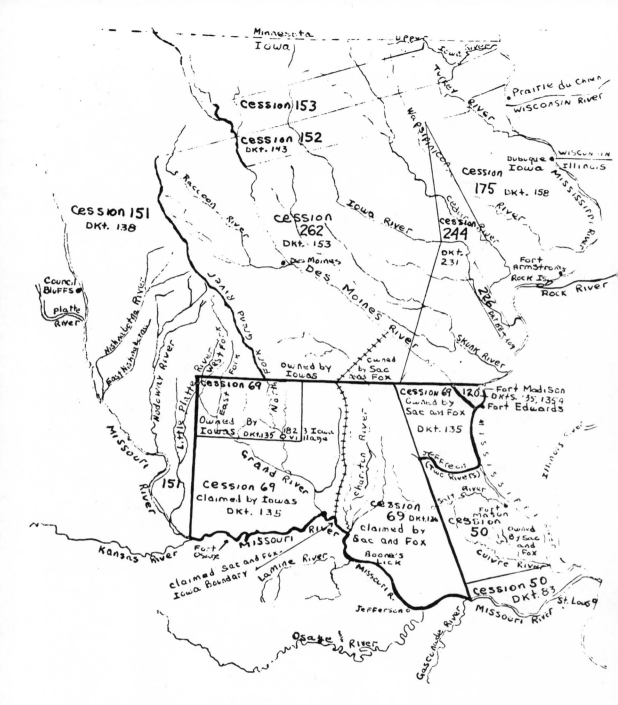

Map 9. A sketch map of the Ioway cessions between the Mississippi and Missouri rivers that was used as a visual aid before the United States Indian Court of Claims (Docket 138 [1955] 22 Ind. Cl. Comm. 232, p. 333). It shows cessions made by treaties between 1824 and 1838 and also the Sac and Fox cessions. Courtesy of the Chief Counsel, Indian Claims Commission, Washington, D.C., May 4, 1973.

would probably be annexed to the state, and their situation, if they stayed, would become intolerable. The settlers were so close that their animals roamed through the Indian cornfields and destroyed them. Missouri wanted the land, and the state meant to prevail. A brief attempt in February to remove the settlers by military means failed. Colonel Dodge and other officers sought out the intruders and told them to vacate their homes in ten days, but such warnings and removals had no permanent effect.

Under constant pressure, the Ioways, the Sacs, and the Foxes of the Missouri decided to deal with the United States, and on September 17, 1836 they ceded to the United States all their lands lying between the state of Missouri and the Missouri river. In exchange for this southern portion of Cession 151, the groups were assigned "the small strip of land on the south side of the Missouri river lying between the Kickapoo northern boundary line and the Great Nemahar, making 400 sections to be divided between the said Ioways and Missouri band of Sacks and Foxes of the Missouri, the lower half to the Sacks and Foxes and the upper half to the Ioways."[52] As compensation the United States would pay each nation $7,500. They would move as soon as arrangements could be made. Five comfortable houses would be built for the chiefs, 200 acres of ground broken; a farmer, a blacksmith, a schoolmaster, and an interpreter would be furnished "as long as the president deemed proper"; and rations would be furnished for one year. The young Mohaska (White Cloud), Nau-che-ninga (No Heart), Wachemone (The Orator), and Ne-o-mo-ne (Raining Cloud), Nau-o-mo-ne (Pumpkin), and seven other leading men of the tribe signed the document at Fort Leavenworth.

In October Agent Hughes wrote to the treaty commissioner, Colonel Dodge, that the Ioway chiefs still wished to discuss with him the subject of the lands that they had just sold to the United States, as well as their claims on lands also claimed by the Mississippi Sacs and Foxes. "They claim an equal undivided half of all the lands lying below the Sioux line (1825) and north of the state of Missouri." They were anxious to cede to the United States all the lands they claimed, and they wanted two chiefs to see the President on this subject. After this they would move to their new homes across the Missouri. "They will travel at their own expense, without the favor which is usually extended to other tribes. Their business is of all importance to them as a nation."[53] This was not the first time that the Ioways had requested permission to visit the President on this matter. In 1831 Hughes had notified Clark that they wished to relinquish and cede land that embraced Dubuque's lead mines in northeastern Iowa:

they have separated forever from the Mississippi Sac and Fox, and they wish to have their money, and property near to them so that they can use it.... You understand the importance of getting a hold on those lands by purchase, and also the difficulty of getting them at all at any reasonable price, should a few years elapse . . . indeed it would be well for those Indians to visit the President, as but very few of them ever have, and all those that ever have seen their grandfather are much easier to understand and manage.[54]

Despite this plea the chiefs were not invited to go to Washington. When they realized that the Sacs had recently ceded land to which they had an ancient claim, they gathered in December, 1836, and composed, with the aid of their agent, the following document and sent it to President Jackson and the Congress.

Petition of Ioway Chiefs

To General Andrew Jackson President of the United States, or his Successor in office, as well as to the Senate and House of Representatives of the United States of America in Congress assembled.

The undersigned Chiefs and Braves of the Ioway Nation of Indians residing at present on the north side of the Missouri River — Upper Missouri, for themselves and at the earnest solicitation of the young men, women and children, of their Tribe, do most respectfully ask leave for they cannot beg although their Nation is small, to present to your honourable Personages, a plain and true statement of their grief, and the oppression that has been in a most unsparing manner heaped upon them by their Red Brothers the Sacs and Foxes of the Mississippi and they regret to say that this Oppression has been in a good degree fostered and cherished by their White Brothers — But they fondly hope that it has been by oversight or mistake, and not with intention on the part of their Brothers, and Conquerers to cheat, neglect and defraud them, only because their numbers are small, at this day, and this reduction of their Tribe has been mainly caused by their association with, and strict adherance to their white fathers and brothers to keep their Treaties and the peace with all Nations. It is a notorious fact that they have stood like squaws, with their Bows unstrung, and scalping knives and Tommahawks burried; with the peace pipe in their hands untill they have been killed and destroyed both by white and Red skins (although once the most powerful and warlike Indians on the Mississippi and Missouri Rivers, they have been cut off and reduced to nothing, a mere handful of that Nation that was once masters of the Land). No Indians of any other Tribe dare build his fire or make a mocasin track, between the Mo. and Mississippi Rivers from the mouth of Missouri, as high north as the head branch of the Calumet, upper Ioway and Desmoines Rivers, without first having obtained the consent of the Ioway Nation of Indians. In fact this Country was all theirs, and has been for hundreds of years. And this fact is susceptible of the clearest proof, even at this late day. Search at the mouth of the Upper Ioway River, (which has been the name of their Nation time out of mind) there see their dirt lodges, or Houses, the Mounds and remains of which are all plain to be seen, even at this day, and even more, the Country which they have just claim to, is spotted in various places with their ancient Towns and Villages, the existence of which no Nation can deny. And even now their Village on the Desmoines is held and occupied by the Sacs — which place the Ioways only left about 25 years ago, on search of Game on other parts of their land, but never intended to abandon their claim to the Same or the bones of their fathers, which are yet to be seen there — and the Country has never been taken from them by Conquest. Your Petitioners would most respectfully represent, that whilst enjoying in peace and in happiness all the blessings and plenty which the great Master of life had freely given to them, On the 11th day of September 1815 their Nation were requested by their great Father the President to meet two of his Commissioners, Genl. Wm. Clarke and Ninian Edwards, to hold a Treaty of peace and perpetual friendship. — A Treaty was made, the Ioways Chiefs & Braves agreed to become the Children of their great father the President. Who was to protect them as his children. That on the 4th of August 1824 their Chiefs were called together, and Genl. Clarke told them in Council that their great Father wanted to buy from them all the Lands they then held lying within the State of Missouri. Amounting to several millions of Acres — and which has been and is worth to the United States Several million of Dollars. They listened to the word of their great father and sold the land for $5000, payable on 10 equal annual payments of $500 each. A Blacksmith and farming utensils & cattle were then promised to them. The Blacksmith and farmer has been furnished them, but the other articles have never been received. Which constituted a part of the consideration for which they were induced and persuaded to sell their Lands and to part with the bones of their fathers, but they still hope that ample Justice will be done to them. Your Petitioners further charge and state that they promptly left the land referred to and settled and remained in quietness on their Lands West of the State of Missouri and north of the Mo River, untill the 19th day of Augt. 1825 [1827], previous to this date they had been informed by their friends Genl. William Clark and the Honorable Lewis Cass, that strife and difficulties and war existed betwixt the "Sioux, Winnebagoes, Menomines, Chippewas, Otteway, Pottawatomies, Sacs & Foxes, and that with a view to produce peace and settle all the Boundaries of the contending Parties for Land the above & named Gentlemen called and convened your Petitioners Nation, and other Nations at Prairie Du chein on the last mentioned date, and after a council a Treaty of Peace was made, in which the Boundaries and Divisions of Land were defined. That at the Treaty your Petitioners gave permission to the Sacs to hunt on their Lands west of the Mississippi and which permission was placed in the Treaty in words and language which they did not understand by which the Sacs claim title to all their ancient possessions and Land. Your Petitioners charge that the Sacs never had any previous claim to the Land west of the Mississippi. And by the use of words on the face of the Treaty your Petitioners are only made to Stand in the attitude of Copartners as to the ownership of the Land which they had held before ever a white man dare make a moccasin track on that section of the Continent of North America. But because these things has been done by the hand of power they are willing to rest in quietness provided half way Justice can be done them. But now wronged, as they are, they would beg leave to refer to the 3rd Article of the Treaty above referred to by which a small portion of their claims and rights are held good and recognized.

Your Petitioners charged that since the Treaty aforesaid they have been informed and believe that Treaties have been held without notice to them, or their knowledge or consent, by which Large tracks of valuable land have been ceded to the United States by the Sacs. To the amount of many Thousands of Dollars. Your Petitioners Pray that your Honourable Bodies will, or by a Committee of Congress may examine to the extent of your Petitioners' claims. And in the end they trust that ample Justice will be done. If not they will have again to appeal to arms. And try to repossess themselves of their ancient possessions.

They have deputed & appointed Frank White Cloud, 1st Chief of the Nation and their particular friends Majr. A. G. Morgan and J. V. Hamilton, or either One of them to make and sign all Treaties in their name, We have sent these Agents & delegates at our own proper costs and charges. We also wish to receive in Lieu of our Rations for One year the Amount thereof in money, at twelve cents per Ration. We could offer many reasons for this but our Agents will fully explain. When their case shall be fully considered they pray Justice and relief may be granted to them. They ask permission to refer to Genl. Wm. Clarke their father who has always been their friend, and upon his word they are cheerfully willing to place all their complaints and claims and they will most cheerfully submit to his decision whether it may be for, or against them and for our peaceable and good conduct for many years. We ask leave to refer to our Agent Genl. Andrew S. Hughes. Justice is all your Petitioners want and this, they fully expect. And your Petitioners ever Pray &c. —

Watche Money	his X mark
Congee	his X mark
Nee Amoney	his X mark
Targo Hongh	his X mark
Rerbedouse	his X mark
O Kig Water	his X mark

I certify that the above was given by the Nation and signed in my presence.

And. S. Hughes,
Sub Agent, Ind. Affrs.

STATE OF MISSOURI)
: SS.
COUNTY OF CLAY)

I Abraham Shafer, Clerk of the County Court within and for the County aforesaid Certify that Mohasko Roubidouse [illegible] acknowledged as chiefs of the Ioway Nation the foregoing Power of Attorney in my office before me. In testimony whereof I have hereto subscribed my name and affixed the seal of said Court at office in the Town of Liberty this 14th day of December 1836.

Abraham Shafer clerk[55]

For the first time we read the Ioways' description of the extent of their land, which included the sites that were mentioned in Chapters 1 and 2 (where they were first thought to be as early as 1700 and before) on the Upper Iowa and Little Sioux rivers and later on the Des Moines. They again accuse the Sacs of taking their lands and the treaty commissioners of misleading them. The commitments made in their treaties have not been fulfilled, and they appeal for redress.

As the Ioways suggest in the appeal, Clark's opinion was sought on the contents of the Ioway petition. On January 5, 1837, he wrote, "Upon my arrival in Upper Louisiana thirty-four years ago, I found the Iowas in possession of an immense tract of country between the Mississippi and the Missouri River, their claim to which so far as my knowledge extends, was undoubted and unquestioned and which they have never abandoned, living on it from [that] time to the present. I ask it as a personal favor to let General Hughes come on to Washington City with his Indians. He may have more influence with them than any man living."[56]

Consent to such tribal visits was hastened by the American Fur Company's complaint that constant strife among tribes was detrimental to business.[57] Plans were made for an October meeting with the Ioways, the Sacs, the Foxes, and certain Sioux bands to discuss the conflicting claims and to settle the warfare among them. Hughes requested that the Sioux and the Ioways not meet at the same time, since the two nations were antagonistic; also, he and Joshua Pilcher, the Sioux agent, were not friends.

During the formation of council plans the Missouri River frontier saw increased tribal interaction and dissatisfaction. In May, 1837, Col. S. W. Kearny at Fort Leavenworth reported an alliance of the Delaware, Shawnee, Otoe, Omaha, Missouri, Sac, and Ioway tribes against the Sioux. In 1831 and 1835 the Delawares and the Shawnees had been removed to their reservations west of the Missouri, south of those of the Ioways and the Sacs, and the Foxes. They had quickly become involved in the strife of the area, as the competition for hunting lands and the Sioux attacks increased. Kearny said the signal for attack by this alliance would be the removal of the Potawatomis from their lands near Council Bluffs. He requested that, in order to avoid a general war, the government not remove them from their location. Some friendly chiefs had informed him that a war against the Sioux was to be merely a pretext to wage war against the white frontiersmen. It was known that the Potawatomis had brought a war belt of wampum from the Sacs. If war should result, the "tribes would wipe out the militia," and "the situation of those Indians is not understood by anyone who supposes that they are to be treated like many friendly tribes and their management left to ordinary persons." General Hughes, he continued, had lately moved the Ioways to their new homes on the other side of the river. The Potawatomis had tried to prevent them from going, telling them that if they did not remove, they would gain more from it. He concluded, "We can take care of ourselves but the Department at Washington is woefully neglecting the Indians around here, though I have twice called their attention to them. When some scalps are taken from the whites by these Indians the report will be loud enough to be heard. The country opposite us is rapidly filling. The intercourse between the whites and the Indians is shameful."[58]

Kearny's statement of poor treatment and neglect is corroborated by Hughes, who noted that all of the Ioways had crossed the river to the new reserve by June 29, and that they badly needed provisions. They had complied rigidly with the treaty, and the government should carry out its part without delay, he added. Provisions had not been supplied, and until such time as they were, Joseph Roubidoux, a trader, would furnish them on a loan basis. Arrangements for the Ioways to be supplied were finally in process, at the end of July, but the matter was to be held in suspension until General Clark returned or till further instructions were received from the department in Washington.

In August the Ioway chiefs set off for Washington with their agent to see the President and to try to settle their differences with the Sacs and with the government. They met with Commissioner C. A. Harris on October 7, 1837. After he greeted the tribesmen and passed the calumet, the commissioner requested that each speak what was on his mind. No Heart, the uncle of White Cloud, spoke first. He said that the Ioways had prepared a map showing the villages of the new nation in all the lands that they claimed or had inhabited in their remembered history. He pointed first to the earliest villages near Lake Pepin and Green Bay. He then indicated the villages near the Otoes and the Omahas on the Missouri and noted the places along the Des Moines where they had lived when the French and Spanish were in the area. The Sacs, he said, were invited to eat and hunt and "divide the game, but never understood they were to have our lands." But they and the Foxes have "always taken advantage of us knowing that we were a small tribe. They steal from us and then sell to you."[59]

He stated, as did the following speaker, Walking Rain, they they did not have an interpreter at the Treaty of 1830 and did not understand the terms of that treaty. Walking Rain added force to No Heart's claim on the lands discussed by pointing out that the rivers bore the names that the Ioways gave them, that neither the Sacs nor the whites had named anything in the disputed lands. He emphatically stated that, because they did not have an interpreter at Prairie du Chien, *they* were not understood when *they* talked.

Keokuk, the Watchful Fox, then defended the Sac and Fox position of acquisition by conquest:

We heard from our forefathers the history of this country. We have heard that the Ioway were our friends. Our forefathers had no difficulty with the Ioway. They say also that the Ioway behaved well during our difficulties with other nations. The country between the Missouri and Mississippi river we fought for. We drove these people [Ioway] off. My forefathers gave these people a battle at St. Louis [1780]. They were called the Missouri Indians. We have killed everyone of them and taken their country too. Those people and the Osages were the only nations friendly to us. We came near to those people [Ioway]. They fled before us. We followed on their track. We have always pushed them before us. That is the reason they have marked so many villages on their map. If I had not begged them to come back they would have been off, I don't know how far beyond the Mississippi. This country I have gained by fighting. Therefore, I claim it. Our people once inhabited the country about the Great Lakes. We were driven off. You don't hear me claiming the country. I was driven off. This is my country. I have fought for it.

The Ioways are last mentioned in the treaty journal entry of October 11. No further reference is made to them, nor are any of their speeches recorded. The Ioway chiefs had withdrawn and refused to attend any further sessions. A treaty was drawn between the Sacs and the Foxes of the Missouri in which they released their rights in the country between the Missouri and the Mississippi rivers.[60] Although the Ioway chiefs were offered similar proposals, they refused to sign them and returned home with Major Pilcher, who had replaced Clark as superintendent of Indian affairs. He was successful in changing their minds when they reached St. Louis, and the chiefs signed an agreement to release their rights in Cession 151 for $2,500; but they would not agree to sign away the rights to lands east of it.[61]

In the spring of 1838, disillusioned by the treatment they had received in Washington and St. Louis, and angered by the neglect of the government in supplying the stipulated provisions for their people, the Ioways declared that they intended to return to their old homes near the Mississippi,[62] along the Des Moines, and to establish their rights to that region. They later offered to settle their claims for $300,000. Agent John Dougherty thought that this amount could be reduced to $50,000 and they would be satisfied. Internal dissension on this issue again appeared within the nation. Disagreement between chiefs caused separation of one faction from another, and Dougherty reported that they had moved to live apart from one another.[63] The government itself faced more than dissatisfaction from the Ioways; Ioway-intermarried whites and their half-breed offspring did not want the nation to cede their lands in central and eastern Iowa, although the Sacs had already done so. Dougherty explained, "They will gain large areas for themselves" if the tribal lands are not sold. Traders and some others urged the Ioways to hold out for more money, "so they will have more to steal from them each year."

Representing another white-motivated interest, area newspapers put pressure on the government for some settlement. The *Far West* column of June 14, 1838, indicated that the Ioways had not been fairly treated:

> and that they will not part with the land until they, in their own opinion get a fair and liberal consideration. So far as our information extends we are confident that a treaty cannot be made on the terms proposed by the government. . . . The Indians refused the treaty indignantly last fall in Washington, they refused it again in St. Louis, and we cannot conceive why it must again be forced on them by the agents of the government; let us give them in God's name a fair value for their father land, as we are determined and must have it, we owe them that much at least in common justice.

Dougherty sent the clipping to the commissioner in Washington and said, "I have no doubt you will at once agree with me that it is from the pen of the same gentleman from whom you received a letter last winter through a member of Congress on the subject of the Ioway and the treaty in question. There is scarcely a word of truth in the whole of this labored article."[64] Ill feeling continued within the nation over the 1836 treaty relinquishment of their lands between the Little Platte and the Missouri rivers. From that area 992 Ioways and 510 Sacs had removed to the new Great Nemaha River reserve west of the Missouri in southeastern Nebraska and northeastern Kansas. However, 130 Ioways refused to abandon their homes "due to some difficulty with their chiefs" and had gone up the Tarkio River to plant their corn. Colonel S. W. Kearny called the band chiefs together to tell them that trouble with the whites would surely result if they did not leave and that they must move or he would have to take them to Fort Leavenworth.[65] Their decision and action are not known.

The Treaty of 1838 concerned the last of the nation's original homelands, now occupied by the Sacs and soon to be vacated by them as a result of their recent cession. The Ioways now proceeded to cede all right or interest in the country between the Missouri and the Mississippi rivers, and between the Sac-and-Fox boundary and the Sioux boundary, as described in the 1825 treaty, as well as all cessions made by the Sacs and the Foxes in these same areas since then. For this they were to be paid $157,000, which would be invested by the government at not less than 5% interest. The interest would be used as annual income for the tribe, "during the existence of their tribe." The concluding articles mentioned provisions and, as usual, funds for education, agricultural assistance, blacksmith facilities, and construction of "ten houses with good floors, one door and two windows." The treaty was completed at the Great Nemeha Agency with their new agent, Anthony L. Davis, present.

Frank White Cloud (chief since his father's death in 1834), No Heart (Notchininga), and eleven other chiefs signed the treaty. Between 1824 and 1838, all lands of their origin were closed to them. Other tribes from the east would temporarily be settled on some of them, just as the Ioways in the westward movement had been placed on ceded Kansas' lands. They now looked at the world from two hundred sections, a strip of land roughly ten miles wide and twenty miles long, on lands never claimed by them which had been relinquished by others.

Until the 1830's few descriptions of Ioway culture — the daily life of the people, their beliefs, attitudes, and behaviors — existed. Knowledge collected before this time seldom dealt with descriptions of house types, villages, religion, clothing, appearance, agricultural and hunting activities, warfare techniques, ceremonial activities, or social organization. The science of cultural description had not yet been developed. So, most precolonial or early historical culture patterns had been altered before they could be studied in detail. Serious efforts to "civilize" the Ioways and change their culture began in the 1820's and rapidly altered the indigenous ways. Although agents were in the best possible positions to observe and report, their reports in early years gave little information on Ioway daily life. Emphasis was placed on change and the elimination of native ways.

Ioway Agent Andrew Hughes was the first to mention limited facets of their daily life. He reported in 1835 that of the 963 Ioways, 781 were agriculturists, and 182 were "employed in the chase." The latter had no permanent residence and wandered on the "waters of the Missouri and the Mississippi." It is possible that this was the Big Neck faction, which a few years before had followed a similar life, although they had planted corn and established temporary villages in different areas. They were decreasing rapidly, and "they have agreed to come and join the tribe, and some are now with us."[66] By March, 1838, the entire group had joined the main body of the tribe at the Great Nemeha Agency.

Both the village agriculturists in the principal villages and the nomadic groups hunted throughout the decade. On January 23, 1835, Hughes told Clark that the tribe was away on its hunt, and "cannot be seen until Spring." Summer hunts occurred also: ". . . at the season of the year when their crops are secure, the party hunt and provide themselves with an abundant supply of wild meat to winter and summer on."[67]

Two years after the Ioways crossed the Missouri, Hughes mentioned that they had constructed bark houses, and that each family had small fields, or patches of corn, pumpkins, and other vegetables.

171

The game had almost disappeared from the small Ioway reserve, the people returned to the eastern side of the Missouri in small family units in the winter of 1838 and hunted and lived along the Boyer River and nearby creeks.[68] The only notice Hughes gave of Ioway ceremonial activities was in connection with his ubiquitous mentions of agricultural output, which were required in reports. They raised a surplus crop in 1838, "which," Hughes said, "they distribute to friendly tribes when they are visited by them, and in return they secure presents of horses and other things as is customary amongst the wild Indians." We assume that this refers to the tradition of intertribal visiting during which gifts were given. The prized gift was the horse, and tribal status was measured by the number given or received.

During visits which extended from a few days to weeks, various dances were performed, specific to the occasion. Also, intertribal adoptions of individuals took place, which promoted kinshiplike relations conducive to peace. Visits occurred at least annually, and served to communicate news and to promote friendly exchanges and build alliances. Artistic designs and useful ideas and techniques in weaving, pottery, and the construction of clothes, tools, and weapons were observed. If accepted, they were altered to fit each group's cultural standards. Stories told by the visiting men often slipped into tribal repertoires, and tribal songs and dances could be adopted or presented as a gift from one tribe to another.

Various travelers visited and observed the Ioways in the 1830's and after. Each individual who wrote about them brought personal interests, biases, and selective perception to the writing table. What one would describe in detail, another would not mention. In some instances two or three observers corroborated each other's observations. In other cases, there is disagreement. Maximillian, Prince of Weid, gathered information about the location of Ioway villages, some description of their physical appearance, and a little about their relationships with the Otos and the Omahas. The artist George Catlin saw the Ioways at the Prairie du Chien Treaty Council in 1830 and visited them at their village in 1832. He had the artist's eye for minute description of appearance and the detail of material culture and activities. In 1844 and 1845 he traveled to England and France with them and an exhibition of his paintings of American Indians. Catlin's writings about this journey had an artificiality, because the Ioways were in a nontribal environment, and their responses and acts, faithfully recorded by Catlin, were minimally representative of their culture, which they created in bits and pieces for their audiences. His writing does give good character studies for several of the traveling troupe, which included the chief Frank White Cloud, and does portray their careful reactions to strange environments. His paintings portray richly details of Ioway clothing and decoration.

172

James Hall and Thomas McKenney wrote about many Indian chiefs and other leaders, including the Ioways, who attended treaty councils in Washington in the 1830's. McKenney was in an especially good position to describe the happenings of the time. He had access to documents and policy information and traveled to different parts of the Indian country. Visiting chiefs were interviewed; and their responses were written down often with a great deal of interpretation, especially in the quotations of their actual words. The chiefs themselves were selective in what they imparted to the strangers. Most stories centered around activities that made them appear as strong men or warriors in their listeners' eyes; warlike exploits dominate the accounts. They are useful but must be read with the understanding that many facets of individual life — family, religious, and subsistence activity and the performance of political, social, and other interpersonal roles — are almost completely omitted.[69]

From 1837 to the 1850's two Presbyterian missionaries, Rev. William Hamilton and Samuel P. Irvin, lived with or near the Ioways. Their purpose was to convert the Ioways to Christianity and to teach them to live in the white man's world by teaching them reading, writing, and other skills. The missionaries learned to speak the Ioway language, and with the aid of a printing press, they translated into Ioway* parts of the Bible, hymns, a grammar, a primer, and other works. They also kept journals and wrote for newspapers, and they were sometimes used as authorities by later scholars. Their interpretations were perhaps biased, especially in matters pertaining to religion, and large areas of the culture were omitted in their reporting. Nevertheless, they are primary sources of the time. They were aware of the difficulties of recording the culture of another people:

> In tracing their history, religion, &c., it will be exceedingly difficult to proceed with certainty and satisfaction, from the difference we find in the notions of different individuals: e.g. to-day we will sit down with an old Indian, who will enter into a plausible detail of their history, or religious belief, or some traditions of their fathers. Another of the same age and patriarchal rights will give quite a different statement about the same things; or perhaps the same individual would to-morrow give his own story quite a different shade. This is the reason why the reports of the transient observers vary so much. It requires long acquaintance, and close observation, to arrive at anything like just conclusions on these points; and it is only by collecting different and conflicting notions, and balancing them, that we can find which prevails. [70]

* Works by Hamilton and Irvin are *An Elementary Book of the Ioway Language, with an English Translation*, 1843; *Original Hymns in the Ioway Language*, 1843; *Wv-ro-hae*, 1843 or 1844; *We-wv-hae-kju*, 1844; *Six Chapters of the Gospel of St. Matthew*, 1846 or 1847; *The Ioway Primer*, 1849, 1850 (2nd edition). These are discussed in Douglas C. McMurtrie and Albert H. Allen, *A Forgotten Pioneer Press of Kansas* (Chicago, John Calhoun Club, 1930).

Maximillian, Prince of Weid, accompanied by the Swiss artist Karl
Bodmer, viewed the frontier world of the interior West in 1832 and
1834. As he ascended the Missouri on the steamboat *Yellowstone*,
Maximillian indicated interest in the Indian people. As he passed
each point of interest, he discussed local tribes with knowledgeable
passengers or persons ashore and recorded what he learned in his
journals. From Major Bean, a former Ioway Indian agent, he gathered
the following story of the "Origin of the Otos, 'Joways,' and Missouris,"
told to him, he said, by an old chief:

ON THE ORIGIN OF THE OTOS, JOWAYS, AND MISSOURIS:
A TRADITION COMMUNICATED BY AN OLD CHIEF TO MAJOR BEAN,
THE INDIAN AGENT

Some time in the year (it was before the arrival of the Whites in
America) a large band of Indians, who call themselves Fish-eaters
(Hoton-ga), who inhabit the lakes, being discontented, concluded that
they would migrate to the south-west in pursuit of the buffalo, and
accordingly did so. At Lake Puant they divided, and that part which
remained, still continued their original name in Indian, but from some
cause or other the Whites called them Winnebagos. The rest, more
enterprising, still continued on the journey, until they reached the Mississippi and the mouth of the Joway River, where they encamped on the
sand-beach and again divided, one band concluding not to go farther,
and those who still wished to go on called this band, which still remained
encamped on the sand-beach, Pa-ho-dje, or Dust-noses; but the Whites,
who first discovered them on the Joway River, called them Joways
(Ayowas). The rest of them continued on their direction, and struck the
Missouri at the mouth of the Grand River. Having only two principal
chiefs left, they here gave themselves the name of Neu-ta-che, which
means "those that arrive at the mouth," but were called by the Whites
the Missouris. One of their chiefs had an only son, the other chief had a
beautiful daughter, and, having both a gentle blood, thought no harm to
absent themselves for a night or two together, which raised the anger of
the unfortunate girl's father to such a pitch, that he marshalled his band
and prepared for battle. They however settled it so far as not to come
to blows, but the father of the unfortunate son separated from the others,
and continued still farther up the Missouri, whereupon they called themselves Wagh-toch-tat-ta, and by what means I know not they got the
name Otos. The Fish-eaters, or the Winnebagos as we call them, still
continued east of the Mississippi in the State of Illinois. The Joways,
having ceded to the United States all their title to the lands they first
settled, have moved West of the State of Missouri, between the waters
of the Missouri and the Little Platte. The Missouris, having been unfortunate at war with the Osages, here again separated, and a part of
them live now with the Joways, and a part with the Otos. The Otos
continued still up the Missouri until they arrived at the Big Platte, which
empties into the Missouri, when they crossed and lived some time a little
above its mouth, but of late years have resided about 80 miles (by water)
from the Missouri, on the Platte River. [71]

Maximillan also recorded that there was an Ioway community seven

miles up the Little Platte River which appeared to be temporary.
Perhaps the mat, bark, and pole structures gave that appearance to
one accustomed to the ancient solidity of European stone, brick, and
mortar. The second village stood on the highland between the Missouri
and the Little Platte, a few miles from Joseph Roubidoux's trading
post near the Black Snake Hills, near present-day St. Joseph, Missouri. The third village or settlement previously stood near the mouth
of the Boyer River, south of Cabanne's trading post.[72] A possible
fourth site was near the Nodaway Slough, where he reported seeing
some huts, near Martin Cantonment, that had been built on an island
in the Missouri in 1818.

Of an encounter with the Ioways he wrote:

We were very glad to see, at the land-place, a number of Omaha and
Oto Indians, and some few Joways, who, in different groups, looked at
us with much curiosity; all these people were wrapped in buffalo skins,
with the hairy side outwards; some of them wore blankets, which they
sometimes paint with coloured stripes. In their features they did not
materially differ from those Indians we had already seen, but they were
not so well formed as the Saukies. Many of them were much marked
with the small pox. Several had only one eye; their faces were marked
with red stripes: some had painted their foreheads and chins red; others,
only stripes down the cheeks. Few only had aquiline noses, and their
eyes were seldom drawn down at the corners; generally speaking, their
eyes are small, though there are exceptions. They wore their hair loosely
hanging down their backs; none had shaved their heads; and, on the
whole, they looked very dirty and miserable. The countenances of the
women were ugly, but not quite so broad and flat as those of the Foxes
and Saukies; their noses, in general, rather longer. Their dress did not
differ much from that of those Indians, and they wore the same strings
of wampum in their ears. The men carried in their hands their tobacco
pipes, made of red or black stone (a hardened clay), adorned with rings
of lead or tin, which they generally obtain from the Sioux, at a high price.

This trading post consists of a row of buildings of various sizes,
stores, and the houses of the *engagés* married to Indian women, among
which was that of Mr. Cabanné, which is two stories high. He is a
proprietor of the American Fur Company, and director of this station....
A high wind prevailed throughout the day, but, within doors, the weather
was warm, 78° at four o'clock. Our vessel remained here the whole
day, and we were besieged all the time by Indians, who caused a very
disagreeable heat in our cabins. Among them was a Joway, called Nih-
Yu-Mah-Ni *(la pluie qui marche)*, who sold us several articles of his
dress. [73]

The year before Maximillian viewed the Ioway villages and some
of their inhabitants, George Catlin visited the Ioways. He later wrote,
"I started out in 1832 with the determined purpose of reaching the
tribes of Indians in North America and of bringing home faithful
portraits of the principle personages, both men and women from
each tribe, views of their villages, games, sports, etc., and full notes

on their character and history."[74] On his journey he found the Ioways living in a "snug little village within a few miles of the eastern bank of the Missouri River above Fort Leavenworth." The tribe numbered about fourteen hundred persons at this time, he noted, and they were far ahead of their neighbors in accepting civilization, depending on agriculture rather than hunting for sustenance. The only dwellings that he described were the tipis made of sewn hides painted with black, blue, and red designs and raised on twenty to thirty poles. Catlin's paintings give his impressions of Ioway physical characteristics. He said that the men for the most part were of average stature. An Ioway who accompanied him to Europe was six and one-half feet tall compared with White Cloud, who was five feet ten inches tall. Catlin attributed the lack of heavy torso musculature in the men to time spent on horseback. He noted, however, that leg muscles were developed fully from dancing and from hunting on foot. They were able to perform feats that "civilized men could not do" in their performances. The warrior's head was shaved or shorn of hair except for a scalp lock, to which ornaments for the various dances and ceremonies were attached.

Catlin's artistic eye noted in great detail clothing, body decoration, and the ceremonial intricacies with which he became well acquainted during the months of a European tour with the Ioways. There were different modes of painting the face and body, a time consuming process. If the final design did not satisfy, the colors were washed off and the painting began anew. Principal colors applied in streaks, hand prints, and overall patches were red, green, white, black, and yellow.

Men's Activities

Catlin offers little information on the day-to-day activities except that men followed buffalo and other prairie animals on horseback, shooting them with bows and arrows. They often pursued game on others' lands, which involved them in almost constant warfare with surrounding tribes. Tribesmen also caught horses on distant plains. Participation in their ceremonial events was an important part of life.

Women's Activities

Catlin's list of women's activities is short. Women were responsible for raising and lowering the tipis when the tribe was on the hunt. They also furnished the tipi interiors and lit the fires, while the men relaxed, smoked, and talked. Catlin was impressed with the artisanship displayed in the long wampum shell necklaces that both men and women wore. Women made the clothing and decorated it with porcupine quills and other objects (see Figure 11). Women were

Figure 11. Ru-ton-ye-wee-ma, or Strutting Pigeon, and her daughter as painted by George Catlin in London, 1844. She was the wife of the younger White Cloud and accompanied him and the other Ioways on their European visit with George Catlin. Courtesy of National Collection of Fine Arts, Smithsonian Institution.

included in some ceremonies, such as the Scalp Dance, in which they moved in the circle with the men and held battle-won scalps attached to a pole or the top of a lance.[75]

Childhood

Catlin said little on the subject of childhood other than that young boys were taught to prepare for war and the chase. Dancing became an important part of male life and was learned early. An infant often would not be weaned until the age of four. He or she was carried on the mother's back in a cradle board decorated with porcupine quills and small trinkets that dangled from the handle to catch the child's attention. Catlin noted that, with the child on her back, the mother's hands were free for other activities. Infants and children were deeply mourned at death, and offerings were placed at their graves periodically.

Ceremonial Activities

Catlin gave greater detail on this aspect of Ioway culture than others. He had observed frequently a few of the many Ioway dances and their associated ceremonies.

Hunting Dances. The Buffalo Hunting Dance was performed before the men went on the hunt. "For each animal these people hunt they believe there is some invisible spirit presiding over their peculiar destiny, and before they have any faith in their hunt for them, that spirit must needs be consulted in a song and entertained with a dance."[76] Nearly every man in the village had a mask of a buffalo's head, which hung in his wigwam and which he put on to perform the dance.

The Ioways hunted both the black and the grizzly bear, from which claw necklaces were made. The Bear Hunting Dance, a supplication to the bear's spirit, was performed before the hunt began. Each dancer used his hands as paws and his body in such a manner as to imitate the bear running and sitting with its paws held out in front of its chest.[77]

Warfare Ceremonies. Catlin listed several Ioway dances and ceremonies associated with the preparation for war and the celebration after successful sorties. All dances were accompanied by drummers and singers seated on the ground.

In the Approaching Dance, the warriors used eye and head gestures, posture, and body movements to indicate the method by which each advanced as he searched for the track, found and followed it, discovered the enemy, and prepared for the attack. When the enemy was sighted, the leader of the war party raised his arm and

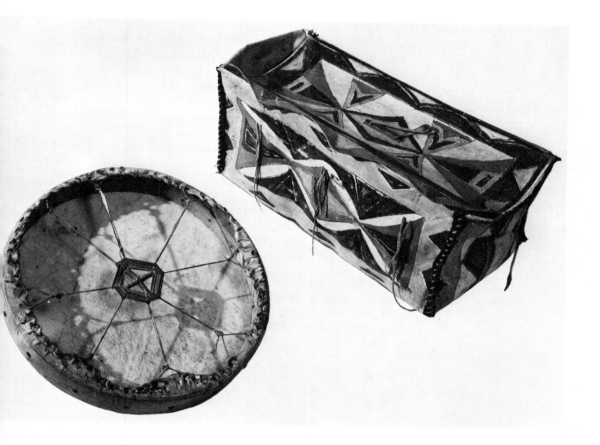

Figure 12. An Ioway hand-held drum (the back side is shown to display the lacing) and an Ioway rawhide trunk, or parfleche, 20 inches long and painted in various colors. Both these items and others similar to them were in Ioway possession until the early 1920's. Courtesy of Milwaukee Public Museum (Accession Nos. 31545 and 30680).

beckoned his party to follow him. During the 1845 performance in Paris and London, the leader carried a rattle of deer hooves. Catlin translated one of the songs:

> O-ta-pa, I am creeping on your track
> Keep on your guard, O-ta-pa
> Or I will hop on your back
> I will hop on you, I will hop on you.
>
> Stand back, my friends, I see them;
> The enemies are here, I see them.
> They are in a good place,
> Don't move, I see them. [78]

The Scalp Dance was performed for fifteen nights after the war party returned. The scalps served as a record of the warriors' ability and were much displayed during the torchlit dance, in which both men and women participated. First the warrior carried his trophies suspended from the tip of his lance. After circling the area, he then gave them to a female relative to carry in the dance. Carrying his tomahawk and scalping knife, he recounted the action of the battle with body motions around the circle or in place.[79]

The Eagle Dance, Ha-hon-e-cra-se, was among the most beautiful Indian dances. Variants were found as far east as the Iroquois.[80] Catlin wrote that, for the Ioway:

> The war eagle of their country conquers every variety of eagle in those regions, and esteeming the bird for its valour, they highly value its quills for pluming their heads and parts of their dresses, and a part of the war dance must needs be given in compliment to this noble bird. In this beautiful dance each dancer imagines himself a soaring eagle, and as they dance forward from behind the musicians, they take the positions of eagles, heading against the wind, and looking down, preparing to make a swoop on their prey below them; the wind seems too strong for them, and the fall backward, and repeatedly advance forward, imitating the chattering of the bird with the whistles carried in their hands while they sing,

> It's I. I am a war eagle.
> The wind is strong, but I am an eagle
> I am not ashamed — No., I am not.
> The twisting eagle's quill is on my head.
> I see my enemy below me.
> I am an eagle, a war eagle!
> etc., etc., etc., etc.

War-dance song verses were many, and Catlin's "etc.s" are an indication of the many omitted portions.

Each dancer carried the tail feather of an eagle as a fan, his tomahawk, and a whistle made from the bone of an eagle. At the end of each section of music and dance, one of the warrior dancers stepped forward and, in "an excited speech," related his victories, horse stealing expeditions, and other achievements. After each such interval the dance resumed.

Of the Warrior's Dance, Eh-ros-ka, Catlin said, "This exciting part of the war dance is generally given after a war party has returned from war as a boast, and often times, when not at war, it is given as an amusement merely."[81] The title, he said, meant the body, the tribe, or war party. The opening song was addressed to an individual chief or warrior of the enemy:

> O-ta-pa
> Why run from us when you are the most powerful;
> But it was not you,

O-ta-pa
It was your body that ran
It was your body, O-ta-pa'
It was your body, that ran.

In the final section of the dance the war song, or Wa-sis-si-cah, is
sung, and the movement of the dance quickens:

How-a   How-a
O-ta-pa
I am proud of being at home
I am proud, O-ta-pa, I am proud
I am at home - my enemy ran
I am proud, I am proud, O-ta-pa.

The intervals in the dancing were filled with "boasts and threats"
against the enemy to whom each song was usually addressed.

Social Ceremonies

The Welcoming Dance was given for visiting tribes and other guests.
This was the dance performed in the Otoe greeting for Major
O'Fallon in 1819. Catlin said that it was performed for strangers
"whom they decide to welcome to their village, but in doing so they
are actually addressing themselves to deceased tribal members,
saying that these strangers, for the moment will come and take their
place. It is a lament for the dead, but also can be for a tribal member
who is absent." All participants and observers stood reverently for
the dance's opening portions. The dances and songs then become
more lively, and the strangers were welcomed in the place of the
departed.

The Calumet or Pipe Dance was the favorite of the Ioways in
Europe. It was used by them at home to conclude a peace parley
with other nations, at which time the pipe was smoked around the
circle. The pipe had a catlinite bowl and a long wooden stem and is
decorated with eagle feathers.* The War Chief of the Ioways always
presided at these councils. During the ceremony he wrapped his
buffalo robe around himself, stood with his arms extended straight
out, and talked of his tribe and its exploits, particularly emphasizing
his own. After an interval, he asked one of the young warriors to light
the pipe. He received it in his right hand, took a few puffs, and then

---

* Catlinite, or pipestone, was named after Catlin, who visited the quarries,
studied and described the mineral, and sent its description and a sample to Dr.
Charles T. Jackson, a Boston mineralogist, who named it in his honor. See Harold
McCracken, *George Catlin and the Old Frontier* (1959), pp. 176-77.

181

passed it to his left hand and continued to talk with his right arm extended.

After the final speeches concluded, the pipe was again lit, passed, and smoked, and preparations for the dance were made. The ritual began when the two chiefs, one from each nation, holding their pipes in their left hands and their rattles in the other, stepped about the circle. After a certain length of time, other warriors from the participating tribes joined in the dance movements. Pipes and rattles were always handed to the dancers by the greatest living warrior in the host tribe. He had the right to boast of his exploits and to include among them, from that time on, his participation in that particular dance of peace and friendship.[82]

Of the Dog Feast, Catlin explained that the Ioways in London sought a dog so that they could celebrate a thanksgiving feast. This was "most acceptable to the Great Spirit," he said.

Games

Catlin enjoyed the stickball games that he observed among various tribes. While in London, the Ioways exhibited their games on the "Lord's Cricket Ground." This was an acre or two enclosed by a rope, inside which the Ioways performed stickball, archery, and other events. For the ball game, goal posts were placed at opposite ends of the field. The ball was thrown up into the air halfway between the goals, and opposing players used small, woven hoops attached to sticks about three feet long to pass the ball down the length of the field to the goal posts. This was a shortened version of the game, Catlin explained. In the villages as many as two or three hundred men could become involved in its excitement.

The Moccasin Game, Ing-kee-ko-kee, was played by two, four, or six players seated in a circle. In between them lay three or four moccasins under which by rapid hand movements each player in turn attempted to hide a small stone, while his opponent, by hitting the moccasin with his hand, guessed where it was. The game was accompanied by rhythmic music and was played for hours. It was a gambling game and objects were bet on its outcome.[83]

The Game of the Platter, Kon-tho-gra, was a women's gambling game. Small wooden markers with insignias on them were thrown into a wooden bowl then shaken out on "a sort of pillow." The bets were decided after the bowl was turned over with the little blocks still hidden beneath it. When they were uncovered, the various up-turned colors and marks decided the winner.

Catlin briefly mentioned other Ioway games and songs, such as the Medicine Song, the Burial Song, and the Farewell Song. The Death Song was sung by one who knew that he was going to die. "It has the doleful effect, having as one has in that country, a knowledge of the certainty of death decreed by a council or a suicide." The song was addressed to the Great Spirit of the soul, "Which entered in at the breast and is going out at the toe."[84]

Ceremonies and Observances at Death

The death of an Ioway named Roman Nose in London was faced by the others with the feeling that it was the will of the Great Spirit and "they must not complain." They refrained from their usual activities, however. The place of death, so far from their village, did not permit them to carry out their traditional ceremonies involving the kin group.

In Liverpool, in his final days, Roman Nose said that he was going to the place where his friends had gone before. When he shut his eyes, he could plainly see them, and he said that death was the exchange of one set of relations and friends for another. "The road might be long, but it did not matter where he started from, the Great Spirit had promised him strength to reach the place." He instructed that the best vermillion and, if possible, some green paint be purchased and put in his pouch with his flint and steel. On his journey he would use the paint to prepare his face to meet his friends and relatives. His arrows in his quiver were to be examined by his friends and replaced if missing or worn. When his death came, the Ioway doctor prepared the body for burial by laying beside it his quiver of arrows, his pipe, and enough tobacco to last him through his journey. His face was painted, his silver medal laid on his chest, and the coffin closed.[85]

At the death of the ten-month-old son of Little Wolf, the child's remains were placed in a small coffin. Each of the men ran a knife through the fleshy part of his left arm, drew a white feather through the wound, and then placed the reddened feather beside the infant in the coffin. The parents brought the possessions they had carried with them from their village or had acquired in England as gifts. All, except the clothes they had on, were given away. Catlin said that, when they were asked if they would like to have the interment in the Quaker cemetery, the Ioways said, "Penn, Penn," a name evidently known to them. English friends consented to the infant's burial in their cemetery at Newcastle upon Tyne.[86]

Other Beliefs

Ioway belief in sacred indwelling spirits is described by Catlin in only a few scattered instances associated with animals. Catlin and the Ioways visited the London Zoo. One Ioway called Senontiyah, the doctor, to come see the wolf, which was his "totem or arms." This

183

may have indicated that this was his clan's legendary progenitor, or that the wolf spirit had visited him in a sacred vision experience and instructed him in ritual behavior and song. The doctor stopped at the cage and began to howl in a low voice; the wolf returned the cry. "The doctor with a tear in his eye offered his imprisoned brother tobacco." Then the visitors saw the buffalo entrapped so far from its home. They were much distressed with its shabby and forlorn condition. The bears they would have embraced if they could have, they said. As for the snakes, they offered them tobacco, explaining that the snake for them was sacred and could not be killed.

Religious Practitioners

Ioway doctors and priests were responsible for curing the ill, prophesying future events, and accompanying war parties to assure success through ritual. They also performed many roles in the ceremonies and dances of the various sacred societies, during which some of them performed mysterious sleight-of-hand acts or "jugglery." On seeing an English magician hypnotize a subject and do other tricks, the Ioway doctor haughtily deplored his lack of skill.

In preparing their work *Indian Tribes of North America,* Thomas McKenney and James Hall interviewed Ioway chiefs and leaders who had visited Washington to make treaties and discuss tribal affairs. Nine members of the Ioway nation are represented in their biographical sketches: White Cloud (Mahaska); Rantchewaime, his wife; White Cloud, his son; Great Walker (Man Who Killed Three Sioux, Shau-hau-na-po-ti-ni-a, Na-ah-ma-hon-ga); Big Neck (Man Who Is Not Afraid to Travel, Wi-nau-ga-scau-ni); Orator (Watchemone); No Heart (Notchiminie, or Notchininga) Neomonnie; and Tahrahon. Each of those interviewed added to the list of known Ioways by relating events in which they participated or by referring to those who were their relatives. Included in the volumes were paintings of some of them by Charles Bird King.

The biographies indicate that warfare and its related activities were an important part of nineteenth-century Ioway life. Each man recounted his many sorties and often gave the names of the war party leader and one or more companions, indicating that such affairs were not composed of large numbers of men. Two, ten, twelve, fourteen and twenty-five members participated in the parties that were described. White Cloud recalled eighteen expeditions. The adversary nations were the Sac, Omaha, Pawnee, Sioux, Kansa, and Osage. Time spent in planning, completing, and recounting their exploits in ceremonies gave depth and fulfillment to their lives. Protection of territory and the survival of their people demanded this determined belief in the importance of warfare.

Apparently at this time the position of *Principal Chief* was hereditary.* When his father died in 1834, White Cloud believed himself too young and refused to assume the place, saying that he would not unless the general council of the nation decreed that he should do so. The elders met and decided in his favor, and at the age of twenty-four he became the Principal Chief. As an elder collateral relative, his father's brother, No Heart, or Notchininga, served as his advisor.[87] Another important figure in Ioway society was the *War Leader,* or *War Chief.* One holder of this position was Watchemonie (or the Orator or General, as his names were given). The war leader was responsible for receiving formally deputations from other tribes at the village. In once instance, Watchemonie told of a Sac war party who had killed two Ioways and came to make peace. Fearing they would not be well received, they called for him to leave the village and intercede for them. They gave him seven blankets to present to the principal chief. After the council's consideration, Watchemonie returned to the delegation with a present of a keg of whiskey. The way was cleared for their safe entrance to the village. The war leader's role enlarged with the interaction that resulted from the advancing white population. Once some young men stole horses from a settlement. The chief asked them to return them, but tribal law permitted them to decline. Adjusting to the new order, and realizing from previous experience that the whites might take revenge on them, Watchemonie purchased the horses and returned them to their owners.[88]

Ioway methods of adjudication are illustrated in a few instances. Serious disagreements were settled by arbitration at a feast given for the disputants with the chief of the band presiding. The pipe was passed to each man present, and if one refused it, a death, it was believed, would soon occur within that family. This strong sanction usually caused the participants to attempt to settle their differences. It is not indicated whether these events took place within a clan, or only ·in interclan disputes in which the principal chief directed the procedure. What the word "band" signified at this time is not certain. It is used in all official correspondence referring to the Ioway divisions, and McKenney and Hall used the term in the Ioway biographies. It is certain that related people were within the group. It is unclear whether they were members of one major clan, and its subgroupings, or several clans grouped together into one unit. For certain, the unit called the "band" could control the behavior of its membership. For example, an Ioway, a cousin of White Cloud and No Heart, wished to go to war to avenge the deaths of his three

---

* Henry Lewis Morgan was told in 1859 by Robert White Cloud that if the chief's son was not acceptable, then the deceased man's brother or his nephew could assume the title. See *Journals of Henry Lewis Morgan,* edited by Leslie White, p. 67.

children from illness. No Heart called the band together in a council where the cousin was offered the pipe and advised to forego the venture. His obstinancy and refusal caused the chief's brother to offer him a large gift of seven horses to compensate for his loss. But the man refused the pipe and the gift. Within a few days his wife died. Hall stated that the cause of death was believed to be his refusal of the pipe. With this death and the suspicion that supernatural intervention indicated that the man's desire for revenge had been correct, he was allowed to go. He gathered his party together and, following the proper ritual, sought and killed an Omaha.

The process of revenge and justice within the tribe is represented in one instance, when the avenger sought the tipi of the man who had killed his father. He slashed it to pieces and killed the man's horses and dogs. The murderer watched him and then handed him a pipe, which was a plea for mercy and amnesty. It was refused, as it could be in such a case. A council to decide his punishment was requested. The vote was unanimous for death. He was taken from the village by the Soldier Society, shot, and left for carrion.[89]

Customs surrounding death included placing the wrapped body on a high scaffold. Depending on the individual's rank and his family's wealth, different grave goods, in some cases a horse and a dog, were deposited near the body. Tobacco and other objects were sometimes placed within the wrappings of the body. After a final ceremony, not described, the relatives gave away all their possessions. A mourning period of six months followed with blackening of faces, reduced activity, and fasting. Female survivors visited the scaffold to wail and sing songs of mourning. At the end of the period, the family was given a feast and told to put away their grief. This signaled their re-entry into the normal activities of the village.

The death ceremonies of a chief were described to the writers:

Shortly after the death of a chief it is usual to hold a meeting for the purpose of consoling the surviving family. The whole company is formally seated, the chiefs in one place, the braves in another, and the relatives of the deceased in a third, while the children and women of the tribe form a circle around. Presents are then made to the family, one giving a horse, another a blanket, and so on. After which the chiefs and braves speak of the virtue of the departed and narrate his exploits. The one who pronounces the most satisfactory eulogy is treated to something to drink. Two or three meetings had been held in honor of the White Cloud who died in 1834. [90]

After a certain period of time following a warrior's death, his brother led tribesmen to the grave, where they sat. They were told that the mourning period was ended, that the black mourning color should be removed from their faces, and that they should resume the use of red paint, the sign of life, and their daily activities.

Watchemonie said that he did this after the death of his brother, The Crane.*

Peaceful intertribal relationships were attained or maintained by visits between tribes. McKenney and Hall were told that the Ioways visited the Pawnees, the Sioux, and the Omahas, among others. Ceremonies were performed, and gifts given to the visitors. Another ceremony was that of adoption of another tribe's member during the Pipe Dance. The Ioways sought to establish and maintain such bonds of brotherhood with the Otos, the tribe with whom they had had the longest periods of peace since the earliest historical period. In the ceremony, young men chose friends within their own tribe, or another, for whom they assumed obligations and responsibilities that lasted until death. Once a relationship had been established by formal ceremonies, gifts were exchanged and deep understandings built. If called on, one would die for the other. White Cloud (Mahaska) and The Great Walker (Shau-hau-na-po-ti-ni-a) were such friends. The latter had a friend in the tribe who had been killed by the Sioux. At that time he blackened his face in mourning, left his village, went to the distant Sioux village, stole into it, killed one man, and left quietly. Later he killed and scalped two Sioux women. He traveled one hundred miles and returned twenty-four hours after he had left. At home he was given two appropriate honorary names: The Great Walker, and The Sioux Killer. He was given the insignia of bravery: two "polecat skins" bound around his legs. At this time White Cloud asked him to be his brother. Shortly after his consent the two went to Washington to sign the Treaty of 1824.

McKenney and Hall wrote about one Ioway woman, Rantche-waime or The Beautiful Female Eagle That Flies in the Air. She was the wife of the elder White Cloud and had died when her son was a baby. McKenney and Hall and Ioway Agent Hughes all praised her character. She was described as beautiful, chaste, gentle, kind, generous, and devoted to her husband and family. Her husband said that her hand was shut to those not in need, but to those who were, it was said, "It was open like a strainer full of holes, letting all she had pass through it. She was known to give away her last blanket, all the honey in the lodge, the last bladder of bear oil, and the last piece of dried meat." Although she was idealistically described, she apparently also was of a determined nature. The story was told that when her husband left for Washington without her in 1824, she followed him at a distance. When he stopped to eat, she came up behind him and gave him a thump with a tomahawk, saying that she

---

* In the 1960's and 1970's a memorial feast was held a year after an Ioway death. The mourning family sometimes carried a framed photograph of the deceased around the assembled group in remembrance. A dinner was served, and gifts given in his memory. This signified the end of the formal mourning period.

too wanted to go to Washington. Thus convinced, he allowed her to continue with the party.

Reverend Samuel M. Irvin

Rev. Samuel Irvin was another chronicler of Ioway life. His long journal concerned mostly his personal feelings, illnesses, family business, and struggles as a Christian missionary. Scattered among his notes were occasional comments on Ioway life.[91] He first saw the people on April 10, 1837, in their village near the Little Platte River, in "a most wretched condition." He estimated a population of 830, considerably fewer than Catlin's exaggerated estimate. However, smallpox had visited the Missouri River tribes, and their numbers had been seriously reduced by it.[92] To the eastern-bred Presbyterian missionary and his wife, the village of the Ioways seemed a flimsy affair with summer houses built of bark over slender poles tied together with bark strings. In winter the hide tipi, made from buffalo or elk skins sewed together with sinew, was a warm dwelling. The tipis went with the people — whom Irvin described as a "strictly migratory and unsettled people" — in their many migrations. Bark villages were abandoned when the houses were worn, and new settlements set up at different locations.[93]

Irvin corroborated the statements of other observers that war was the main interest of Ioway men, and successful sorties enabled them to earn titles and honors. After the Ioways moved across the Missouri to the Great Nemeha Agency, Irvin accompanied a party to make peace with the Omahas. They showed him a place south of the Little Nemeha River, where they claimed to have had a victorious battle with the Pawnees. They also described a routing in which they had caught the Sioux attempting to steal horses and scalps from them and their close neighbors, the Otos. Near the present town of Peru, Nebraska, they claimed to have surrounded a grassy area at the river's edge, set fire to it, and killed the Sioux as they tried to escape. The status of an Ioway woman was enhanced by a relative's participation in such a war party. Irvin noted on one occasion an old, gray-haired woman riding through the village, her hair streaming behind her, announcing to all her satisfaction at the success of her grandson, crying, "Did I think I should ever live to see so happy a day!"

Agricultural pursuits were largely woman's work during this period. Their main farming utensil was a squaw axe, "a miserable piece of iron with a beveled edge and an eye like a garden hoe which a man today would not know what to do with." Additional food resulted from the hunts on which the tribe might be absent six months of the year.

Irvin said the Ioways had some view of a future state, in which "even the best to the ordinary vissisitudes of the present life would occur." At the burial of a child at the mission, the mother placed a bowl of beans and corn and a spoon near the grave. After the tribal hunt she returned and asked the missionary for some bread to place there. In the spring she planted melons and corn at the site.

The balance of Reverend Irvin's comments were concerned with Ioway reaction to and involvement with him as an agent of change in education, religion, and agriculture as he endeavored to promote their so-called civilization.

Rev. Samuel M. Irvin and William Hamilton, 1848

Indian Agent H. R. Schoolcraft, who played a great role in obtaining the cessions of Indian lands, compiled the six-volume work, *History and Statistical Information Respecting the History, Condition and Prospects of the Indian Tribes of the United States,* under the provision of an act of Congress on March 3, 1847. To acquire information, Schoolcraft sent questionnaires to individuals involved in Indian affairs. In 1848 Irvin and Hamilton noted the difficulty that they had in answering some of the questions. They had lived among the Ioways for eleven years; yet they said that they knew little of their ways and hoped in the future to spend more time in collecting their history and traditions. Eventually they did, and Hamilton, especially, produced significant work that is discussed later in this section.[94]

In the Schoolcraft work, the Ioways told the missionaries, "Our fathers tell us that a long time ago, it rained a long time, perhaps, twenty or thirty days; and all animals and all Indians were drowned. The Great Spirit then make another man and woman out of red clay, and we came from them. The Great Spirit told our fathers all this, or told the first man he Made."

For the Ioways, the Great Spirit created all things. The earth was flat, surrounded like an island on all sides by water. They began their travels on an island where all other Indians lived also. To obtain sustenance they all divided into families and scattered to become distinct tribes. The island or place where they started was to the east beyond the water. Like the Winnebagos they described what may be Baffin Bay or the Great Lakes. In order to cross this large body of water they swam or used skin boats. Their first stopping place was at the mouth of a great river with a large sandbar that blew dust on them. From this they received the name Pa-ho-ja, Dusty Noses. Later they moved from place to place as shown on the map drawn by Waw-non-que-skoon-a (See Map 2). An old Ioway, at least sixty years old, said that sixty-six years earlier (which would place the time in the 1780's) the Ioways lived on the east side of a river that runs westward from a lake to the Mississippi (at about this time the Ioways may have had villages or camps in Illinois):

189

At that time we had 400 men fit to go to war, but we were small compared to what we had been. Our fathers say as long as they can recollect, we have been diminishing. At one time we owned all the land east of the Mississippi. Our fathers saw white men on the Lakes about 120 years ago; about the same time we got our first guns. We were afraid of the white man at first, they seemed like the Great Spirit. Our fathers also, at the same time for the first time received iron axes, hoes, kettles, and woolen blankets. We, the old men of our nation, first saw white men between forty and fifty years ago near the mouth of the Missouri. [95]

Ioway villages were constructed on bluffs or high places so that watch could be kept for the enemy. In the winter camps were built in woods or sheltered places for warmth and protection from the wind.

In 1848, the tribe was still organized into clans, some of which had become extinct by that time. The Eagle, Pigeon, Wolf, Bear, Elk, Beaver, Buffalo, and Snake clans each had distinct ways of cutting and wearing the hair. The styles of the eagle, wolf, bear, and buffalo were worn by young boys, but at maturity men all wore their hair similarly, with only a lock or braid remaining at the top: a small area of hair extended around it for about two inches on the front and sides and down the back of the head. It was cut once a year.

What tribal government remained at this time was in the hands of the chiefs, led by White Cloud and four others in descending order of importance (No Heart was second chief). White Cloud was not considered a good chief by the missionaries. He drank to excess, they said, and did not cooperate with them by sending the tribe's children to their school. For other chiefs they have greater praise. Since the death of The Orator (Watchemonie) in 1844, the tribe had not had an Orator or Speaker. The tribe was again divided into two parts with one part living away from the agency at an undesignated locality. According to tribal tradition, scarcity of food had much to do with the tribal division into two or more segments. But in the missionaries' opinion the "rivalry and ambition among chieftains and war leaders, has no doubt had also much to do in this affair."

When it was necessary to visit another tribe to arrange for peace or for other purposes, the Ioways proceeded cautiously. The principal men traveled until they sighted the village. Here they paused and sent one man ahead. He carried a pipe stem-first, singing a song as he went, to call attention to himself. On entering the village he was taken to the first chief's dwelling. If he smoked the proffered pipe, all would go well, but if he refused, the Ioways believed that dire results would be directed toward him by the Great Spirit, such as the death of the chief or a family member. It was almost a certainty that the pipe would not be refused. The remaining party could then enter the village where they went to the chief's dwelling, and "manifestations of friendship are given by shaking the right hand, while the left is passed down the other arm, from the shoulder, and rubbed forceably over the breast." A council later, would attempt to resolve differences. If they were successful, dancing, feasting, and concomitant ceremony lasted several days.[96]

The missionaries noted the Ioway reluctance to speak about their religion and ceremonies. Their own attitude toward the Ioways' "heathen" beliefs is illustrated in other places (for instance, Reverend Irvin's diary). This was conveyed to the Ioways, who responded with the simple logic that, if the ministers tried to covert them to Christianity, then they must assume that the Ioway religion was in error or inferior to their own. Hence their reluctance to discuss their religious beliefs.

The missionaries also noted that ceremonies and songs were more numerous than they had supposed. They were taught from father to son, and "they have not been altered in the least for many generations." Concerning Ioway beliefs in supernatural animal spirits, they said:

> ...a kind of religious adoration to some animals, reptiles, and birds exists. There is a small bird, a species of the hawk, which they never kill, except to obtain some portions of its body to put with their sacred medicine. They say it inhabits the rocky cliffs of mountains, and is very difficult to take; that it has a remarkable faculty of remaining a long time on the wing. This faculty seems to obtain for it the respect of the Indians, as it seems to soar with ease toward what they suppose is the land of the blessed. [97]

Snakes held a special place in the pantheon. Snake doctors existed, who talked to them and made them offerings of tobacco, or "such things as may be at hand," "and propose peace and friendship between the snakes and the children of the nations." A story was told that, when the Ioways began to build their new settlement west of the Missouri River, near the mouth of the Wolf River, in 1837, a young man came to the Snake Doctor and told him that he had seen a rattlesnake on the point of a nearby hill. The "great snake doctor" immediately left the village, taking tobacco and other articles with him. When he found the snake, he had a long talk with it, gave it the offerings, and returned to the village. The doctor then told the residents that they could live in safety, as peace was made with the snakes.

The stars held supernatural power, as a story recorded by the missionaries recounts:

> Long ago, a child, when very young, observed a certain star in the heavens, which he regarded more than all others. As he grew up, his attachments for the star increased, and his mind became more and more set upon it. When able, he went out to hunt, and while traveling, weary and alone, not having very good success, this favorite star came down to him, and conversed with him, and conducted him to a place where he found bear, and plenty of game. After this he was always a great hunter.

The missionaries mentioned various objects used by the Ioways in their everyday lives. Wooden bowls, ladles, corn grinders or pounders were handmade. Shields, skins, horsewhips, saddles, and warclubs were decorated with "the devices of bears, buffaloes, etc." The journeys of war parties were sometimes recorded in the same way on their shields and other objects. Each man was an individual artisan who manufactured his own arrow points with a file and metal.

Reverend Hamilton, true to his word that he would study Ioway culture in greater detail, did so in the years following his report to Schoolcraft. The information that he recorded was used and acknowledged by such later scholars as Henry Lewis Morgan, Alanson Skinner, and J. O. Dorsey. Dorsey described Ioway religious beliefs, which he compared to those of the Winnebagos, the Otoes, and the Missouris:

> Mr. Hamilton wrote thus in one of his letters, "It is often said that the Indians are not idolators, and that they believe in one Supreme Being, whom they call the Great Spirit. I do not recollect that I ever heard the Iowas use the term Great Spirit since I have been among them. They speak of God (Wakanta), and sometimes of the Great God or Bad God. But of the true character of God they are ignorant. Many of them speak of God as the creator of all things, and use a term that signifies, Creator of the Earth." Sometimes they call him Grandfather. But they imagine him to be possessed of like passions with themselves, and pleased with their war parties, scalp dances, thefts, and such like sin. . . . They sometimes speak of the sun as a god, because it gives light and heat. The moon they sometimes speak of as a god, because it seems to be to the night what the sun is to the day. I asked an Indian the other day how many gods the Iowas had, and he promptly replied "Seven." [98]

One Wakanta was Tatche, the Wind, that seemed to be divided into the South Wind, which was considered good, and the Northeast Wind, which was thought to be maleficient. Another Wakanta was the Thunder and Eagle Being, combined in some manner. Thunder was visualized as a large bird, and when his voice was first heard in the spring, it was time for a certain feast to be given. The Wakantas of the Underground, in one cited instance, appeared to have malevolent intentions toward man. Water Wakantas were occasionally observed by the Ioways. No Heart told Reverend Hamilton that he had observed a water god in the Missouri at the time of a man's drowning. The god had taken the man to be his servant. In another instance, a young Ioway girl drowned when a canoe capsized. Those nearby heard the god cry out, and they said he had taken her with him. The Wakantas were sometimes in conflict. Those of the water were attacked by the Thunder Beings in the air when they arose from the surface. Certain animals with godlike attributes could be called Wakantas. The buffalo and snake were among them. Humans could become Wakantas, but, according to Dorsey, Hamilton had not discovered the conditions and steps for this.

Animals were sacrified from time to time, but to which of the seven Wakantas is not known. Hamilton saw numerous dogs hanged as sacrifices. No Heart told him that at least fifty years before that time, smallpox decimated the tribe, and so many died that great offerings were made. "We threw away a great many garments, blankets, etc., and offered many dogs to God. My father threw away a flag which the British had given him. When we had thrown away all these things, the smallpox left us." "To throw away" in the Ioway language, Hamilton explained, meant "to sacrifice." No clan animal, however, could be sacrificed or eaten by its members.*[99]

The Ioways possessed sacred bundles that served different purposes, but it was not clear how ownership was determined. A group of seven war bundles were interrelated as brothers and sisters. War bundles were taken on war parties, and, when the warriors returned, the bundles were opened and used in the ceremonies and dances that followed. Each bundle contained a war club, skins of animals and birds stuffed with medicine, wild tobacco, and other war medicine. Some bundles contained round stones, which warriors could rub on their bodies to prevent injury. Buffalo medicine bundles were used to heal the sick and wounded. They contained small sticks with deer hooves attached, which were shaken while the doctor treated the sick, a piece of buffalo pelt, and, often, a piece of elk throat skin. Deer medicine bags contained the sacred otter skins used in the Otter Dance. At one time there existed seven other "bad medicine" bundles that were used for altogether different purposes. Some bundle contents were intended to deprive the enemy of power — he became unable to run or shoot and could be killed. The Adjudication or Trial Bundle consisted of seven layers of skin inside which lay a "mysterious object" by which the Ioways "try men, or make them swear to tell the truth." No one living in 1848 had ever admitted to seeing the object, which was thought to be of iron or stone. No woman was allowed to see the bundle, and Hamilton was told that he would die if he gazed on it.[100]

Another facet of Ioway religious behavior Dorsey labeled "Dancing Societies." These associations were connected with the sacred bundles and other sacred procedures described by Hamilton. Only three of the various Ioway groups were mentioned: the Otter Dancing Society, the Red Medicine Dancing Society, and the Buffalo Dancing Society. In the otter dance, participants carried otter medicine bags containing a pebble or other small objects and other sacred items. The bead, which represented a spirit, was shot by the dancer, in some manner through the mouth, at another participant. This bead was said to be "kept in the breast of the dancer and expelled or coughed up at the

---

* In 1964 an elderly member of the Eagle and Thunder clan said that no one in his clan could harm the eagle to gain its feathers. The clan members were dependent on others to obtain their eagle feathers in earlier days.

proper moment. He who was thus shot in turn did cough up the mysterious object, and at the end of the dance each member swallowed his own shell or pebble."

Red Medicine Dancing Society members traveled some distance toward the prairies near the Rocky Mountains, it was said, to find an object "about the size of a bean or small hazel nut of a red color." The Ioways considered that it contained a mysterious spirit. The doctors would crush and boil the beans in a large kettle. Members would drink it hot, and "it produces a kind of intoxication making them full of life, as they say, and enabling them to dance a long time." This is identified as the mescal bean, *Sophora secundiflora*, presently found in western Texas and southern New Mexico.

The Buffalo Dancing Society, which supplied the tribe's medical practitioners, used a sacred bundle in curing ceremonies. Only men who had visions of the buffalo spirit could become members of this society.

The Ioway adopted the Green Corn Dance, which they said they received from the Sacs, who had acquired it from the Shawnees. Men and women participated in the dance on summer nights.[101]

Maximillian, Catlin, McKenney and Hall, and Irvin and Hamilton give brief glimpses of the Ioway culture of the 1830's and 1840's. None of the observers attempted to make a complete discription of Ioway culture, and a major portion of it has been lost. Alanson Skinner added many details in his *Ethnography of the Ioway Indians* (1926), but this too has many gaps that may never be filled. Much information for the period preceding cultural intrusion by whites was not remembered by the few remaining Ioways who might have been able to recall and illustrate the unknown portions of their past.

The Inverted Triangle: The Agent, the Trader, and the Indian

True respect and admiration for the Indians existed among some of the white men who were sent or sought to live among them, but the racial prejudice and ambitions of others, often fulfilled by coercion and exploitation, left little occasion for the achievement of noble purposes. Schematically, the Indian stood at the base of an inverted triangle. On one side the agent, or other governmental representative, wheedled and pressured him to make land cessions and forcefully urged him to be "civilized" and discard his culture. On the other side stood the trader. He often exerted pressure on the Indian not to cede his lands, but he did urge him to hunt, sometimes on lands that were not his own. The trader also advised the Indian and succeeded in greatly influencing Indian opinion in ways that contradicted the agents' plans and instructions.

After the fur trade began to diminish, and Indian lands were largely ceded, the Indians used annuity money to pay for their needs. Year after year, annuity payment time brought the trader as well as the Indian to the payment table. In many cases the money went almost directly into traders' hands to pay debts that grew higher and higher from prices calculated for maximum profit. In many treaty agreements large sums subtracted from the final settlement were paid to traders for debts contracted by the tribe. In some instances, the agent and the trader worked together at the expense of the Indian, to make the most of their situation, but in others the agent fought against the traders as Ioway Agent Hughes did.

With the abolishment of the government factory system in 1822, the American Fur Company looked forward to expansion of its interests and profits among the Indian nations west of the Mississippi. Two of the original purposes of the factory system had been to prevent exploitation of the Indians and to restrict the sale of whiskey. After 1822, the Intercourse Acts and other legislation did little to prevent exorbitant prices and whiskey distribution because enforcement was difficult. Some agents complained loudly and frequently of abuses. The fur trading company was impervious to such criticism. On December 25, 1830, Pierre Chouteau of the American Fur Company, St. Louis, wrote to Hughes:

> I have been informed that Mr. Vance Murry Campbell, a United States Indian interpreter, has formed and Established a Trading house, and that he was actually trading with the Indians under your Agency; Should this report be correct I hope you will lose no time in putting a stop to a violation of the Indian Regulations, and to bring to Justice the officer under your immediate control. [102]

Four days later Colin McLeod wrote to William Clark from the American Fur Company's Black Snake Hills post near the Ioway village on the Missouri River that R. Farnham had hired him to trade there, but when he arrived he found Campbell carrying on the trade, as well as transporting merchandise into the Indian lands for trade, "a privilege that would not be allowed me four years ago: when the subagent said that it was against regulations." He accused Hughes of wrongdoing in allowing a United States interpreter to operate a trading house, and wrote "there can be no danger in loosing when backed by the publicks money or bad credits transferd as Indians' presents, accounts made out, and money drawn or horses paid for by the Government and the Indian.... The accounts of this little subagency would make a modest man blush. As to drawing pay for Mr. Campbell as Interpreter, your own examination of the account will determine." [103] Hughes informed Clark on January 18 that he had received and answered the first letter from Chouteau. Hughes believed that stricter rules of conduct had to be established between private traders and agents of government. "It is a fact that the American Fur Company have as their employees, or under their immediate influence the whole Indian country." The prices that were demanded made it impossible for anyone to accept the United States wages, unless he had other resources. It was almost impossible to obtain the services of an interpreter without the agent being dependent on a trader. Hughes explained that Campbell had come as a licensed trader from a certain company, not the American Fur Company, to assist them in their business. But since he spoke Ioway, he had been hired by the agent as an interpreter since no other was available. Since December 21, when Campbell was released from his position as interpreter, Hughes had had no interpreter.

He continued, that it was the purpose of the trading companies not just to deal in merchandise but through this means:

> to have the entire influence and control over the Indians, their object and interest seeming to be to urge the Indian on to the chase. The interest and benign views of the Government are different, so that it is not infrequently the case that the power and influence of the trader are felt to overbalance any influence which the agents of government may have over the Indian, and thereby defeat a faithful agent in carrying into effect views which the government has. Agents are sent for one purpose, and the traders come for another, the consequence is that the man who will do his duty, will incur the opposition of the traders who are armed with immense capital and influence, that unless the Government shall interpose the arm of its power, it is useless to send Agents to the Indians, and by pointing out the limits of power and duties of each, there need be no collision.

Hughes said that he was continually involved in controversy with the traders. "So far I have retained a friendly relation to the Traders, but at some sacrifice of the dignity of the office I hold." He suggested the necessity of regulations to prevent the growing power of the traders and restore the agents' control over the Indians.[104]

In January, Clark received another letter from Hughes, stating that McLeod and his employer were offended because he had steadfastly refused to allow them "to sell one drop of whiskey to the Indians," and "constantly complained to them of their high prices." As an example, powder that should not have cost more than $26.25 a hundredweight, including shipping costs, was sold to the Ioways

McLeod found that Hughes would not bend the rules to accommodate the trade and, according to the latter, "has sought to discredit him." Hughes had directed the Indians not to buy any goods from traders in anticipation of annuity payments, which had added to McLeod's wrath. When the American Fur Company exerted pressure, Hughes in disgust talked of resigning but did not wish to do so without clearing his name. He requested an investigation of the company and of himself by the secretary of war.[105]

In another instance, Bushnell, a trader for the Missouri Sacs and Foxes, met with those tribes the next month at the Ioway subagency at a council called by their chiefs. Present were Hughes, the chiefs, Bushnell, and two interpreters, Frank Labussux and Nathan Smith. During the council, Matosee, a chief, pointed at Bushnell and said,

"There is the man that makes us pay ten dollars for one blanket, and gives us nothing but these poor things for our skins. Why, My Father, do you allow this? You can see it for yourself. There is the man. He cannot deny my words. They rob us and steal from us and keep us poor."[106] Mr. Bushnell retorted it was not his fault. Prices were high. When credit was given, half of them did not pay, and he did not force them to take goods. One countered, "If you would give us $1.00 for our deer skins, we could pay, but you do not. You take them and pay what you please." Others gave examples of enormous price gouging and asked Hughes to write to their Great Father to take pity on them. Hughes responded that he had no power to interfere, that it was the responsibility of Congress to change the laws. The feud between the American Fur Company and Hughes enlarged during the winter and spring of 1831. McLeod accused Hughes of permitting Campbell to trade on the Grand River, away from the authorized trading house, and said, "he took five rats for a dollar in trade and four on credit." As a counter remark, an employee of Campbell, Aristippis Brown, said that he had never seen Campbell carry any goods when he visited the Indians. On March 4, W. R. Powe wrote to Hughes to deny that he ever told McLeod anything about Campbell, but he said "that he has seen McLeod and Bushnell packing up goods and starting off to the Indian country, and has heard them slander Hughes to the Indians." In a conciliatory letter to Hughes, McLeod confessed that he did not have all his facts straight in his earlier accusation. In spite of the apology, Hughes asked for his removal on the basis that he and others were encouraging the Indians not to treat with the government for sale of their lands.[107] To add to the impact of his request, he sent a copy of the American Fur Company's accounts of goods sold on credit to the Ioways "to the total of $950.00 for which is demanded payment at the time of annuity. The amount charged the Ioways is without parallel. Just examine the account and see the charges. I have made a calculation that in this account there is a clear profit of at least $650.00 and in addition to this they make as much or more profit in skins they make on the sale of goods."[108]

In June, Clark received a letter from John Ruland indicating the increasing problems with the traders' purveying spirits to the Indians. "Almost every Agent has complained of the American Fur Company traders on account of the distribution of whiskey by them among the Indians." By regulation boatmen were entitled to a certain amount, but they consumed very little of the whiskey allotted them. Most of it was sold to the Indians. In speaking of Hughes, Ruland said, "If the Ioway subagent could have entered into the views of those traders in the vicinity of his post, and winked at their violations, we would not have heard criticism of him."[109]

At the close of this turbulent year of agent and trader relations, Hughes informed Clark of their latest machination. The traders had obtained county licenses in the adjoining settlements, "where the Indians are enticed to come and buy whiskey. The country is in an uproar. Indians are drunk everywhere." In some cases they traded their guns and ammunition and clothing for whiskey.[110] John Dougherty saw two other difficulties that resulted from trader influence on the Indians. In November, 1831, he observed that Indians were urged to hunt game where it could be found. Increasing warfare between tribes could be partly attributed to their discovery of other nations hunting in their territories. Also, the constant search for game to pay their mounting debts discouraged them from turning to agriculture, which would be necessary when the game was depleted. He suggested that the government-controlled factory system be reintroduced to supply goods at cost "in exchange for agricultural products the Indian could grow."[111]

After years of frustration and suggestions from the agents, the Indian commissioner, the superintendents, and others concerned about the course of Indian affairs, a wholesale restructuring of the law, concerning not only Indian trade but also the whole range of governmental relations, was made in 1834. A board of Indian commissioners had been appointed by Congress in 1832 to describe Indian conditions and to make suggestions for improvement. Incorporating the suggestions of all parties, the House introduced new legislation in May, 1834, which resulted in the final passage of the Intercourse Act of June 30, 1834. Provisions applicable to the Ioway-trader-agent relationship were: (1) The licensing of traders became the responsibility of superintendents and agents, and licenses could be revoked for improper conduct; (2) fines would be imposed on nonlicensed individuals; (3) purchase of guns, traps, other hunting equipment, tools, cooking utensils, and clothing from Indians was prohibited; (4) no white men could hunt or trap on Indian land except for subsistence (this was to halt peltry hunting by many traders' employees); (5) military forces would be authorized to remove illegal settlers, apprehend criminals, confiscate and destroy all distilleries (Indian and white), apprehend violators of the Intercourse Act, and terminate hostilities among Indian nations by direct intervention. Many other areas of Indian affairs were covered, including new regulations for the Office of Indian Affairs and its personnel. The powers of the agents were extended, particularly in trader licensing. Improved hiring procedures were outlined for blacksmiths, farmers, interpreters, and mechanics. Annuities were to be paid to chiefs or their representatives and not to any nontribal person. Agents were to purchase all goods and supplies by sealed bids if possible, and no agency employee could participate in Indian trade.

Included in suggestions for the reform of Indian affairs was the establishment of a western territory for placement of eastern emigrant tribes, but the legislation was not passed. Such a territory was thought necessary for Indian protection from the influences and intrusions of the white population. F. P. Prucha comments, "without the organization of the western territory for the Indians there was little hope that the pledge given to the Indians upon removal that they would be protected in the permanent enjoyment of the western lands could be fulfilled or that the new Intercourse Act would enjoy much better enforcement than its predecessors."[112] As a result of the new law, Hughes licensed John Owens to trade among the Ioways in December, 1834. But the American Fur Company continued to watch Hughes closely, ready to report any suspected misdeed. Pierre Chouteau, representing the company, wrote William Clark in 1835 that Joseph Roubidoux had complained that Jeffry Deroin, Hughes's interpreter, was trading throughout Ioway country, and not at a licensed trading house. The following year, Roubidoux and John B. Roy replaced John Owens as Ioway traders at the Black Snake Hills post.

Hughes finally lost his battle in January, 1838, and was removed from his position. Various reasons were given or assumed. One was that Pilcher, now superintendent of Indian affairs at St. Louis, did not personally like him; another was that he had obstructed the St. Louis Peace Treaty of 1837, and that certain irregularities had been found in his records, that is, the listing of more persons on his roster than actually were there.[113] Hughes denied all charges to the end. The Great Nemaha Agency was without an agent until June 5, 1840.

Warfare in the 1830's: A Cultural Imperative

With the decrease in game and the increased tribal demand for trade items, competition for the declining animal supply acerbated inter-tribal antagonisms. If there had been hazy boundaries, or zones of mutual use in the hunting territories, these were modified even further as the Indians scrounged for hunting territory and the government insisted on boundary maintenance. To protect the remaining fur-bearing areas, intensive efforts were made to drive out intruders. Small tribes joined forces to contest the intrusion of more powerful neighbors. With killing came the necessity for revenge for honor. Whenever possible, either by counsel or threat, the United States agents and military personnel endeavored to prevent, control, or punish those who indulged in warfare. Indian hostilities often served as reason to increase the numbers of forts and military personnel across Indian country.

Restrictions imposed by the government and the consequent loss of Indian tribal autonomy struck at the core of the Indian male-dominated society. Males had originally spent much time in hunting for food and peltries. Antagonism and frustration grew, when game scarcity and land cessions decreased their areas of mobility. Government civilization programs tried to turn them to agricultural pursuits, seeking to place them placidly behind plows to grow rather than catch their food — although agriculture traditionally was women's work. As hostility increased, warfare served as an outlet for energies

199

and frustrations, and as a validation of manhood in some tribes. Traditionally this culturally controlled activity called for ritual preparation before the war party rode out from the village and, it was hoped, returned triumphantly to be lauded by the warriors' kin groups. When this too became impossible, Ioway manhood suffered and deteriorated tragically.

In 1831 the Ioways along the Boyer and Nishnabotna rivers adjacent to the Missouri fell victim to the Omahas, who had murdered the son of Crane, an Ioway chief, and had captured a woman and three horses. The Ioways were especially aroused, since they had recently sent, in a gesture of friendship, a message to the Omahas informing them that a Sac war party was on its way to their village. For the murder of Crane's son, the Omahas cited the Ioway murder of an Omaha, the previous winter, near Cabanne's trading post. They accused "Ioway Jim," a tribal outcast who had been forced to live among the Otos. The Omahas visited the Ioways, who told them that the accused was no longer a member of their tribe and that they were not responsible for his actions. However, they went with the Omahas to the Otoe village to ask for his surrender, which the Otos refused. Therefore, the Omaha death went unavenged until the moment of Crane's son's death. The Ioways stated that they would not seek revenge and expected the United States to obtain the murderers from the Omahas and "Ioway Jim" from the Otos and undertake the punishment of both.

Shortly after this incident, a Sioux war party stole seven Ioway horses. Big Neck, whose band had now joined the main group, formed a war party and pursued them in order to retrieve the animals. The Sioux took a stand, and during the battle Big Neck and Little Star were killed and Waucoochee wounded, "all of whom were distinguished men of the nation," Hughes reported. He added that in both incidents the Omaha and the Sioux acts were premeditated. Although the Ioways indicated that they would await redress, they were said to have made ample arrangements with the Kansas and the Sacs and the Foxes to avenge their dead, if the United States should not carry out their commitments and secure the Sioux and Omaha aggressors.

After a time, and despite the chief's promises to the agent, one hundred young men in a war party sought the Omahas who had killed the uncompromising Big Neck, a tribal hero for his bravery against the whites and against Indian enemy nations. The chiefs pursued them, and all returned without harming anyone or gaining honor. Clark then instructed Dougherty to arrest the Omahas involved in the attack.[114]

In Illinois the Sac and Fox Tribe under Black Hawk were involved in their tragic war with the United States. The Missouri Sacs and Foxes and the Ioways, living near each other on the Great Nemaha Reserve, did not seem to have any inclination to join them in their struggle. Still, as a precautionary measure, the tribes were informed that four companies of rangers would be patrolling between the

western branch of the Grand River and the Des Moines to the east
and north. The tribes were told where they might hunt "so as to
create no suspicion on themselves as taking part in the war." The
Ioways replied that their young men had already gone up the Des
Moines to hunt buffalo, and others were on the Nodaway and the
Little Platte. "If this statement be true, they will not meet our troops,"
said the Agent. But he found animosity toward him in July when he
returned from a trip. A group of Ioways and Sacs and Foxes came
to his home, ordered food, and were "insolent to my wife." He took
four Sacs and Foxes and two Ioway chiefs and placed them under
guard as a guarantee of good behavior by the others. He noticed that
all the young men were absent at a council he called, and he hard
that the Sacs and the Foxes of the Mississippi were in the area. He
reported fearfully that, "These tribes are heart and soul in with the
enemy and nothing but their annuities prevents them from scalping
people." Hughes was angered by his Indians. In the spring they had
told him that they knew nothing of Black Hawk's contemplated
aggressions. Now they told him in the council that they had known it
all the time. He suspected an uprising at any moment after that. In
subsequent correspondence Clark calmed, then reprimanded, him for
his panic, reactions that had included taking twenty-two hostages to
Fort Leavenworth.

In 1833, the Ioways had not received notification of proper redress
for the Omaha attack two years before and they sent out a war party
of twelve, who returned triumphantly with six Omaha scalps and
two prisoners, a woman and a child. For this act, Major Bennett Riley
came and marched eight Ioways to Fort Leavenworth. It was said that
Big Elk, the Omaha chief, had come to the Ioway village to make
peace with them in February and had spent several days there on
friendly terms.

The Kickapoos had recently been moved west of the Missouri,
north of Fort Leavenworth. Reports of altercations between them
and the Ioways and the Sacs and the Foxes were received in 1834.[115]
The Ioway and Omaha situation had not improved by 1835, and they
were summoned to a council at the Bellevue Agency. Here Dougherty
and Hughes presided over a peace council where differences were
again discussed and the Great Father's orders for peaceful coexistence expounded. The chiefs' marks were affixed to a paper that
stated that "all outrages should be forgiven and forgotten, and peace
shall be firmly established between our respective tribes and forever
maintained amongst us."[116] "Forever" lasted until June, 1837, when
a secret war party took an Omaha scalp "without provocation." "The
deed is disapproved by the chiefs, but Major Dougherty and I can
settle it," Hughes declared.

Warfare among all tribes continued in 1837 and 1838, and peace
councils were held at different agencies and in Washington.[117] To
ameliorate a Sac and Sioux dispute of long standing, it was again
suggested that the Winnebagos be removed from their Wisconsin

homes and placed in the "neutral strip" between the two tribes. They flatly refused the offer as suicidal. The hostile relationship between the Ioways and the Pawnees received government notice in 1839, when Dougherty held a council at Bellevue for the Ioways to pay the Pawnees "to cover their dead." An Ioway was said to have waylaid a Pawnee and taken his scalp. "For the body the Pawnee were paid $200.00 in goods, and the Ioway obtained the title of a distinguished warrior among his nation."[118]

A Society Faltering

During these two decades of treaty making, certain behavioral patterns indicated that disruptive forces were present within the social organization of the Ioway. Antisocial acts are present in all societies, and the types of pressure exerted on the Ioway culture dictated that certain strains would manifest themselves in overt disruptive acts within the tribe and with outsiders. Reports included murders and other crimes within the tribe, depredations on the white community, increased warfare, increase use of alcoholic beverages, sexual relations by purchase with non-Indians, increased hunger and starvation periods, and continued tribal fractionation into separate dwelling groups. Causes for separation were based partly on leadership disagreements over tribal policy toward the United States, beginning as early as 1809 when Hart Heart accepted a medal and was appointed or recognized as chief by the President.* Differences surfaced and separated the tribe during the War of 1812 and after the signing of the 1824 treaty, when Big Neck's band lived apart on the Grand River. Conflict continued when some Ioways refused to move west of the Missouri River after the establishment of the Great Nemaha Reserve.

The problem of whiskey consumption continued to increase. Clark stated in December, 1831, that the only way to control its abuse was to prohibit it altogether. Whether or not this was true, he said, "It is known that not an Indian could be found among a thousand who would not after a first drink sell his horse, his gun, and his last blanket for another drink. . . ."[119] In 1833, Agent Dougherty sought the Ioway men accused of the murder of the six Omahas. This incident was recalled by Maximillian of Weid on his journey up the Missouri:

Some of the Engages came on board and reported that the Joway

---

* This practice ultimately brought much distress and conflict to Indian nations and tribes, as it created two groups of leaders, one recognized by the United States government and the other chosen in the traditional way by the people. The former were sometimes bribed and manipulated to suit the government's purposes.

Indians whose village was about five or six miles distant had made an
incursion into the neighboring territory of the Omahas and killed six of
these Indians and brought a woman and child as prisoners whom they
offered for sale. Major Dougherty to whom the agency the Joways
belonged immediately landed to rescue the prisoners, accompanied by
Major Bean and Mr. Bodmer. But they returned at eleven o'clock at night
without having accomplished their object because the Joways during
his reproaches had completely intoxicated both themselves and their
prisoners. The Joways had exchanged their blankets and other effects
for brandy. . . . White settlers have already established themselves fifteen
or sixteen miles within the Indian territory who make whiskey and sell
it excessively cheap to the Indians by which these people are ruined.[120]

Agent Hughes charged that spirits were manufactured at one
American Fur Company post and constituted over one-fourth of the
total consideration given to the Indian in exchange for furs. He ended
by saying that, "When a wagon of whisky comes into the country,
the agent cannot seize it, the Indians won't, and by the time the army
troops can be summoned from Ft. Leavenworth, it is all disposed
of to the Indian, and the offenders gone."

Another facet of social disorganization in this decade came to
light with Hughes's report that certain Ioways would consent to the
purchase of their daughters by traders. They were then

made strumpets for a few weeks or months, and after being thus
debauched and abandoned by their supposed husbands as miserable
homeless wanderers amongst their tribes with an infant on their back,
despised by the young men of their nations, forever wretched and ruined.
One of the young squaws, a leader in the art of spinning was purchased
by Mr. Roubideau, a man of family in St. Louis, and after some months,
she was abandoned and died in childbed. It is a fact that the Indians
do entertain some prejudice against the whites, and one of the chief
reasons is the above. [121]

What may have been an Ioway retaliatory response was revealed in
a letter from C. B. Creekmore to Agent Hughes in 1832: "I have had
two horses stolen by the Ioways. The Indians have often come to my
house, and other of my neighbors and insulted our wives and families,
in proposing to have carnal communications with them, they offered
to give my wife a gun, and they attempted to commit a rape on the
wife of one of my neighbors. They offer to buy our young women
from our people."[122]

As 1837 approached, and the time for the removal of the Ioways
from the eastern to the western side of the Missouri, the tribe became
increasingly demoralized. The whites kept the Ioways continually
drunk and "deprived them of their Horses, guns, blankets, etc.,
etc.," like so many vultures. The Ioway villages "present each day a
scene of drunkenness and riot, with noses, lips and faces cut."[123]

When the Ioways had moved to the other side of the Missouri,

The Ioway
Indians

the situation became desperate. The agent reported that the Ioways "are in a state of actual starvation. No annuities have arrived, nor anything else. What is to be done? Humanity as well as a reasonable compliance with the treaty demands it."[124] Reverend Irvin wrote in his diary that, soon after the new land was settled, the houses that were built for the chiefs were dismantled, the doors, windows, floors, and fence rails were taken, and "All that could be were sold for whiskey and trinkets." The cattle and hogs delivered to them to raise were devoured. Under the influence of whiskey a brother and father would fall at each other's hands. In September, 1838, Father de Smet at Bellevue observed that, "Colonel Kearny came to Bellevue with two hundred Dragoons.

> They took four prisoners among the most distinquished Ioway for depredations on their white neighbors. Preparations were made to whip them. The colonel reluctantly pardoned them at the intervention of Mr. Hamilton the missionary."[125]

At the end of the decade Major Bean, their former agent, wrote of them:

> The Ioways and Sacs are as different a people as you could possibly imagine from what they were when I was their subagent in 1827 and 28. In place of the mild, friendly well disposed people then, I find a distrustful, illnatured, fierce and insolent people.[126]

8. The Entreaty Period

As for the future, he had hoped somehow to be able to combine the life he had known since childhood, with the new outlook he was acquiring as a student. But with every year this ideal faded, for his learning estranged him irrevocably from his past, from the villagers, and from his family.

Alexander Solzhenitsyn, *August, 1914*

THE CRACK IN THE IOWAY cultural armor had widened. After 1833 White Cloud the Elder would not participate in warparties or scalp dances, saying that he had signed treaties of peace and would not break his word.[1] No Heart, his brother, also turned his face from many of the old ways (see Figure 13). Both men had been exposed to or influenced by the white men's schooling and decided to accept the invitation to send some of their nation's children to the Choctaw Academy at Blue Springs, Kentucky.[2] White Cloud and others accompanied the children on the long journey, recalling a similar time in 1824 when tribal sons had attended St. Regis. After he escorted the children, White Cloud was presented a medal and a certificate:

> Choctaw Acady. 9th Aug. 1831
> To all good people of the United States as well as to all red skins who may see this. Be it remembered that on this day the bearer White Cloud, 2nd Chief of the Ioways has given evidence to the Americans that he has listened to their advice and council and has brought to this Academy some children from that tribe to be taught and instructed in the arts of civilized life — that he and his friends who accompany him are the first from his region of country who have appeared here [sic] and for which he is entitled to the kind consideration of all white and red men and in token thereof has recd. a medal from us. [3]

Figure 13. Notchininga, or No Heart (1797-1862): *left,* the portrait painted by Charles Bird King when Notchininga was in Washington in 1837; *right,* in later life. Notchininga served as head chief of the Ioways after the death of White Cloud in December, 1851. Courtesy of National Anthropology Archives, Smithsonian Institution.

Other changes in Ioway culture were also apparent. John Dougherty observed in the spring of 1838 that the tribe was living less in "bands or squads" and that individual plots were broken rather than a large common body of ground.[4] But only the elite few among the ruling class may have leaned toward the new ways. The first village at the Great Nemaha Reserve was constructed of wooden poles and bark in the old manner. Rev. E. McKinney in 1846 observed:

> In the summer the houses are of bark. They are built for the accomoda-tion of several families and are about 30 by 20 feet long, seven feet high at the eaves, and 15 feet at the "comb" of the roof. The sides and the ends are generally composed of split slabs stood on end or slightly driven in the ground. The roof was made of pieces of bark laid on pole frame and secured by a sort of crosswork of poles tied together with bark strips. The door is either a mat of rushes hung up against the opening in each end, or a bark shield a little larger than the entrances.

There was no chimney or fireplace; smoke escaped through an open-ing in the roof. Storage and sleeping platforms were built around the interior walls.[5]

In October, 1841, the chiefs in council decided that the village was in an unhealthy location and should be relocated. When a suitable site was found, work began on new bark houses, which were com-pleted by March, 1842. That autumn, Subagent W. Richardson was instructed to take a census with the assistance of the chiefs. He did so "with each family having been examined separately with particular care." The total tribal membership was 472 with 111 "heads of families." Family size varied from 1 to 10 persons:

Persons in Family	Number of Families
1*	1
2	11
3	33
4	23
5	26
6	6
7	3
8	3
9	2
10	3

*U-ki-ma, a male over 40 years.[6]

Richardson did not indicate the residence patterns of these families, and so it is impossible to ascertain their interrelatedness. Warfare and disease had decreased the population so that there may have been a disruption of the older kinship dwelling pattern and, as a result, a coalescence of numerous smaller units under one roof or in nearby dwellings.

Ioway and white intermarriage and sexual liaisons had occurred for many decades, and the 1842 census included a Widow Dorion and a Rubideaux family (both were names of Ioway traders). Such unions were sometimes consumated for the benefit of the woman's family in hopes that some might benefit from the affluence and influence of the white man. Into such a situation young Rudolph Frederick Kurz, a Swiss artist, willingly and romantically wandered in 1849.[7] Like other Europeans, he came to study and paint the Indians of the West. When he first met the Ioways near St. Joseph, he was entranced by their physical beauty and friendly manners. He extolled them by saying "Forms more beautiful than those I found among the Ioway Indians I cannot imagine, although I have been accustomed during my studies from life for many years to all that is finest in the human form." His obvious interest and approval, plus his bachelor status, made him the recipient of two offers of marriage from the Ioways. The first on New Year's morning, 1849, came from a woman who brought him a quiver of arrows for his collection. At the time of the sale she advised him "partly in words and partly in signs" that she had "a young and beautiful daughter that she wished me to marry," and he was invited to the family tipi that night.[8] "Being fond of these people and having given no occasion for mistrust or quarreling, I did not once consider the danger of rambling about the forest at night." On arriving at the dwelling he found the entire family inside around the fire. The woman indicated an attractive but "exceedingly young girl of about 13 or 14" wrapped in a shabby blanket, whom she said was to be his wife. The youngster began to cry, and Kurz tried to comfort her with candy and other trifles. The woman then sent for a young man who had graduated from the Choctaw Academy and who spoke good English. He explained the marriage transaction. The mother was to receive a pony and a new blanket; the bride, a complete set of new clothes, good food, and no beatings; and the remaining relatives, a sack of meal weighing seventy pounds. Kurz, dumbfounded by his rapid progress to marital status, sat without a word. The woman took his silence for assent, and, thus encouraged, added that she would like to have some sugar and coffee added to the bargain. The young girl, uneasy about the termination of her unmarried state, fled from the tipi and could not be found. Relieved, Kurz started home but, fearing that he would become lost in the darkness, returned to the tipi, where "Anene's brother, Kennachuck (all members of the same band or lodge call one another brother and sister, and father and mother, whether that relationship exists or not), prepared a place for me to sleep and gave me a pillow." He later made known that he did not wish to complete the arranged marriage. He was told that such marriages were customary with or without the girl's consent. "One or two horses is the price that makes a binding contract. When horses are not included, the marriage had no binding force either for the wife or her parents." If the girl runs off, the original or equally valuable horses must be returned.

Kurz's next and final betrothal was to Witthae, the daughter of a chief. Her father, Kirutsche (which is similar to Kiratci, a hereditary name in the Eagle and Thunder clan) had accompanied Catlin to Europe in 1844. Whether Kirutsche was his true name or his European name is unknown.

During one visit Kurz was given the small portrait of King Louis Phillipe that had been presented to Kirutsche in France. For a year the artist had been encouraged to sit beside the daughter in public gatherings. Although Witthae gave no response to his attentions, her parents encouraged him to continue his suit. In January, 1850, the chief visited Kurz to discuss marriage between his daughter and the artist. In the proposed marriage contract the chief promised that he would see that Kurz received two thousand acres of land. He said that the land would be "secured" to Kurz by the chiefs. The chief himself wanted to be employed and not waste time. He confided that working by himself was not feasible if he wished to gain anything from it. His relatives would expect him to share with them, and "he could not possess anything for himself alone, while the others were hungry." To avoid this situation the father suggested a partnership in the purchase of a stonecutter's business, which they would work themselves. He was emphatic in his proposal; Kurz recorded, "I was never to begin giving any of our possessions to the others, because then they would expect us to share with them without doing anything in return." They decided that they would plant no corn that they would have to share with needy relatives. The stone could not be taken from them, and "besides the stone-cutters place was on the Missouri, a long distance from their village." Kurz agreed to the proposition, saying, "He who ventures nothing, gains nothing." "Furthermore," he said, "my parents-in-law pleased me quite well; they were industrious, good tempered and honest":[9]

So, when Witthae came with her mother on January 10, I received her as my wife. Her mother served hot coffee, fried meat, and bread. White Cloud, chief of the Iowa, came as guest to witness our union. Next day I purchased her outfit that she might clothe herself in new garments throughout. I bought the usual short shirt or blouse of red calico, a woolen underskirt and pantalettes, a red blanket, a choice of large pearl beads for necklaces, and many colored bands for her hair and for her costume. Later I bought wool for knitting and smaller beads for girdle and garters. Though Witthae herself would rather have adopted the European mode, I preferred that she dress as an Indian girl. I liked the Indian style of dress both for its charm and its utility.

Everything went well until the mild winter weather made further slaughtering of hogs inadvisable; then, since the Iowa could no longer profit by the bits of meat trimmed from the slaughtered swine, one family after another went away — Kirutsche and Wuotschime among them. Floating ice made their passage across the river very dangerous.

Soon Witthae began to feel like a captive bird. She had no one but me to entertain her. All my efforts to cheer her up proved unavailing. She became melancholy, obviously homesick. She gazed continually with tear-dimmed eyes into the distance beyond the river. Wrapped in her blanket she sat, dreaming of her earlier freedom; paying no attention to my assurances that I would take her over to her people as soon as the weather permitted.

Luckily, her mother's sister came one evening, bringing her daughters with her. Witthae was once more cheerful. In the hope of relieving my wife from further attacks of homesickness I invited her aunt to remain with us a while and help us to spend the time until we should settle down in a place nearer Witthae's people. It was arranged, moreover, that Kirutsche was to come to us upon his return from a visit to some friends in the Fox Indian tribe and assist us, when we transferred our residence to the land promised.

Then, imagine my astonishment, some mornings later, when I found that my bird had flown. Witthae had gone, taking her relatives and her belongings with her. I was in the front room shaving, when, all at once, it occurred to me that there was an unwonted stillness in our living room. After I had finished I went in there. I could hardly believe my eyes, in spite of undoubted proof to the contrary. There was no possibility of doubt: their goods and chattels had been taken along with them. I pondered: should I hasten after her, stop her, plead with her to be gracious and come back to me? Never! I loved her; I had taken her in sincerity with good intention; I had treated her well; I hoped, therefore, that she would come back. But at evening she had not returned. I thought it beneath my dignity to go after her.

Two weeks later my mother-in-law came, but did not bring her daughter. She said Kirutsche would bring her back.

"If she does not wish to come of her own accord, she may remain at home," I told her mother. Wuotschime was very much grieved. I held to my resolve. That was the end of my romantic dream of love and marriage with an Indian. [10]

Before the intrusion of white individuals, such as Kurz, into the Ioway kinship system and marital agreements, a strict class system dictated that individuals marry within their classes. Chiefs' children married each other, and Noble Braves' offspring married, except in rare cases when they could marry in the class above if their fathers were distinguished Warriors. Commoners were confined to marriage within their own class. [11]

In the older marriage system, Witthae would have been taken by her mother's brother to their lodges. There the women of the family would have dressed her in a splendid costume and sent her back to her father's lodge with a gift of as many as twenty horses from her suitor's uncles. With the arrival of the horses, her father would say to the eldest son, "Let your sister present these horses to her brothers and brothers-in-law. If any remain, distribute them among the chiefs and braves."

After that, the girl's father gave a feast, a large portion of which was said to have been contributed by the groom's family. They also brought gifts of blankets, clothing, and other valued articles. During the day the girl's uncles lectured her on her marital duties and cautioned her not to speak to her father-in-law. This and the similar stipulation that the young man limit his communication with his mother-in-law was part of an affinal avoidance pattern.*

After the feast the couple spent several days with her parents. They then returned to the groom's father with gifts of horses and other things from the bride's parents. Through the feast, the ceremony, and the exchange of gifts the marriage contract was completed, and the couple assumed the roles of hunter, warrior, gardener, hide and food preparer, artificer, and eventually parents.

The marriage ceremony among Braves was less ostentatious. The groom's parents held a feast for the bride, and then fifteen or twenty horses were distributed to the guests, who were expected, at appropriate times within the year, to return gifts of equal value. In this way wealth tended to flow and be reciprocally distributed.

Commoners, who were often as poor as chiefs were rich, could exchange only a horse or two or sometimes none. Little food or goods were available for the ceremony, and the couple began their lives together in a modest way.[12]

Kirutsche, Kurz' father-in-law, faced a dilemma, when he indicated a desire both to follow and to break with Ioway tradition. Chiefs were expected to be wealthy, but they were also expected to share their wealth. With the changes in Ioway economics that resulted mainly from the decreased hunting revenue, the chiefs were forced to seek new avenues to maintain their economic position. Kirutsche could not, as in former days, feed all the poorer tribal members or relatives who were for psychological and economic reasons unable to sustain themselves. He decided to produce wealth but to ignore kin-group demands. It is not known whether his reaction was typical, but his seeking Kurz for a son-in-law as well as a business partner indicated an attempt to adapt to changing conditions in order to maintain status.

Without the great fur wealth of former days, the institution of multiple wives no longer held the economic advantage that it once had when more hides needed processing. However, polygyny continued to exist in the 1840's. Reverend Irvin reported that White Cloud in 1841 had three wives, one of whom was half Ioway and half white. Old Plume had two wives, who grieved piteously at his death. "These old women attended him throughout his final illness. I cannot think that I have seen more tenderness exhibited in the most tender relations of civilization." On the other hand, White Cloud's half-Ioway wife did not fare as well. Although seriously ill,

---

* In the 1960's limited affinal avoidance was mentioned as proper behavior by older Ioways in Oklahoma.

she was neglected both by her husband and by the other two wives
and members of the family and was accused of feigning illness.[13]

Marriage could be dissolved by divorce. All the grounds for divorce are not known, but adultery and abandonment were given as reasons. The children of a divorced couple might live with either set of grandparents. If horses had been exchanged, the man was expected to return them to the bride's family before they would officially nullify the marriage and allow him to remarry.[14] In Kurz's case, divorce was final when his wife abandoned him. Under the traditional culture pattern her parents could have forced her to return to him, but when he rejected that offer, they accepted the situation. He then left the St. Joseph area and traveled upriver to a northern trading post. When he returned to St. Joseph, Witthae attempted a reconciliation, which he refused.

Chief Kirutsche was not alone in seeking solutions to status maintenance. Other chiefs found their traditional means of acquiring wealth reduced and sought other ways to gain it. Foremost was the continual attempts to be the recipients and distributors of the yearly tribal annuity. The 1834 Intercourse laws stipulated the chiefs' right to do this. From the viewpoint of an outsider, Reverend Irvin, they abused their responsibility:

> The chiefs go to the traders, and buy a large amount of goods, or a number of horses, or a quantity of provisions, or even whiskey, which is given to a few of their favorites called braves, and a few particular friends, while the poor and industrious get no benefit at all.

He continued that, in this manner, chiefs bought the loyalty of braves, and commoners accepted this as the way it should be. They urged the chiefs to go into debt in hopes that they might be given a gift which was theirs by rights.[15] Thus in the early Ioway reservation period, the chiefs held that, in order to maintain position, they should control most of the annuity and not divide it equally among all. Had this not been done, the visible part of their status that was symbolized in their feasts and giveaways for visiting nations, marriage and death ceremonies, war party homecomings, and sacred society events would have disappeared, and they would have found themselves in an untenable position.

Tribal government now controlled only those facets of political and social life not under United States regulation. Wealth in the form of annuity was distributed by the agent, and he could manipulate the chiefs by his method of distribution and by his threats to withhold payments. He could often control their acts as well as those of other tribal members for whom he held the chiefs responsible. Ioway agents in the past had had chiefs arrested and held hostage for acts, commited by tribesmen, that were considered violations of laws and regulations. Therefore, it behooved the chiefs to be compliant and not to allow great freedom of action among their people. What tribal powers the chiefs now exercised are unknown. They were probably the responsible decision makers in settling local disputes, delegating certain secular powers, presiding at tribal councils, initiating war parties, maintaining certain sacred ceremonial events, determining hunt times and locations, and leading visits to and receiving visits from other tribes (the last two events would be subject to agent approval in coming years), and rejecting and accepting new technological ideas.

Councils with agents in this decade indicate that conflict had increased and that communication had become difficult. Many interpreters, for example, Reverend Irvin, a novice speaker of the language, were unable to give the fullest meaning to either side. The agents' reports were made with their positions and well-being in mind, and their writings of what was said by each party and what was decided are the only evidence in existence. The repeated Indian requests to go to Washington to discuss their problems firsthand reflected this filtering of their opinions and demands.

In September, 1841, an Ioway council discussed the annuity distribution and Ioway debts to traders. No Heart spoke first. He began in a deferential manner by saying, "We are not now as we once were. Once we were so poor and ignorant that we made fire by rubbing sticks together, but we have improved." He supposedly went on to state his complaints that the whites were stealing from the Ioways, and his wish that the young men of the tribe would do better this year than they did the last and not get into trouble. The Ioways wished to abide by the laws and to pay all of their lawful debts.[16]

Turning to the subject of the pending annuity, Wa-sha-mon-ie, a brave, said, "We would like to have a small sum of money put aside that some few individuals might get $10.00 a piece." Five of the other braves present also took this position, but not in a challenging manner, for the chiefs were present, and they would not consent to this innovative suggestion. There is no comment on their request by the chiefs.*

Wachamonya, a chief, rose and changed the subject. He charged that traders were overcharging the nation. Fervently he said, "If the traders do not like what I say and will not sell us goods cheap, I am going to tell them to take their goods and go away. We like to talk on this subject because the traders are present and can hear what we say. . . ."

No Heart now began a serious discussion on another matter, a default in payment from a previous treaty, in which the tribe was to receive $2,500 but had received only $1,500. The remaining $1,000 was to have come in the form of twenty bolts of strouding put in the

---

* Brave Wa-sha-mon-ie or Chief Wachamonya may have been the Wash-ka-mon-ya or "Jim" of the European journey of 1844-1845.

214

care of trader Sarpy to forward to the nation. He had never done this
and was requested to fulfill the agreement.

Earlier in the council the agent spoke sternly to the assemblage on their consumption of whiskey. He chided them and pleaded with them to stop using it. He then said that if he heard of one drop of whiskey being on the reserves, "I will suspend payment for six months. I am tired of this drinking. My patience is thin. You all know better. I do beg you to be sober at least for a few months that you may see how much better you will be. . . ." As usual there was no immediate response, but later a brave attached to his remarks the sentence, "You have asked us to be sober five to six months, and I hope we will obey you."

During the interval in which the trader situation was discussed, the chiefs thought about their comments on the braves' request for individual payments. Finally, one chief, the Pope, spoke of his right to control a portion of the annuity. Gradually he became angry, until Reverend Irvin cautioned him to restrain himself. He became more excited and said that he was the greatest man in the nation and what he said must be done. Old Pumpkin then grew angry and struck himself on the breast, saying that *he* was the father of the nation and the greatest man. The discussion grew more heated, but with their frustration vented and their objections given, the disputants resumed composure.

In the August 15, 1843, council the chiefs continued their requests for the monies due them from past treaties. When this money was granted, it was to be used for the establishment of the manual-labor boarding school, the dream of Hamilton and Irvin,[17] and for various other civilizing purposes. The September council meeting discussed the distribution of the yearly annuity. The previous year it had been distributed to the individual families, and now the chiefs were determined to object strenuously to this. The matter came up immediately. Walking Rain said, "I have been asked by the chiefs to speak. When you spoke of this matter of paying money to heads of families, we thought it was for one year. We have talked this over and think our plan best. We have some serious objections to this manner of paying annuities. Many times we are compelled to make national debts and give presents to our friends. Our chiefs would not be able to give credit or give presents."

No Heart, second in authority, told the agent that they had agreed not to sign the paper accepting the annuity on the former basis, that not only the chiefs but the nation were opposed to it. Agent Richardson accused them of deceiving him, saying that they did not understand what the document meant, that there was to be individual distribution of annuity. He said: "You know my opinion of the manner in which you squander your annuity. If you must have plain talk. The chiefs and a few braves spend the whole of it. The poor, the weak, and the best behaved men and squaws get little or nothing.

I come to speak of a threat that one of your chiefs made to me. There he is. I want all of you to hear me. I understand that he, White Cloud, said that if I attempted to pay the money to heads of families, that he would take the money from me to pay the debts. . . ." He added that White Cloud should know that he did what is best and that he did not want to harm one of his sons, but if it were necessary he would do so. He thanked the others for the respectful attitude that they had had toward him. White Cloud apologized for his threat, saying that he had been drinking when he made it. "I hope you will forget all about it, and not call me a squaw as you have done." He added that he had never been angry with the agent.[18]

A tentative compromise for the yearly annuity was attempted. The agent would pay the total annuity to the chiefs that year if they would sign a paper that said that the next year's annuity would be distributed among the people. They did not sign it at that time, and it is not evident if they ever did consent. Documents do not indicate how the annuity was paid that year, and there is no further council discussion of it.

In the spring of 1844 Reverend Irvin, the paid interpreter as well as missionary, resigned the former position to protest the unfair treatment that the Ioways had received in the payment of $1,500, a large portion of their annuity, to a white claimant. According to Irvin, who had been with the nation at the time of the so-called incident of 1838, the Ioways had not been at fault, the man was now swindling them, and the government was unjust in allowing this claim to be paid.

The policy of allowing claim payment to settlers and others had been established by the Intercourse Act of 1834, and it had become a profitable business. Claims were submitted for property stolen or damaged by Indians. Indians would deny, and whites would "prove" by deposition and affidavit. In many cases the small annuity shrank considerably in payment of these obligations. Few individuals could or would vouchsafe for Indian veracity in answering the accusers. Increasingly, the annuity became a golden harvest to be gathered into the pockets of unscrupulous traders and claimants seeking damage payments.

Agents continued to come and go. William P. Richardson was removed in July, 1845, and was replaced by Armstrong McClintock. In June, 1846, he was replaced by William E. Rucker, whose term lasted until March 1, 1848 when Alfred J. Vaughn became agent. In December, 1849, William Richardson again became agent and served until 1861.

In 1845, in the period between Richardson and McClintock, Reverend Irvin reported that the long-requested boarding school was being built on the reservation. An especially fine building, it stands today near Highland, Kansas. It was 106 feet long, 37 feet wide, and three stories high (see Figure 14). The first story was of dressed

Figure 14.   The Ioway and Sac and Fox Mission School as it stands today near Highland, Kansas. Here the Reverend Samuel Irvin and the Reverend William Hamilton taught Ioway, Sac, and Fox and other Indian children. Courtesy of Kansas State Historical Society.

limestone, the upper stories of brick. Smooth wide boards made the floors, and handsome doors, window sashes, and glass panes were brought from Pittsburgh. Bedding, clothing, and kitchen furniture were on hand, and only a few additional funds were required to complete and open the school. The missionary was well pleased, but he was concerned about the behavior of the Ioways since Richardson's departure. "His efficient and judicious course had thrown around them a strong restraint, but since his removal they feel completely unbridled and are bold to exercise their freedoms. It is indeed a thousand pities that so many interests vital to peace and prosperity of these nations should be sacrificed to party spirit," he said as he commented on the political aspects of agent appointment and removal.[19]

Reverend Irvin was an assiduous teacher. Reverend Hamilton and he had compiled and printed on a small press brought from the East various books and booklets in the Ioway language. A grammar used in reading classes for young Indians had both Ioway and English words and sentences that were intended to convey ideas and values of white society. Each sentence also contained a message that aimed to change the Indian value system:

> *Oxen* are good to work. They work on wagons. They pull the plow and assist very much to farm. Some oxen are very patient and good. Some are like men, they break into fields and steal corn.
>
> *Hogs* are useful animals. White people raise a great many hogs. People who raise hogs have plenty of meat. Indians who hunt for their meat often times have none. They ought to quit hunting and go to work and raise hogs. They would not always be hungry.
>
> *Dogs* guard our houses at night. They chase hogs out of the fields. They hunt deer and other animals. They can follow the track of animals. Some dogs are not worth anything. Indians eat dogs. White people do not eat them.
>
> *Horses.* Here are two horses. Indians are very fond of horses, but they do not treat them well. They ride them very fast. And in winter, because they do not give them much to eat, they get very poor, and many of them die. There are a great many horses running wild on the prairies. [20]

During the first half of the decade the Ioway chiefs and leaders had attempted to retain their prerogatives for a price by accepting farmers, smiths, schools, debt settlements, and other government-directed policies. Signs of attrition and political breakdown were apparent outbursts of the old chiefs in the councils, in White Cloud's threat against the agent, the continuing problems with alcohol, the chiefs' posture of entreaty before the agent, and their weakening struggle to maintain control of the annuity. However, the face-to-face meetings with the agent, the swallowing of pride, and the displays of humility were not the entire life of the chiefs. These occasional councils, unpleasant as they were, were submerged in day-to-day activities among their people. Irvin's and Hamilton's journals tell of many events that indicated Ioway attempts to preserve their culture in spite of the annoyance of reservation restrictions.

One Tuesday morning in April, 1841, Irvin did not go to the village to teach in one of the abandoned bark houses that he used for classes. He had heard that the village was engaged in a Buffalo Dance, and he knew that the children would be involved and could not be cajoled to attend school. On this same day, a white man came across the river to borrow a horse, so that he could visit the Kickapoos. He brought with him a gallon of whiskey and a deer skin to

pay for the horse. After he had departed, the chief became suspicious
and sent the Waiakida or Indian soldiers to arrest and return him.
They caught him, captured and tied him, and took him to the chief,
who kept him until the agent came and declared that he was a
fugitive from justice, a counterfeiter.[21]

As in all societies, the Ioway had laws protecting the nation or its
members from the transgressions of others within it. Each chief was
entitled to select two "honored braves," outstanding warriors who
had participated in rituals such as name changing and tattooing.
These men, known as *Waiakida,* served as guardians of public order
and well-being. They obeyed the orders of the chiefs with ultimate
responsibility to the Principal Chief. Their principal responsibilities
among others were: (1) to prevent village quarrels by either persuasion or physical restraint; (2) to patrol or scout the village periphery to prevent attack; (3) to prevent a premature war-party charge
against the enemy; (4) to control the line of hunters on the bison
hunt; (5) to aid in assigning camp areas during tribal movements;
(6) to keep the village quiet during the great ceremonies; and (7) to
inflict punishment when decreed by council, usually by public
flogging.[22]

For carrying out the above responsibilities, they enjoyed the following privileges: (1) to live in the chief's dwelling at certain times;
(2) to have an honored place at all ceremonies and other events;
(3) to be exempt from vengeance for acts performed in the name of
law and tribal justice; (4) to wear the sacred feather bustle; (5) to
be privileged to receive the Pipe Dance;* (6) to have multiple wives
and to have their daughters tattooed; (7) to attain membership in
the *Kiaugera wace,* or Braves Society, which entertained visiting
tribes; (8) to marry a chief's daughter if invited by her family;
(9) to bestow the sacred eagle feather on some other honored brave
and to give a horse or equally valuable gift.[23]

On the evening of February 17, 1841, Irvin wrote that a party of
Waiakida rode by on their way to the village. They were "drest and
painted in good stile." They had been given the responsibility to
chastise the first person who became drunk, and recently one or
two of the villagers had been flogged. In a previous council meeting
the agent had threatened to stop the payment of annuity if he saw
anyone drunk. Thereafter, according to Irvin's diary, the chiefs
"made a law some time ago that the first one who would get drunk

---

* The Pipe Dance in this instance may refer to the ceremony of adoption by which
various bands or clans within a tribe, or from other tribes, would visit one another
for the purpose of adopting a member of a prominent family through a series of intri-
cate ceremonies, as in the case of the Pawnee Hako, described by Alice Fletcher in
BAE, 22nd Annual Report, Part 2 (1904). Intertribal adoption served to build kinshiplike relationships that maintained peace among tribes or certain groups within
them. See also Alanson Skinner, "Societies of the Ioway, Kansa and Ponca Indians,"
Anthropological Papers, AMNH, XI, Pt. IX (1915): 706-709.

within twenty days shuld be whipped by proper persons who ware appointed from among their own Braves for that purpose. The time has now expired and they are now to have permission to drink for three days. Then they contemplate suspending all drinking for 30 days, and then after that for 40 days and so forth until the miserable business will be ended."[24]

On April 14, another important ceremony took place. Again Irvin had left for the village to teach only to find that a tattooing ceremony was in progress. He commented:

Moste all of the people old and young gone to a great danse to the object of which was to put some spots as marks of honour or distinction in the foreheads of some young girls. This is done by the old father of Ceremonies who does it by applying powder on the skin. Nearly the whole village and nation was assembled and moste of the young women and even small girls and children were painted and took an active part in the danse. I could not but admire the courage of some little girls who would go forwards alone before the whole assembly and danse before the musick undaunted. A severe reproof to backward Christians who are affrade to go forward in the cause of Christ.[25]

Tattoos identified those of highest rank and distinction. Kurz described one young woman with a trapeze-shaped tattoo that ran from the base of her throat to her abdomen. Another was marked with a small circle on her forehead. Dots, diamonds, stars, lines, and small feathers appeared on the cheeks, neck, breasts, and legs. Warriors were given stripes around their wrists to indicate the number of scalps they had taken. The markings held religious as well as social significance. The Wakantas of the Air were said to have given the marks and their meanings to the Ioways, and those who wore them were protected by them.

At the beginning of time there were said to be two tattooing bundles, one for each moiety or tribal division. The first bundle began with the extinct Deer clan's member, Taaine, who had a dream in which an Air Wakanta told him that he must call the chiefs together and tell them of his vision. He was directed to make a bundle. First he held a feast announcing that he was going to make war on the Cranes. A small hunting party went with him and killed some cranes and deers to obtain fetal fawnskins. These hunters formed the first sacred tattooing society and made the bundle and cared for it according to the Air Wakanta's direction. They then held ceremonies to tattoo those who merited it. Feasting and payment to the society was an expensive process, and only men of wealth and status could afford to have their families tattooed. All chiefs' families were thus marked. At each ceremony it was customary to invite ten commoners from the different clans to attend. A herald or spokesman took part, and the bundle owner was present and honored with gifts of horses, blankets, and other gifts. Later it was necessary to substitute or include "a five dollar bill."[26]

Skinner was told in 1912 that the Ioways wore tattoos as whites wear diamonds. A tattooed girl was considered noble, and no one was permitted to be rude to her or to call her names. No common man could approach her. If any little girl quarreled with her, she would be scolded severely. Several elderly members of the Bear and Buffalo clans in the 1970's were given these marks when they were children.

Reverend Irvin did not deliberately attempt to record a calendar of Ioway ceremonial events, but if he observed some special occasion in his visits to the village, he might remember to note it in his journal. Other than the Buffalo Dance and the tattooing ceremony, his entries disclose the following events between 1841 and 1844: [27]

Thursday, February 11	"a sacred dance"
Sunday, February 14	"a great bear dance"
Sunday, February 28	Feast at White Cloud's. Otoes have been sometime in a visit. The Chief had bought some goods from a trader to give them.
Wednesday, March 3	"a wholly day for them"
Thursday, March 4	Otoes visit, and the Ioways gave them presents.
Sunday, March 14	"all engaged in a great feast and dance in behalf of a great war party which is in contemplation to be in the spring in company with a number of other nations against the Sioux"
Tuesday, April 13	"Buffalow dance"
Wednesday, April 14	Tatooing ceremony
Thursday, April 22	Village nearly emptied, all went up to Noncheningas to the Great Scalp Dance.
Tuesday, April 27	Otoes visit, and Scalp Dance closing.
April 26th	Some of village on hunt to "get meet for a feast to conclude the big scalp dance"
January 15	Pawnees visit, "a great adieuie has been made"
Tuesday, August 9	"Today they are going to smoke horses to the Sacks. Great preparations ... dressing ... painting."
Wednesday, August 17	Raccoon feast at Wachamonyas. Boiled with green corn.
Monday, January 29	"all engage in attending a great pipe dance which the Otoes were making for the Ioways Temperature 2 degrees below zero, and dancing naked in the open air"

Irvin mentioned that the Ioways were going to "smoke horses" for the Sacs of the Missouri. This event, called Ni-ut-a-ha, was reserved for tribes with which the Ioways had special friendship. After a visit had been announced, the chief called a council to obtain pledges of horses to be given away. If ten or more were pledged, a certain Pipe Bundle would be used. It was placed in a special place while the symbolic feast was prepared by boiling a kettle of water and placing tobacco in it. As the tobacco laden steam rose to the sky, the mixture was slowly emptied on the ground as an offering to Mother Earth. The Pipe Bundle was opened reverently, and the pipe in its beautifully decorated stem leaned against a special holder in the ground. Now the horses were presented to the selected visitors. After all was done, the Sacs arose. The chiefs thanked the Ioways and issued an invitation for them to visit them in the future. After they were gone, the Ioway chief prepared a feast for the horse contributors. At its conclusion, grease from the meat was rubbed on faces and chests as a type of blessing. The pipe bowl was rubbed with grease and put away in the bundle.[28]

Another ceremony observed by Reverend Hamilton was sponsored by White Cloud. He wrote in his journal:

March 4, 1852 — Met He-wat-ho-choo who said, I am going to Boka's to a feast. The Thunder came last night and he is making a feast for it. (Last night thunder was heard for the first time this spring.) I went to Boka's. He and Thief were sitting together singing and shaking their sacred gourds, and seemed to keep time with great precision. While singing they kept their eyes nearly closed. Before them was a stick about four feet long with several small branches. It was painted a light blue, and was ornamented with an eagle's feather painted red, a strip of an otter's skin and part of a human scalp. This latter, however, I did not observe, but he afterwards told me it was there. Some two or three were sitting near them, and the opposite side of the tent was vacant, and ready for the guests. A kettle of sweet corn and Buffalo meat was setting beside the fire. As the guests came in they took their places quietly. Some of them passing around the stick containing the offerings to the Thunder. As some were late coming, the two who made the feast stopped singing and shaking their rattles. When all had arrived who were invited, Boka, or White Cloud, as he is called, made a short speech addressing each one by the title, grandfather, brother, uncle or friend, according to the relation he sustained, telling them that the Thunder had arrived and he had made a feast for it and an offering. Some of the others also made remarks. Neumonya spoke to me saying, "It is very ancient custom handed down from our forefathers." He-wat-ho-choo took a small piece of meat from his bowl and put it on the end of the stick containing the offerings. When each man's bowl was filled Boka told them to eat, while eating he said to me, I have made a feast for the Thunder and an offering. I intend to go on a War Party when the grass grows, to the Pawnees and take a scalp. This offering can give me success.

When they had finished they began to leave one by one, passing round the circle, and addressing each one as before according to the relation they sustained.

After the feast was over, Boka told Thief to take the stick containing the offerings and throw it away near a certain tree. Then turning to me he said, It is thrown away for the Thunder. Formerly we used to make a feast for four days, when it first came from its main village it could not get far north, but now we only feast one day. That medicine bag is the one Old Pumpkin used to have. It contains a great many things.

Is it full of scalps?

No, not now. It used to be full, but since you came among us you have kept us from going on War parties, and as we make various offerings *The Entreaty* of the scalps, they are getting scarce. We used to have plenty. This *Period* medicine bag is very ancient. We have had it from the beginning. When we first became many.

How many are there in all? There are seven. [29]

The missionaries' journals and diaries reveal that Ioway and white cultures existed side by side, meeting but infusing slightly to the frustration of the agent and missionaries. In the end the acculturational victory would be the white man's, but in the mid-nineteenth century the Ioways continued to keep their inner world in order as much as possible. Chiefs and doctors fulfilled their ceremonial and civil obligations to their people as well as they were able. War parties left secretly and returned. Adjustments and regulations were made in their own council in an attempt to live within the constricted situation in which they found themselves.

At this time religion and medicine were interdependent in Ioway society. Doctors' societies existed, and one of their ceremonies was described by Hamilton:

June 20, 1851 — Mode of Treating Wounds

To-po-muk (two death heads) had secured a cut just between the great toe on the top and side of his foot, severing the principal tendon. He had one doctor attending him. This doctor was sucking the blood to draw out the corruption. He first filled his mouth (with) warm water, and then applied it to the wound. After continuing this operation some time, he took a butcher knife and scarified the part which was most swelled. In the meantime another doctor, Buffalo Bulls Eyes (Cee-tus-te), came in and the two worked his foot for some time, rubbing it with a rag. After they had finished washing the foot, Wau-kun-yee untied his medicine bag, took out some medicine, grass or herbs of some kind, and having put some live coals on a flat stone, such as they use to pound on, he sprinkled his herbs upon the coals, making a smoke and rather agreeable odor. He then commenced warming his hands over the smoking medicine and would apply them to the leg below the knee and would draw them towards the foot and toes. This he repeated several times until it was quite all wiped, and as he seemed to think, much improved. While he was attending to this operation Cee-tus-te sat behind him for awhile, and then came and sat near me singing and talking very rapidly alternately. I could scarcely distinguish his words. He seemed to be encouraging the other in his drying operations and to pray, in their own blind way, or sing for success. At the same time I thought he was bidding the demon depart. I said to him.

What did you sing and say? You spoke so fast I could not comprehend you (and I thought it was designed on his part).

I was talking, said he to the Buffalo under the ground. They hear, and tell what medicine is good. I have seen them: the Iowas have seen them with their faces mudded, and their fore legs, and having weeds on their horns which they dig up, when they thrust their horns into the ground; and he went to the door and pulled up some weed to show me how they carried them. [Written in margin:] This was doubtless the Buffalo Medicine. They have different kinds as Otter.

Do you mean said I, The Buffalo or their Spirits?

Their spirits. It is just the same as you teach us. You talk about God, and about obedience to him, and heaven and hell. We talk about these things in our way. It is sacred, just the same as you teach us.

Do you suppose they can hear you?

Yes, they hear: and if they would say we will not listen to you, the person will soon die.

But I wish to know what you said?

Come here and sit beside me, said he to the other, and we will sing it. There are seven songs that we sing when a man is wounded. They then commenced singing, telling me at the close of each of the first four songs what he said. The song consisted only of a short sentence, which was often repeated. When a person was wounded and very sick they would sing.

1. I am wounded. I am wounded. Ha-a-a-a.
2. Look at me. Look at me. Ha-ya-a. Ha-ya-a-a-a.
3. Let me stand. Let me stand. Ha-ya-a. Ha-ya-a-a-a-.
4. May I walk. May I walk. Ha-ya-a. Ha-ya-a-a-a-.
5. Let me go there. Let me go there. Ha-ya-a. Ha-ya-a-a-a-.
6. Let me run. Let me run. Ha-ya-a. Ha-ya-a-a-a-.
7. Ditto   Ditto   Ditto. Ha-ya-a. Ha-ya-a-a-a.

When we sang these songs they hear us. It is true. Sometimes when a Buffalo is shot in the breast, he becomes very sick, staggers from one side to the others (imitating the motion while he spoke) then two other Buffalo get one on each side, and support it and urge it along, perhaps, and helping it until they get it away. When they doctor it. They have a basin of earth in which they place the water. This they use in blowing on the wound. If there is no water nigh, one runs off to a stream and drinks water and runs back again and pours it out of his mouth into the basin. They bring the weeds also on their horns and using the water in the basin they blow as we do on the wound.

They then said they would take a smoke and blow upon the wound which they did. The manner of blowing is something like this. They use water or concoction of some roots. If water only, they generally have some root or bark in the mouth. Taking a sup of water they put themselves in a favorable condition, and send the water out of the mouth with a whizzing sound making it like a mist, blowing frequently for four or six times before they replenish the mouth. They generally blow from behind the wound, so as to drive if possible, whatever is bad out of the wound. These operations they continued alternately for some time when one of them commence singing again, and protracted this song for a length of time. [30]

Sacred songs, prayers, dances, and curing techniques contributed to Ioway healing. Reverend Irvin's attempts to attend the ill fitted in with their expectations of his role. Bleeding was then an accepted means of curing, and from time to time Irvin's journal indicated that he used it. This method would never have been permitted if a similar practice, by which the evil causing the ailment was removed by breathing or sucking it out, or by cupping the area involved with small animal horn tips, had not existed among their own doctors. Irvin's journal described visits he made to the ill:

In the forenoon Mr. H. and I went to see some Indians at the village who ware sick and gave some medacine. We talked some with, and prayed for the sick....

March 3rd. I went to see the principal chief who was quite sick, and whos eyes ware verry sore. He has been drunk a long time and will loose his eyes soon if he does not reform....

April 17th. An Indian came to our station and said that an Indian woman had died and that it was the wish of the connections of the deseased that we make a coffin and bury the body in english style.... we did so, but the old man wished a smale hole left in the end of the coffin and had all her dress affairs interred with her. In this case they have shown more religios reliance than usual....

January 25, 1842. Attended old Plums and held meeting. His mind is nearly gone. [Later Irvin wrote, "He has died and his widows wanted our aid in his interrment."]

Efforts to convert the Ioway are described throughout the journal:

[February 14, 1842.] On yesterday we went to the camps a short distance below to hold meeting.... The few who attended seemed to show more of an enquiring disposition than is common. It is common for them to give their assent to what is said wheather they understand what is said or not. Their enquiries are at times amuseing. Today one enquired wheather if some good Ioway should get nearly up to heaven, if thare was any danger of him falling back again. It was also asked who put the wood in the big fire in hell. They show great ignorance, but it is pleasing to see them enquire.

March 13 . . . at the Indian encampment . . . could not get many together, and those who ware present soon got weary of the exercises and went away.... It will shurely be a long time at this rate before the poor Ioways can be brought into a knowledge of sacred things. [31]

The missionaries' efforts to educate Ioway children were more successful than their attempts at religious conversion. The early years found them holding classes in the village itself. After the construction of the boarding school their pupils never totaled more than forty at one time. Irvin noted so many things that interfered: the ceremonies which the children had to attend, the summer agricultural tasks, the hunts, and occasions when young boys were taken away to learn to be warriors. One one such occasion he noted the boys were all away, and he taught a "good number of girls."

In May, 1842, Irvin noted:

On yesterday as I was going on my way to the village I met a large no. of the Boys, many of whom ware my schollars they sade they ware going on a war party they ware equiped in warlike stile one had on his back the medicene bag, and they ware quite in a good humour. I proposed that they should say a lesson to this they readily agreed and we took our seet in a shade near the edge of the prairie After performing for a time the usual exercises of the school I went on to the village and they went on their way on my way home I meet the same party returning in all the tryumphes of war. They said they had kill and scalpt an Indian that they had been verry brave &c. they had the likeness of a scalp suspended on a pole the customary mode of returning from war. They ware singing and dancing, whooping and hollowing in war like stile. This was a war party in mineature. They seemed to enter quite into a martial spirit and ware much pleased with what they had done. Here we may see heathenism in the bud. In these fallse and wicked amusement the children meet with the moste cordial approbation of their parents. They can perform but few things which will be more interesting to the parents. Such as the father so will be the sons. [32]

Of the forty attending the boarding school in 1846, twenty-five could read the Scriptures.[33] In 1848, half of the teaching continued to be bilingual. In order to learn other skills, the boys were employed in farm labor, and the girls worked in the kitchen and performed other household and sewing tasks.

During this period several young Ioway men had attended the Choctaw Academy in Kentucky. Kurz commented on the benefits of this type of education, or the practicality of it, for the life that they faced when they returned to the tribe. He said, "There the boys learned the English language, reading, writing, arithmetic, some geography, and history, and a trade, chosen from shoe making, tailoring, etc...." He then speculated on the view, generally accepted many decades later:

What use can be made of such esoteric trades in a community where there is not a chance of employing them, nor the capital to set oneself up in business, nor where even if they were to try to pursue their trade in other places, they would not be hired. The plan will not prove a success so long as the Indians are not given the same political rights as the white population in America.... When these Kentucky proteges come back to their tribes they soon learn the truth of their prospects. They then become the most unhappy, the most indolent, the most disregarded among their people. With their new fashioned ideas they find no means of support; they are not farmers, huntsmen or protectors, still less warriors. In a word they are ruined as Indian braves. [34]

Attempts to change agricultural patterns by substituting farm techniques utilizing oxen, ploughs, wagons, and scythes continued alongside traditional women-directed efforts. Irvin reported in May, 1841, that women had started to plant corn, beans, pumpkins, and melons. Children helped when they were needed. But before field preparation could begin, certain rituals had to be performed in order to assure a good crop and harvest. According to the Buffalo-clan origin story, the clan was given ownership of the sacred corn. Before the ground could be planted, the chiefs and doctors of that clan performed certain rites in which they implored divine assistance for the plants that would feed the people.[35] After their supplication they carefully planted a few seeds. Only then could women complete the planting.

Thus, when agents and others tried to change the Ioway agricultural system, they interfered with basic religious and philosophical beliefs. The consistent resistance of Indian men to playing women's roles in agriculture is more easily understood in this context.

Before this time, when the tribe was on distant hunting grounds, the first frogs croaks signaled the return to the summer village and planting. The most ancient stories say that the Pigeon and Buffalo clans led the tribe back to their villages. When they arrived at the spring site for a new village, the Snake clan members indicated the village grounds. The Snake doctors sought nearby snake inhabitants and requested their permission for the Ioways to dwell there. After settlement, the agricultural cycle could begin. In August the villagers moved into temporary camps around the fields to drive off predators and to harvest the corn, which was roasted in large pits in the fields and carried back to the village in woven mat or hide containers. When the appropriate time in the cycle was reached, the Green Corn Dance, acquired from the Sacs and the Shawnees, took place. Later in the fall, when the air became chilled after sunset, and the elk's whistle was heard on the wind, the Bear and Wolf clans now in authority prepared for movement to the hunting grounds and winter camps.[36]

This is the way it had always been, but by the 1840's the young men of the tribe encountered difficulties in following traditional patterns. The game was almost gone, and, where it could be found to the west, the powerful Pawnees, Sioux, Cheyennes, Arapahos, and Kiowas hunted and made the journey dangerous. The Waiakida were ever watchful, not only for the buffalo they hunted, but for the enemy hunting them.

Government efforts continued to turn the Ioways from the old life and to make them live like white men. They were not stupid, and they tried to walk a narrow path between rejection of new ideas, which would perhaps bring unknown reprisals for failure to comply, and acceptance of sufficient innovations to satisfy the agent, missionaries, and others who sought to change and control them. The values of some phases of the new life did not escape them. They realized early that a knowledge of English would benefit them directly in their dealings with white men. At the same time, putting their children in school all day changed them and made them less amenable to native ways. Young men who returned from Choctaw Academy were plainly different and often could not seem to find themselves again. The dilemma faced by the acculturating Ioway

Indians was realized by Thoreau in 1850 when he wrote in his journal:

> A squaw come to our door today with two papooses, and said, "Me want a pie." Theirs is not common begging. You are merely the rich Indian who shares his goods with the poor. They merely offer you an opportunity to be generous and hospitable.
>
> Equally simple was the observation which an Indian made at Mr. Hoar's door the other day, who went there to sell his baskets. "No, we don't want any," said the one who went to the door. "What! do you mean to starve us?" asked the Indian in astonishment, as he was going out the gate. The Indian seems to have said: I too will do like the white man, I will go into business. He sees his white neighbors well off around him, and he thinks that if he only enters the profession of basketmaking, riches will flow in unto him as a matter of course; just as the lawyer weaves arguments, and by some magical means wealth and standing follow. He thinks that when he has made the baskets, he has done his part; now it is yours to buy them. [37]

Acceptance of certain aspects of white or "European" culture did not compensate for the loss of their own. The Indians resorted to various devices — ameliorative, temporary measures — to adjust to the frustrations and restraints of reservation life. One method was to escape physically from the stressful agency environment by visiting other places and tribes. Such a meeting was attended by the Ioways in 1843. Far to the south of them, in present-day Oklahoma, lived the powerful Cherokees, who had faced all the bitterness of removal from their eastern lands and saw the need to unite Indian nations far and wide to withstand the continuing greed of American settlers for Indian land.

The Cherokees had sent messages to thirty-six tribes in a wide area from the Rocky Mountains to the Mississippi River, calling for a council at Tahlequah, their capital in the forested, hilly regions west of Arkansas Territory. Eighteen tribes responded, bringing together over one thousand tribesmen. Among them were Great Nemaha Agency Ioways, led by Wo-hum-pa, known for his bravery against the Sioux. There were five in all including women. Mrs. Hannah Hitchcock of Ft. Gibson on the Arkansas wrote that as a little girl in 1843 she noticed the Ioway at Tahlequah because they wore bright little bells strung all over their clothes that tinkled merrily when they walked. Following their traditional ways, on the first Sunday afternoon just before dark, the Ioways marched in greeting around the large encampment. Interested delegates joined them until many were in the procession. They paused at each cabin on the square and sang, danced, and blew on their cane flutes, ending their performance with the Ioway cry of greeting.[38] They continued around the encampment until they reached their own lodge. They had thus woven a chain of friendship around the entire assemblage.

The council lasted a month. It was filled with prayers, speeches, and agreements. One agreement "pledged the signatories not to cede any of their land to the United States without the consent of the other parties."[39]

Another Ioway journey was observed by J. J. Audubon, who traveled up the Missouri River in 1843 to describe and portray animal species. On April 25, he boarded the steamboat *Omega* in St. Louis and recorded that Sarpy, the trader, came aboard with a group of fur trappers, some drunk. He called the roll and threw each one an outfit, which was "a blanket containing the apparel for the trip. He was ordered at once to retire and make room for the next," and, "they were ordered off as if slaves." During this frantic scene, Audubon observed some Ioways and other Indians who had come aboard, who, "poor souls, were more quiet, and had already seated or squatted themselves on the highest parts of the steamer, and were tranquil lookers on."[40]

Some miles upstream,

we came alongside a beautiful prairie of some thousand acres, reaching to the hills. Here we stopped to put out our Iowa Indians. . . . We saw Indians on their way towards us, running on foot, and many on horseback, generally riding double on skins or on Spanish saddles. Even the squaws rode, and rode well, too. We counted about eighty, amongst whom were a great number of youths of different ages. I was heartily glad that our own squad of them left us here. I observed that though they had been absent from their friends and relatives, they never shook hands, or paid any attention to them. Major Richardson came on board and paid freight, and said that this was the country of the Iowa and Fox, numbering over 1,200, and that his district extends seventy miles up the river.

As Audubon proceeded up the river, he saw more and more tribesmen of other nations. On May 12, he described their destitute appearance: "I pity these poor beings from my heart. . . . Ah, Mr. Catlin, I am sorry to see and to read your account of the Indians *you* saw — how different they must have been from any that I have seen."[41]

Perhaps the most spectacular visit of Ioway tribal representatives was their journey to Europe in 1841-1845. They were acccompanied by promoter G. H. C. Melody, their interpreter Jeffry Deroin, and, later, George Catlin (see Figure 15). His knowledge of the Ioways spanned ten years. It was reflected in his regard and interest when he met them again in London and they accompanied him on his exhibition of Indian portraits and artifacts. Secretary of War J. M. Porter had consented to the trip and had asked White Cloud to select the others who should go.[42] Those chosen were: Neumonya (Walking Rain), the third chief; Senontiyah (Blistered Feet), the "medicine man" or doctor: three warriors, Washkamonya (Jim), Nohomunya (One Who Gives No Attention), Shontayiga (Little Wolf), and

229

Figure 15. An engraving of the Ioways made in London in 1844 when they were with George Catlin, who is shown on the right. Reproduced from W. H. Miner, *The Iowa* (Cedar Rapids, The Torch Press, 1911). Courtesy of Kansas State Historical Society.

Watanye (One Always Foremost); Rutonyeweme (Strutting Pigeon), White Cloud's wife; another woman, Rutonweme (Pigeon on the Wing); Okeweme (Female Bear that Walks on the Back of Another); Tapatame (Sophia), White Cloud's daughter; Koonzayame (Female War Eagle Sailing); Watawebukana, the ten-year-old son of Neumonya; and Corsair, the baby son of Shontayiga (see Figure 16). While White Cloud was absent, his uncle, No Heart, assumed his responsibilities, and he is named as chief in the documents of this interval.

When the party arrived in London, Melody and Catlin reached an agreement, and White Cloud informed them that his purpose was to earn money to aid his nation. Catlin kept notes each day on what was

No. 9.

Figure 16. Catlin's sketch of the fourteen Ioway who went to Europe in 1844-45. The following identifications are Catlin's:

Chiefs
1. Mew-hu-she-kaw, White Cloud; first chief of the nation
2. Neu-mon-ya, Walking Rain; third chief
3. Se-non-ty-yah, Blister Feet; great medicine man
   Warriors and Braves
4. Wash-ka-mon-ya, Fast Dancer
5. No-ho-mun-ya, One who gives no attention
6. Shon-ta-yi-ga, Little Wolf
7. Wa-tan-ye, One always foremost
8. Wa-ta-we-bu-ka-na, Commanding General; the son of Walking Rain, ten years old
9. Jeffrey Doraway [Dorion, omitted]
   Squaws
10. Ruton-ye-we-ma, Strutting Pigeon; White Cloud's wife
11. Ruton-we-me, Pigeon on the Wing
12. Oke-we-me, Female Bear that walks on the back of another
13. Koon-za-ya-me, Female War Eagle Sailing
14. Ta-pa-ta-me, Sophia, wisdom; White Cloud's daughter
15. Corsair, a papoose

231

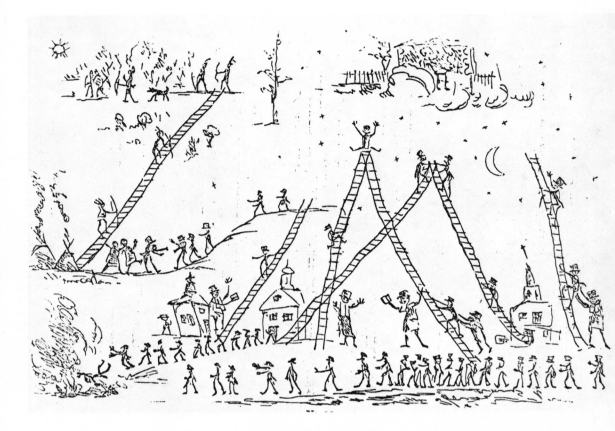

Figure 17. An Ioway drawing copied by Catlin in London, 1844. It illustrated the white man's ascent to heaven. God sits in a house in the clouds
in the upper right. Hell is in the lower left corner. The Ioway heaven is in
the upper left corner. Reproduced from George Catlin, *Notes, Eight Years
Travels in Europe,* Plate 11.

said and what happened, as well as reactions to the Ioways. Arrangements were made for daily Ioway dance performances. Other hours
of the day were filled with sightseeing expeditions to show them the
marvels of civilization.

During the London visit, ministers and representatives of different
religious faiths often visited their rooms to see them and sometimes
endeavored to convert them. The number of different ways in which
the white people approached God, Heaven, and Hell confused the
Ioways. It seemed curious that they should have invented so many
approaches to what the Ioways knew should only be viewed in one
way (see Figure 17). Neumonya, the war chief, finally talked to a
group who had attempted to present another way to redemption.
Catlin's record of the dialogue follows:

As to the white man's religion which you have explained, we have heard it told to us in the same way, many times, in our own country, and there are white men and women there now, trying to teach it to our people. We do not think your religion good, unless it is so for white people, and this we don't doubt. The Great Spirit has made our skins red, and the forests for us to live in. He has also given us our religion, which has taken our fathers to "the beautiful hunting grounds," where we wish to meet them. We don't believe that the Great Spirit made us to live with pale faces in this world, and we think He has intended we should live separate in the world to come.

My friends, — You speak of the *"good book"* that you have in your hand; we have many of these in our village; we are told that "all your words about the Son of the Great Spirit are printed in that book, and if we learn to read it, it will make good people of us." I would now ask why it don't make good people of the pale faces living all around us? They can all read the good book, and they can understand all that the "black coats" say, and still we find they are not so honest and so good a people as ours: this we are sure of; such is the case in the country about us, but *here* we have no doubt but the white people who have so many to preach and so many books to read, are all honest and good. In *our* country the white people have two faces, and their tongues branch in different ways; we know that this displeases the Great Spirit, and we do not wish to teach it to our children.

The reverend gentleman inquired —

"Do you not think that the Great Spirit sometimes punishes the Indians in this world for their sins?"

War-chief. — "Yes, we do believe so."

Rev. Gentleman. — "Did it ever occur to you, that the small pox that swept off half of your tribe, and other tribes around you, a few years ago, might have been sent into your country by the Great Spirit to punish the Indians for their wickedness and their resistance to his word?"

War-chief. — "My Friends, we don't know that we ever resisted the word of the Great Spirit. If the Great Spirit sent the small pox into our country to destroy us, we believe it was to punish us for listening to the false promises of white men. It is white man's disease, and no doubt it was sent amongst white people to punish *them* for their sins. It never came amongst the Indians until we began to listen to the promises of white men, and to follow their ways; it then came amongst us, and we are not sure but the Great Spirit then sent it to punish us for our foolishness. There is another disease sent by the Great Spirit to punish white men, and it punishes them in the right place — the place that offends. We know that disease has been sent to punish them; that disease was never amongst the Indians until white men came — they brought it, and we believe we shall never drive it out of our country."

The War-chief here reached for the pipe again for a minute, and then continued —

"My Friends, — I hope my talk does not offend you; we are children, and you will forgive us for our ignorance. The Great Spirit expects us to feed the poor; our wives and children at home are very poor; wicked white men kill so many of our hunters and warriors with *fire-water,* that they bring among us, and leave so many children among us for us to feed, when they go away, that it makes us very poor. Before they leave

233

our country they destroy all the game also, and do not teach us to raise bread, and our nation is now in that way, and very poor; and we think that the way we can please the Great Spirit first, is to get our wives and children something to eat, and clothes to wear. It is for that we have come to this country, and still we are glad to hear your counsel, for it is good." [43]

The presence of the Ioways in England drew large crowds, and they were invited to the houses of the great. After Benjamin Disraeli showed them his house, it was found that the doctor, Senontiyah, was missing. After a search he was found seated in the middle of the bathroom, where he had lighted his pipe and was surveying the room. He said that it was a good contrivance to have in his country. The principle was the same as the sweat lodge, but the contraption of the English "vapour and shower bath" was more ingenious.

As the days went by, the number of impressions grew. As the Ioways observed Catlin's journalistic efforts, some means of recording their own observations was discussed. Washkamonya, or Jim as Catlin called him, decided to keep a notebook of interesting facts that they wished to recall and discuss when they were among their kinsmen again.

The Ioways attracted so much attention, wherever they went, that it was decided to buy them English clothing so that they could visit places unobserved. Accordingly, everything, including wigs, was purchased. Senontiyah, curious about the practices of his religious peers, decided to attend a church. He had practiced removing his hat, as was customary before entering a church, but in his excitement he forgot to do so until he sat down in one of the pews. He hastily sought to remove it and succeeded in snatching off both hat and wig, which exposed his scalp lock and his red-painted head. In an instant he clapped the wig and hat back on his head and remained seated without apparent loss of composure. He later continued his comparative study of religions by visiting Westminster Abbey and St. Paul's Church.

Certain sights shocked Ioway sensibilities. Among them were the coal mines, where they saw women and children used as beasts of burden to pull carts on their hands and knees through tunnels. Crowded prisons horrified and alarmed them. The grandeur of York Cathedral represented the greatness of civilization, but the proverty of many London, Birmingham, and York inhabitants began to distress them seriously. When they questioned Catlin about the reasons for so many poor people, the subject of taxes and debts arose. The latter were understood, but not the result, the incarceration of debtors in prison for nonpayment. They reasoned that such a punishment only deprived the mother and children of a man to supply food and shelter, and they could see no reason for it. The poorhouses were explained as a means of taking care of such indigents, but the Ioways merely shook their heads. [44]

Jim's notebook now contained a sizable list of figures that argued against the benefits of civilization. He had compiled figures on the annual consumption of spirits. His numbers, carefully copied from his daily *London Times*, said that 29,200,000 gallons were sold annually in Great Britain and Ireland and that 24,000,000 pounds were spent to buy that amount. He then added a note that 50,000 drunkards died each year, and one-half of the insanity, two-thirds of the pauperism, and three-fourths of the crime were the consequences of its use.

"This," Jim said, "was one of the best things he had for his notebook," thinking of the missionaries at home as well as those who visited the Ioways in London. He said, "those black coats were always talking so much about the Indians getting drunk, that it would be a good thing for him to have these figures to show, and that he intended to have Catlin write near these figures at the end of the tour, that fourteen Ioway Indians were one year in England and never drank any of this firewater, and were never drunk in that time."

In order to pay for a subscription to *Punch*, Jim decided to take some of the many Bibles the group had been presented and see if the publisher would exchange them for a *Punch* subscription. He was told that such a trade would probably not be acceptable and that the *Times* would keep him well informed. And it did. The next item that struck the eye of the visiting Ioway anthropologist was an open letter to the Queen, which requested protection of the young women of the kingdom who daily were taken advantage of and induced to enter a life of infamy. A regular trade had been established, with stage coach stops watched by female agents for the purpose of "entrapping innocent young women." The Queen was asked to promote laws to protect the daughters of the poor. This article was circled, cut out, and entered in the notebook to be taken home and shown to the "black coats" who extolled the inate virtue of white women and decried the lack of it in their red-skinned sisters. Side by side in Jim's book were the number of churches, the number of ministers, and the number of crimes of all types that were committed in the country.

The last visit in Europe carried the Ioways across the channel to France to visit King Louis Phillipe of France and the residents of Paris. They looked forward to this visit because of their memories of the French Grandfathers of the previous century. Again they visited and were visted by the renowned, including Victor Hugo and George Sand, but the greatest excitement came with an invitation to visit the royal family at the Tuilleries. They were met, Catlin said, by "half a dozen huge and splendid looking porters in flaming scarlet livery and powdered wigs, who conducted us to where we were met by one of the King's *aides-de-camp*," who escorted them to the King. After Catlin presented each Ioway to the royal family, "a sort of *conversazione* took place":

> His Majesty in the most free and familiar manner (which showed that he had been accustomed to the modes and feelings of Indians) conversed with the chiefs, and said to Jeffrey, "Tell these good fellows

that I am glad to see them; that I have been in many of the wigwams of the Indians in America when I was a young man, and they treated me every where kindly, and I love them for it. — Tell them I was amongst the Senecas near Buffalo, and the Oneidas — that I slept in the wigwams of the chiefs — that I was amongst the Shawnees and Delawares on the Ohio; and also amongst the Cherokees and Creeks in Georgia and Tennessee, and saw many other tribes as I descended the Ohio river the whole length, and also the Mississippi to New Orleans, in a small boat, more than fifty years ago."[45]

The king then displayed two gold medals that he would present to the two chiefs when their names were engraved on them. Neumonya, spokesman for the principal chief, presented to the king a beautiful pipe decorated with blue feathers that represented peace, which they had carefully prepared for the occasion. Concluding a gracious speech, he said, "Great Father and Great Mother, we will pray to the Great Spirit to preserve your precious lives; we will pray also that we may return safe to our own village, that we may tell to our own children and to our young men what we have seen this day."

Jim's statistical bent did not languish during the Paris visit. Senontiyah, the doctor, was a bachelor who noticed the fair sex in his quiet way. He reported that there seemed to be an uncommonly large number of women who led dogs on little strings or ribbons. He said he thought that they liked dogs better than children because there was more evidence of dogs. In another sociological study, Jim and the doctor took to their carriage to compile the following observations of that facet of Parisian society:

Women leading one little dog	432
Women leading two little dogs	71
Women leading three little dogs	5
Women with big dogs following, no string	80
Women carrying little dogs	20
Women with little dogs in carriages	31

They were told there was a dog market and a dog hospital. The doctor thought it would be a very good thing to have a hospital for their mistresses also.[46]

All things considered, and after long discussions on comparative societies, they came to the conclusion that the French reign must be superior to that of the British, for they observed no beggars on the streets and the whole effect of Paris was one of greater brightness and cleanliness. They had almost concluded that the French were a more sober lot than the British when they visited a winery where they viewed a vast repository of 800,000 casks under one roof. A visit to the Foundling Hospital opened Jim's notebook again, and he added that, of 26,000 children born in Paris during the past year, 9,000 were illegitimate.* The knowledge that there was no one, not

* The accuracy of these figures is not verified.

even a distant uncle, who cared enough to provide for even one little one, put more black marks on the growing list of French frailties. At this point the doctor asked why the thousands of ladies in Paris, who cared so much for little dogs, could not be induced to care for these little children. At this, the comparative gap between the English and French societies grew slim indeed. Catlin declared at this time that Jim's notebook would soon be filled with information to "teach to the cruel and relentless Indians" the benefits of civilization.

The Ioways returned to their homes in July, 1845 (see Figure 18). The effects of their sojourn on them as individuals cannot be found in documents, but the hypocrisy of civilization stood revealed in a wider panorama than before. Perhaps their bitterness grew deeper as they saw the inevitability of their future on the Great Nemaha Reservation (see Map 10), a place bereft of the adulation, applause, and genuine interest in their cultural expressions and their unique existence that they had experienced in Europe.

The only known acknowledgment of the Ioways' return from Europe was a remark in Reverence Irvin's annual report that told of the completion of the boarding school and of White Cloud's encouragement of its efforts. During White Cloud's absence charges were made against Agent Richardson, who resigned in protest in June, 1845, and was replaced in August by Armstrong McClintock. He called councils with the chiefs in October and November, 1845. No Heart protested the payment made of $1,500 to a white man who claimed that Ioways had killed his cattle. He denied the tribe's responsibility and then asked for an advance of $5,000 of their 1846 annuity to pay their debts to trader Joseph Roubidoux. The annuity payment procedure arose, and the chiefs requested the money in coin. McClintock agreed and thus reversed the previous decision made by Richardson. The economic situation had deteriorated, and provisions were scarce. The return of two hundred Ioways who had been residing near the Potawatomis on the headwaters of the Nodaway, worsened the situation.[47]

In January, 1846, McClintock called for a company of dragoons from Fort Leavenworth to expel unwanted persons from the reservation. He was within his rights to do so, since they were former employees of the Richardson faction and had been fired. In April, Supt. Thomas H. Harvey, who had received a report of McClintock's request for troops, visited the agency to investigate. He talked with the interested parties, and in council the chiefs took the opportunity to state their grievances. White Cloud and No Heart noted that they felt that the tribe had not been fairly paid for their land cessions. "We were told that the annuity was like an appletree giving a great harvest each year to our tribe. We find that this is not so." One-Who-Looks-Back, who had returned with the group who had been with the Potawatomis, said that his group had never received any share of the land cession benefits, that the chiefs had always received all

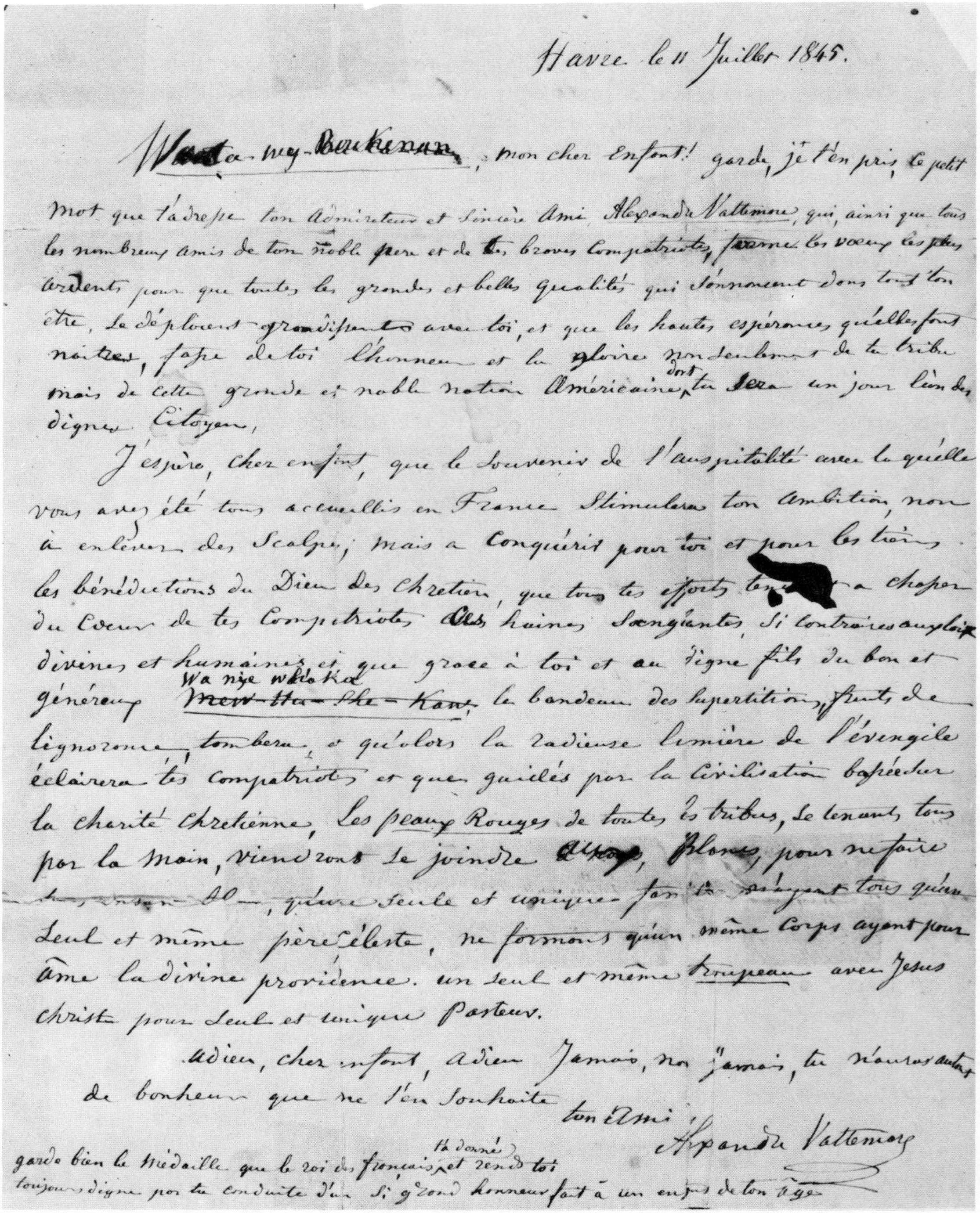

Havre le 11 Juillet 1845.

Watawey-Beukanan, mon cher Enfant! garde, je t'en prie, le petit mot que t'adresse ton Admirateur et Sincère Ami Alexandre Vattemore, qui, ainsi que tous les nombreux amis de ton noble père et de tes braves Compatriotes, forme les vœux les plus ardents pour que toutes les grandes et belles qualités qui sommeillent dans tout ton être, se déploient, grandissent avec toi, et que les hautes espérances qu'elles font naître, fasse de toi l'honneur et la gloire non seulement de ta tribu mais de cette grande et noble nation Américaine dont tu sera un jour l'un des dignes Citoyens.

J'espère, cher enfant, que le souvenir de l'hospitalité avec laquelle vous avez été tous accueillis en France stimulera ton Ambition, non à enlever des Scalpes; mais à Conquérir pour toi et pour les tiens les bénédictions du Dieu des Chrétiens, que tous tes efforts tendent à chasser du Cœur de tes Compatriotes les haines Sanglantes, si contraires aux lois divines et humaines, et que grâce à toi et au digne fils du bon et généreux Wa-nye-wa-ka-ka Mew-ha-she-Kaw, le bandeau des superstitions, fruit de l'ignorance, tombera, et qu'alors la radieuse lumière de l'évangile éclairera tes Compatriotes et que guidés par la civilisation baptisée la charité Chrétienne, les peaux Rouges de toutes les tribus, se tenant tous par la main, viendront se joindre aux Blancs, pour ne faire, qu'une seule et unique par un seul et même père céleste, ne formons qu'un même corps ayant pour âme la divine providence, un seul et même troupeau avec Jésus Christ pour seul et unique Pasteur.

Adieu, cher enfant, adieu Jamais, non jamais, tu n'auras autant de bonheur que ne t'en souhaite ton Ami

Alexandre Vattemore

garde bien la Médaille que le roi des français t'a donné et rends toi toujours digne par ta conduite d'un si grand honneur fait à un enfant de ton âge

Figure 18. A letter written by Alexandre Vattemore to young Watawebukana, son of Neumonya, on July 11, 1845, as the Ioways left France for home. The writer, who had become interested in the Indian group, gave fatherly advice to the young boy. Courtesy of Indian Archives Division, Oklahoma Historical Society.

of it, and that now the people wished to share in it.*[48] Ignoring this remark, No Heart said that the tribe had received $2,500 worth of blankets from Roubidoux,† and that he was owed $5,000. Harvey replied that he had refused to pay Roubidoux and had requested their Great Grandfather not to advance their annuity until the proper time when they could pay their debts. At the end of his inquiry he told McClintock to rehire the fired employees. In response to this and other suggestions the agent resigned, saying that he had been treated unjustly. He was replaced by William E. Rucker.

In November Harvey returned again to check on the agency and the Ioways. He held council with the chiefs, the braves, and the common people. Little did the chiefs know that a serious challenge to their authority was about to take place and that Harvey and Rucker planned to downgrade their authority before the people. He remembered from the last council that some braves and common families wished to share in the annuity to supply their basic needs and chose to use public opinion as a tool finally to decide the issue. He reported:

> I thought these that were in favour of it when I asked them, must rise. I was determined to get their vote without giving them an opportunity of becoming excited by the discussion of the subject. I told the chiefs I hoped they would be the first to rise. When I put the question, no one rose for an instant. Little Wolf, a distinguished Brave, was the first to rise. His rising gave an instantaneous impulse to the whole nation with the exception of two of the principal chiefs and their immediate personal friends who sullenly kept their seats. . . . I called Little Wolf** forward and praised him before the nation.[49]

Harvey went against tradition by calling for a popular vote on how the annuity would be divided among the people. He then moved on to

---

* At that time it was general government policy not to pay annuity to splinter groups that refused to remain with their tribe on a designated reservation.

† The name Robidoux or Roubidoux, is spelled in various ways throughout the documents, as are Neu-mon-ya, Dorion, or Deroin, Laggarash, or Naggarash, and others. In some places the names were hyphenated, and in others they were not, as can be seen in the quoted sections of this text.

** Little Wolf, or Shontayiga, was already distinguished in the eyes of the United States. President Tyler had awarded him a medal for intervening and saving a party of Omahas, on their way to a peaceful visit to the Ioways, from an attack by an Ioway war party, presumably from a faction of the tribe living apart. Little Wolf, Roman Nose, and Jeffrey Dorion took the Omaha chief, Big Elk, to the agent's house for protection. Both the young men and interpreter Dorion had accompanied White Cloud to Europe. The original commendation certificate signed by Tyler, dated October 23, 1843, is in the Indian Archives Division, Oklahoma Historical Society.

his next assault, that of removing the privilege to contract debts. He read White Cloud's list of debts, some of which were to citizens of Missouri who were present. He looked directly at the people and told them that he was there to benefit all of the Ioways and not just the few, and that he was determined to break up the fraud that had been perpetrated on them. He would pay only those debts for which bona fide receipts from previous agents existed. White Cloud asked Harvey to give the balance of the annuity to Roubidoux. "I abruptly told him I would do no such thing. I was going to pay it to the people." Thus affronted publickly, White Cloud returned to his seat. The final amount for each individual was $2.50, and Harvey reported that they were delighted with the payment. "Next year after the payment of the second installment of the debts to Robidoux, the amount of payment will be doubled."[50] From this day forward, the power of the Ioway principal chief decreased. The government agent had challenged his and other chiefs' rights to distribute the annuity and to purchase goods that had helped to maintain the chiefs' and, indirectly, the tribe's status, particularly with tribes with whom they had reciprocal gift-giving relationships. This advantage won by the government had been gained by playing on the people's need for money in a time of economic difficulty, although other factors, such as factionalism, may have been operating.

The government policy was to distribute as annuity the interest earned annually on the principal. The bulk of the promised treaty cession profits was therefore held by the government and was used as it saw fit. Theoretically the money was held in trust, not to be paid to the Indian nation until the government decided that it should be. The Indians were aware of this injustice, but repeated requests for the amount due them were rarely acknowledged in the nineteenth century. Tribes became more and more impoverished, as they endeavored to survive on a smaller land base with an annuity which was sometimes as low as the $2.50 per individual paid to the Ioways in 1846.

Map 10. Various Ioway villages, houses, and other landmarks on the Great Nemaha Reservation in 1843. From Ioway Point on the Missouri River a road leads southward. The following locations are indicated on the road: the houses of Washamonya, White Cloud, No Heart, Pumpkin, Plum, Wauhookshinga (?), and Craig; Hewathoche's village and house; the Ioway School House; and an unidentified house. On the Ioway Branch are the Roubidoux trading post and Neumonya's house. Down the road are Campbell's and Akia's houses. A road branching northeast leads to Neumonya's village and the old abandoned Ioway village. Father to the south on the main road are the brickyard, No Heart's new house, the Ioway blacksmith, and the interpreter's house. The Ioway farmer lives north of the Mission, which is bounded on the south by the Sac and Fox reservation boundary line. Courtesy of the National Archives (RG 75 Series 234 Roll 307 0618).

A
MAP
Shewing the location of the princi-
pal improvements within the Great
Nemahaw sub agency. A. D. 1843

BY

W. P. RICHARDSON. *Ind. S. Ag't.*

MISSOURI S.

MISSOURI R.

IOWAY

LAND.

SAC

LAND.

MISSION.

S. AC
Agency

FARM.

In April, 1847, White Cloud with Chiefs Wascamoni, Chetaninga, Wapacahona, and KiHeKa and Braves Wakiing and Watacona, dictated a letter to John Keith, a white settler, who sent it to Washington for them. Among other requests they wished to have new missionaries. They said that in ten years they had accomplished nothing. They lived in a fine building built with Ioway funds. When Harvey visited, they collected a large number of children. After he left, the children went home, but the missionaries brought them back, took the clothes they had given them, and sent them home naked. The ten children left there did not like it, for they were not well fed. White Cloud stated that the missionaries took $700 without authorization from the annuity to buy clothes and food for the children. Other Ioways had not been able to pay their debts, yet the missionaries took that money. They also wished the annuity to be paid to chiefs and braves. They also wanted the return of interpretor Jeffrey Deroin, (Dorion) who had been removed by the Agent.

Jeffrey (or Jeffry) Dorion (or Deroin) was married to White Cloud's niece. Harvey had ordered him off the Ioway reserve for unfounded reasons, according to George R. Gibson, who wrote that the order was probably due to his willingness to espouse Indian causes against the missionaries, "who if let alone would soon have all the annual sums paid to them by the Government, and that too when the Ioways are in a starving and famishing condition. They have built a very fine house, and have a large rich farm, and it appears to be a moneymaking business at the expense of the Indians, and without a particle of profit to them." Gibson said that he knew neither the agent nor the missionaries, but this was his impression. See Gibson to D. R. Atchison, May, 18, 1846, *GNA* (RG 75, M 234, R 307, NA).

After his confrontation with Harvey, White Cloud sought means to restore his status as the leader of his people. On May 14, 1848, two years after the superintendent had shamed him before the nation, he organized and led a war party of ninety-five against the Pawnees. They ambushed a traveling group and killed three men, six women and two children. On May 25, they returned to their village amidst great rejoicing, and the great War and Scalp Dance cycle began. Since that time, the agent reported, riot and rejoicing continued. He called a council and demanded an explanation. No Heart said that they had tried to prevent the war party but that White Cloud, "in a state of habitual drunkenness," with the aid of the son of Little Wolf and Nohohatche, was responsible. White Cloud replied, "The Pawnee steal our horses. If the white soldiers can kill the Pawnee, why can't we? They are also our enemies."[51]

The United States commissioner of Indian affairs then decided that he had to remove White Cloud from any government-recognized position of authority, and he did so. Nevertheless, the act of leading a war party that successfully added honor to the names of many men who had not had an opportunity to count coup did not disgrace White

Cloud in his nation's eyes. His action, a traditionally sanctioned effort that was socially integrative, called on a large number of Ioway men to stand together on a principle, the tradition of warfare and honor. White Cloud, by his leadership in this act, regained the status that he felt he had lost in the April council with Harvey. It was now not necessary for him to be recognized by the United States in order to control or to influence tribal opinion. The agent reported in September, 1849, that White Cloud still controlled the tribe and had been bold enough to threaten "the missionaries, myself and the whites."

Ioway discontent and anger had other roots. The westward movement of land-seeking settlers had begun. Gold had been discovered in California. Kurz observed that "thousands of gold seekers and immigrants enroute to Oregon, thronged the taverns and streets of St. Joseph."[52] The California Road from St. Joseph ran through Ioway lands. Farmers and adventurers of all sorts brought their diseases and used water, grass, and timber extensively. The Ioways saw this as a breach of contract in the negligence of the United States to maintain the integrity of their land.

In October, the Sacs, the Foxes, and the Ioways attacked the Pawnees. A company of Fort Leavenworth dragoons was sent to seize the participants or their leaders. The soldiers encountered White Cloud with a party of thirty to forty Ioways on their way to a friendly visit with the nearby Sacs and Foxes. They were stopped and White Cloud arrested. All returned to the Ioway village where Principal Chief Neymonya was asked for the head of the Pawnee woman who was taken in the attack. He said he did not know where it was and was accused of selling it for whiskey. He and White Cloud were arrested and escorted to the village of the Sacs, whose principal chief had led the attack on the Pawnees and had taken the head. He, too, was arrested. The Indians were taken as prisoners to Fort Leavenworth and held for a time.

In council in January, 1850, No Heart was the new principal chief. Missionaries Irvin and Hamilton described him thus: "Na-Che-ning-a, or No-Heart-of-Fear, is the second chief of the Iowas (1848), and the principal business-man of the nation. He is at this time chief speaker. Not remarkable for strength of mind, but under good influence will always be a fine man. Shows some concern for the welfare of his people, a friends to the whites, and anxious to have his people adopt their customs. Very friendly to education. The School and mission own much to him for his friendship and influence." (Schoolcraft, *HCPIT,* 3, 265). At the council No Heart spoke of the Ioway problems as follows:

> Father, We are glad to see you and have a talk with you. We want to talk about white people traveling through our country. They travel through here every year, and last spring there were thousands of men, wagon and oxen who went through. They drank our water, ate our grass, burnt our timber, and what is worse, brought a bad sickness [cholera] among us

which killed many of our people, making us very sorry. We have not done these children of our Great Father any harm, nor have we complained, but now want you to ask our Great Father to add at least five hundred dollars a year to our annuities to pay for this. This will make our hearts glad and make the road wider for other white people. Father, try hard, very hard to get it.

Neumonya, now serving as second chief, affirmed these and other thoughts, and Agent Richardson stated that these were valid suggestions. [53]

Happier times came briefly in 1851, when two bands of three hundred Winnebagos left their reservation for an extended visit with the Ioways. Richardson reported that they wished to stay in the area because their land in the north was cold and barren and had little game. They wished to stay particularly because of their ancient friendship for the Ioways "to whom," Richardson observed, "they seem much attached." The Ioways for several payments had asked Richardson to pay the Winnebagos as if they were their own people, and the Winnebagos, in turn, had requested that a portion of their annuity be obtained and that they be placed on the Great Nemaha Agency roll. After discussing this the agent said, "I am satisfied they will intermarry and soon become permanently identified with the Iowas, if permitted to reside on their lands, as they desire." [54]

The visit of their respected grandfathers, the Winnebagos, must have been a joy for the Ioways. Indeed, their very presence gave shimmery substance, like a shaft of sunlight, to the past, when they emerged together from the legendary land on the north. How many old stories must have been told and how reverently the old dances performed in their attempts to commune with the Wakandas,* the ancestors, and their glories.† Perhaps the relationship thus expressed reflected their absorption with traditional reality and cultural reintegration. As Reverend Hamilton reported on the state of the mission, "Though they frequently listen with a good degree of attention, no saving change appears to have been wrought in the hearts of any of them, and they continue, as heretofore, attached to their heathenish practices." [55]

Agent Richardson's concerns grew greater. The problem of claims against the annuity never ceased. Nonreservation individuals owed money for goods purchased by the Ioway were present at every payment. Richardson often could not distinguish whether a claim was justified. He declared at last that annuity payment should be closed to all except the Ioways and licensed traders. His temper grew

---

* J. O. Dorsey stated that the Ioways had sacred songs in the Winnebago language. "It is probable that these are the property of a secret order, as they, too, show how some of the gentes [clans] descended as birds from the Upper World." See Dorsey, "Osage Traditions," BAE *Sixth Annual Report*, 396.

† The memory of their past connections with the Winnebagos continues. In 1972 an elderly Ioway chief in Oklahoma traveled north to visit some Winnebago "distant relations."

short on another matter in 1852. A group of Ioways, led by Robert Whitecloud, had gone to Washington to be part of an exhibit and show. Superintendent Mitchell received a letter from the agent that said:

> Sir, I hope you will send the Iowas who are in Washington City home and order the Agent to give the men a good flogging. I had repeatedly told these people not to listen to the vagabonds who were endeavoring to seduce them from their homes to exhibit them as they would wild animals. The chiefs remonstrated against their going, and the very persons who led them off, promised me most faithfully, that they would not go. I refer to Robert Whitecloud and Robert J. Wood. White Cloud, the deposed chief, died about 20 days since.[56]

This outburst from Richardson contains the second known reference to his use of flogging for punishment. In a letter written in 1849 in which agency farmer Foreman, deploring the conditions of the agency under Vaughn, noted that such lawlessness was never allowed under Richardson "who laid on the stripes for waywardness."[57] Whether any chiefs were thus abused is not known, but White Cloud would no longer need to see or feel the degradation of his people in this or any other manner. He died in December, 1851, approximately forty years of age.

On April 18, 1853, Daniel Vanderslice replaced Richardson. He faced a multitude of intruders into the Indian lands under his jurisdiction. With phagocytic intent the whites gathered around the small or large cell of Indian land and infused themselves in any manner possible when opportunity presented itself. Vanderslice did what he could to remove those illegally present.[58]

He held council in June with the Ioways, the Sacs, and the Foxes, who were preparing for the summer hunt. He urged them to avoid all collision with the tribes that they would meet on the plains and to show good conduct toward the emigrants that they would encounter on their way to the Far West. Tribal members who remained at home were stinted for sustenance, but the wheat that the Sacs had planted and the flour that the traders had sold to the Ioways on credit would sustain the people until the hunters returned and the gardens were ready.

Although they followed the traditional hunt and other customs, the Ioways were becoming sophisticated at going outside the system to seek assistance when their appeals to the government went unanswered. In 1853, they sought the advice of A. W. Mitchell, a St. Joseph attorney, in the matter of agent fund handling.[59] Outside sources often suggested a course of action for selfish reasons, particularly in the case of traders who sought redress for the Indians for their own benefit. Others were sincere, well-intentioned persons who appeared as minority voices from time to time to take up a cause, sometimes with success and oftentimes not. Selfish whites unfortuntely appear to have been in the majority as they placed increasing pressure on the Great Nemaha Agency Indians to sell a portion of their lands. This culminated in October, 1853, with a request from the Kickapoo and the Sac and Fox tribes for sale of some of their lands. The desire was not a whim, but an expression of need for a greater income. Their lives now largely revolved like a treadmill around the annuity payment. Their debts increased, and the payment was never large enough to eliminate them and to sustain the Indians' yearly needs. It was impossible to survive in this manner, and Jefferson's earlier expectation came to pass. The land was the only resource that the Indians had to extricate them from economic duress. If they sold land to the United States government, there would be at least an increase in the annuity. Also, they always hoped that a larger lump sum payment would be made from the principal held in trust by the government.

Pressure on the Ioways to sell their land was also increased, as the agent continued to inquire if all the agency tribes would not care to sell. He notified the commissioner of Indian affairs on February 10, 1854, that the Ioways had consented to sell three fourths of their reserve. If a treaty could be negotiated, then the rest of the reserve could be allotted in severalty to heads of family in eighty-acre lots and to all other members of the tribe in forty-acre portions, "but without their privilege of selling or transferring, or in any way alienating it without the consent of the government." He indicated that the Ioways now indicated a disposition to go to work and that he would do all that he could to promote this attitude, since "the habits and improvidence of the Iowas have reduced them to the lowest ebb as regards a mere subsistence, and they must necessarily suffer much long before their summer crops mature. While the miserable conditions to which they have brought themselves is chargeable to their want of thrift, it is painful to be a witness to their abject poverty, without having the means to relieve them."[60]

To the hypocrisy of the agent is added the knowledge that a balance of $2,000 had accumulated in the agricultural fund. The Ioways on several occasions had stated that they did not wish their money used for this purpose, but to no avail. Perhaps at that time some means could have been devised to transfer and use those funds to alleviate their "abject poverty."

On June 13, 1854, chiefs No Heart, Little Wolf, Wahmoonnaka, and Naggarash with the agent and an interpreter, went to Washington for the inevitable land cession. They agreed to sell a major portion of their "small strip" of land designated in the 1836 treaty. The treaty stated that the amount now left to them lay within boundaries "beginning at the mouth of the Great Nemeha down the Missouri River to the mouth of Noland Creek, thence due south one mile due west to south fork of the Nemeha River thence down the fork to the Great Nemeha River. . . . [This] it is hereby agreed shall be the future and permanent home of the Ioway Indians."

The tribe was to be paid from receipts from the sale of the land. *The Entreaty* They were to receive some funds in several lump sums, and the rest *Period* was to be invested for them by the United States. The undetermined proceeds of the land sale were to accrue and to be distributed at the discretion of the president. The Board of Foreign Missions of the Presbyterian Church was granted 320 acres of land for improvement of the mission and 160 acres of timbered land. Interpreter J. B. Roy received 320 acres for his services. Part of the fund set aside from the October, 1838, treaty was to be used to continue the agricultural program. A sum not exceeding $100,000 dollars was to be paid to the Ioways or expended under the direction of the President for the erection of houses, breaking and fencing lands, and purchasing stock. Fifty thousand dollars of the amount was to be paid, if deemed expedient, during the year following the next October (1855). The remainder of the $157,000 paid for the Platte Purchase was to be invested for educational and other benefits.[61]

At last the Ioways thought that they might obtain additional funds, although it was at a dear price. They agreed to allow roads and highways to be built through their remaining land, and certain railroad companies would be permitted rights-of-way. The chiefs promised that within six months the people would remove themselves to the remaining small portion of land.

Agent Vanderslice had many ideas about the management of Indian affairs. In response to a query on his opinions, he noted that it was time to.replace Indian native dress with American rural clothing. Always practical, he felt that it would cost less and would make the Indians feel more civilized, and, in dressing like white folks and removing their native decorations, they would stop remembering the past. It was also necessary to teach the Indians to value individual property ownership, to be thrifty, and to save for the lean times. Most importantly, land was to be handled individually instead of collectively, and families were to live on individual farms.[62]

Self-inspired from putting his thoughts on paper, Vanderslice called a council. "It was agreed that the system of congregating in villages should be broken up, and hereafter each family must settle upon separate and distinct tracts or parcels of land within their reservation." He added in his report that the fewer there were together, the less would be the tendency to "idleness, drinking, gambling, and other low and groveling debaucheries."[63]

If this could be accomplished, his plan could be successful, he believed. The village was the nucleus of tribal life. If they were separated and placed on individual allotments remote from each other except by foot and horse, the Ioways would lose that closeness derived from intimate contact, and the stubborn adherence to traditional ways would surely be eliminated, he reasoned. If further suggestions were accepted and carried out, the agent would sit on councils of elected tribal officials whose positions would be subject to official approval and have the power to veto any laws or regulations made by that body or to suspend any decisions made until approval was obtained from the President through the agent. "In fact the whole of their municipal affairs would be under the patronage and control of the United States until a change in the Indian character is sufficiently marked and their civilization as far advanced that they can take their place as fellow citizens with their white neighbors," he concluded.

All but a few Ioways had moved from their ceded lands and had received their usual annuity by November 7. In council they stated that they awaited receipt of the first payment that had been promised for October 1, 1854, if it had been approved by the President. The agent visited the Ioways in December and found that they made little progress in autumn agricultural pursuits and in house building. Instead he found that the able-bodied men had gone off on a winter hunt rather than stay at home and "tend their responsibilities there." He complained that the large annuity paid them had not been prudently used. Many had bought horses, at high and, in a few instances, extravagant prices. They did have some fine horses, but instead of purchasing good and substantial work horses, they paid $100 to $150 for good runners. Most of these they had with them on their buffalo hunt.

By May, 1855, according to the agent, conditions had improved. Greater attempts had been made at farming, and sufficient crops for the coming year were in the ground. The blacksmith shop, where their wagons and ploughs could be repaired, pleased those Ioways now determined to undergo civilization. Much of the agent's time was spent in advertising that intruders on the Ioway-ceded trust lands would be removed. Squatters had moved in even before it was ceded, and the loss of valuable timber, secretly cut and hauled away, reduced the value of the land. One bold man had built his house only three and a half miles from the agency.

The large payment promised in the previous year's treaty was to be paid in October, 1855. The agent warned all to be prudent in their expenditures and, certainly, to be wary of falling into the hands of the whiskey traders lurking on the reserve boundaries. If they behaved well, the Great Father would pay them again in the spring. His lecture was not completely heeded, and he wrote with chagrin that some of the best Indians had been on a druken frolic for several days. He criticized non-Indian authorities for little cooperation in the prevention of liquor sales. The laws were stringent, but enforcement was, as always, inadequate.[64]

For some time the families of the Ioway "half-breeds" had been concerned about their rights as prescribed in the Treaty of 1830. The whites had invaded their reserve on the north of the Ioway lands, and they asked that the land be assigned to them in severalty to prevent further intrusion. Half-breeds involved were Joseph Dorion, Joseph Robidoux, John Robidoux, Farrah Rodidoux, Francis Dupuy,

Elisha P. Dorion, Francis Bushnell, John B. Roy, Charles and Alex Dorion, G. Vanderslice and Charles L. Malese.* In November, 1855, Robert Whitecloud, whose mother, Mary, was half white, petitioned that the half-breeds receive fee simple title to their lands. Other signers of the petition included George, Sophia, and William Campbell, Frank LaFleshe, the son of Neconomi (who had married into the Omaha tribe after the disolution of her union with Dr. Gale), Stephen Story, Sarah Ballard, J. H. Beddow, Daniel Vanderslice, and Joseph and Francis Robidoux.

Before their rights could be ascertained, the identity of those qualified to receive land was to be decided. In May, 1856, Manypenny appointed Joseph L. Sharp as a commissioner to determine all Omahas, Ioways, Otos, Yanktonais, and Santees of any degree of mixed white or Negro blood. If a claimant was rejected, the reasons had to be entered in the record.[65] A year later Sharp completed the list, which included 185 Yanktonais, 105 Otos, 62 Omahas, 58 Ioways, and 17 Santees. By the end of 1860 land had been allotted to each person who qualified, although there had been many boundary disputes with settlers. Lewis Neal was the first individual to receive a patent.[66]

According to the agent's reports and letters, the Ioways began in 1856 to conform somewhat to the expected norm, moving so far as to attend some of the councils with the agent in "citizen's" clothing, which, they said, indicated that they wished to become white men. Some of the chiefs requested that their lands be sectionalized so that they could select a piece of land and claim individual title. How many others of the tribe agreed to this concept is debatable. The chiefs continued their requests for the promised brick houses. The agent tried to dissuade them, asking why they could not live in log houses like other white men. But they had seen officials' homes in Washington, St. Louis, and Europe. They had been promised brick houses, and they continued to insist.

The mission school claimed a victory. Kirwin Murray, a young man who had spent many years there, married an Indian girl also reared at the school. He was considered a success, "decent with respectable manners, and associated with the best portions of the [white] community," and a good example to other Ioways.

The 1857 mission report proudly stated that under the direction of James Williamson a large harvest had been produced with the aid of only Indian boy scholars. Eighty acres of corn, five acres of potatoes, five acres of garden, ten acres of oats and wheat, and thirty tons of hay had been harvested and stored. "The girls do well in the house;

---

*Besides bearing the names of their European progenitors, Indians took English names of persons known to them. They were also assigned arbitrarily such names as Julius Caesar, Benjamin Franklin, Jay Gould, George Washington, James G. Blaine, and Abraham Lincoln.

almost all the domestic work for our large family is done by them," Irvin added with satisfaction. Proud as he may have been, the reduction of the Indian children to manual-laborer status to fill the barns of the mission and to cook and clean house as servants did not satisfy Ioway parents. A growing faction of anti-agent and anti-missionary Ioways took their children from school. The census includes few of that nation among the thirty-four pupils, which included four Snakes, four Pawnees, seven Blackfeet, six Sioux, and one Cheyenne.

By 1859, the tribal population was 431. Efforts at agriculture continued with 68 fields and patches. Hay was cut and put up by some for winter stock feed. But the agent was not satisfied with Ioway progress on the road to civilization. He was aware that their values did not match his own, and he noted that:

> The first object should be to remove those prejudices against labor which are so deeply fixed upon their minds while in childhood by the recital in the wigwam of the traditions, tales, and fabulous accounts of chiefs and braves, of heroic conflicts with the enemies of their tribe, and of their strategems and maneuverings while on the "war path" in encompassing their foes; and also of their great exploits in hunting the buffalo and grizzly bear. The mind of the male child is filled with visions of their future success in attaining thus a high rank in their tribe. It is the goal of their ambition, and it is not without its influence upon the young female, who encourages with her smiles and admiration the successful warrior and hunter.[68]

The proposed sale in 1857 of previously ceded Ioway lands elicited keen interest. Told by certain individuals that their lands would be sold for very little and that they were to be defrauded, the Ioways asked unsuccessfully in April to visit the President to discuss the matter. They were refused, and the sale proceeded. The sale of 94,078 acres by June brought $184,864, while 1,122 acres were left unpurchased.[69] The agency farm constituted a portion of the acres unsold. Henry Lewis Morgan revealed in 1862 a dark side of Agent Vanderslice when he wrote:

> The government has spent a good deal in opening experimental farms among the Indians. The one of the Iowas was an unsuccessful experiment. Several thousand dollars were spent in opening the farm. A large appropriation was made for this purpose. Afterwards $1600 a year were spent for seven or eight years in carrying it on. It contains 660 acres, something more than a section, and is immediately east of the Mission House, in one of the choicest farms in Kansas. Above 200 acres were fenced and improved, several small buildings erected and the property could have been sold in three or four different years for $25 per acre. This is the general testimony at Highland, including S. M. Irwin. It took about all the farm raised besides the $1600 to carry it on. The Indians got no benefit of the crops, and none from instruction. It was a failure in all respects.

The Department at Washington directed the advertisement and sale of the farm for the benefit of the Iowas to whom the proceeds belonged. Vanderslyce, the agent, held on to it until his term was about out, although opportunities are known to have occurred to sell it at $25 per acre; and finally when the reaction set in on the price of land, he advertised it for sale in accordance with the instructions sent him long before, but was careful to do it in such a way that no one should know that it was to be sold. It was not known at Highland, about three miles from the farm, and the nearest village, nor at Iowa Point, nor anywhere else. On the day of sale a friend of the agent stopped at Highland on his way to the sale but said nothing. He was one of the persons selected to bid. The farm was sold for $1500 to a friend of the agent, and a few days afterwards it was consigned to Mr. Vanderslyce for $2000, who now owns it. There were several men at Highland able and willing to pay them two or three times this sum for the land had they known of the sale, among them Mr. Johnson, Genl. Bayliss, and probably Mr. Irwin. In this manner the Iowas were defrauded of a valuable piece of property by the agent, and that Vanderslyce is admitted to be one of the best agents the Iowas ever had. Think of that! This is so moderate a piece of iniquity that even now he passes as an honest man.

The trust lands of the Iowas which were worth $10 per acre on an average, were sold by the government at a valuation ranging from $1.50 to $2.75 per acre. They were seized by Squatters, and the government refused to interfere and thus allowed the Iowas to be despoiled. So much for experimental farms, and the history of this farm is the history of all.[70]

The beginning of the Civil War found the state of Kansas with "her soul in arms and eager for the fray." It was said that the war was the thought, the occupation, and the experience of Kansans for four years, and all races contributed volunteer members to its armed services.[71] At the war's beginning, Great Nemaha Agent J. A. Burbank ordered two flags for the tribes at his agency. He said: "Some of the citizens have been trying to get the Indians to join a military company. I refused to let them join any company until so ordered by the Great Father. I told them to remain on the reserve and raise something to eat, and if their Grandfather wanted them to fight he would send them guns and provisions."

On the south, in Indian Territory, the Choctaws, the Cherokees, the Chickasaws, the Creeks, and the Seminoles found themselves internally divided in their loyalty. Confederate agents came into the territory, and units of their army occupied federal posts on Indian lands. Confederate Indian emissaries were sent to the Kansas Indian reservations to bring those tribes under the Confederate banner if they could. Agent Burbank reported in July, 1861, that a delegation of southern Indians had invited the leaders of the Ioway and the Sac and Fox tribes to a great council: "Fearing that all was not right, I got a spy to watch their movements, and have learned that two Iowas, one Sac and Fox, and two Otoes have been selected by their respective tribes to visit the Comanche Indians. I have good reasons to believe that the secessionists and half-breeds are at work to raise the Indian tribes *en mass* to assassinate the whites, or plunge them in a war against the government."[72]

A year went by without the dire predictions being fulfilled, and Burbank was informed in the spring by the commissioner that it had now been decided not to call up for enlistment Indians of the Great Nemaha Agency until they had planted and raised a crop of food and then probably not at all. Until further notice the Ioways were to stay home. However, the men of the Ioway nation were now caught up in the fervor of the war and asked again if they could not be enrolled as soldiers. Burbank forwarded their request to the superintendent, who sent it to the commissioner with the comment that he was adverse to Indians in military service.[73] Burbank reported that after a brief episode with the southern Indians the Ioways, the Sacs, and the Foxes were now steadfastly loyal to the Union. Naggarash's Band did not want to be involved in the white man's war at all; others who did want to go would not go unless they were mounted. "I have held three councils with them and they refuse to go afoot," Burbank reported. If this resistance could be overcome, he believed that he could raise about sixty men for service. The old warrior and Head Chief No Heart had said, "I am too old to follow the war path, my red Brethren. My Great father wants me to go on the war path. My Red Brethren have called on me. My people are ready to go. I have called my young men together. There is about fifty in all that are ready to go. But they would not go to war without horses. The other tribes would laugh at them and think them poor if they went off to war afoot. He requested money from their annuity so that horses could be purchased for the young men.

By summer the young men were allowed to enlist. By October some had joined the 13th Kansas Regiment. In a short time three others requested that the agent buy them cavalry horses so that they could join the 2nd Regiment, Nebraska Cavalry. The commissioner ordered Burbank on December 6, 1862, "to let the chiefs in council authorize this expenditure and I will interpose no objection."

During the summer of 1863 a young Ioway named Cap Dorion enlisted in B Company, 14th Regiment, Kansas Volunteers. Apparently he had a debilitating disease, for soon after his enlistment he was placed in the Fort Leavenworth hospital. Believing that he could not recover unless under the care of the Ioway sacred society doctors, he left the hospital without leave and returned home. Once there the agent reported that he seemed unfit for further military service and requested that proper steps be taken to discharge him. The request was granted by Brigadier General E.R.S. Canby on December 14, 1863.[74]

In January, 1864, the commissioner was authorized to raise two additional Indian regiments. Burbank informed him that "a number of Indians of this agency are anxious to go. I think I could raise a full company by getting a few from the Otoes and Omahas who speak the same language as the Ioways. Allow me therefore to request that I may be authorized to convene the chiefs and enroll those who are willing to go into service." The next month Burbank received permission from Commissioner Dole to proceed.

After the war's end the mustering-out process began but not without difficulty. A regiment with many Ioway men in it had been sent to Lawrence, Kansas, to be released. The Ioways were Joseph Robidoux, Henry Buffalo, John Burbank (renamed after the agent), William Wolf, George Campbell, John Hill, Samuel Whitecloud, George White, Henry Lee, John Ford, Will Squirrel, Line Dorian, Farrer Robidoux, James Kin-ne-houk, Joseph No-Heart, William Ward, William Whitewater, George Washington, Joseph Vetter, John T. Hawk, and Daniel Whitecloud. Growing impatient with the time-consuming process and wishing to return home after such a long absence, the young men requested that they be allowed to leave early. They gave power of attorney to a certain officer to collect their pay and bring their discharge papers to the agency. "When Captain Henry came, he brought $1,100 dollars and gave it to them stating that it was all the money he received for them, and also stated that he lost his carpet bag with the statement of their accounts and all their discharges."[75] A later investigation proved that the captain had defrauded the Ioways, and he was prosecuted.

It can never be said that the Ioway nation did not contribute its share of manpower to the Civil War. Of the total population of 293 in 1864, 14 men were in the 13th Kansas Regiment, 23 in the 14th Kansas Cavalry Regiment, 1 in the 1st Nebraska Regiment, and 3 in "a Missouri Regiment," making a total of 41 in service and leaving only 21 men on the reserve. These few men and women were able to do all farming necessary to maintain the young men's families as well as their own.

Agent Vanderslice had said disapprovingly that young boys were trained to look forward to the status of warrior and that it was that and only that which mattered to them. For the Ioways the white man's war brought a sanctioned means to attain manhood in the true, traditional manner. The Ioways who remained at home re-integrated their traditional values and worked with new zest to sustain all their members while their young men were gone on the war trail.

After the Civil War the Ioways made various determined efforts to live like white men. Agents Vanderslice and Burbank, in carrying out the government's civilization policy, had succeeded in one way or another in convincing a portion of the leadership that it was necessary to substitute one way for another way of life. It is not known how much of the traditional life was retained because Burbank made only vague references to it, but there was a marked acceptance of new practices by the younger leaders who returned after the war.

Death had removed the older chiefs, who had acted as sources of tradition, and the influence that they had disseminated disappeared. No Heart's death in 1862 and Tohee's statement that the chiefs were young men foretold more rapid acculturation of the tribe. Cross-cultural influences were evident in the presence of mixed Indian-white leaders such as Robert Whitecloud.

Residence patterns largely changed from band villages to scattered agricultural farms during this period. Vanderslice and Burbank promoted this as part of a policy that envisioned the eventual allotment of land to heads of families and others. The number of individual farms and patches increased from twenty-one in 1861 to thirty-four in 1864. Grain, hay, vegetables and peach, apple, and cherry trees were planted. Animals and fowl were raised. At the same time, the Ioway tradition for differential wealth continued. The chiefs were in a favored position in their relationship with the agent and had the first opportunity to gain the means of increasing their wealth. They received the majority of the farming implements from the agent. An agency school had been constructed, and daily average attendance was said to be between forty and fifty students for all resident tribes.

The budget included payment for the service of a weekly minister. Another innovation was the use of a white physician, Dr. Thomas C. Shreve, at nearby White Cloud, Kansas. Among those visiting the doctor were mixed-blood families such as the Godfreys, Dorions, Dupees, Dupuys, Whitecloud s and Robidouxs. Among the war veteran patients listed were Sandy Reed, Joe Burbank, and Henry Washburn. During the war, experience with army medical service may have influenced the Indian acceptance of non-Indian medical practitioners. Innovators like Chiefs Tohee and Mahee, who now were farming completely in the "white way," chose to use Dr. Shreve's services and medicines. Some patients were fairly consistent in their visits. Others used the doctor's service a single time. Approximately 130 Ioways visited him between 1865 and 1866.[76]

Besides visiting the doctor in White Cloud, the Ioways were seen daily wearing "citizens" clothing while they drove their wagons to different towns to sell their vegetables. Burbank had other ideas for turning the Ioways into entrepreneurs. He suggested they weave willow baskets and grow broomcorn to make brooms. He encouraged the men to dig the coal found on the reserve. A few men sawed, hauled, and sold wood for fuel and timber. Seining the river for fish was possible after approval to buy a seine was obtained in 1863. White economic values were accepted so rapidly that the agent reported that more oxen, yokes, and ploughs were needed. The present owners would not loan theirs for fear of their being broken. If they did loan them, they expected to be paid for it. The old value of sharing one's possessions apparently did not hold in this case, and the adopted concept "never a borrower nor lender be" took precedence.

It was understood that the agent was responsible for leading the Ioways to the "true light of civilization." He would therefore em- phasize success and would regard as failures those Indians who clung to the old ways. Of course, some tribal members did not learn the new agricultural techniques, live in log houses with glass windows, visit the doctor in White Cloud, wear non-Indian clothing, send their children to school, nor listen to the white preacher. Agent reports indicate that some traditional patterns continued to be followed during the Civil War period:

1860 — Eighteen Iowas visited the Mississippi Sacs and Foxes and received some horses in the "smoking the horses" ceremony. The agent declared, "I have tried to prevent all such visits as they are demoralizing to all parties concerned." [77]

1861 — The Ioway police, or *Waikita* were instructed to punish those who became drunk under the new law passed by the council forbidding intemperance. In October the Mississippi Sacs and Foxes came to visit.

1862 — Several tribes visited the Ioways for presents. "They always have a feast, give presents and drink alot," said the Agent. The chiefs endeavored to retain their right to distribute monies or goods received as annuity. The agent gradually removed this practice from their control.

1863 — Cap Dorion returned from service in the army to be treated by the Ioway doctrs. [sic] A band of Winnebagos led by Chief One Horn came to settle down near the Ioways.

1864 — Some of the Ioways visited the Winnebagos.

1865 — An Ioway requested that the killing of his brother by a Kaw, or Kansa Indian, be paid for in the traditional manner or that he be allowed to revenge his death in the customary manner. Ioway chiefs, in New York after visiting on tribal affairs, bought beads, blankets, and ribbons as well as non-Indian articles of clothing.*

In 1859 and 1862 the great Nemaha Agency was visited by Henry Lewis Morgan, one of the great students of the American Indian, who had come to the West to study Indian culture and, in particular, to describe the kinship systems. In 1859 Robert D. Whitecloud was his chief source of information about the Ioways, and Reverend Irvin, then operating a private school, also discussed the tribe with him. Whitecloud listed the clans as the Wolf, Bear, Eagle, Pigeon, Buffalo, Snake, Elk, and Beaver (extinct). Clan members did not intermarry, and each clan carried its own personal names, which were never used by others. Whitecloud's name was *Wanyemera*, or Sitting Holding Something. He had had various names bestowed on him during his life and had changed his own name once or twice, he said.[78]

He listed the dances performed at that time as the Buffalo Dance, Otter Dance, Scalp Dance, Braves Dance, Society Dance, Feather

* H. L. Morgan visited the Ioways in 1862 and reported that most wore Indian dress, with few exceptions. See Leslie White, *Journals of Henry Lewis Morgan,* 137.

Dance, Dance with Joined Hands (Green Corn), Ancient Dance, Taking the Kettle Out, Dance for the Dead, Night Dance, Medicine Dance, Grizzly Bear Dance, Medicine Drinking Dance, and Enlisting Dance. One dance described entailed partaking of a morning draught of an herb potion that had cooked during the previous night. It had an emetic effect on each participant that cleansed them, he said. He had endeavored by payment of horses to become a member of the group who did that dance, but had not succeeded in being accepted.

Ioway religious beliefs included the presence of benign and evil forces that controlled men's lives. The spirits of good dwelled in the sun, the moon, and other aspects of nature. The buffalo, too, was sacred and had the magic power to reclothe its bones in flesh after death.[79] Immortality existed after death. Witches, representing the evil forces, were also very real. Medicine men were effective and could "put a bone in a man's back and take one out," he said.

Burial was either in a hollowed-out grave or in a cairn. If a rock cairn was constructed over the deceased, grave goods were included within it. A wooden grave post was erected near it and a tall staff with an emblem was placed close by. Morgan visisted an Ioway cemetery on the reserve in 1862 and noted that the interment method was used there. Of approximately twenty to thirty graves, some had grave posts at their north ends. Slender poles, some fifteen to twenty feet tall, stood by a number of graves. Some graves in the cemetery had frames of timber around them, while others were protected by erect slabs. Others had round timbers laid along them to cover the burial. Earth mounds over some graves were four feet high and several feet long. Morgan did not note the practice of scaffold burial. He visited the recent grave of Chief White Horse, a signer of the 1861 treaty. It was surrounded by a picket fence and was located on the summit of a prairie hill, one mile east of the agency. The grave post was six inches thick and was "painted with vermillion and on the north side was a row of red marks, seven in number, showing the number of scalps he had taken."[80] The opposite side showed eight marks, added by his friend who had placed the post there. On another side of the post was a painting of an Indian on a horse that indicated that White Horse lay there. Nearby was the tall slender staff with an emblem of a cross in the center.* Among other appurtenances of the grave was a bundle of sticks about six inches long with dark blood stains left by the mourners, who had "cut their arms and drawn blood" in the same manner as the London mourners of Little Wolf's baby.

Morgan was interested in the transfer of power after a chief's

* Such a flag, white with a square green cross, fashioned by hand, flew over a grave in the Ioway cemetery near Perkins, Oklahoma, in 1965. Remnants of other staffs and torn cloth flags were also present. The significance of the green cross was not given.

death. He was told that the son followed the father, but if he was not acceptable, a brother of the deceased or a nephew was chosen. War and peace chiefs still were chosen. Interpreter Elisha Dorion told Morgan that No Heart was now chief, although the previous chiefs, White Cloud and his father, had been head chiefs. "Robert the son of the latter was set aside, and No Heart was made chief in his place. When No Heart dies, Robert may get it yet. He has the right to be a chief."[81] Whitecloud, who spoke perfect English and was considered by Morgan a fine man of great natural abilities, said that "the government and missionaries are continually interfering to put upon them chiefs whom they would not recognize in their domestic affairs."*

The secretary of the interior, now responsible for Indian affairs, noted in 1862 that the rapid expansion of American civilization did not allow adequate land for Indian hunting. The acquisition of this land was required for agricultural purposes, and "although the consent of the Indians has been obtained in the form of treaties, it is well-known that they have yielded to a necessity to which they could not resist. Instead of being treated as independent nations they should be regarded as wards of the Government."[82] Another statement on prospective policy was that "reservations should be restricted so as to contain only sufficient land to afford them [the Indians] a comfortable support by actual cultivation, and should be properly divided and assigned to them, with the obligation to remain and cultivate the same."[83]

President Lincoln, the Great Emancipator, sometimes reflected his frontier heritage in his attitude toward the American Indians. His childhood had been spent in those states where Indians had not yet been completely removed west of the Mississippi and where tales of their so-called atrocities filled the mind of the children of the period. In 1830 he volunteered for service in the Black Hawk War against the Sacs in Illinois. As president he ordered the execution of thirty-nine Sioux and life imprisonment for one other for their attacks and "massacre" of settlers in Minnesota. He stated that the people of that area were interested in the complete removal of Indians beyond their boundary as a guarantee against further hostilities.[84] In his 1863 annual message he announced that 3,841,549 acres of land had been opened up for homestead settlement, military bounties, railroad uses, and other purposes. In speaking of recent Indian treaties that transferred large and valuable tracts to the government, he said:

It is hoped that the effect of these treaties will result in the establishment of permanent friendly relations with such of these tribes as have been

---

* It is possible that Robert Whitecloud, like his father, had resisted the agent and had not been appointed as a chief for that reason. Previous reference has been made to the agent's disapproval of a trip he made to Washington.

brought into frequent and bloody collision with our outlying settlements and emigrants. Sound policy and our imperative duty to these wards of the Government demand our anxious and constant attention to their material well-being, to their progress in the arts of civilization and above all, to that moral training which under the blessing of Divine Providence will confer upon them the elevated and sanctifying influences, the hopes and consolations of the Christian faith. [85]

During Lincoln's administration Ioway and other tribal cessions continued. The Ioway and the Sac and Fox tribes succumbed to pressure to cede their lands and made another cession treaty in 1861.[86] The latter ceded all the land they acquired by the Treaty of 1854, and the Ioways agreed to cede the western portion of their remaining lands in Nebraska and Kansas for the Sacs and the Foxes of the Missouri to use in lieu of their former reserve. The Ioways would be paid for the land that they ceded from the proceeds of sales of the Sac and Fox cession. Any annuities that resulted from the treaty stipulations were to be paid in goods rather than in money. All monies from other treaties would also henceforth be paid in this manner. One-half of the net proceeds of the land sales and interest thereon, at the rate of 5% would be paid to the Ioway tribe in the same manner as their annuities were paid under the 1854 treaty.[87]

Although the Ioways signed the treaty, in a later council they drew up a petition that stated that they now believed that Article II should be changed to read "one half of the net proceeds of the Sac land sale should be turned over to the Ioway tribe immediately in the form of agricultural implements, such as horses, wagons, oxen, and other needed articles." The Ioways said that they suggested the change because they desired to learn to live like white men but had no means to do so. Their present small annuities did not provide sufficient capital for improvement.[88]

Government acquisition of additional Kansas Indian land became possible by an act of Congress. On July 31, 1863, Secretary of the Interior J. P. Usher informed the commissioner of Indian affairs that in its last session Congress had passed an act that specified "that the President of the United States be as is hereby authorized to enter into treaties with the several tribes of Indians respectively now residing in the State of Kansas, providing for the extinction of their titles to lands held in common within the said state, and for the removal of such Indians of said tribes as hold their lands in common to suitable localities elsewhere within the territorial limits of the United States, and outside the limits of any state." The commissioner was instructed to "carry out the objects of this enactment as soon as possible." [89]

In January, 1864, Ioway and Sac and Fox Agent Burbank was called to Washington. Indian land title extinction and removal of Indian tribes were subjects of foremost importance in his talks with the commissioner. In a letter written after his return he said: "That in

258

pursuance to your verbal instruction, I have called the tribes together and presented your point of view." He asked them to reflect on it and return to council. The Ioway stated that they preferred to let the Winnebagoes have the land ceded to them in 1861 and remain where they were, and "come in as white citizens."[90]

Part of the agent's and the commissioner's plans involved the Otoes. It had been suggested to the Ioways that they be removed to Otoe land if they would relinquish their own. An emissary had been sent to the Otoes, who had agreed to sell land for Ioway settlement. The tribes involved expressed a desire to visit Washington to confirm the terms of the proposed treaty, but they were not invited. A treaty draft was instead sent to them. On March 6, 1864, the Ioways agreed to sign, but after further consideration the Otoes refused. For the time the Ioways were left alone by the treaty makers and could wait apprehensively for the next approach.

The tribe faced many other difficult government relationships and problems. The constant struggle continued with annuities, either because of the form in which they were distributed or because the payments were late. They did not know the financial status of their trust funds. Despite intermittent queries, Treaty agreements were constantly violated in regard to financial payments promised for specific articles aside from the annuities. The Ioways did not acquire the actual cash as it accrued from the sale of Sac land. Their money invested in southern bank bonds did not always draw interest, or they were not paid interest on it during and after the Civil War. There was never enough money, and there should have been.

The Ioways made at least five requests to go to Washington to try to understand and solve their problems by direct confrontation with either the President or the commissioner. It had become general policy to refuse Indian requests to visit Washington unless it was imperative to persuade them to agree to a land cession. If possible, treaties were handled at the local level.

Notchininga, or No Heart, died on September 2, 1862. The uncle of the deposed chief White Cloud had seen many years of change for his people. He belonged to the ruling Bear clan and served as chief after White Cloud's death in 1852. The death of a chief customarily placed a member of the same clan in his position. At that time five men carried the name of White Cloud: Robert, Samuel, Jefferson, Frank, and James, some of whom were of intermarried, non-Ioway descent. At the time of Notchininga's death, the chief's role did not pass into their hands. A council was called for October 23, 1862. The agent reported that Tohee, who had been appointed a chief by the agent, said: "Tell our great father our head chief is dead, and now the chiefs are young men, and we want to see if our people cannot become like white people. Our head chief is our chief, and if our great father will look at the treaty he will see who ought to be our head chief. Some of our young men want to be head chief. We think we ought to know who is the head chief."[91] It is not certain if this is what Tohee said, but it does indicate a contest or power struggle for the position, the existence of factions, and the challenge to the old way of passing on authority. The chief perhaps had to be a full-blood Ioway; some Whiteclouds who were eligible were not, or they were ineligible for other reasons. Tohee alluded to the former treaty signers and indicated that among them is one who should hold the chief's position. The treaty signers for the 1861 treaty in order were No Heart, Naggarash, Mahee, Tohee, Tahrakee, Thuromony, and White Horse. The 1854 treaty signers were No Heart, Little Wolf (Shontayiga), Wah-mon-a-ka, and British (Naggarash) the second signer of the 1861 treaty. The 1838 treaty was signed by Frank Whitecloud, No Heart, the Plum (Kongee), Mockshigatonah, and Senontiya, who went to Europe as doctor. According to cited evidence, the Bear and the Buffalo were leading clans, and the principal chief came from the Bear clan. (Clan affiliations for many of the above individuals are unknown.) Burbank informed the commissioner of No Heart's death in November by saying that he was unwilling to designate a successor until he was advised. Obviously the decision was not to be left to the Ioways. Two years earlier, the agent had placed Tohee and Mahee on the council. This is not to say that they would not have been hereditary or traditional choices, but it is not certain. Tohee's later descendents say that they are of the Buffalo clan, leaders of the tribe in fall and winter.

It is assumed that the greater the number of hand-picked chiefs on the council, the easier the agent's job became. In this regard Burbank wrote to the former Agent Vanderslice for advice. He replied that the question of who should be chief is readily answered by seeing that the next oldest chief take his place, and "as Nag-ga-rash was the second chief during the life of No Heart, he became the first Chief at his death, and as such you are justified to recognize him."[92] Accordingly, Naggarash (Laggarash) became chief, and not Robert Whitecloud as H. L. Morgan and Dorion had discussed during the former's ethnographic inquiries.

The Great Nemaha Agency was under the jurisdiction of the Central Superintendency with others in a region near St. Joseph, Missouri, where the superintendent's office was located. W. M. Albin, the new superintendent in 1864, spoke against some practices in the agency system. The first criticism was aimed at the annuity goods order system, which could easily be subject to fraud if the agent and chiefs were in collusion, as both could be bribed. The agent and chiefs sat at the pay table, and the latter signed the receipts for money. According to Albin the fraud could be perpetrated as follows:

The agent issued an order to the Indians according to the previous payroll, not considering births, deaths, or emigration. Some chiefs could be induced or bribed by the agent to do their bidding, to sign for the whole tribe, one-third of whom might not receive any benefits. The money was paid to the trader in consideration of the receipts given. In nineteen out of twenty cases the traders wanted to defraud the Indians, and the Indians were not satisfied when they saw that their agent had become the champion of the trader. Albin declared, "We should carry out in good faith the contract we made with the Indians when we purchased their lands, and pay their monies into their own hands."

Another evil existed in the handling of the "surplus," Albin said:

The surplus is another evil by which the Indian is swindled in untold thousands. It may not be perfectly understood that the stealing found of the agents principally consists in this surplus, as for example, supposing the amount of the annuity is 60,000 and the number of Indians is 1,000. There would be 60.00 for each. However, supposing the Indians are paid 50.00 a piece, this will leave a surplus of $10,000 which the agents and chiefs being in copartnership divide between them, generally with a decided advantage to the agent.[93]

The commissioner, piqued by this criticism of personnel and policies, reprimanded Albin severely for revealing the glaring wrongs and injustices of the system. Albin replied to this censure that he had not meant any disrespect to the President or to any of the persons in charge of Indian policy.[94] Albin's criticism is bulwarked by Morgan's disclosures of the Great Nemaha Agency:

I have made this a subject of inquiry both with Mr. Irwin and Mr. Williams who is in charge of the Iowa school. The evidence increases that it does but little good, that it is not only a failure but disgraceful for the immorality and dishonesty with which the business is managed. It is a position of great temptation for the agent to speculate in the funds which pass through his hands, and the opportunities are numerous enough. At the Iowa agency (Mr. Burbank) there is a school and improvement fund $5,000 per annum, the annuity about $7,000. The improvement money is spent on a school near the agency which is now said to be doing well, about 25 scholars, and on the Blacksmith Shop before mentioned. There is no Indian farm now carried on here. The first abuse is in making out the census or pay roll. This is done three or four months before the annuity is paid and tickets are given to the heads of families, corresponding with the classification of persons on the roll. So that each Indian knows how much he will draw on his family ($22 each). Mr. Irwin mentioned that in making out the roll sham names are sometimes introduced, e.g., Noheart and Wolf. Chief secured a ticket for himself — including his family, and a separate ticket for his wife and a sham family. This they told Mr. Irwin and said they took the tickets because the agent and traders told them to. They were in debt and the agent and traders took this method to aid them. Thus they were made dishonest and also placed under obligations to the agent and traders.
Another method is to include deceased members of the family, e.g., if he has but four in his family he will secure a ticket for seven or eight. When the roll is paid these Indians are required to sign a false receipt, and the agent certifies that it is correct, when he knows it to be false.

Remedy for this is to require the agent to swear to the census and punish the perjury. A proper oath can be framed. Mr. Irwin says he has known a number of times a census of four and five hundred Iowas returned when but 300 could be found.

The next abuse is in the system of licensed traders. At present the Iowas have one licensed trader who is a brother of the agent, Mr. Burbank. He has a hand in the census and all the affairs of the agency, and is substantially a partner of the agent. He always knows when the annuities are to be paid, that is, he knows some months in advance, and is the first to know. It is generally understood here that the information comes from the chief clerk in the office at Washington. If this is true, he receives fees from all of these agents and is hand in glove in all these rascalities. As soon as it is known when the payment is to be made, the traders begin to give as large credits as the Indian desires up to the full amount of his ticket. The store is open through the year, but the credits are not large until near the time of the payment. The credits thus given usually amount to the entire annuity. A few sometimes get a little, but the most of them not a cent, besides being a little in debt on the next year.

Payment day. The Indians assemble. The agent calls by heads of families and the Indian responds. His ticket is compared with the roll (this census or roll is never sent to Washington until after the payment is over) and if right the money is counted out by the agent and laid on the table. The trader sits there and says you owe me just this sum and without any account or settlement he takes the money and puts it into his trunk or bucket. The Indian makes his mark on the receipt and leaves without touching the money. Another Indian presents a ticket calling for $80. The traders says you owe me $90. I will take this and you will owe me on the next year. The Indian signs the receipt and walks away.

The Indian has no account, keeps none and does not seem to care anything about it. He buys a number of articles and cannot keep the sum of them, but with a bill he might be made to understand it. The wares sold are partly useful and partly trinkets, and the profits of course very great. We went over some of these prices. It is evident that the Indian cares nothing for the annuity, but most for the credit, and the whole thing is so managed as to make it of little use. Licensed traders ought to be prohibited on the old reservations if there are villages near, or the number should be increased so as to make one a restraint upon the other. After the annuity is paid the pay roll and receipts are sent to Washington.[95]

In addition to this fraudulent situation, Morgan disclosed that, when Vaughn was the Ioway agent, his son was the trader's partner. The Ioway farmer was paid $500 annually and spent only five months of the year there and seven at home in Missouri. Blacksmiths sometimes paid "30% to the agent as was the case of the Kickapoo Agency, and is probably the rate upon all the rest."[96]

Without a doubt the agent had become a powerful figure. He could assume the role of chief executive of tribal affairs with veto power over the Indian council's suggestions and decisions. He interpreted and carried out government policy in the manner he chose. He listened to Indian complaints and sent as many of their remarks as

he wished to Washington or to the superintendent. Often he did not
convey their words at all, for much of their criticism was directed
against himself. In some cases Indians were punished by flogging.
The agent's willingness to champion Indian rights was based on his
personal interest and was limited by fear of the censure he might
receive if he became too critical of the system, as Albin did.

Many agents tried over and over to inspire their charges to accept
the new ways that they believed were the only means by which the
people could survive in the new order. But others were in the
business to profit, and they carefully covered their deeds by one
means or another.

For official and public consumption Burbank appeared to have
had Ioway interests at heart. Many of his official letters voice great
concern for their welfare. He attempted to have laws passed that
would convict liquor dealers. He worked consistently in his first
years to stop the theft of Ioway timber. He was constantly frustrated,
because Indian testimony was not accepted in court and these crimes
continued throughout his tenure. He inquired about their funds. A
late arrival of the annuity was officially criticized, and an entreaty for
larger amounts of money to buy needed farm equipment and supplies continued throughout his years as agent. On the whole he
appears to have been one of the most sympathetic Ioway agents, but,
as revealed by Morgan, he too was exploiting the Ioways for his own
advantage.

In May, 1864, the Sac lands went on the public sale list, and in
October the Ioways requested $15,000 due them from the sale.
However, it was not forthcoming, and in September the chiefs
gathered and, in a petition, stated that the agent had sold their lands
without their consent, and that they had not received any money.
Although they inferred that the agent had not been honest, the
superintendent examined the agent's accounts on August 22 and
noted to the commissioner that they seemed to be in order and the
funds dispersed properly and economically except for a six-dollar
gold pencil, which "however useful they be to agents, can scarcely be
said to be necessary for any tribe of Indians."[97]

Burbank met with the commissioner in September, 1865, to answer
charges brought against him by the Ioways. The commissioner
requested that he write a letter to record his defense. In the letter
Burbank called the charges false and foolishly audacious. To the
accusation that he had sold the Ioway lands without their consent,
he replied that Vanderslice had been their agent when they agreed to
sell them, but he had been the agent when the actual sale occurred.
The second charge was of mercenary complicity with the trader, his
brother. His response to this was weaker, merely that "I can only
offer his affidavit and mine to substantiate this fact if desired as soon
as time will permit," and that "I can fully establish the fact by
competent witnesses that it has been my active policy to prevent
their [Ioway] going into debt. I have always counseled them to save

their money. Nag-ga-rash is the most prodigal of Indians, and has caused me more trouble than any one member of the tribe, on account of his proneness to run into debt."

To the accusation concerning his consent to the giving of the annuity money to the trader at the pay table, he said: "At no time has the money been paid by me into the hands of anyone other than those entitled to receive it. The trader being present, of course, avails himself of the opportunity to collect his just claims from the Indians themselves, and in no case have I permitted the Indians respectively to pay out all their money to the trader, no matter to what amount they were indebted to him. As to squandering their money, my accounts fully declare the falsity of such charge."

He concluded by saying that he was unwilling to believe that Laggarash (Naggarash) or Kihega, in a sober state, if at all, would permit their names to be used in these charges. He stated that the charges had been made up by malcontent whites who wished to have him removed and to have a favorite appointed in his place.[98] Burbank was not removed, and Ioway discontent and rancor reached new intensity as the following letter reveals:

December 18, 1865

Sir:

On last Saturday evening the chiefs, braves, and warriors of the Iowa Tribe of Indians came very unexpectedly to my office, entered and sat down. I immediately asked the Interpreter whether they had come to hold a Council and stated that if they had, I was ready to listen to them. They made no reply for some time, and I told them it would soon be dark and if they had anything to say to me to proceed. The chiefs said nothing. About that time I noticed that what is known as the Ky-he-ga band of Iowas were all thoroughly armed with Revolvers, Tomahawks, and Knives, and began to suspect that there was something wrong. After awaiting some time Ky-he-ga got up and said that they had heard some news and had come to talk to me and said that the young men had something to say to me.

James Whitewater then commenced by saying that they had come here to tell me things, which their chiefs were afraid to say. He said that they were dissatisfied with all of their Employees, and would have a new Agent, that they had come here to throw me out, and take charge of the office themselves. Several others followed in the same strain and from what I could understand of their language I was satisfied that they intended to murder me, take possession of the Office and get up a fight with the balance of the Tribe. One young man, George Washington, came forward, demanded that I should deliver to him the key to the office. Having no weapons and no White men with me I immediately got up and started for the Agency house hence, a distance of some three to four hundred yards from the Office, telling the Interpreter to state to them that I would return in a few minutes, with the intention of getting my revolver, and if possible find one or two of the employees expecting to return to the Office, and with their assistance and the Kin-a-hook band, defend myself and protect the property of the U.S.

As soon as I got up I heard one or two gun caps burst but managed to get out of the house. George Washington followed me snapping his Revolver at me which fortunately did not explode. I immediately commenced running and hearing the War whoop hallowed for help, some ten of Ky-he-ga's band followed me. I succeeded in getting into the house before the Indians got to it. I found my pistol but it was so rusty that I could not use it. Then tried to hide if possible. The Indians broke open the house door until they found me, and on seeing me fired two shots. I finally managed to quiet them and returned to the office with them. By this time all the Iowa Indians had left the office except Ky-he-ga's band. They then demanded the keys of the office which after some parley I was forced to give them or be murdered. I then went to the house, sent to White Cloud [the village] for assistance and telegraphed to Ft. Leavenworth for Troops. Some 20 of the citizens of White Cloud arrived here about midnight. The key having been left with the Indians who remained in the Office, it was then taken from them. The office and council house being under the same roof with a door between them, I decided to place all of the Indians in the council house, put them under guard, close all the shutters and station the men in there and send word to the Iowas to come to the office to hold a council early in the morning. About 10 AM the Iowas came straggling along. As soon as they entered the office the men would come out of the council house disarming them, concealing them in the council house. In this manner we soon secured all the Tribe and took thirteen revolvers with some knives, etc.

After the tribe were all secured I arrested the following persons of the Ky-he-ga's band who are the Ringleaders, vizt Kyhega, James Whitewater, George Washington, Sandy Reed, Nau-kan-hotshee, Minda-tha-wa-th, Hotchisee and Little Buffalo. These I placed under arrest and sent the balance of the tribe home. The Hon. Judge Dundy arriving in the evening I turned them over to him for hearing. During the night, and next morning he heard the evidence and decided to bind them until the next term of the U.S. Court except Little Buffalo whom he released.

About noon a Lt. O. G. Robinson arrived here from Ft. Leavenworth with thirty men of the 2nd U.S. Cavalry.

Judge Dundy turned the prisoners over to him to be taken to Ft. Leavenworth for safekeeping. The Sac and Foxes of Mos. having come here at the same time I presumed that they were mixed up in it, but find that they were home, some of them, except Wa-pe-ca-ca.

The cause of this outbreak was the refusal to take a young brave, a member of their Band to Washington. My instructions from the Department were to take four chiefs and the Interpreter, consequently it was not in my power to take him if I had wished to. They were determined that he should go, and their proceedings at this time, with information which I have since obtained, lead me to believe that they had agreed among themselves whether to force me to comply with their demand or kill me. The persons who were engaged in this outbreak and are now under arrest are the ones referred to in the Report of Oct. 12 for the month of September as being inclined to cause trouble by stealing from the Citizens in the vicinity of the reservation. This matter is all ended for the present and the peace and quietude of this agency hereafter on my judgment depends altogether in the manner in which they are dealt with.

The chiefs were not aware of this intended outbreak and were entirely innocent of the intentions of the Ky-he-ga band.

The revolvers which I have taken I will send to Fort Leavenworth for safe keeping until I can consult you further about them. [99]

Such an attack showed that the resentment felt by some Ioways had overcome their great fear of agent and troop retaliation. Kihega and Naggarash had signed a recent letter of complaint against the agent, as had White Cloud and Kihega three years before in 1862. Kinahook's band appeared to be loyal to Burbank or afraid to act. The agent said that he intended to seek their aid in the incident. He explained that his not choosing a young man from Kihega's band to go to Washington caused the uprising, but it is known that many accumulated grievances played a part in this last known Ioway attack on United States authority. Many dissenters, among them, Sandy Reed, James Whitewater, and George Washington, were young Civil War veterans. Their war experiences had made them different young men from those sent off by the agent four years earlier. No longer did they have a childlike or submissive view of the agent and his authority. The days of the Father and the Grandfather had ended for many.

The outburst opened official ears in Washington and the frequent Ioway requests for an audience were finally acknowledged. Representatives were invited to visit in January, 1866 (see Figure 19). The chiefs expressed their desire to see the President, but excuses were given that he was extremely busy with the affairs of all his children, and they were told they should talk to his representatives. They gently broached the subject of their selling the remaining sections of their land and consented to consider the matter at their leisure. After they had voiced their complaints, the government representatives promised to do what could be done (considering all the circumstances, of course). Following the conference, the Ioways consented to go to New York. They visited the mercantile establishments of Buckley and Sheldon on 77th and 75th Streets near Broadway and Drinker and Anderson on Duane Street where they were allowed to purchase, at the government's expense, ribbons, scarlet cloth, sashes, assorted yarn, shirts, vests, carpet bags, a compass, boots, pants, calico, beads and broaches.

In 1867, the chiefs informed the agent, who had reminded them of their promise to consider selling their remaining land, that they now were interested in signing a treaty to that effect. They said that they would sell their land and move south to Indian Territory to be with the Sacs and the Foxes. Actually they were afraid that the government would soon force them to sell, and they believed that they could advantageously sell their lands before pressure was applied. The negative white attitude toward Indians during this period in this region was pronounced. Wars with Plains tribes on the frontier frequently made life difficult for reservation Indians and for white settlers, who often suspected all resident Indians of aggressive tendencies.

After the Civil War a great river of soldier families and other land-hungry or restless individuals flowed west of the Missouri. The Homestead Act of 1863 enabled many to take land and settle on it.

Figure 19.   The Ioway chiefs visiting the Commissioner of Indian Affairs in Washington, January, 1866. *Front row, left to right:* Mahee (Knife), Tohee (Briar), Cass Dorion, Naggarash (British), and Tarrakee (Deer Ham). *Second row:* Elisha Dorion, Kahegainga (Little Chief), and Black Hawk. The photograph is thought to be by Zeno A. Shindler. Courtesy of Kansas State Historical Society.

Railroads had received large amounts of land for rights-of-way. As towns sprang up, dirt roads stretched across the country to connect them and then to go beyond them in wagon trails toward the west. The Indians of Kansas and Nebraska were again in the way. Pressure for removal, as expressed by elected officials and others, brought about the reluctant and bitter departure of the Delawares, the Ottawas, the Kickapoos, the Chippewas, the Munsees, the Potawatomis, the Sacs and the Foxes to the Indian Territory. Here they were placed on lands that the great southern tribes had been forced to cede in treaties after the Civil War because of the southern sympathies of portions of their leadership. For the time, however, the small Ioway nation, whose population had slipped below four hundred, was allowed to remain near their agency at No Hart, Nebraska.

9. The Quaker Years

IN HIS INAUGURAL address on March 4, 1869, President Grant declared, "The proper treatment of the original occupants of this land, the Indians, is one deserving of careful study. I will favor any course towards them which tends to their civilization and ultimate citizenship."[1] Criticism of the state of Indian affairs had been growing. Maj. Gen. John Pope, Commander of the Department of the North West, speaking of the effect of the national policy on the Indians, said:

> He has lost all the high qualities of his native state, and has simply been reduced to the condition of an idle, drunken, gambling vagabond. The mortality among these annuity Indians living on reservations, has far exceeded that among the wild tribes and bids fair to extinguish the whole race in a wonderfully short period. I think it will not be disputed by those familiar with the subject that our Indian policy has totally failed of any humanizing influence over the Indian, has worked him a cruel wrong and has entailed a very great and useless expense upon the Government. I have passed ten years of my life in service on the frontier, and the facts herein stated are the result of observation and experience and are familiar to every officer of the Army who has served in the West.[2]

Responding to the pressure of influential groups, President Grant sought advice on Indian policy reform, and Congress created the Board of Indian Commissioners, a nonpartisan group with authority to inspect all Indian office records, the agencies and personnel thereof, to be present at annuity payments, to confer with Indian councils, and to advise superintendents and agents of their duties. Its members could suggest changes in duties, responsibilities, and methods. Indian goods were to be available for inspection at the time of purchase and distribution. The Board would hear complaints against agents and refer them to the secretary of the interior. All officials of the Office of Indian Affairs were instructed to cooperate with the board and "to give the most respective heed to their advice within the officers' positive instructions from their superiors and to cooperate with them in the most earnest manner to the extent of their proper powers in the general work of civilizing the Indians, protecting them in their legal rights, and stimulating them to become industrious citizens in permanent homes instead of following a roving and savage life."[3]

Two years earlier, during President Johnson's administration, the Peace Commission had been formed to investigate Indian conditions and to placate through councils and treaties the frontier Indians of Nebraska, Kansas, Indian Territory, Texas, and Colorado, who were effectively resisting the westward movement of whites. Government acquisition of Indian land continued, and the Peace Commission sought to eliminate the aggression that resulted from this and other causes. Their reports blamed not the Indians but the United States government and its citizens for most hostilities manifested by the Indians. They suggested, among other things, improving the Indian service and inviting the nation's religious organizations to volunteer their services in providing advice and care to Indians.

President Grant turned to the Society of Friends, or Quakers, and successfully enlisted their support of his new reform program. Six agencies in the Central Superintendency — the Great Nemaha, the Oto and Missouri, the Pawnee, the Omaha, the Winnebago, and the Santee Sioux — were placed under their wing.[4]

Ioway discontent had reached another peak in 1869. The tribe had sent petitions and had repeatedly and unsuccessfully requested permission to visit Washington to discuss their unsettled accounts and to voice their opprobation of the muddling and mishandling of their affairs. Now, however, with the growth of railroads west of the Missouri and with an eye toward land accession, the government consented to their pleas. Once there, the main concession was not made by the government but by the Ioways, who consented to a railroad right-of-way through the reservation at $2.50 an acre.

In the spring, 1869, the Society of Friends selected Thomas Lightfoot of Montgomery County, Pennsylvania, to be the first Quaker Ioway agent. In accepting the position, he replied, "Please forward commission and full instructions where to go and what to do." He did not yet know the ways of bureaucracy, and when railroad men asked for certain reserve lands and Indian timber to build the railroad, he gave his consent. He reported this to the superintendent and was reprimanded for his unauthorized action. Soon after this, a Quaker delegation visited the agency to note his progress and to council with the Ioways, who spoke strongly against congressional ratification of the treaty concerning railroad rights. Certain members claimed that Chiefs Naggarash, Tohee, Mohee, Kihega, Chatomonah, and Tarrakee had signed the treaty in violation of their wishes and were to receive lands individually for signing. Ioway women were especially adverse to removal from the ceded lands, and went so far as to affix their names or marks to the petition requesting that the treaty not be ratified. Agent Lightfoot said, "D. R. Holt, a trader, was in Washington at the time the treaty was made and he asserts that other parties were willing to pay the Indians $5.00 an acre, but the Commissioner who had them in charge would not allow them to receive propositions from any other than the Railroad Companies."[5]

After the Quakers returned to the East, Benjamin Hallowell, a member of the Friends Executive Committee, visited with President Grant on November 11, 1869, and read the Ioway and other treaties to him. At the conclusion of the reading the President stated, "There is so general dissatisfaction on the part of the Indians with the treaties that have been recently made with them, that I propose to withdraw all those that are not ratified from before the Senate, and begin anew if necessary."[6]

In January, 1870, Hallowell became alarmed when he discovered that the treaties were once again offered by the Department of the Interior for ratification. He had assumed that President Grant's disapproval had been sufficient to prevent this. He wrote to Commissioner Ely Parker that he could not understand the action, considering the opposition of the Indians, the agents, the superintendents, and the President. On February 4, 1870, Grant sent a message to the Senate: "For the reasons stated in the accompanying communication from the Secretary of the Interior, I respectfully request to withdraw the treaties hereinafter mentioned which are now pending before the Senate . . . concerning treaties concluded with the Sac and Fox of the Missouri and the Iowa tribes of Indians, February 11, 1869."[7] For the moment the Ioways retained their twenty-five sections of land.

The Quaker policy was also directed to saving the Indian from fraud and extinction. They did not necessarily object to land cessions, since individual land ownership was believed to be one basis for "civilization," and they agreed that most Indian tribes held more land than was necessary for their use. They also thought that Indian culture served no useful purpose in its indigenous forms and must be surplanted by "American" cultural characteristics. Elimination of native practices was to be bloodless, gradual, and thorough and was to be brought about by education and persuasion.

The Friends established stores that would serve the Indian interest and eradicate the older system's fraud. Commissioner E. P. Smith received the Ioway Quaker Store report in 1875. The agent and the trader were comanagers; the trader received $800 a year and a share of any profits that should accrue. Any profits above a certain percentage were to be spent for Indian advancement:

Under Agent Lightfoot the Indians have been diverted from following their former custom of indulging in beads and other fripperies and to make the most of their annuities. It is sufficient to say that the Iowas instead of suffering semistarvation for six months of each year have had a sufficiency until the last plague of grasshoppers, when on information received here the storekeeper was requested to furnish means for the alleviation of the destitute which was attended gratis. The second advantage of this system of establishing stores in the Indian country is that there is no inducement to make excessive charges as the trader is no gainer for anything beyond the amount of his guaranteed profit.

The Ioway store manager was a retired Philadelphia merchant. He had already accumulated a profit of $4,200 to be used for the Ioways' benefit, with any excess applied to the establishment of another agency's store.[8]

In addition to certain profits returned to the tribe from their store, Agent Mahlon Kent, the Ioways' third Quaker agent, set about garnering additional revenue by leasing Ioway-held coal resources. Cattle leases were made, and sales of timber allowed, to increase tribal income and self-sufficiency. The Ioways, it was planned, would develop a business sense in the Quaker tradition.

In 1871, certain members of the tribe requested that their lands be surveyed and allotted individually. Fears grew that their land might be lost to them entirely, as had been the case in much of their previous history. Their fears were based on fact, and severalty seemed a way of preserving something of their inheritance. On February 14, 1871, D. R. Holt, an influential Nebraskan, wrote to the Hon. John Toffe in Washington: "Our Indians want to make a new treaty. The Iowas and the Sac and Fox of the Missouri have 60 sections of the best land in the state. Will you please call upon the Commissioner of Indian Affairs and have him invite them to come to Washington immediately."[9] Senator Toffe informed the commissioner that "many earnest appeals have been made to me by the people of that state on the matter." Indian officials on the local level had also been considering the matter. Agent Kent's and Superintendent Janney's opinion was that allotments of eighty acres for heads of families and forty acres for single adults over the age of eighteen were adequate amounts for the Ioways to retain. "A larger amount than this would extend the tribe" and disperse them at too great distances from one another.[10]

In July the secretary of the interior informed the commissioner: "I have considered your report upon the application of the Ioway Indians for the survey and allotment of their lands under the 6th Article of the Treaty of May 17, 1854, and I approve your recommendations to meet the expenses necessary to make the survey and allotment by a Sale of the lands ceded in trust by the Sac and Fox of Missouri to the United States under the treaty of March 6, 1861."[11] This land had been ceded as a home for the Sacs and the Foxes after they sold their remaining Great Nemaha Reserve lands. The Ioways had received no payment for this cession and were therefore interested in the sale of the land now held in trust. The land was offered for sale, all bids were in by October 1, and the land was all sold. In November and December the

Ioway chiefs requested, then petitioned for, a summary of monies derived from the sale and requested that the amount owed them be paid directly. "The annuities received are insufficient to enable us to progress in these improvements as rapidly as we desire."[12]

No reply came. In January, 1872, the chiefs sent another request and also asked for a survey and individual allotment of their own land, in order to "make comfortable homes and more thoroughly adopt habits and customs of the white man because we have given up buffalo hunting and are depending upon our land for our support." Naggarash, Tohee, Mahee, and Kihega signed this petition, but they received no answer for some time.

This lack of response pointed up the paucity of tribal influence following disposal of most of its land to the government. The Ioway chiefs were discovering that the Quaker agents with their new policy were no more pliant or tractable in many ways than were previous agents. Reports of the 1870s reflect the increasing lack of power of the councils of the chiefs. In 1870, the chiefs requested information on how much annuity the tribe was supposed to receive each year according to all previous treaty agreements and land cession sales. The new agent Thomas Lightfoot stated that they had asked repeatedly and felt they had a right to an answer. In 1871, the chiefs petitioned to have Samuel Whitecloud hired as an apprentice carpenter, "so that in time we may be able to have the business carried on by hiring men from our own tribe." This request was ignored. Then the council, calculating on its own, said that $11,000 was due it. They requested that it be paid them in order that they could pay their debts to D. R. Holt, a trader. They also assented to the government's proposal for division of funds for education, a physician, purchases of equipment, and individual annuity payments. From the $12,133.75 annuity, $7,838.75 was to be distributed to the people for payment of their debts and other purposes. The remainder was to be applied to the above-mentioned articles.[13]

In 1872, the chiefs again submitted a petition to request information on the status of their land sale. In July, they requested the replacement of the agency mowing machine. Robert Ward, Jefferson Whitecloud, and others signed this request.

Growing disillusionment with Agent Lightfoot developed. The Ioways complained that the numerous requests and petitions that they had sent had not been answered and that the agent paid no attention to their needs. (The Sacs, also under this agent, said that he had told them "that he did not care about us when we tried to get him to stop our timber from being cut, saying it's too far for me to go and see about it. He wants us to become civilized, but we don't want to become citizens. We have always been Indians and want to remain so." They wished to move south to the Indian country, and the Otoes and "our friends the Ioways want to go with us also." They had no answer to their request to move. Sac-a-pee declared that "since this Quaker has been in charge of this agency he pays no attention to the Sac and Fox chiefs. He says he will do as he pleases. Our chiefs are afraid of the Agent. When they say anything to him, the Agent says, 'that will do' and they hang their heads and say nothing."[14]

In December the Ioway chiefs again petitioned the President for answers to their queries about surveying and allotment of their lands and the amount of the total proceeds of the previous year's land sale. Their request for their funds was denied, and the land sale money was converted into 6% bonds held by the government for the tribe.

Agent Lightfoot was replaced by C. H. Roberts in 1873. The Ioway council was persuaded to request that $2,000 be placed in his hands for the purchase of house building materials, livestock, furniture, and agricultural implements. The "civilization" portion of their payment increased from an annual $1,750 to $4,700.

Attempting to have greater say in their affairs, the chiefs unsuccessfully petitioned in 1874 to have Joseph Vetter, a member of the tribe, appointed as their trader. They claimed that they did not trust outsiders. Their request was denied. In the summer, Agent Roberts urged that the Ioway chiefs agree to a code of laws which provided that all fines for infractions be divided among the law-abiding members. Central to this provision, the agent noted, was the increased consumption of ardent spirits. The agent reactivated the Indian police, and from the annual annuity the chiefs agreed to pay each of the five new appointees $40 per year. Higher-level officials agreed that such a force made the agent's job much easier because direct confrontation and arrest were carried out by tribal members.

In 1875, drought and grasshoppers greatly reduced the crop yield, and Agent Kent first inquired of the commissioner of Indian affairs if he could reduce the cash annuities to the Ioways without their consent in order to pay the increased costs of the agency and the school, which counted on its crops to feed its students and personnel. He then presented the idea to the chiefs, who promptly rejected it.[15]

In November the chiefs requested that $400 of their funds be set aside to bail Henry Washburn, a tribal member, out of jail. He had been accused of committing grand larceny at nearby Hiawatha, Kansas. The request was denied.

At the request of the council of chiefs, the Indian police were deactivated in 1877. The agent consented to this with their promise that self-curtailment of agent-defined illicit activities would be assured. However, spirits were still consumed, and the agent called the chiefs and headmen together to take the pledge not to imbibe intoxicants. Ioways found drunk were to be arrested and fined. By the end of the year there "was a general absence of disorder again." Agent Kent was pleased with this and added that the authority of the chiefs was practically nullified as the tribe advanced in civilization.

The agent-controlled Indian police continued to function in 1879. An example of their activities is shown in the record of Frank Mahee, age 27, who was appointed that year. His roster for the month listed the following: October 12, protected fields and took up [intruder's] cattle; October 21, helped arrest Sam Wilson, a whisky smuggler, and guarded prisoners; October 30, helped arrest Millie D. for boisterous behavior. Others on the force included Henry Washburn, who resigned after a week's duty, George Washington, Moses, and Dan Godfrey. Although these young men were from the leading families, some time later the agent forced them to resign and placed some of them in jail.[16]

Traditionally an agent had little sympathy or respect for the authority of Indian leaders, and he consistently sought to minimize their role and effect and to replace it with more power for himself and his regulations and the laws of the United States. It seemed to be the most plausible way of reaching a solution to the "Indian problem," as it came to be called. Many Quaker agents at this time served out of a sense of duty and because they had been called to do so. For many it was a discouraging piece of work, and they returned to their former lives saddened by their lack of success. Some grew callous after an early eagerness to assist their Indian brothers in sincere Quaker zeal. Regardless of an agent's ability and character, that which they sought to do in most instances opposed the Indians' traditions and conceptions, and frustration and the use of force was the consistent fruit of many of their efforts.

There is no record from this decade of the ceremonial life and other traditional ways of the Ioways. Certainly, among the more conservative tribal members, attempts to carry on and to transmit the culture of their ancestors continued. Some families worked on communal farms during the summer and lived in hide tipis during the winter of 1871. However, it was hoped by the agent that with the furnishing of stoves they would no longer have the "excuse for doing this and would construct log houses to live in." Among the acculturating full- and mixed-bloods, such resistance to change did not occur as they sought to attain a certain level of acceptance and favor with agency personnel and the surrounding white communities in their emulation of white ways. Agents' annual reports placed great emphasis on these individuals and ignored nonconformers for the most part. The 1879 report stated that sixteen hundred fruit trees had been planted and that there were numbers of cattle, barns and stables. Many families had wells near their doors. Five Ioway families had more than fifty acres under cultivation. These farms were not yet held by individual title but were claimed by precedent of former use. Sewing machines owned and rag rugs made by hand were proudly mentioned. A few Ioway women were said to have homes that in cleanliness and good taste compared favorably with those of their white neighbors.

Thus civilization of the Ioway advanced and with it reports on their educational attainments. A slight increase in the enrollment of the day school and the Industrial Home, as the boarding school was now called, was emphasized. The latter was devoted mainly to agricultural pursuits, with the Indian boys serving as a ready labor supply. The Friends of Philadelphia supplied the school with books and clothing.

A few Ioways utilized higher educational facilities. One youth was sent to a local university, while several others were sent to Carlisle Institute in Pennsylvania. The agent's 1878 report claimed that 110 of the 213 Ioways could read English.

One tradition that seemed impossible to eradicate was the custom of intertribal visiting, which the agents deplored. From the Indian point of view it remained a great escape from reservation life and a means of maintaining identity and use of older customs. Agent Roberts in 1874 spoke in strong terms against it, saying, "Tribal visiting is one of the greatest obstacles in the way of civilization and improvement. In my humble opinion some measures should be adopted to prevent such visiting, at least among the partially civilized tribes." Agent Kent in 1877 stated that tribal visiting had a

"demoralizing effect perpetuating injurious traditions which should be buried in complete oblivion. The tribe preparing for a visit collects together all available means, sometimes leaving children and aged women in a suffering condition, to prepare a feast for the party visited, that it may be liberal in its donations, thinking that they will be benefited by an accumulation of worthless animals which they sometimes return, and which continue to be a burden to them so long as they are retained. This practice will not have a tendency to make these people useful citizens, and where Indians have made a reasonable degree of progress it should be prohibited by Law."[17]

In Kansas in 1877 the Kickapoos, who had planned to visit the Ioways, were prevented from doing so by their agent, who said that he certainly would not give permission to any tribe in his agency to visit any other. For most tribes now, the buffalo hunt, the war party, horse capturing, and coup counting were largely things of the past. With this new plan to prevent intertribal visiting, even reminiscences at ceremonies and feasts became impossible between tribes whose friendship bonds stretched back through time.

Examples of the erosion of kinship bonds were discovered. Before he died, one Ioway requested that Agent Lightfoot's wife, Mary, be given guardianship of his children so that they might be cared for. The agent sought the superintendent's advice, saying that the mother and other relatives of the children had agreed to the request. Earlier, orphaned children had been raised within the remaining family, but illnesses such as tuberculosis, cholera, and smallpox increased the number of parentless children. Limited subsistence sources for some families necessitated their seeking other means of providing for these young children. The Society of Friends established the Orphans Home, or Industrial Home, to care for the growing number of children who needed care. In a short time the original enrollment of fourteen grew to between thirty and forty members, including children from the Sac tribe. These children, of course, were more quickly taught the new ways since they had no traditional sources to teach them the ways of their people.

In the late 1870's, Ioway tribal structure was changing. The tribe was about to split and never be reunited. In 1879, Agent Kent reported that "several families have abandoned good houses and have moved to Indian Territory." Various factors account for this removal from a land they knew to one totally outside their experience in terms of geography, climate, and history. There were now among the Ioways a large number of Ioways who were half white or more, some of whom had been appointed by the agent to positions of leadership, as indicated by the council petition signatures and the nature of their comments in council. There was also the growing separation between traditional and progressive (or "civilized") tribesmen, a division not always based on degree of blood. The resented intrusion of non-Indian interests on the reserve was exemplified by the leasing of land to white farmers and by others' illegal use of grazing and other lands.[18] The old bonds with the Sacs and the Foxes now in Indian Territory, continued. They wanted their Ioway friends to share their life there. Some Ioways may still have longed for the former freedoms of a life gone by, unrestricted by the federal government and the encircling and intruding white communities and their citizens.

One touchy area of social adjustment was Ioway intermarriage with whites, which could result in difficulties, depending on the place that the family sought in society. Various degrees of assimilation and stress occurred among such individuals and their offspring. Some tried to follow the white man's road, as it was called, and others the Indian way; some vacillated in between. Intermarriage increased as white men sought access to the reserve and its potential for economic advancement. Some husbands were ne'er-do-wells who had to be arrested for theft and drunkenness. Others sought wealth through their children by Ioway women by obtaining, directly or indirectly, a share in the annuity or use of the land. Some abandoned their children and their wives. Others tried to fit in and become like Ioways, to adjust to a different way of life. Perhaps a few, like Kurz years before, married for romantic reasons.

Mixed-blood children originally had been stigmatized to some degree by the Ioways, but, as their numbers and influence increased, they gained an important voice in tribal matters. Chiefs' unions with non-Ioways produced children of varying degrees of Ioway blood, who upset traditional norms on inheritance of position. In the White Cloud line, three sons were allotted land in the Half Breed Tract. Mahaska, or White Cloud, Robidoux claimed the chieftanship several decades earlier. The first chief in the 1870's, Nag-ga-rash, had a son, George Washington, who also acquired land in this tract, as did several other leaders' offspring.

One basic difference between the mixed-bloods and the conservative Ioway full-bloods was their views of land use and ownership. The majority of mixed-bloods agitated early in the decade for survey and allotment so that each member could claim individual title rather than share the land in the traditional way. It is supposed that white

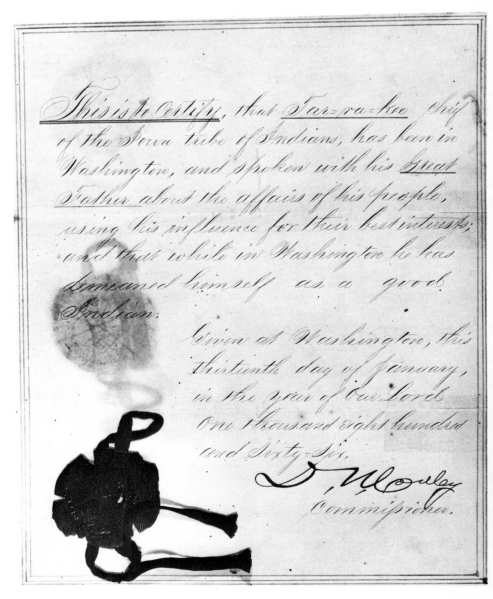

Figure 20. Certificate presented to Ioway Chief Tarrakee, January 13, 1866, in Washington by Indian Commissioner D. N. Mosely. Courtesy of Indian Archives Division, Oklahoma Historical Society.

husbands who wished to own land in the tradition of their culture promoted this idea. Even some wealthy, status-minded full-blood leaders accepted the idea of severalty, as previously discussed petitions seem to indicate. This was not the case with Tarrakee (or Tarakee), one of the five chiefs signing official documents in these years. He had been to Washington and had received a commendation document (see Figure 20). He was about fifty years of age in 1878, measured five feet eight and weighed 179 pounds. He was the fourth chief of the Ioways until 1876, when he was removed because of his "persistent interference with the transaction of ordinary Agency business." As early as January 10, 1872, he had sponsored a letter stating his opposition to severalty of the Ioway reserve saying, "I am a full blooded Indian of the Ioway nation. I understand that a movement is afoot to divide or sectionalize our land. We are, that is, a large majority of the Ioway tribe is opposed to doing this, and earnestly ask that our land be not divided. A few half breeds want it divided so that they can sell to the whites as they have done before, but we want it all sold and want to move south into Indian Territory."[19] After 1876, Tarrakee's name does not appear on any known documents or petitions, and it is believed that he disagreed with other policies of the growing half-breed faction, particularly in the acceptance of white ways that intensified during the Quaker period.

The idea represented by Tarrakee's stand is not that the Ioways did not want to sell the land (which most did in some way), but that the full-bloods or others, wanted to sell all of it and move away, while the acculturating mixed-bloods wanted their individual shares, to do with them what they pleased and not have to act in common with the others. Since their ideas of severalty fitted the government's future plan for the reserve, they held the balance of power with the agent supporting them. Nonconformers like Tarrakee soon saw Indian Territory as a place to escape to from the unpleasantness of the Great Nemaha Agency.

Indian Territory was located in an area south of Kansas, west of Missouri and Arkansas Territory, and north of the Red River. In the 1820's and 1830's it had been designated by treaty for settlement of five eastern tribes, the Cherokees, Chickasaws, Choctaws, Creeks, and Seminoles. Before they moved there, it had been the home or hunting ground of the Wichitas, Caddos, Tawakonis, Kichais, Osages, Comanches, Kiowas, and other tribes. After the Civil War, the Five Civilized Tribes, as the eastern tribes were called, were required to relinquish large sections of their assigned treaty lands because of their loyalty to the Confederate cause. In demanding these cessions, the federal government envisioned the settlement of other tribes on the ceded land. In his third annual message on December 4, 1871, President Grant had declared, "I recommend to your favorable consideration also the policy of granting a Territorial government to the Indians of Indian Territory.... Such a course might in time be the means of collecting most of the Indians now between the Missouri and the

Pacific and south of the British possessions into one Territory or State."[20]

Indians in Kansas and Nebraska, such as the Ioways, were considered in the 1870's likely candidates for removal to Indian Territory, particularly because their lands were eyed as fine areas for settlement. The Sacs and the Foxes did move to Indian Territory after the Civil War, and some continued to urge the Ioways to join them there.

Pressure of another sort came from white settlers, who in 1870 petitioned the Senate to ratify the treaty of 1869 which the Ioways and Quakers had urged the President not to present to that body. In the petition, signers from Brown, Doniphan, and Pawnee counties in Kansas and Nebraska requested that the whole reserve be sold, since it is "detrimental to the Indians to stay among whites where they can procure liquor." It was added that the Ioway chiefs wanted to have the treaty ratified but were afraid to say so because of the agent.

The effort to have the Ioways removed was unsuccessful, but whites sought access to the reserve in other ways. One farmer brazenly fenced in a section of Ioway land, called it his, and refused to remove the fences. Agents took the fence down, but he replaced it. He claimed that he had not obtained all of the land to which he was entitled, and the only way he could get it was to take some of the Ioway land. After a two-year series of letters among the farmer, the agent, the commissioner, the superintendent of Indian affairs, and the United States attorney, he finally agreed to leave the fence down as soon as a hedge grew tall enough.

Other farmers on the periphery of the Ioway reserve allowed their cattle to graze on Indian land although warned numerous times against it. The agent finally decided to allow grazing leases; he explained that, if he did not, settlers' cattle would be run on Indian grass anyway.[21]

Another kind of intrusion came from several intermarried white men who had not been overly successful in their own society and who did not fare any better among the Ioways. Several were removed from the reserve for drinking, stealing, and generally disruptive behavior. One, P. Solomon, like a bad coin, returned each time after his expulsions, and the United States attorney in Nebraska informed the agent that "there is no way to keep him off."[22] The problem of illegal whiskey sellers continued, and agents complained that the punishment was never severe enough to prevent the return of the intruders. The Ioway police arrested those caught selling spirits, but many were not convicted.

On March 7, 1876, Agent Kent wrote to Superintendent Barclay White, "three of the five chiefs and about one-half of the heads of families of the Iowa Tribe, having formally requested to have the lands of their reservation allotted to them in severalty and believing it will increase their prosperity, and advance their agricultural interests, I hereby ask permission of the Department to allot said lands in the

following manner. . . ." He then proposed to allot eighty acres to each
male or female head of family, forty acres to each single male, reserve
the timber lands in common, and set aside one section of land for the
school, agency, and employees' dwellings. The superintendent approved the plan, but the commissioner rejected it on the grounds that
it did not have the unanimous approval of the chiefs or people.
(Tarrakee was one of the chiefs who did not approve the plan.)

In his 1877 report the agent said "that considerable exitement has at
times arisen relative to sending a delegation to Indian Territory with a
view of selecting a location; but recently a unanimous decision was
made that they would not take such a step so long as it must be done at
their own expense." In spite of this decision, the following year some
Ioways packed up their belongings and moved to Indian Territory. The
agent makes no note of this until his 1879 report, when he mentions
it and says that other Ioways extended their farming to cultivate the
land left vacant by the others: "Several good houses are tenantless,
made so by reason of the exodus."

On August 13, 1878, Levi Woodward, the Sac and Fox agent in
Indian Territory, answered Comm. E. A. Hayt's July 25 letter about the
new Ioway arrivals at his agency. Woodward said that four families
of Indians from the Great Nemaha Agency had arrived in a destitute
condition on August 6. When their immediate needs were supplied,
they appeared to be well satisfied and proposed staying among the
Sacs and the Foxes if they were allowed the privilege.[23] In the first
group, twelve Ioways brought with them three wagons and three sets
of harness, as Agent Kent had advised. They wrote to their friends and
asked that they join them. The Ioways arrived too late to plant gardens, and they bought provisions for the winter. "The traders here are
willing to extend them credit if they have assurance that they will
remain here and draw annuity." On hearing of the Ioway presence in
Indian Territory, the commissioner informed Kent that, before other
Ioway left the reserve, he was to tell them that they had permission
to join their friends and relatives only if they did not return to their
Nebraska lands.[24] The situation became even more contradictory. The
next month the commissioner informed the agent that his office had
been unaware that there were any Ioways among the sixteen who had
left the agency with the three wagons, "whom you stated to be Sac and
Fox Indians, until Agent Woodward informed the office that only four
of them were, the rest being Ioways, and it was your statement that
mislead this office." The commissioner, quoting Kent, said, "You say
that these Iowas have long been anxious to go to the Indian Territory,
that their course having always been to oppose all improvements,
throw all possible obstacles in the way of the Agent in his attempts to
make the Indians self supporting, etc." Kent was then criticized for
giving them passes to go since it was the policy of the Indian Office
not to issue passes unless there were promise of return, except in cases
of absolute necessity. The Ioway case did not fit into that category.

Kent then asked the commissioner if the Ioways could be allowed to stay in Indian Territory, and the request was refused. He said that Kent knew of their indebtedness to their trader and that he should not have let them go under those circumstances.[25]

The first party of Ioways were joined by a small family group of eight in October, 1878, bringing to twenty-four the number who desired to live among the Sacs and the Foxes and who urged others to come join them. Agent Woodward notified Agent Kent on October 23 that John Po-huh-kaw, "their chief died here on the 22nd, and they wish their home agent to be informed. They had doctored him themselves until it was too late for the medicine given by the Agency physician to do him any good. . . . The Indians think he died with an old complaint brought on by having been bewitched at some time previous."*

Po-huh-kaw was not listed as a chief at the Great Nemaha Agency. He was one of the signers of the petition for allotment in March, 1871, and among the eighty-one Ioways listed in debt to trader Holt in 1870. He may have been a clan chief, but it is not certain which clan members came in the early migrations to Indian Territory.

In June, 1879, twenty-two Ioways arrived after an eighteen-day trip. The young Ioway men said that they planned to get to work immediately to hew logs for their houses and for rail fences.[26] They revealed that Agent Kent had not given them all of their annuity money when they left. They claimed that he had retained $2,000 to purchase farm equipment, which he knew they could not bring with them. They wondered if the Indian Department had authorized such an expenditure, since they had not. They added that at the time of the annuity payment the previous spring they had received only half of their money. Agent Kent had told them that they would receive the rest of it in the fall. When the time came, they had not yet received it. The agent had also withheld the small payment given the chiefs, and they wanted to know why this was done. Hotchisee, one of the protesting leaders, had received a commendation certificate attesting to his character from the commissioner in the spring.

It is unknown which men in leadership positions after White Cloud and No Heart were hereditary or appointed chiefs. Tohee, Mahee, and Kihega were listed as braves in 1861, but the government definition of that term is uncertain. They were later called chiefs and appointed by the agent as such. They came to Indian Territory eventually. An interesting list describing some of their characteristics and activities, given in 1871, also included the deceased No Heart and Kratenthawah:

---

* In modern times, an elderly Ioway explained that one must beware of owls that keep coming too close to the house. The old people would kill them. Asked if he would do so, he said, "Yes, I'd kill it. If they kill that owl, like they say, it's a Spirit, whoever it is might get sick over there. He's the one or she's the one who performed the owl themselves." See Martha Royce Siegel, Ioway Field Notes, 1965.

393 — Nan-chee-nin-ga, or No Heart (of Fear)
    Height, 5 feet 10 inches, weight, 170, died in autumn of 1862, age 65.

385 — Nag-a-rash, or British
    Height, 5 feet, 8 inches, weight 193, age 68 years. Head measure, 22⅞, chest 47½.

Became first chief of Iowas in 1862. Has always been in favor of education and civilization. Has made four visits to Washington, the first time being in 1847 when he went from St. Joseph, Mo. to Baltimore in a wagon starting in the spring and arriving in the fall. Stayed in Baltimore two weeks, sold horses and wagon and took cars to Richmond, Virginia. Traveled through Va. during the winter on exhibition and came to Philadelphia the following April and staid five months then came on to Washington, and remained two weeks. He made 40.00 shooting with bow and arrow at 5, 10, and 25 cents pieces. Returning came by cars to the mountains, then by canal to Pittsburgh, by steamer almost to Leavenworth, where the river was so low could get no further, and had to hire a mule team to St. Joseph. Was away 17 months. Has also made two trips to New York. Was once in a battle, together with Otoes, Pawnees, Kickapoos, Potts, Sac and Fox with Snake Crows, Cheyennes, Arap. Commanches, and Kiowas, which began about 4 oclock in the morning. He shot 160 balls, 150 of the enemy were killed and 50 dead horses found on one acre of ground.

388 — Mah-hee, or Knife
    Height, 5 feet 10, weight 172, age 56, head 22¾ chest, 39½
    Third Chief of Iowas

When young lived in Mo. then moved to Iowa Point now in Kan. was always sociable and a friend of his Agent. At one time carried the mails for the Agent from the Agency to St. Jo and Leavenworth, Kan. A distance of 30 to 60 miles respectively. One time when returning from a hunt on the frontier he was informed by his Agent that his people were going to Washington to make a treaty to sell out. He said he wanted to move only a short distance, to about the mouth of the Nemaha river where they are now located, so he could raise grain for his own family. The agent told him to select the best brave or land [?] in the tribe and move to where you want to live, and while the Chiefs are in Washington you shall have a field broken, and those who go on the plains shall not have anything done for them. Mahhee was always a hard worker, but at one time was dissapated and while under the influence of liquor, killed his own father, but since that time has entirely reformed, and he now does not even take an occasional drink. One time when upon the warpath, he had a hand to hand fight with a Pawnee Brave, who was too strong for him and threw him. He says, I got up and ran a little ways, and came back with my knife and scalped him. Whenever we are on the war path, no matter who we meet, white or Indian, we kill him.

395 — Tah-ra-kee, or Deer Ham
    Height, 5 feet 8½ inches, weight, 179, age 50
    Head 22, chest, 41½
    4th Chief of Iowas, until 1876 when he was broken on account of his persistent interference with transaction of ordinary Agency business.

391 — To-hee or Bear, which should be Briar, is also same as
395 — Tah-ra-kee or Deer Ham.*

390 — Ki-hega-ing-a or Little Chief
    Height, 5 feet 10, weight 192, age 43, head 22¾ chest, 43.
    5th Chief of Iowas.
Enlisted in the army during the late war in July, 1863, was in the service, two years, was in one skirmish with Rebel guards of whom one was killed and nineteen wounded, traveled through Arkansas while in the service, at the commencement of the war was told by the Agent if he enlisted, he should be made Chief when he returned, in place of his brother Thor-o-mon-ne, who was dead, which was accordingly done.

387 — Kra-ten-tha-wah, or Black Hawk
    6th chief of the Iowas, about 6 feet, weight 170, slender, died January 1, 1871, aged about 30. [27]

President Rutherford Hayes in his first annual message in 1877 stated that the United States was at peace with all tribes after a series of deplorable encounters of the past years:

> To preserve peace and by just and humane policy will be the object of my earnest endeavors. The Indians have been the aboriginal occupants of the land we now possess. They have been driven from place to place. The purchase money paid to them in some cases for what they called their own has still left them poor. In many cases when they had settled down upon land assigned to them by compact, they were rudely jostled off and thrust into the wilderness again. Many, if not most, of our Indian wars have had their origin in broken promises and acts of injustice upon our parts, and the advance of the Indian in civilization has been slow because the treatment they received did not permit it to be faster and more general. We can not expect them to improve and to follow our guidance unless we keep faith with them in respecting the rights they possess. . . .[28]

President Hayes continued to seek the assistance and advice of the Friends to bring rectitude to the Indian service. But in spite of the President's determination, toward the end of the decade the relationship between the Society of Friends and the Indian Department became strained, and the department considered withdrawing from this phase of its commitment to the Indians. A principal reason for their concern was the removal of their appointees without proper hearings. This and other matters brought the situation to a head in April, 1878. The President received a letter from the Executive Committee of the Friends. It protested a Board of Inquiry report of the Central Superintendency, for which they had been given responsibility

---

* Both Tarrakee and Tohee signed the Treaty of 1861; therefore it appears that they are not the same individual. See Kappler, *Treaties*, 2; 811.

for agent selection and other matters. A letter to the Commissioner stated:

> ...The general course of the Indian Department for the past few months has given us an impression that our cooperation instead of being heartily desired is a burden to the Department. Support was only possible with cooperation, and we believe the time has come for us to relinquish all responsibility for the nomination of officers and their official conduct in the Department. [29]

When he was informed of this situation in May, President Hayes said that if any complaint arose against any individuals appointed by the Quaker Executive Committee, the committee should be informed and the accused parties should have full opportunity to exonerate themselves. In spite of this, the relationship grew increasingly hostile and unworkable under Comm. E. A. Hayt. In May, 1879, the commissioner left the committee with the distinct impression that he proposed to do as he thought best regardless of their recommendations and contrary to the instructions of the President. The committee then called upon the President, explained its reluctance to continue its work under these circumstances, and relinquished its responsibilities in this particular area of Indian affairs. President Hayes accepted their decision.[30]

The Friends did not entirely abandon their efforts to aid the Indians. They continued to emphasize missions, education, and medical assistance. Although the Ioways brought charges against their Quaker agent in 1877, a mission was established for them in the next decade in Indian Territory.

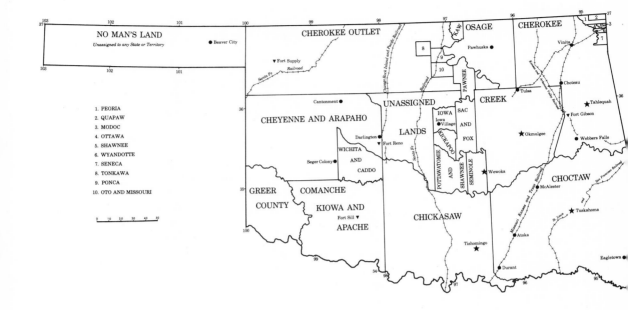

Map 11. Indian Territory, 1866-1889. The Ioway Reservation created by executive order, August 15, 1883, lies north of the Kickapoo and west of the Sac and Fox reservations. On September 22, 1891, it was opened to settlement following the completion of Ioway allotment. Reproduced from John W Morris et al., *Historical Atlas of Oklahoma* (Norman, University of Oklahoma Press, 1967), map 33.

10. The Final Removal

Why have they left their good homes in Nebraska for such a tract as they think they have here?

Lawrie Tatum, April 18, 1885

The leading idea of the white settlers relative to the location of the Indians seems to be anywhere but here.

Agent H. C. Linn, Great Nemaha Agency,
August 31, 1880

THE INDIAN OFFICE persisted in its ambivalent position toward Ioway migration to Indian Territory. Acting Commissioner E. J. Brooks wrote Agent Kent in August, 1880, "The Office entirely disapproves of their plan to leave their fine farming lands in Nebraska for any location in the Indian Territory." He added that if they did so, they would receive no annuity nor assistance in their new location. As a result of this policy, the Sac and Fox agent reported that the thirty Ioways in Indian Territory were destitute. He said, "They came here with the knowledge of the Honorable Commissioner, and I was ordered to enroll them here, and Agent Kent was ordered to drop them from his rolls. Something should be done for them...."[1]

In January, 1881, Acting Commissioner C. M. Marble, when told that an additional forty-five Ioways had arrived at the Sac and Fox Agency, affirmed Brooks's statement that only those Ioway at the Great Nemaha Agency should be paid their annuity.[2] By this time, of the total of 222 Ioways, ninety-two were now in Indian Territory. But the next commissioner, E. S. Stevens, reversed the former official view and in May, 1882, ordered the Sac and Fox agent to make a roll of the Ioways so that they could receive their annuity. He was satisfied that injustice had been done to them.[3] By fall, the money had not arrived and they continued to suffer. They had wandered on the Sac and Fox reservation during the first few years, but in 1882 they had settled on land "west of the Sac and Fox between the Deep Fork on the south and the Red Fork on the Cimarron on the north," where they hunted and built their dwellings. Agent J. V. Carter recommended that this area be made their permanent home. Another request for the annuity brought the reply that it would be received with interest earned on that amount previously unpaid.[4]

In July, 1883, the agent forwarded a petition from the Indian Territory Ioways. It requested that their land in Kansas and Nebraska be sold and that they be granted lands in Indian Territory.[5] Fearing that the government would force them to remove to Indian Territory, some of the Great Nemaha Agency Ioways were uneasy but wished to send delegates to the south to investigate areas that could be settled. They were told that they could go if they used part of their annuity to pay for the journey. They were also informed that, if any Ioways moved, all would have to move. When they discovered this, the majority of the Ioways preferred to stay on their lands. A delegation of southern Ioways came north in the summer to urge their relatives and friends to move south and thus created greater indecision.

In Indian Territory the long-awaited reservation was established by Executive Order on August 15, 1883. Within the area that they had settled, the Ioways received a home of 228,418 acres of red rock outcroppings, and generally poor soil with hillsides and ravines covered with cedar and low scrub oak, so dense in places that a horse could not make its way through it. The land was minimally productive. Its greatest assets were its beauty and the presence of small game and cattle grazing potential in open areas (see Map 11).

With the establishment of their reservation and the arrival of their annuity money, the southern Ioways became more amenable to their situation, and again they requested the sale of their Great Nemaha Reserve. They stipulated that the northern Ioway half-breeds were not to be part of any allotments prior to sale, since they had all been given lands before and had squandered them. They had been taken back into the tribe, and "another allotment, they claim will be a repetition of the above."[6] An important part of the agreement by which the Indian Territory reservation had been assigned to them was their consent to sell the northern reserve. Until that was done, they would not have true title to their new home. Proposed Senate Bill 1108 provided for the survey and ultimate sale of the northern lands. Comm. Hiram Price said it was satisfactory except that "if the tribe decided to remove, some individuals having improved farms would desire to remain." He prepared an additional section to the original document to provide for these individuals. On March 3, 1885 (23 Stat. 351), the act to sell the Sac and Fox and Ioway lands in Kansas and Nebraska was passed. Certain lands were to be restricted from sale on approval of both tribal councils.[7] This provided for those who wanted to remain.

The agents called for councils to vote on the act. Of fifty-eight eligible male voters on both reservations, at the Sac and Fox agency all twenty-six Ioways voted affirmatively to accept the act's provisions; in the north, eleven voted for the sale of land and the Ioway removal to Indian Territory, twelve voted against it, and six were absent.[8]

Fewer than half of the northern voters were in favor of removing. They saw no reason to leave their fine farms, and their decision was understandable and wise. Section III of the act provided that those who wished to stay and take allotments could do so. The southern Ioways, on the other hand, favored the sale, for the land was of no further use to them. They wanted most of all to have assured title to their reservation, and with the land cession they hoped that their annuity would increase. But lack of provision for northern Ioway minors' and orphans' rights offered a stumbling block. The northern Ioways asked that "action be delayed until Congress can remedy the defect in the law."[9] All the Ioways waited for what would happen next.

The Executive Order of 1885 established a home for the southern Ioways and carried a provision, apparently unknown to them, that other tribes could be settled on their reservation. On September 29, 1884, the commissioner wrote to the Ioway agent that arrangements had been made to settle the Tonkawa tribe from Texas on Ioway lands. The agent, somewhat surprised by this, wrote that the Ioway chiefs opposed this and wanted the land reserved for more northern Ioways. The commissioner replied that the Tonkawas had as much right as the Ioways and that they would be settled there. He added that the reservation held 228,152 acres and there were fewer than eighty Tonkawas and eighty-eight Ioways. "Those in Kansas and Nebraska being reported to be 132, making of total of three hundred Indians . . . which will give 760 acres of land to each Indian."[10] The figure of 228,152 acres was a revision of the earlier estimated 228,418 acres.

In spite of Ioway opposition, ninety-two Tonkawas arrived from Fort Griffin, Texas, and were placed on the reservation along Bell Cow Creek, after previously assigned lands on the Deep Fork were found to flood frequently.[11] Lawrie Tatum, formerly the Quaker agent to the Kiowas and the Comanches, visited the agency and found the Tonkawas in destitute condition. He wrote:

If they have no home in Texas, they will probably be better off on the poor, poor land of Oklahoma than they would be in that state. . . . We also went to see the Ioway Indians. I pity them and would like to know more about them. Have they a title to the tract of land on which they are living, or is it positively assured to them on a sale of their land in Nebraska? Why have they left their good homes in Nebraska for such a tract as they think they have here? Are they fully informed of their conditions? Would be much obliged to you for answers to the above questions. I think that they are located in the most unhealthy place that I have seen in the Territory."[12]

The Tonkawas' stay near the Ioways was of short duration. On June

16, 1885, they were moved to the Oakland Agency on the old Nez Perce reservation a short distance to the north.*

On January 26, 1887, the amended act (24 Stat. 367) was passed. It provided for the allotment of land in severalty for any Ioway who elected to stay on the Great Nemaha Reserve. A family head would receive one-hundred and sixty acres, a single person over eighteen and an orphan under eighteen would receive eighty acres, and all minors would receive forty acres. The land was to be held in trust for twenty-five years, after which the owner would be given its patent.[13]

During the summer Inspector R. S. Gardner explained the provisions of the amended act in councils with each of the Ioway groups.[14] The majority of both councils voted to accept the act's provisions, including the selling of the land to the United States. The secretary of the interior instructed the commissioner of the General Land Office to begin the land survey, after which allotment to those desiring to stay could begin. The survey that followed was later rejected by the Land Office as imperfect, and by 1890 that act had not yet been carried out.[15]

Agents' reports and reminiscences of Indian Territory pioneers and settlers following Indian land allotment gave brief flashes of southern Ioway traditionalists' attempts to balance their lives between two worlds. Now the agent and his interference could not be ignored, and it was impossible to find a place with no painful memories of their lost sovereignty. From this decade forward, two agents reported annually for the Ioways, one in Indian Territory from the Sac and Fox Agency (later renamed the Shawnee Agency) and the other from the Great Nemaha Agency, which was consolidated with the Pottawatomie Agency in Kansas in 1882.

The Northern Ioways

At the time of removal of a portion of the tribe to Indian Territory, the northern reservation was well established in a rich agricultural area adjacent to the Missouri and Great Nemaha rivers. Today the corn grows tall, soybeans thrive in dark green rows, and sunflowers flourish in experimental fields. Sturdy cattle and handsome farms attest to its continuing productivity throughout the past century. Agents' reports show early indications of the growing affluence of the Ioway people there and of the attitude of the whites, "who have long

---

* The Nez Perce under Chief Joseph were allowed to return to a reservation in Washington in 1885 after many were lost to disease in the alien climate and conditions of the Oakland Reservation in present-day north-central Oklahoma. Commissioner Price to Agent, June 3 and 26, 1885, Sac and Fox Agency, *Tonkawa Indians file*, OHSIA.

looked with covetous eyes upon this small tract of land and spare no
effort to dispossess the Indians of it." In spite of the whites' cupidity,
the Ioways were peaceable and well disposed toward them, and
general intercourse was the same as would be seen in any thriving
agriculture community. Only a few incidents ruffled the calm pastoral
scene. Occasionally, certain men indulged in the intrigue of whiskey
smuggling, and professional horse thieves were abetted by a few
unscrupulous Indian citizens. Later in the decade cattle were again
grazed on unfenced Indian land. In some instances in Kansas it
became profitable for a white farmer to buy a small amount of land
adjacent to an Indian reservation and then to run herds of ten to
fifteen hundred head for others on Indian lands. The agent eventually
was able to stop this by charging one dollar per head and enforcing
regulations for grazing.

On the whole, however, Agent John Blair reported in 1888 that the
Indians and the surrounding whites traded and visited with each
other, much as the whites did among themselves, and they appeared
to sustain very pleasant relations toward each other. His 1883 statement that "the Iowas were a very prosperous tribe of Indians, the
white blood predominating to a more or less degree" may have
influenced the course of this interaction.

Not all of the mixed- and full-blood Ioways lived, as the agent
described them, in well-built, frame houses with barns, orchards,
fields of grain, well-kept farms, and cattle and other livestock contributing to their wealth. In 1884, Agent Linn reported that all Ioways,
with the exception of about ten families who had not adopted all the
habits of civilization, lived in houses. In 1885, the twelve who voted to
go to Indian Territory represented one-fourth of the tribe and were
called "blanket Indians," a term that had come into use describing
those Indians who resisted acculturation.

Land tenure attitudes and practices were described:

Each family has its fixed habitation and a patch or field contiguous to it
under some kind of fence. The individual right to these is unquestioned
and recognized as sacred by the tribe. Should the owner's means enable
him to erect more commodious buildings or enclose more extensive fields,
the recognized right expands and extends with the possessions. The first
occupant of vacant territory is considered the owner. The stock of all graze
without restraint on the unappropriated commons, and all members of
the tribe are entitled in equal degree to appropriate to his own use
whatever he can of its proceeds.[16]

Most of the northern Ioways wore citizens' clothing, sent their
children to school, sold their agricultural surplus, and sometimes
hired outside help to aid them in farming. They leased their land
occasionally but preferred to farm it themselves. Aside from performing some older dances (probably carried out by less-acculturated
tribal members), the Ioways could not be described as greatly dif-

ferent from their white neighbors. Compared with members of nearby tribes, the Ioways were considered at this time among the most progressive and successful in becoming "civilized."

The Southern Ioways

In Indian Territory another situation obtained. From the time of the first migration southward the economic status of the Ioways there deteriorated from its former state. As stated previously, they were considered destitute. They had brought little with them, had received no annuities or other income for some time, and had no fixed place to live for several years. Only 10 percent of their reservation was considered arable. But from the Ioway point of view, the agricultural and economic potential of the land did not matter as much as an outsider such as Lawrie Tatum would think. They had not come to Indian Territory to become first-class farmers with surplus cattle to market. If they had wanted that, they would have stayed on the great farming lands of Nebraska and Kansas. Instead, they built small bark-house villages, erected tipis in winter, and in some cases constructed log cabins. They wore a combination of citizens' and Indian clothing and tended to speak their own language rather than English (which most could speak when they wanted to). Their children did not attend school until one was constructed. A few small fields, where they grew corn, melons, beans, and other food crops, adjoined their village. They gathered herbs and food plants in the fields and along the streams. They started to dry corn for nearby tribes in 1883, but were unsuccessful, because the dry season caused the corn to become hard too soon. Horses continued to be valued with each family slowly accumulating between two and five — not on the scale of former times but enough to give the pleasure of possession. They continued their ways of doctoring, and they were frequent victims of malaria and lung ailments. They had brought with them many sacred bundles and other objects necessary to perform rituals, dances, and other religious acts. They continued to use and to cherish them as long as they had them. Early in the twentieth century, in order to supplement low incomes, many Ioways sold objects to museums, including sacred bundles from the Buffalo and Bear Doctors' Societies; tattooing bundles; pipe bags holding beautifully carved pipes with decorated stems, war bundles; ceremonial objects; and household articles in use at the time such as wooden spoons, ladles, and bowls, hide scrapers, hide work bags, woven nettle fiber bags, painted parfleches, a wooden mortar, bows, arrows, quivers, cradle boards and clothing.[17]

A set of nine bone dice used by women, six ball sticks, and a small bundle used for "love, gambling and horse racing luck" were purchased. During the 1880's the agent endeavored to withstand the great gambling "mania" that swept through his agency. In 1884, the com-

Figure 21. The Ioways continued to build their traditional pole and bark-covered houses after they moved to Indian Territory. The location of this village is not certain, but it is thought to have been near present-day Wellston, Oklahoma. Tipi poles stand against one dwelling, while farm implements indicate the acceptance of non-Indian farming practices. The photograph was taken in 1887. The houses are similar to those described by Rev. Samuel Irvin fifty years earlier. Courtesy of Research Library, Photographs Collection, Oklahoma Historical Society.

missioner wrote, "It is imperative that this vice of gambling cease and stringent measures must be adopted at once to put a stop to it at your agency. You will therefore inform your Indians that hereafter this offense will not be tolerated, and any Indian found guilty will be severely punished, and will be compelled to forfeit every article of property put up or offered for gambling purposes."[18]

Nevertheless, the game continued in 1888, and the agent said, "I have failed to find one that thinks it is wrong to gamble, and they seem surprised that the Great Father will allow white people to have horse races and play ball over the States for money, if it is wrong."[19] In 1889 he added that "white men come near the Agency at the time of annuity payment expecting to make a rich haul [gambling], but as a rule the Indians are too much for them." This was probably one of the few times that the Ioways outmaneuvered their deceptive white brothers.

Agents' reports on the Ioways briefly noted the presence of tribal doctoring, visits to "smoke horses," adoption rituals, and other ceremonies that continued during the 1880's. No details are given, so it is not known how much change took place in the new environment, with fewer members to assume traditional roles. Gradually any event that was reported was termed a "pow wow," so that it cannot be ascertained what dances and ceremonies were being continued.

Early Settlers' Accounts of the Ioways

Glimpses of some aspects of Ioway culture before the turn of the century are found in reminiscenses collected in the 1930's from individuals who lived near them in Payne and Lincoln counties in Oklahoma.

> *Villages* — Then near, but east of Guthrie, there was a small tribe of Iowas. Their little village was built up of tepees similar to those in Mexico. These teepees were round and covered with grass and straw. Their beds were built up high off the ground. The Iowas put four posts in the ground, forked at the top, then they placed small limbs at the head and the foot and the sides. These were made secure with strings made of pieces of hide. Then they made slats of hewn poles, and used straw mattresses with buffalo hide for cover. They dug small pits in the center of their tepees where they cooked in the winter, and they cooked out of doors in the summer [see Figure 21].[20] The Iowas Indian village, in what is now Lincoln county only a mile from the Logan county line, was perhaps a half mile east of the lower lake. There were about 70 Indians who lived there, some in a stockade, some in bark houses, and some in tepees. . . . A Quaker missionary lived and worked with them before the Iowa country was opened, and perhaps, after. His name was John Murdock.*[21] The Iowa village consists of nine houses used for living purposes, including Chief Tohee's, and a larger one making the tent which is used exclusively as a dance house. In this rude structure all their feasts are held. A feast consists of a meal either of game, or on some extra occasion, a dog.
>
> *Early Families* — The village in summer was of bark houses or lodges and occupied what we termed apartments, from ten to twenty people building a lodge large enough for a so called family home. Some who familied together included Kerwin Murray, Jeff Whitecloud, John Ford, John Grant, Tom White, Terrace Roubidoux, John Mohee, Old

---

* The missionary's name was John F. Mardack. The Quakers had continued their interest in the Ioways. In 1889 a mission with a church and mission house was established at the village near Wellston. The mission house served as a home for missionaries and a boarding home for Ioway school children. Following allotment in 1894, a closer mission was established southeast of Perkins. It operated with a majority of non-Ioway members until 1915, when another church group, urging baptism as the only means of obtaining Christian status and salvation, alienated all of the Ioways from the Quaker church and brought the half-century relationship to a close. See *Chronicles of Oklahoma*, 33, 178-79.

Man Tohee, Jerry Squirrel, Billy, Dan, and Dave Tohee, the Wolf family, Dick Dupee, Abe Lincoln, Mag Lincoln and Nellie Tohee.

Winter Residence Pattern — In the winter months they would disband the family lodges and in a smaller family pitch their canvas teepees in a heavy timber for protection against the elements.[22]

Dances — We could hear the Iowa Indians beating their tom-toms almost seven miles away when they were having their stomp dances.[23]

Tattooing — The Whiteclouds and Tohees have a royal tattoo circle the size of a half dollar or larger.[24]

Burial Practices — We were driving cattle about 3 miles east of Wellston when some bones fell out of a tree on us. On investigating we found several skeletons of Indians. We were told the Iowa Tribe always placed their dead on scaffolds in the tree tops.[25] We went to one of the funeral services. They built a small scaffold in a tree top and placed their dead in sitting positions. The women drew their shawls over their heads and moaned. At this service there was already two bodies on this scaffold, one, that of an old man in a sitting position with his back to the tree who looked like he was petrified, and there was a child who looked like a little mummy.*[26]

Annuity Payments — The Iowas with their chiefs, Whitecloud and Grant, the Sac and Fox, the Tohees, the Cheyenne and Arapaho, and at least one tribe from north of us used to be paid off in Guthrie. They never seemed to have any more money going home than they did coming. They must have owed most of it to some store in town. Sometimes the government issued them blankets and other clothes. But before leaving town they had usually traded these things off.[27]

Tribal Visiting — Across the river, four miles from our home was an Indian settlement of the Iowa Tribe. They held many camp meetings at this place and other tribes would gather there and stay for weeks at a time. At one time the Sac and Fox and the Otoes were gathered here for a meeting with the Ioway.[28]

Religion — The remnants of the once mighty tribe of Iowa Indians dwindled to 70 fullbloods, who live mostly in Lincoln and Payne counties. They are still considered to a great extent idol and ancestor worshippers, in spite of having the gospel preached to them for the last 50 years.[29]

---

* An earlier account of scaffold burial for the Ioways was given in 1840. Thomas C. Duggins, a surveyor of the 1836 Platte Purchase in Missouri, observed, "We saw their ancient towns and wigwams, burying grounds and their late camps. I was out one day hunting on the river and came upon a recent Indian grave on a scaffold eight feet high, eight feet long and forty-one inches wide wrapped in buffalo skin, and laid on a grass mat of their own make, and lashed to the scaffold with cords. Immediately under the corpse was a place like a grave in which was buried his private property, jewels, beads and etc. It was placed near the bank of the river with its head toward the rising sun where stood a large black oak on which a cross in a very large shape had been cut. This was an Indian of the Iowa tribe as this is their manner of disposing of their dead and of the Roman Catholic persuasion. We saw others that had been scaffolded and had fallen down, and partly destroyed, others buried under the ground, which had been ransacked, I suppose to get their property. They exhibit considerable ignorance in burying their dead." See *Missouri Historical Review,* 56, 124.

The last statement indicates that the Ioways were attempting to maintain their religious ceremonies in 1897, when the statement appeared in an area newspaper.

The Ioway per capita roll of 1883 gives some indication of their tribal organization in Indian Territory. Three bands were led by Chief Tohee, Hotchisee, and Mohee (it is not clear whether the latter is the Mahee who appears in records before removal to Indian Territory). Tohee's band, the largest, had sixty-three members. Hotchisee had twenty, and Mohee accounted for seven.[30] In such a small, interrelated population expected marriage choices were difficult to make, and soon the Ioways were intermarrying with other tribes, first with their linguistic kindred the Otoes, whose reservation was not far away, and later with the Sacs, the Potawatomis, the Pawnees, and members of other neighboring tribes. As far as can be determined, the three bands represented the Buffalo, Bear, the Eagle and Thunder, and Wolf clans. Later, other clans' members joined them to form amalgamations of clans, eventually losing their distinctions and traditional roles.

At this date, 1883, Tohee was sixty-seven years old, Mohee was seventy-five, his son Frank was thirty, and Hotchisee was forty-nine. Jefferson Whitecloud was thirty-eight and was listed as a member of Tohee's band. He had been living among the Otoes with his wife and two daughters until 1883, when he enrolled with the Ioways. Joseph No Hart was twenty-seven and had joined Tohee's group. In 1882, Tohee resigned in favor of his son, William, now surnamed Falk, to whom he delivered "his papers." Hagarahche, or Joe Vetter, was appointed second chief by the council. The agent informed the commissioner that the Ioways were desirous that he should be informed of these important appointments.[31] For the most part, the Bear and Buffalo clans, from which the Tohees were descended, supplied the head chief after the Ioways were in Indian Territory. Another Bear clan member, Jefferson Whitecloud, served as chief for a short period of time before his death.

Other White Clouds (or Whitecloud, as it was written) remained on the northern reservation or intermarried with the Otoes in Oklahoma. James White Cloud, who served in the Civil War and was the grandson of Joseph Roubidoux, died in 1940 at the age of one-hundred, after serving as chief of the northern Ioways for eighty-four years. The northern Ioways claimed that he was chief of all the Ioways during much of this time. His son Louis, was selected as chief. His grandson, James Mahaska (White Cloud) Rhodd, was chief in the 1970's, although the tribal government then consisted of a general council formed under the Indian Reorganization Act of June 18, 1934, which also provided for a tribal constitution and bylaws. Rhodd has been a council member of the Iowa Tribe of Kansas and Nebraska, as that portion of the tribe is now called.

Living in Oklahoma in the twentieth century and considered as chiefs of the Iowa Tribe of Oklahoma were Blaine and Solomon

Figure 22. Mary and James White Cloud, northern Ioways. James White Cloud was born in 1848, served in the Civil War, and later was chief of the Ioways in Kansas and Nebraska. He died in 1940. Courtesy of Kansas State Historical Society.

Nawanoway Kent, descendents of Tohee through their grandmother, Tohee's daughter (see Figure 23). From time to time there has been discussion about hereditary rights to this position among other tribal family members. In reality there is no officially recognized position of "chief." These men have served as elected members of the tribal business council. The Oklahoma Indian Welfare Act of June 26, 1936, provided for a constitution, bylaws, and a business council. This governing body is elective, and its members have been descendants of chiefs and other prominent Ioways.

Indian Territory tribal council meetings in the 1880's were held in a large bark village house. Land use and village affairs were discussed, and appeals to the government for annuity payments and action on other unfulfilled commitments were drafted. Important decisions concerning the leasing of their grazing lands to outsiders were made, petitions for sale of their northern lands considered, and appeals to visit the President framed. Later in the decade, an obdurate refusal to participate in the allotment of their reservation was carried out in discussions day after day with the Jerome Commission. Other duties and functions such as religious dances, tattooing ceremonies, adoption of Sacs and Otoes as children, brothers, and sisters, visits and giveaways* of presents to other tribes (when the Ioways had collected enough goods to make a good showing) kept the chiefs and head men in a position of responsibility and respect, although frustrations and disappointments were numerous.

In 1886, Hotchisee, described as principal chief, notified the commissioner that two traders were fitting up houses twelve miles west of Wellston on the Ioway Reservation and moving goods into them. They planned to hire an Absentee Shawnee, it was said, and Hotchisee considered him a bad man and did not want him in the Ioway country. Hotchisee was one of the chiefs who had been active in the post-Civil War period, as had the older Tohee, Mahee (Mohee?) and Kathermina. They all had migrated to Indian Territory, and they had informed the agent at that time that they were full-blood Ioways. They gave as reasons for bringing their people to the new home that the whites were too close to them and their reservation in the north; that there were constant depredations by those whites; that the increase in drunkenness among their young men alarmed them; and that game was scarce in Kansas and Nebraska and restrictions were imposed

---

* The term *giveaway* is used to describe modern Indian ceremonies at which a member of the tribe, a family member, or a member of another tribe is honored by bringing together blankets, shawls, yard goods, towels, sheets, foodstuffs, and money. A family or an individual stands before the assemblage and asks diferent individuals to come and to receive a gift from those that are piled in front of them. A spokesman calls the people forward and explains the family's or the individual's reasons for honoring the individual. He is handed the gift and he thanks and shakes the hands of each of the family members standing there.

Figure 23.   Left to right: Blaine Nawanoway Kent, Commissioner of Indian Affairs Glen L. Emmons, and Solomon Nawanoway Kent during a visit to the Commissioner's office in the late 1950's. The Ioway leaders were visiting Washington in regard to tribal affairs. From the author's collection.

on them when they wanted to hunt. They had told the agent that their people "would die of starvation before they would go back."[32]

As they had stated, their desire to be away from white intruders had motivated their move to the new land, but as was evident in Hotchisee's letter, they were not successful in escaping white intrusions in Oklahoma. He added that too many others, who did not have the right to do so, lived on Ioway lands in houses in which he wanted Ioways to live. They wanted, he continued, to have young Ioway men employed and not so many outsiders. He wished the soldiers would be sent to remove the intruders.[33]

This problem existed as early as 1879, when the commissioner had answered Agent Shorb's letter saying, "You make mention of certain white persons, 'leeches', who are laying around from day to day to sop a little blood from the government or the Indians, etc." You are directed to order all such persons to leave the reservation at once, and in case of refusal, report their names to this office, and the necessary authority will be obtained to remove them beyond the limits of the Indian Country."[34] President Hayes proclaimed in 1880, "I do further warn and notify any and all persons who may so offend that they will be speedily and immediately removed thereby by the Agent according to the laws made and provided that no measures will be spared to prevent the invasion of said territory."[35]

Words in far-away Washington were to no avail; the problem of intruding whites continued. In 1887, the commissioner informed the secretary of war that a small detachment of cavalry or scouts should be stationed at the Sac and Fox Agency to remove the intruders and break up the cow camps that were illegally housing men who used the Indian lands for grazing cattle. Fort Reno, located to the west in Cheyenne and Arapaho country, supplied men, who in July arrested thirteen intruders. After they departed, the problem resumed its serious proportions.

The use of land also brought problems to the Great Nemaha Agency Ioways. In the 1880's two unnamed chiefs were described as "non progressive and obstructive." They had attempted to control and to limit in the traditional manner the amount of land that some young men wished to cultivate and to use for pasture, according to the agent. Their objections were not given, but presumably they ran counter to the agent's wishes. Intermarried whites had also enlarged their holdings by fencing in some of the best land, probably without the consent of the chiefs. At this time there were tribal adoptions of those non-Ioways, who thus received formally, or informally, equal status in the tribe, with the rights to participate in certain benefits. The commissioner responded to this situation by saying that young men's ambitions should be fostered, but that intermarried persons not adopted by the tribe had no rights or title to land, except if tribal custom allowed a husband to control the wife's land.[36] It is suspected that these intermarried whites and mixed-bloods now controlled much tribal business, including the decisions on land use. The two chiefs who tried to obstruct them may have been among those who removed to Indian Territory and complained to the agent there about the whites on their northern reservation.

Besides the intruders in Indian Territory, others saw the profitable prospects in Ioway lands. One group included C. T. Wells, Eddy B. Townsend, and Clarkson C. Pickett, who requested a license to trade with the Ioways and the Kickapoos in 1884. By coincidence, Townsend had in 1882 been a special Indian agent with investigatory powers. He had been assigned to visit the Sac and Fox Agency and had suggested that certain lands be set aside for the reservation to which the Ioways were assigned. Now he returned in another guise, seeking to capitalize by use of Ioway income and land.

The application to trade at Wellston was sent to the commissioner, who replied to Agent I. A. Taylor. He reminded Taylor that Wells, after which Wellston was named, had been accused of selling intoxicating liquors, such as strawberry extract, to the Indians. The agent was requested to investigate these charges and to prove or disprove them. The investigation was completed in short order, Wells found innocent, and the license issued on August 11, 1884, with the admonition that "All kinds of preparations composed in part of alcohol are to be excluded from the stock and a departure from this order we will promptly report."[37]

But Townsend and Pickett had other plans besides merely trading with the Ioways and the Kickapoos. On February 5, before the trading license was issued, another agreement was made between the Ioways and the two men to lease a major portion of the Ioway reservation for cattle grazing. William Tohee, Hotchisee, Frank Mahee, Joe Vetter, Brochomee (Kahthinonmy), and Hogarache passed a resolution in council on January 1, 1884, for the purpose of "more profitably utilizing their unoccupied lands and raising additional revenue."[38] The agreement included the use of the entire reservation except for "such lots and parcels of land as the Ioway may individually or collectively improve or cultivate for their own use and benefit." Since this was only a very small portion of the total 228,152 acres, it can be seen that most of the reservation was to become a cattle ranch, if Townsend and Pickett desired. The five-year extendable lease included other provisions, such as cattle-company use of Ioway timber for fences and buildings. No fewer than 2,000 head of cattle were to graze at any one time, and the sum of $.60 for each head was to be paid semiannually to the tribe. The cattle company would pay for any damage to any unfenced Ioway property, which in fact placed many Ioways in small fenced parcels of land surrounded by a large cattle operation. In addition, the company promised to pay the tribe $1,000 at the outset for the purchase of farming implements and seed for the coming spring planting.

In June, 1885, the Ioways granted the company the additional right to fence the entire western line of the reservation from the Deep Fork to the Cimarron, to fence a one-mile-square pasture, and to cultivating up to 150 acres within the reserve. White men employed by the company and their families began to live within the area. Hagarahche, Haywecoorah, Brochomee, Jefferson Whitecloud and David Tohee were appointed to see that the individual Ioway debts to the trading company would be paid with the advanced money, supposedly to be expended for agricultural implements and seeds in the original lease agreement. Future debts incurred at the trading post would be paid from the cattle lease money, and "should this be insufficient to cancel the individual indebtedness of our tribe, we desire to use so much of our next annuity payment in the same manner as may be necessary to relieve us from our present debt and embarrassed condition."[39] Without knowing the costs of items sold in the trading post, the extent of the Ioway debts, or the number of cattle to be paid for under the lease, we cannot say whether this arrangement was to be more beneficial to the Ioways or to Townsend, Pickett and Wells. But one suspects that it may have been more profitable for the latter.

In spite of the contract, Commissioner Atkins returned the agreement unapproved in July, 1885, saying that the department could not recognize such grazing leases in the territory.[40] This reply reflected the official view of the Office of Indian Affairs, stated in its Circular 140, October 18, 1884:

> Information having reached this office that certain persons are availing themselves of their positions as Indian traders to influence by gifts and other means, leading men of Indian tribes to lease them large tracts of reservation lands for grazing purposes, all such practices are hereby strictly prohibited.

To circumvent this, Townsend and Pickett removed their names as traders. Only Wells was licensed the following year. The lease between them and the Ioways continued for its full term until 1889. At this time the cattle company was behind in its lease payments to the Ioways. An arrangement was made to pay the required $.60 per head per year for the 3,244 cattle that were then grazing.[41]

From all indications it had been a profitable arrangement for the cattle company. Certainly its costs had not exceeded its profits. But the time for Indian land allotment had arrived in Indian Territory, and the cattle companies disappeared. The Ioways were able to pay their debts for a while. They had managed to hold their lands in common, as they desired, even though most of them were used for cattle grazing. They had built their villages and lived together in them but had avoided fences and intruders in vain.

11. Allotment and Its Aftermath

That the severalty policy was a terrible mistake was apparent shortly after its application.

William T. Hagan, *American Indians*

THE DAWES SEVERALTY (Allotment) Act, enacted in 1887, was to assign to individual Indians tracts of land varying from forty to one-hundred-sixty acres and to pay them for surplus reservation land after allotment was completed. The surplus land, minus tracts for cemeteries, schools, and other uses, was to be opened to white settlement. Overtly it was a continuation of the philosophy of turning the Indian into a farmer and a true American citizen. However, others saw it as a means of gaining more of the Indian birthright in spite of a century of promises to protect those rights — promises that somehow never were kept.

Wheels for implementation of the act moved slowly, but popular acceptance of its provisions was apparent. A territorial newspaper, *The Norman Transcript,* on November 30, 1889, said:

> The time has gone by when either tribes of Indians, cattle barons, or other syndicates can be permitted to appropriate and hold the public domain in great tracts when so many people are without even a spot of ground upon which to rest without being trespassers. The earth is the home of all men and no portion of the population should be permitted to monopolize it.

The Jerome Commission, named after its leading negotiator, David H. Jerome, came into Indian Territory in 1890 to convince the Ioways, the Pawnees, the Poncas, the Tonkawas, the Wichitas, the Cheyennes, the Arapahos, the Sacs, the Foxes, and others of the benefits of individual parcels of land, rather than common ownership of the entire tribal reservation. Any surplus they could sell to the United States.

The commission came to the Ioway village near present-day Fallis and Wellston on May 8, 1890, and set up their meetings in the Quaker Meeting House. Commission members alternately cajoled and threatened the Ioway leaders as portions of the proceedings indicate:

> *Warren E. Sayre:* Do you want land alone, or land and money?
> *Hogarache:* I don't want to do anything. We will stand the consequences.
> *Sayre:* But under the law, you must take one or the other. Which will you take?
> *Joe Vetter:* I don't want to have my name on your list.
> *Jerome:* Now, Vetter, you must determine for yourself and your wife and children. . . . It is for your own good to do what we want you to do. You are a man, not a boy.
> *Vetter:* We are *Indians* — and whenever we own anything, someone comes along and takes it. It is nature for everyone to keep everything that he has. We have some little money in the United States Treasury and we are depending on this money to keep us. We made a treaty a long time ago, and we are afraid of this. [1]

Ioway arguments were unsuccessful. By May 20, the commission, to its satisfaction, had completed the agreement with the Ioways. Each member was allotted 80 acres of reservation land to be held in trust for 25 years by the government; the period of time could be extended by Ioway tribal request. Taxation on this land was to be prohibited for the same length of time. Ten acres were reserved for a school, church, and cemetery. The tribe was to be paid $24,000 immediately for materials for houses and agricultural implements. A series of payments extending over 25 years brought the total amount of money owed to the Ioways to $84,000. The total reservation size had been declared to be 228,418 acres. After allotment, 221,528 acres of surplus lands remained for the government.[*2] Altogether 109 Ioways in Oklahoma received a total of 8,685.3 acres of their land. Later, on the Great Nemaha reserve, 159 allottees received 11,768.77 acres.[†]

---

* According to B. B. Chapman in "Dissolution of the Iowa Reservation," *Chronicles of Oklahoma,* 14 (1936): 475, the total acreage of the resrvation was 279,296 acres. One hundred and eight Ioways were allotted 8,605.3 acres, leaving a surplus of 270,681.27 acres. He gives his source as F. M. Goodwin to J. B. Tanner, April 24, 1924, C. Cls., *Printed Records,* vol. 560, no. 34677, pp 73-5. The number of acres given in the text is derived from the source cited in text, Senate, Ex. Doc. 171, p. 2.

† Different numbers are given for the number of northern Ioways who received allotments. The *Annual Report of the Commissioner of Indian Affairs, 1892,* p. 271, gives the figure as 159; the same source in 1894, p. 20, gives the figure as 143. In 1895, the number needing allotments was given as 45. Charles Kappler in 1916 reported to the commissioner of Indian affairs the list given in the text and said that several more also did not receive land.

Many Ioways there, including Florence Morris DeRoin, Roy DeRoin, John LeClair, Dan White Cloud, Clarence Murphy, Pauline Murphy, Ellsworth Murphy, Delphine Murphy, Thomas Murphy, Clara Murphy, Correne Partelow, and George Rhodd, were not allotted land because of a government oversight. Plans to allot to them lands with the Otoes or Kiowas in Oklahoma did not develop.[3]

A year after the agreement, the allotment teams arrived at the Ioway village in Indian Territory. Only a few Ioways wanted the dreaded process to begin. Blaine N. Kent, a descendant of the allottees, explained how his people felt about it:

> They had their own land of so many acres a piece that they must go and live on. They were living down in the village there, my mother's father, uncle's people, and the other chiefs. They, they were trying to find the locations where their land was, their allotments. My grandfather doesn't feel very good over that. No, he did not feel that it should have been such a thing as allotment act. He feels that it should have been in reservation. With allotment they only have so many acres that each one was allotted during that time. That leaves all the younger generations without land, without a home. If it was in reservation they would go out and establish a home on it taking their choice where they should establish their home. And still the land belongs to the tribe and the folks. There the generations could come along and would have a place to go, and live and try to make a living.[4]

The special agent for allotment, John C. Robinson, arrived in April, 1891, and began by telling the Ioways that they had sixty days to choose their land. If they did not do so, then he would select parcels for them. Forty-two, or more than half, refused to select sites. A local newspaper said that they had "sulked and held off and had not taken lands. Mr. Robinson made quick work of this and selected and set aside the lands for them in two days." Most of the sites were along or near the Cimarron River, south of present-day Perkins, Oklahoma. Those who did select land did so in a block in order to duplicate their common tradition. However, as late as the last quarter of 1892, several Ioways refused to accept their allotments or the sums designated in the agreement.

The so-called surplus Ioway reservation land was soon settled by whites, who entered the reservation on September 22 in the Run of 1891, as it was popularly called. Early accounts give the pell-mell aspect of the land opening where 15,000 persons pushed their way into Ioway, Sac and Fox, and Potawatomi lands. One settler remembered:

> I came to Oklahoma from Buffalo, Kansas, when the Ioway and Sac and Fox country opened. Got a claim two miles west of Perkins on the Cimarron River. I took a claim joining Charley Tohee's Indian allotment. His 80 and the claim I took is all in the Cimarron River now. The day of the run there was lots of excitement. People set the grass afire to hunt corners and by 3 o'clock we couldn't hardly see the sun. There was lots of

corner stones moved 15 to 20 rods to fool people in the run. We ran only across the river, and lots of them were with wagons, and carts, and horseback, and afoot. And if a horse or man fell down, they rode over him like he was not there.[5]

In his annual report, Agent S. L. Patrick reported on the results of the run:

Since my last report a great change has taken place. Within the year 1,280,000 acres of land under the jurisdiction of this agency have been thrown open to settlement, nearly all of which, except that allotted to the Indians, has been claimed and is now occupied by white settlers, many of whom have in this short time planted and raised enough crops for home consumption. Thriving towns have sprung up; business and speculation is brisk. Thus, in less than one short year American "pluck" has converted this "howling wilderness" into a populous thriving farming community.[6]

At the time of allotment the Ioways lived in a village near a good spring with nearby grazing areas for their ponies and adequate space for their corn fields. The village area, however, was not considered good for agriculture, so it was not allotted, even though the Ioways attempted to keep the area, which had their cemetary nearby.

The chiefs and their families chose adjacent parcels so that they could construct a village. Established some two miles southeast of Perkins on the south side of the Cimarron River, the village was built of bark houses and tipis, according to one who lived there as a child in the early years of the century. The dwellings belonged to the members of the chief's kin group and served as the locus of Ioway tribal government and tribal ceremonies (see Figure 21, Chapter 10). "Squaw patches," as they were called by the Ioways, were located nearby, and a few men obtained farm implements and began to farm and to care for their horses. In 1895, the tribe raised 10,000 bushels of corn and cut 100 tons of hay for their 44 horses, 5 mules, and 20 cows. In 1897, they cultivated 1,200 acres by themselves, 1,000 acres were farmed on shares with white farmers using their land, 2,500 acres were fenced by lessees for pasture,* and 10 acres were in orchards. The agent commented, "As a tribe they are doing well. They were raising about all they needed to live on and appear to be happy and well satisfied."

A few years after the allotment, the Ioways had not received the initial $24,000 promised to them in the Jerome Agreement. They petitioned Congress for the appropriation. Originally the amount was to be paid in stock, tools, and other items, but the tribe now wanted cash. Comm. D. M. Browning notified Agent E. L. Thomas

---

* Leasing of Indian allotments was permitted under 26 Stat. L 795, February 28, 1891; 28 Stat. L 305, August 15, 1894.

on December 5, 1893, that the recommendation had been made but that Congress had not appropriated the money. The Ioway council then decided to send a delegation to Washington. In 1894, Chiefs Dan Tohee, John Grant, John Ford, and Joe Vetter and interpreters Kirwin Murray and Joe Springer went there to insist upon payment of the $24,000 due them. Surprisingly, they were successful.

The Ioways at home were not the only ones elated with the outcome of the trip. Area merchants rejoiced. A Guthrie newspaper declared that the Ioways had received a small payment of $40 each and that within the week they would receive the "big $24,000 payment. The merchants of the city are out on a lookout for their credits, and will collect for goods sold to the Ioway." Two days later a newspaper head-lined, "Guthrie Got Her Share":

> Our merchants at the Ioway payment are satisfied with their payments. P. Hellman, F. Thwing, M. Golden, B. F. Berkey, Dano of the "Rush" and H. C. Beamer returned from the Sac and Fox Agency today, where they attended the Ioway payment. They are well satisfied with their collections. Every man getting his money who was on the ground in time.... Each Indian received $268.66. After the completion of the pay-ment, the Indians indulged in a great blowout and expended their money lavishly. [7]

Hoping for another success, the Ioways again petitioned in 1895 to obtain the remainder of the amount due them under the Jerome Agree-ment in order to invest it in a practical manner. Their Memorial to Congress said in part:

> We see in the settlement of Oklahoma the rapid increase in the value of land. We have learned much by our association with the white settlers, and we see what may be done with the money due us, because we have an opportunity to invest the same in lands that could be bought cheap now, that would double our investment, and place us in the future in a position to live on our own resources, and not become the wards of any person, county or nation. [8]

This time their request did not meet with success. The people be-came discouraged, evidencing great dissatisfaction with the life they were leading. The Otoes visited, and, after counseling with them, some Ioways abandoned their homes near Perkins and moved to the Otoe Agency. Eventually many did so and intermarried. Their descen-dants can still be found in the Otoe area in Oklahoma, and some were placed on the Otoe rolls.

In December, 1895, other Ioways unsuccessfully negotiated with the Osages for a lease of a tract of land on that reservation. They next attempted, through an attorney, John A. Sampsell, to lease fifteen thousand acres from the Kaws. They stated that they wanted to estab-lish a village and a cattle ranch there. The *Guthrie Times Record* reported, "They say they are tired of living apart on their allotments scattered among the whites who will not associate with them, and who use every opportunity to cheat them, and being citizens, they propose to live as they please, and be no longer bossed by the Indian Bureau."[9] This plan did not meet with success either.

New frustration came from sources other than unfulfilled treaty promises and resentment from allotment living. Oklahoma Territory established on May 2, 1890, encompassed the lands of the allotted Ioways. In certain ways, its government considered them citizens, seeking to tax them as it did the new white settlers around them. This was not supposed to happen according to the Ioway allotment agreement. Antagonism began in the spring of 1895. In 1898, the Ioways decided to resist taxation by not allowing any assessments to be made by territorial officials. However, John Embler, for some unknown reason, permitted the tax assessor to perform his assignment. That first attempt to tax the newly allotted Indians was thought a small victory. The territorial government view was that since Indians enjoyed the privileges of citizenship, such as the use of the roads, they should therefore be subject to taxation. However, the Ioways contended "that they are nothing more than the slaves of Uncle Sam, and in substantiation of this point, point out that an Indian cannot make a visit to a member of another tribe without securing a permit from the Indian Agent. An Indian off his reservation is subject to arrest."[10]

Article IV of the 1891 act pertaining to Ioway allotment said, ". . . And during said period of twenty-five years said lands, so allotted and the improvements thereon shall not be subject to taxation for any purpose by any State or Territory. . . ." Agent Lee Patrick reported in his annual report to the commissioner on August 31, 1898, what had happened:

> Under the recent ruling of Judge Keaton, of the United States district court in Pottawatomie County, Oklahoma, rendered in January, 1898, the assessors of the various townships have been instructed to assess for taxation all improvements found upon Indian allotments, such as fencing, buildings, etc. The rate of taxation in this country is so high that in many cases the taxes on improvements will be more than the cash rental paid on the land. This will be a severe drawback to any advancement contemplated by the Indian. He dreads taxes as much as his predecessors did the white man. The result will be that he will not want any improvements made on the land by a lessee, nor will he put any there himself. Action should be taken at once by the Department of Justice to prevent the collection of these taxes. Unless some action is taken, the Indians will surely quit making improvements on their lands and thus defeat the object of the Government.[11]

This was not the only difficulty that the Ioways encountered with territorial and federal authorities. The Oklahoma territorial legislature passed a law prohibiting polygyny. Increasing pressure came also from the federal government to legalize all marriages to meet the new Department of the Interior regulation.[12] J. C. Doulet, an attorney hired by the Osages, another tribe affected by the legislation, proclaimed in August, 1897, "I know I can knock the stuffing out of that statute.... the law as far as they are concerned is *ex post facto,* and strictly unconstitutional." In late November, the *Daily Oklahoman* relayed a story from a Wichita, Kansas source that nearly one-half of the Ioways had left their allotments near Cushing, Oklahoma, to return to their former homes in the Nemaha valley on the Kansas-Nebraska line:

> They had camped near the junction of the Ninnescah River and had committed depredations in the country around until the farmers threatened to kill some of them off. They have rebelled against the antipolygyny law as well as having to work out the $3.00 road tax. They would suffer the severest punishment rather than handle a shovel or road scraper. This fear of white man's law has started them afoot on a seven hundred mile journey in the face of bitter cold weather.[13]

The outcome of this journey is not known.

Another assault on traditional patterns took place in April, 1899. The Boards of Health of Lincoln and Payne counties in Oklahoma were asked to "abate the nuisances of the Ioway Indian graveyards." The Ioways persisted, it was claimed, in their custom of depositing their dead in small houses on the surface of the ground. If this report is true, the scaffold had been replaced in this decade by a small wooden or bark, lodge-type structure closer to the ground. It is possible that scaffold burials continued apart from the burial ground. Shortly after this announcement, a newspaper wrote that the Ioways were dissatisfied and wished to spend the summer on the Nemaha River.

Attempts to leave Oklahoma Territory and return to their old homes were not successful. The desire to escape reflected dissatisfaction and disillusionment with reservation and allotment life that was duplicated in many parts of the United States. Various psychological responses resulted from the general frustrations and anxieties of the time. The Ghost Dance or Messiah Craze that swept across the country was a sign of the stress in the 1890's. The government viewed the movement with alarm, and agents and military men were widely alerted.[14] The Ghost Dance originated with the Paiute medicine man, Wovoka, in 1888 and spread rapidly as a messianic movement among the Indian tribes of the United States. It exhorted the adherents to prepare for divine intervention in the restoration of their inheritance and a return to the ways of the old days, free from white influence, control, and abuse. Dances in a circle with men and women participating, singing songs, and communing with heavenly spirits in trance-like states were common. The Pawnees, from whom the Ioways obtained the dance, used it principally to communicate with their deceased relatives. During this time, Ioways and members of many tribes had succumbed to disease and malnutrition, and this dance with its self-induced trances helped to relieve the grief.

The Ioways obtained the dance in a proper and ceremonial way, according to a descendant of a man who received it. With gifts and instructions, it was transferred to the Ioway leaders by Old Man Mathews and Old Man Morgan, and other Pawnee leaders. When the dance was held at the turn of the century, the Ioways invited the Pawnees to attend; and they in turn invited the Ioways to their dance grounds. According to an elderly Ioway, the dance was accepted and was used for religious purposes. Revelations occurred, or, as it was expressed, "It reveals to them after so long doing the dance, but the reason why I do not know, since I never had anything like that happen. It reveals to them, but they don't come back in person and talk to them or anything like that." Few details of the Ioway Ghost Dance were given. Usually four leaders, but sometimes six, shook the gourds, sang, and beat the small drum. A special pipe was used during some interval in the dance. Five dance grounds were described in the area south of Perkins, Oklahoma. Sometimes as many as one hundred participants were involved in two concentric circles or in separate circles. The dance was held for four days and nights. While singing and moving in a circle shoulder to shoulder, the participants sang songs that were directed toward the heavens, to that village where they believed their dead reached out their arms to comfort their suffering parents and children below.[15]

Their dead included many of the tribe's children, and in 1892 it appeared that every family lost at least one child in an epidemic that swept through a population that hovered around ninety. Agency physicians did what they could when they were consulted, but they were not always reliable. They continued to come and go. One was removed in 1891 for habitual drunkenness and neglect of duty. In the following year, his replacement was charged with collecting money from the Indians; and in the year after that, he was charged with "earnestly soliciting all the outside practice he can" and neglecting the Indian people. Later in the decade, one doctor was evidently emotionally distressed: "On the second day on duty he wrote letters to His Eminence, Cardinal Gibbons, the Honorable Auditor of the Treasury, and to Miss Cornelia Vanderbilt, to whom he avers he is engaged. . . . It bears out what has been quietly thought relative to this gentleman from the day he arrived."[16] The Indians could fortunately fall back on their own remedies, but they were no match for the epidemics that took such a toll of their numbers.

During the last decade of the 1800's and into the 1900's, in the face of new pressures and obligations to the federal government and territorial laws, the Ioways endeavored to maintain as many aspects of their culture as they could. Ioway men hunted from time to time, but after allotment this became more difficult. The agent had to issue a pass, and fences and white farmers prevented use of favorite hunting grounds. In December, 1899, the Creek agent at Muskogee, Indian Territory, wrote to Agent Lee Patrick that "two parties of your Indians

Figure 24. An Ioway house standing on an Ioway allotment near Perkins, Oklahoma, in the 1960's. It was covered with metal sheets and used for storage in its later years. From the author's collection.

were hunting in Creek country. One between Bristow and Cushing, and the other on the Deep Fork west of Okmulgee. While there is no particular objection to the Indians of your agency hunting in this territory, I call your attention in order that you may do what you think is proper in reference to having them return to their homes."[17]

In remembering the hunting of those days, Blaine Kent recalled how it was:

My Grandfather hunted, well, over there, northeast of Avery, or south-west of Cushing about five miles northeast of Avery, there as far north as those places, he was hunting deer or wild turkey or whatever he could find such as wild hogs and prairie chickens. That was the Sac and Fox reservation, but the Sac and Fox came over on the Ioway reservation, and hunt as long as they want and go back to their reservation. Also the Ioway can do the same thing, go on their reservation, camp out, stay there as long as they want to. No one will say anything about it. Furthermore, not only these two tribes, but the Kickapoos, Shawnees and Potawatomies, all these tribes on adjoining reservations. There is nothing said about who could hunt there or anything like that. They could do that until allotment came, then they made things so when the Allotment Act, they just couldn't go here and there, because the allotment means the reservation is going into something like a checkerboard.

Once I got in my car and went east of Drumright about seven miles. What got me out there was that I thought of my father and mother, and also my grandparents, and some of the elder people of those days. Especially I thought of my father and my mother. During that time I was just a little feller, but I remember some things. I was old enough to ride a horse. I went out there. I turned off, got off the highways and sat there in the car, thinking and studying. I had in mind that my folks used to camp along that creek there, and also some of the other relatives. I saw my father after they set up camp and got everything settled down, he would get on a pony, and take his Winchester and go down that creek out to hunt deer. He'd go east from there, but I don't know where he goes, he goes through the hills, the timber, and cross the creek and hollers. We call it now the Creek reservation, they were plenty of wild game there, and nothing was said about the Indians going there. It was free for all Indians, any kind of meat that they want, they could find. Then he'd come in and say, "well, I killed a wild hog. It's hanging up way there on a tree. I'm gonna have to go get it, and I've come back for help. They'd hook their horses to a buggy, and they'd go there and haul the wild hog. Some of them weighed, I imagine, about 500 pounds. When they brought the meat in they would take care of it, cure it over the open fire. And when they got enough supply of meat, then they would go back home till they ran out again, and then they'd go back. Two or three families went together. Grandfather's, Charley Tohee's and Maggie Lincoln, John Moses' family and Joe Dupee's, but he was a younger man than the rest. And Dan Tohee and his family.[18]

Attempts to maintain other traditions continued. In 1897, the Sacs and the Foxes returned from their visiting with the Otoes at Red Rock in Noble County. They brought sixty ponies to the Ioway village, where they held a dance and gave some of them away. Dog feasts, first mentioned by Catlin, were held probably more frequently in 1897 and 1901 than local newspapers noted. A new variant of the old stick-ball game, called baseball, caught on rapidly late in the century and saw many young Indian athletes competing with one another, including Jimmie Thorpe, as he was called. The Otoes and the Ioways played a series of games in 1897 during their annual visit.[19] In 1899 a "big religious dance occurred on the Ioway dancing ground," and tribes from as far as Kansas participated. During this period began the growth of friendly relationships between neighboring tribes, who at one time may have been enemies. The interaction brought about similarities in attitudes, ceremonies, dress, and other manifestations called pan-Indianism. Boarding schools introduced Ioways and members of other tribes to each other, and intermarriages aided and contributed to a widening intertribal communication.

Severalty had been promoted as a means of setting the Indian on his own path of economic self-sufficiency. Little education, experience, and capital were provided to accomplish the goal. In fact, economic life for the Indian became increasingly agent-controlled in the years that followed. Much government policy was promulgated to protect the Indian who was deemed unable or "incompetent" to handle his own affairs. Regulations, however, were not always able to prevent the machinations of the unscrupulous lessee, and land speculator, intruder,[20] merchant, lawyer, and sometimes agent. For example, a letter written by the commissioner to an agent in 1896 suggests collusion between the agent and merchants:

> Sir:
> I am in receipt of a communication, under date of the 16th instant, in which the following language appears:
> 'There is a thing carried on here which seems to me to be a wholesale robbery, or just as bad. When the time for making the Government payments to the Indians by the Agent, he notifies them that on a certain date payments will be made. Come to the agency one tribe at a time. The Pottawatomies must travel from 35 to 70 miles, extremes of this reservation. It takes a week to make all the payments. They buy their provisions, etc., there and spend much of their money before leaving. The Iowas from 35 to 50 miles. The last time were gone over a week, boarding down there. My investigations have shown me, that is, satisfied my own mind, that there is a league of some kind between the agent and one or two store keepers to get the Indians' money. Certain gamblers are always there too. Other arrangements to get their money. One man is putting up a large quantity of pork to sell to the Indians when they come for their money. They are paid in checks and these store keepers get them, if the gambler is not ahead. The Indians and some of us have tried to get the Agent to go to some town near the center of the tribal reserve and there make payments. He declines. Tecumseh is central for Pottawatomies. Perkins is within two hours drive of all the Iowas. It is the same with other tribes. All are treated alike under this agency. Cannot the Department order the Agent to go to a central location for each tribe? Why should a whole tribe go so far instead of one man's coming to them?'
> I will thank you for a report as to the truth or falsity of the statements referred to, and if they be true, you should request authority, whenever you pay annuities, to visit the proper places to make these payments, thus removing all grounds for such complaints.[21]

The agent's reply to this letter has not been found.

Another individual who sometimes benefited from the Indian was the territorial lawyer, who was now appointed by the court and approved by the government to assist the Indian in his financial affairs if he were a minor, an orphan, or an incompetent. The guardian, as he was called, would frequently be asked for funds to cure an ailment, as in the case of an Ioway child who was going blind. Sometimes such appeals brought little or no response, even after many requests. Many guardians fulfilled their obligations in an honorable manner. Some had funds for as many as a dozen wards under their control. The situation reached such scandalous proportions in 1899 that the commissioner of Indian affairs sent a letter to all agents, notifying them of changes in the system that would correct abuses. He said at this time that "the Indian wards get very little or no benefit from what is rightfully due them."[22]

From another quarter the Indian and the merchant continued their uneasy alliance. The Ioways took their business to nearby towns such as Perkins, Cushing, Chandler, Stillwater, and Guthrie, where they established credit for their purchases (see Figure 25). Indebtedness grew alarmingly in this and the next decade, according to a list kept by the agency. The total amount owed by one individual to four merchants was $993.66, a large sum. The total indebtedness of twenty-eight persons was slightly over $5,200.[23] An area newspaper noted in 1899 that the last annuity payment of the Ioway fell far short of covering their debts. The tribe continued to attempt to collect treaty funds due them in order that they might pay their debts. Yearly income averaged $25 and $75 per family for lands leased. This was insufficient for purchased goods, such as clothing and household articles.[24] Employment opportunities, too, were limited.

What were some effects of allotment in 1891 on the Ioway allottees in Kansas and Nebraska? A short time after land leasing was permitted, farms that were productive by the efforts of their Indian owners were leased and operated by white farmers. The agent's report for 1896 stated that leasing had "demoralized them in a business way, and from being considered the most prosperous and progressive," the Ioways were now considered "the least self supporting."[25] In 1897, Agent James noted that over 4,000 acres had formerly been cultivated by the Ioway, while in that year only 1,000 had been utilized. In his opinion, leasing originally had been intended for old and disabled people, but now it had become a "mania," and land as well as their dwellings were leased to white people.* They spent much of their time visiting in Oklahoma and Wisconsin. For a time "they were disinclined to send their children to school." They showed a slight interest in a Moravian Mission, the only one functioning during this period "a Sister Mollie of the Holiness Church" was also said to be among them.

In 1899, Agent W. H. Honnell expounded his response to allotment's stepchild, Indian land leasing. "It had brought a complete demoralization of the Indian." It had stopped their habits of work. They sold their stock; they surrendered their homes and lived in shanties and wigwams: and they spent their time in visiting and riotous living. Some

---

* Taking the opposite stand regarding leasing, Agent Lee Patrick, in 1899, declared that the "leasing system has proved of great benefit to the Indians." See *Annual Report of the Commissioner of Indian Affairs* (1899), p. 304.

Figure 25. The Ioway Indians visiting Guthrie on September 16, 1889, some five months after its establishment during the land run of 1889. The Ioways often went to trade at this town after "payment" time. Courtesy of Research Library, Photographs Collection, Oklahoma Historical Society.

Indians of the agency had become promoters, who induced their friends and relatives to lease their lands to white men, by which they "deceived and robbed their fellow tribesmen."[26]

Thus ended a decade of allotment, which brought the Ioways of Oklahoma, Kansas, and Nebraska to a new century. Some looked forward to the challenges of the future, but for many, if there was a positive expression or reaction to the larger world around them, it cannot be discerned in the memories of their descendants or in the government reports of the time.

Ioways attempted to cope with the life of that time by leaving their allotment areas for extended visits to other tribes and by the treks the southern Ioways made to their older Kansas and Nebraska homes. They sought to lease land, where they could live together in the traditional way and share their preferred culture. The acceptance of the

315

Figure 26. Helen Kent Mathews and her grandson at Pawnee, Oklahoma in 1964. There is a striking resemblance between her and Ru-ton-ye-wee-ma in Figure 11. She is the daughter of Blaine N. and Rosa W. Kent. From the author's collection.

Ghost Dance and, in the next decade, the peyote rituals of the Native American Church speak of disillusionment and search. Continued efforts to seek proper payment of funds due them from the United States government and their economic disadvantage in the white world added to their difficulties. Perhaps the joy to be found in life lived on in the young. The old men passed on what they knew to them. Black Wing in 1966 recalled the exultation of learning how to make a sacred thing, the drum:[27]

> I learned to make a drum alright. Some old fellow learned me how to make a drum, and also my Grandpa, he learned me, told me. But I didn't just go ahead making a drum because I'd seen somebody make one. No. When they, Grandpa and my folks make known that I should learn to make the

drum, well then, they were chiefs all right, but still they had to go to some-body else, some of the other people around us in the tribe. They had to put up a feast and let them all know that I'm going to learn to make the drum. That I will learn by my Grandpa. So then, by that, people know and understand the meaning. When you learn you don't go before people, but we went out to ourselves, and got everything ready. So he made a little drum, and he and I made a little drum. He helped me, but I was doing the biggest part of it. I was around 10 or 12 years old. Of course, it didn't take us one day. Oh, I don't know how long. Maybe a week. We came back in the evening. I was just trying to think where we were living. I believe we were back over . . . up the creek there on Dad's place at the village.

When we finished it, my folks called my other Grandfather, one of the Chiefs, my mother's uncle. He said, "Well, he has finished this drum." He meant me. And so after that he pronounced this among the others, talking about it, and I was authorized to go ahead and make another drum, and after so long my folks did the same thing again. This old gentleman that they had called on to show me how to make the drum, his name was John Moses, and he was a good deal older than I was and Dad. He was one of the men that they had authorized way back yonder the same as my Grand-pa, but he weren't no chief or doctor, or anything like that. He was the tribe's drum maker. So my father told him that he wanted me to learn to make the drum from him also. So then he said, "Alright." After so long we began. We went out again, like we did when Grandpa took me out. He got everything ready, and I learned how to make a drum from him. It was about the same type of drum. After that they done the same thing and announced it. So then from that time on I was authorized two times to make drums. There must have been about two years between the first and second drum, and I didn't learn it at the same place the last time. This time it was southwest of the Community Building here about a mile from it.

So then we had several men who were authorized to make a drum: John Moses, Charles Tohee, I seen him make a drum; then Thomas Lincoln, my father's nephew, he learned from my dad. Then my brother learned, too. I will come and teach anyone that comes and asks me to, but it's not my place to go and say, I am going to teach them. It's their place to come and make themselves known. Right now there is just two of us who are authorized.

And the teaching of this drum. There's a teaching behind that, but the reasons behind that, I cannot tell you, and I will not go into that, except that the drum is round, and that represents the world, and the sound of the drums means that you are making yourself known to the great Creator, by the four corners or points of the world. The sound of the drum is the same as your voice worshipping the Creator. It is a sacred thing, this making the drum.

Epilogue

It is a right, which natural reason dictates that everyone who receives a promise should have power to compel the promiser to do what a fair interpretation of his words suggests.

Hugo Grotius,
"The Interpretation of Treaties,"
The Rights of War and Peace, 1625

ONE MAJOR GOAL of twentieth-century Ioways has been to gain restitution for those treaty obligations that were not fulfilled by the United States in the previous century. They have also sought equitable payment for the lands that they ceded at below-average prices for those times. With the establishment of the Indian Claims Commission by Congress on August 6, 1946, the Ioways and hundreds of similarly concerned tribes began the arduous process, which resulted in the 1970's in the payment of judgment funds to all enrolled Ioways across the United States. Approximately two hundred and fifty Ioways of Oklahoma and seventeen hundred who claimed to be members of the Kansas and Nebraska group shared the monies. Old Man, in Oklahoma, said that he and his father and brother worked all their lives to bring justice to their people. He hoped, he added in the decade before, that he would live to see the results. He did so in his seventy-ninth year. Most recently, a northern Ioway, Marvin Franklin, was apponted as acting commissioner of Indian Affairs on February 6, 1973.

Abbreviations

American Historical Association Annual Report	*AHAAR*	Kansas State Historical Society	KSHS
American State Papers, Indian Affairs	*ASP, IA*	Letters Received	LR
Bureau of American Ethnology	BAE	Letters Sent	LS
Bureau of Indian Affairs	BIA	*Messages and Papers of the Presidents*	*MPP*
Great Nemaha Agency	GNA	*Michigan Pioneer and Historical Collections*	*MPHC*

American Historical
Association Annual
Report — *AHAAR*
American State Papers,
Indian Affairs — *ASP, IA*
Bureau of American
Ethnology — BAE
Bureau of Indian Affairs — BIA
Great Nemaha Agency — GNA
Historical and Statistical
Information Respecting
the History, Condition
and Prospects of the
Indian Tribes of the
United States, H. R.
Schoolcraft. — HCPIT
Illinois Historical
Collections — IHC
Indian and Pioneer
History Collection — *IPHC*
Iowa Journal of History
and Politics — *IJHP*
Journal of American
Folklore — *JAFL*
Journal of Illinois
Historical Society — *JIHS*

Kansas State Historical
Society — KSHS
Letters Received — LR
Letters Sent — LS
Messages and Papers of
the Presidents — *MPP*
Michigan Pioneer and
Historical Collections — *MPHC*
Minnesota Historical
Society Collections — *MHSC*
Mississippi Valley
Historical Review — *MVHR*
Missouri Historical
Review — *MHR*
Missouri Historical
Society — MHS
National Archives — NA
Nebraska Historical
Society — NHS
Office of Indian Affairs — OIA
Oklahoma Historical Society — OHS
Oklahoma Historical
Society Indian Archives — OHSIA
Territorial Papers — *TP*
Wisconsin Historical
Collections — *WHC*

NOTE: Certain French names in the text are spelled as given in the *Dictionary of Canadian Biography,* Vol. 1 (1966), Vol. 2 (1969), edited by Francess Halpenny and Andre Vachon, University of Toronto Press.

Notes

Prologue

1. Alanson Skinner, *JAFL,* Vol. No. 38, 481, 502; William Whitman, *JAFL,* 51; 201-204.
2. J. O. Dorsey, in *Handbook of American Indians,* ed. F. W. Hodge, Vol. 1; 612.
3. Alanson Skinner, *Ethnology of the Ioway Indians* (1926), 191-92.
4. H. R. Schoolcraft, *Historical and Statistical Information Respecting the History, Condition and Prospects of the Indian Tribes of the United States,* Vol. 3 (1853):361 ff. (This will hereafter be cited as HCPIT.)
5. Thomas McKenney and James Hall, *History of the Indian Tribes of North America,* Vol. 3 (1870); 15.
6. Emma Tohee Kent, Testimony before the Indian Claims Commission, February 27, 1952, Docket 138. In Martha Royce Siegel, *Field Notes, Ioway* (1965).
7. G. H. Pond, "Ancient Mounds and Monuments," *MHSC,* Vol. 1, 114.
8. Dorsey, in *Handbook of North American Indians,* Vol. 2; 278.
9. Schoolcraft, *HCPIT,* Vol. 3, map.

Chapter 1

1. Mildred Mott, "The Relation of Historic Indian Tribes to Archaeological Manifestations in Iowa," *IJHP,* Vol. 36, No. 3 (1938), 227-314; Mildred Mott Wedel, "Oneota Sites on the Upper Iowa River," *Missouri Archaeologist,* Vol. 21, Nos. 2-4 (1959), 1-181.
2. Waldo R. Wedel, "The Oneota Aspect," *An Introduction to Kansas Archeology,* BAE, Bull. No. 174, 600-15; M. Wedel, "Oneota Sites," 6; Dale R. Henning, "Development and Interrelations of Oneota Culture in the Lower Missouri River Valley," *Missouri Archaeologist,* Vol. 32 (1970), 148-52; M. Wedel, "Ethnohistory: Its Payoffs and Pitfalls for Iowa Archeologists," *Journal of the Iowa Archeological Society,* Vol. 23 (1976) 1-43.
3. M. M. Wedel, "Oneota Sites," 6, 7.
4. W. R. Wedel, *Introduction to Kansas Archeology,* 601, 603.
5. James B. Griffin, "A Hypothesis for the Prehistory of the Winnebago," *Culture in History, Essays in Honor of Paul Radin* (1960), 817; Alanson Skinner, *"Ethnology*

of the Ioway," *Bulletin of the Public Museum of the City of Milwaukee*, Vol. 5, No. 4 (1926), 271-72; M. Wedel, "Oneota Sites," 35.

6. M. M. Wedel, "Oneota Sites," 53.

7. For detailed pottery description, see M. Wedel, "Oneota Sites," 111-19 and Table 2, 128-34; Dale R. Henning, "Oneota Ceramics in Iowa," *Journal of the Iowa Archeological Society*, No. 11 (1961).

8. James A. Brown, "The Prairie Peninsula, an Interaction Area in the Eastern United States," Ph.D. dissertation, University of Chicago, 1965, p. 27.

9. M. M. Wedel, "Oneota Sites," 30-31.

10. Ibid., 54-55, 125.

11. W. R. Wedel, *Introduction to Kansas Archaeology*, 603; M. Wedel, "Oneota Sites," 15-28, 37.

12. M. M. Wedel, ibid., 44-46.

Chapter 2

1. Pawnee legend, related by Garland J. Blaine, 1964.

2. H. R. Schoolcraft, *HCPIT*, Vol. 3 (1868), 262.

3. Henry Lewis Morgan, *The League of the Iroquois*, (New York, Corinth Books, 1962), 14.

4. Emma H. Blair (trans.), "Flight of the Hurons and Outaouas," in *Indian Tribes of the Mississippi and the Great Lakes Region*, Vol. 1, 169.

5. Mildred Mott, "The Relation of Historic Indian Tribes to Archaeological Manifestations in Iowa," *IJHP*, Vol. 36, No. 3 (1938), 237.

6. Extract from a letter by Father Louis André, written from La Baye de Puants, on April 20, 1676, *Jesuit Relations and Allied Documents*, Vol. 60, 203.

7. R. G. Thwaites (ed.) "Relation of 1670-1671," by Claude Dablon, *Jesuit Relations*, Vol. 55, 183.

8. John S. Sigstad, "A Report of the Archeological Investigations, Pipestone National Monument, 1965-1966," *Journal of the Iowa Archeological Society*, Vol. 17 (December, 1970), Table 7a.

9. Mildred Mott Wedel, "Ethnohistory: Its Payoff and Pitfalls for Iowa Archeologists," *Journal of the Iowa Archeological Society*, Vol. 23 (1976), 27.

10. *Jesuit Relations*, Vol. 54, 219.

11. Pierre Margry, *Découvertes et Établissements des Francais de L'Amérique Septentrionale*, Vol. 2 (1886), 215; from Bib. Natl., Clairambault 1016:171 (archival Ms. translated by Mildred Mott Wedel).

12. *Jesuit Relations*, Vol. 62, 71-95.

13. *The Dictionary of Canadian Biography*, Vol. 1 (1966), 516-18.

14. *Ibid.*

15. *Ibid.*

16. Blair, *op. cit.*, 367.

17. *Ibid.*, 367-68.

18. *Ibid.*, 368-69.

19. *Ibid.*, Vol. 2, 183.

20. *Ibid.*

21. Mildred Mott Wedel, "Oneota Sites on the Upper Iowa River," *Missouri Archaeologist*, Vol. 21, Nos. 2-4 (1959), 54.

22. Blair, *op. cit.*, 1, 371.

23. *Ibid.*, 372.

24. *Ibid.*, Vol. 2, 15-16.

25. *Ibid.*, 82.

26. *Ibid.*, 82-83.

27. *Dictionary of Canadian Biography*, Vol. 1, 518.

28. Blair, *op. cit.*, Vol. 2, 88.

29. *Ibid.*, 88-89.

30. *Ibid.*, 112.

31. Louise P. Kellogg, "The French Regime in Wisconsin and the Northwest" (Madison, Wis.: 1925), 258.

32. W. J. Eccles, *France in America,* 101.

33. M. M. Quaife (ed.), "Memoir de La Mothe de Cadillac," (Citadel Press, 1962), 15.

34. *Dictionary of Canadian Biography,* Vol. 1, 427-28; Mildred Mott Wedel, "Le Sueur and the Dakota Sioux," *Aspects of Upper Great Lakes Anthropology, Papers in Honor of Lloyd A. Wilford,* Elden Johnson (ed.) (St. Paul, Minnesota, Historical Society, (1974). Many of the references below are from Mildred Wedel's article and other sources which she has graciously allowed the author to use. She has translated and retranslated French documents that impart fuller, correct information for this period of the French in the Mississippi and Missouri valleys.

35. M. M. Wedel, "Le Sueur and the Dakota Sioux;" Grace Lee Nute, "Posts in the Minnesota Fur Trading Area, 1660-1855," *Minnesota History,* Vol. 11; 252.

36. Margry, *op. cit.,* Vol. 62, 63-64, translated by M. M. Wedel.

37. (MSS. Fr. n.a., 21395: 5, translated by M. M. Wedel.

38. *Ibid.;* Jean Baptiste Bénard de la Harpe, *Journal Historique de 'Etablissement des Français à la Louisiane,* A. L. Boimare (ed.) (1831), 40-41, translated by M. M. Wedel.

39. Claude Delisle, *"Memoires de Mr. le Sueur,"* Archives de la Marine, (2JJ56-9:52), Arch. Natle., Paris, translated by Mildred Mott Wedel.

40. André-Joseph Pénigault, "Relation," in Margry, *op. cit.,* Vol. 5, 414-26, and *WHC,* Vol. 16, 195.

41. Delisle, "Memoires" (2JJ56-9:55), tran. Mildred M. Wedel.

42. M. M. Wedel, "Le Sueur and the Dakota Sioux," 157-71.

43. Delisle, "Memoires," (2JJ56-9:55), tran. Mildred M. Wedel; La Harpe, *op. cit., Journal Historique,* A.-L. Boimare, (ed.), (1831), pp 61-62.

44. Mildred M. Wedel, personal communication, July 24, 1973. Translation of C. Delisle, Archs. Mar. (2JJ56-9:94).

45. Mildred M. Wedel, personal communication and translation.

46. Gabriel Marest to Pierre Le Moyne d'Iberville, July 10, 1700, *WHC,* Vol. 16, 180.

47. Delisle, "Memoires," (2JJ56-9:82), tran. Mildred M. Wedel.

48. Baron Marc de Villiers du Terrage, *La Découverte du Missouri et l'Histoire du Fort d' Orleans, 1673-1728* (Paris, Librairie Ancienne Honoré Champion, Libraire de la Société de l'Histoire de France, 1925), 32.

49. *Ibid.,* p. 34.

50. *Ibid.* Mildred M. Wedel translation.

51. Petition of the Ioways to the president, December 14, 1836, Great Nemaha Agency (RG 75, M 234, R 362, National Archives).

52. L. P. Kellogg, "Fox Indian Wars During the French Regime," *Proceedings* of the State Historical Society of Wisconsin (1907), 142-88.

53. Vaudreuil and Bégon to French minister, September 20, 1714, *WHC,* Vol. XVI, 306.

54. Kellogg, "French Regime," 287-289; *WHC,* Vol. 5, 78-80.

55. Kellogg, *op. cit.,* 303-04.

56. Noel M. Loomis (ed.) and A. P. Nasatir (trans.), *Pedro Vial and the Roads to Santa Fe* (1967), 19, 45.

57. Alfred B. Thomas, *After Coronado,* (1935) pp. 226-30.

58. Pierre F. X. de Charlevoix, *"Journal Historique,"* (1744), excerpt in *WHC,* Vol. 16, 413-14.

59. Thomas, *op. cit.,* 228.

60. Margry, *op. cit.,* Vol. 6, 450; trans. Henri Folmer in "French Expansion Toward New Mexico in the Eighteenth Century," unpub. Ms. (1939), 123.

61. Marcel Giraud, "Étienne Véniard de Bourgmont's 'Exact Description of Louisiana,'" *Bulletin of the Missouri Historical Society,* Vol. 15, 3-19.

62. Villiers, *op. cit.,* 61-62; Giraud, *op. cit.,* 16.

63. Villiers, *op. cit.,* 63.

64. Giraud, *op. cit.,* 19.

65. Villiers, *op. cit.,* 103, tran. Mildred M. Wedel.

66. *Ibid.,* 108, tran. Mildred M. Wedel.

67. Margry, *op. cit.,* Vol. VI, 388 ff., tran. Henri Folmer, *op. cit.,* 127.

68. Margry, *ibid.,* 396, Folmer, *ibid.,* 154.

69. Margry, *ibid.,* 423, tran. Mildred M. Wedel.

70. *Ibid.,* 425, tran. Mildred M. Wedel.

71. *WHC,* Vol. 17, pp. xii, 15, 17; J. Van der Zee, "French Discovery and Exploration of the Eastern Iowa Country Before 1763," *IJHP,* Vol. 12, No. 3, 345.

72. L. P. Kellogg, "Fort Beauharnois," *A Quarterly Magazine of Minnesota History* (September, 1927), 234-55.

73. *WHC, op. cit.,* 60.

74. Kellogg, "Fox Indians," 177.

75. *WHC, op. cit.,* 206.

76. *Ibid.,* 218-19.

77. Iowa Docket 135, *Before the Indian Claims Commission,* 24-25; Docket 153, *Before the Indian Claims Commission,* 39.

78. Berlin B. Chapman, *The Otoes and Missourias* (Oklahoma City, Times Journal Publishing Company. 1965), xi.

79. Iowa Docket 153, *op. cit.,* 32-41.

80. *WHC, op. cit.,* 442.

81. Vaudreuil to French Minister, July 20, 1757, *WHC, ibid.,* 195.

82. *Ibid.*

83. *Ibid.,* Vol. 18, 197.

84. *Ibid.,* 196.

85. *Ibid.*

86. Louis Antoine de Bougainville, *The American Journals of L. A. de Bougainville, Adventure in the Wilderness* (Norman, University of Oklahoma Press, 1964), E. P. Hamilton ed., trans., 151.

87. "Memoir of Bougainville," *WHC,* Vol. 18, 178.

88. Notes of Auguste Chouteau, February 21, 1816, Ancient and Miscellaneous Surveys, 331A, 4:258-264, National Archives.

Chapter 3

1. *IHC,* Vol. 10, xxix.

2. *New York Colonial Documents,* Vol. 10, 1091-94.

3. *IHC,* Vol. 11, 126.

4. Sir William Johnson, "Reasons for Establishing a British Colony at the Illinois with Some Proposals for Carrying the Same into Immediate Execution," July 10, 1766. Public Record Office, London, Colonial Offices 5, Vol. 67, in *Foreman Transcripts* (OHSIA), 117-25.

5. "The British Occupation of the Illinois Country," *IHC,* Vol. 10, xxxiv.

6. *WHC,* Vol. 1, 1-36.

7. *Ibid.,* 29-30.

8. *Ibid.,* 32.

9. *Ibid.,* 33.

10. *Ibid.,* 38.

11. *Ibid.,* 39.

12. Sir William Johnson, *Papers,* Vol. 9, 781.

13. St. Ange to Dabbadie, August 12, 1764, *IHC,* Vol. 10, 292-94.

14. *Ibid.,* Vol. 11, 125.

15. Chouteau, Notes, February 16, 1816, (RG 75, Ancient and Miscellaneous Surveys, 4:258-261, 262, 263, 264, NA).

16. E. Wilson Lyon, *Louisiana in French Diplomacy, 1759-1804* (Norman, University of Oklahoma Press, 1934), 41.

17. *Ibid.,* 42-44.

18. *WHC,* Vol. 18, 299-300.

19. *Ibid.,* 306-07.

20. *Ibid.*

21. *Ibid.,* 301-04.

22. A. P. Nasatir, *Missouri Historical Review,* Vol. 24, 427-33.

23. *WHC, op. cit.,* 296-98.

Chapter 4

1. A. P. Nasatir, "Invasion of Missouri, an Incident in the Anglo Spanish Rivalry for Indian Trade of Upper Louisiana," *MHR,* Vol. 24 (1929-1930), 430-31.

2. Laurence Kinnaird, "The Revolutionary Period, 1765-1781," *Spain in the Mississippi Valley, 1765-1794, AHAAR,* Vol. 2 (1945), 104.

3. *Ibid.,* xxii-xxiii.

4. *Ibid.,* 218.

5. A. P. Nasatir, "Anglo Spanish Frontier on the Upper Mississippi, 1786-1796," *IJHP,* Vol. 29, No. 2 (1931), 156.

6. *Ibid.,* 157.

7. Charles Gayerré, *History of Louisiana,* Vol. 3, 46.

8. Kinnaird, *op. cit.,* xvii.

9. "Report on Indian Tribes receiving presents at San Luis," November 15, 1777, Archivo General de Indies (Seville), Papéles de Cuba, legajo 2350, *WHC,* Vol. 18, 358-68.

10. *Ibid.*

11. Francisco Cruzat to Don Luis de Unzaga, November 21, 1776, in Kinnaird, *op. cit.,* 235.

12. Nasatir, "Anglo Spanish Frontier on the Upper Mississippi," 159.

13. A. P. Nasatir, "Anglo Spanish Frontier in the Illinois Country During the American Revolution, 1779-1783," *JIHS,* Vol. 21, No. 3 (1928-1929), 291-358.

14. Kinnaird, *op. cit.,* 298.

15. *Ibid.,* 310-11.

16. Nasatir, "Anglo Spanish Frontier in Illinois Country," 302-03.

17. Kinnaird, *op. cit.,* 320.

18. *Ibid.,* 308.

19. *American Archives,* series 4, 5, 1696.

20. *Ibid.,* series 5, 3, 514-18.

21. Paul C. Phillips and J. W. Smurr, *The Fur Trade,* Vol. 1, (Norman, University of Oklahoma Press, 1961), 640.

22. *WHC,* Vol. 11, 113.

23. *The G. R. Clark Papers,* IHC, Vol. 8, 124.

24. *Ibid.,* 626.

25. "Gautier's Journal," *WHC,* Vol. 11, 102-07.

26. T. Donaldson, *The George Catlin Indian Gallery* (1885), 145.

27. *The G. R. Clark Papers, op. cit.,* 71.

Chapter 5

1. *IHC,* Vol. 8, 390.

2. *WHC,* Vol. XI, 149.

3. Sinclair to Haldimand, June, 1780, *WHC,* Vol. XI, 155.

4. *WHC*, Vol. XI, 156.

5. Laurence Kinnaird, *Spain in the Mississippi Valley*, Vol. 2, 403.

6. *WHC*, Vol. XVIII, 414.

7. Kinnaird, *op. cit.*, Vol. 3, 84.

8. A. P. Nasatir, *JIHS*, Vol. 21, 352.

9. *Ibid.*, 355.

10. Kinnaird, *op. cit.*, 117-18.

11. *Ibid.*, 160-66.

12. *Ibid.*, 390.

13. *Ibid.*, 410-11.

14. *Ibid.*

15. Paul C. Phillips and J. W. Smurr, *The Fur Trade*, Vol. 2, 239.

16. Kinnaird, *op. cit.*, 369.

17. A. P. Nasatir, *Before Lewis and Clark*, Vol. 1, 163.

18. *Ibid.*, 184-95.

19. *Ibid.*, 197.

20. Hunter Miller, ed., *Treaties and Other International Acts of the United States of American, 1776-1818*, Vol. 2, 247.

21. A. P. Nasatir, "The Anglo-Spanish Frontier on the Upper Mississippi, 1786-1796," *IJHP*, Vol. 29, 214.

22. *Ibid.*, 231.

23. a . P. Nasatir, *Before Lewis and Clark*, Vol. 1, 317-18.

24. Cyrus Thomas, *Handbook of North American Indians*, Vol. 2, 372-91.

25. *Kinnaird*, op. cit., Vol. 3, 347, 354.

Chapter 6

1. Charles Gayerré, *History of Louisiana*, Vol. 3, 399, 456-57.

2. *MPP*, Vol. 1 (1907), 351.

3. This document is in the Indian Archives Department, Section X, Iowa Indians, OHSIA.

4. Taisont to de Lassus, August 18, 1799, in *Pierre Chouteau Collection*, MHS, St. Louis.

5. *Ibid.*, September 18, 1799.

6. *Ibid.*, October 3, 1799.

7. *Ibid.*, October 10, 1799.

8. H. H. Sibley, "Memoir of Jean B. Faribault," *MHSC*, Vol. 3, 168-77.

9. *WHC*, Vol. 9, 152-53.

10. F. Perrin du Lac, *Travels Through the Two Louisianas*, 56-57.

11. Alceé Fortier, *History of Louisiana*, Vol. 2, 317 ff.

12. *Ibid.*, Vol. 2, 319.

13. N. Biddle, *Journals of the Expedition of Captains Lewis and Clark*, Vol. 1 (1962), 4.

14. *Amos Stoddard Collection*, MHS, St. Louis.

15. Stoddard, *Sketches of Louisiana*, 366-67.

16. C. Royce Cessions, 289, 152, 50, 69, 151, 262, 153, 120, 244, 175, BAE, Vol. 18, Pt. 2.

17. R. G. Thwaites, (ed.), *Original Journals of the Lewis and Clark Expeditions in 1804-1806*, Vol. 1, 45.

18. *Ibid.*, Vol. 1, 51.

19. *Ibid.*, Vol. 1, 92.

20. *MPP*, Vol. 1, 352.

21. *Ibid.*

22. *Ibid.*, Vol. 1, 372.

23. Elliot Coues (ed.), *The Journals of Lt. Z. M. Pike*, Vols. 1, 2, 3; Donald Jackson, *The Journals of Z. M. Pike*, Vols. 1 and 2.

24. David Bushnell, *Villages of the Algonquian, Siouan, and Caddoan Tribes West of the Mississippi*, BAE, Bull. No. 77.

25. R. F. Kurz, *Journal of Rudolph F. Kurz*, J. N. B. Hewitt (ed.), BAE, Bull. No. 115, 43.

26. S. M. Irvin, *Diary*, KSHS.

27. "Abstract of the Nations of Indians on the Mississippi and Its Confluents from St. Louis, Louisiana, to Its Source Including Red Lake, and Lower Red River," in *The Journals of Lt. Z. M. Pike*, Vol. 1.

28. Donald Jackson (ed.), *The Journals of Zebulon Montgomery Pike with Letters and Related Documents*, Vol. 1, 208-209.

29. C. E. Carter, (comp., ed.), *TP*, Vol. 13, 228-30.

30. *Ibid.*, Vol. 13, 245-47.

31. J. A. Wilkinson and William H. Harrison to Secretary of War, October 19, 1805, in *ibid.*, 245.

32. Carter, *op. cit.*, 298-99.

33. *MPP*, Vol. 1, 386-87.

34. Office of the Secretary of War, Indian Affairs, Letters sent 1800-1824, *NA*, Letterbook 186, 145-47; original copy in French, Oklahoma Historical Society.

35. Carter, *op. cit.*, 488-89.

36. M. Lewis, "Observations and Reflections on Upper Louisiana" *Original Journals of the Lewis and Clark Expedition*, E. Coues (ed.), Vol. 7, 374-75.

37. J. Dubuque to Messrs. Rochebléve & Podlier & Co., June 3, 1807, *WHC*, Vol. 19, 318.

38. Frederick Bates, *The Life and Papers of Frederick Bates*, MHS, Vol. 1, 162-63.

39. *Ibid.*

40. *MPP*, Vol. 1, 434.

41. *TP*, Vol. 7, 531.

42. *Ibid.*, 540-41.

43. *Ibid.*, Vol. 14, 216-19.

44. Bates, *Life and Papers*, MHS, Vol. 2, 102.

45. *Ibid.*, Vol. 1, 83; *Missouri Gazeteer*, July 26 and August 2, 1808.

46. Governor Lewis to Secretary of War, *TP*, Vol. 14, 196.

47. *Ibid.*, 196-203.

48. Jefferson to Governor Lewis, August 21, 1808, *TP*, Vol. 14, 219.

49. *Ibid.*, 221.

50. H. H. Sibley, "Memoir of Faribault," *MHSC*, Vol. 3, 174.

51. John Mason to Secretary of War, November 12, 1808 (NA, WD, SWDF, M 256).

52. Bruce Mahan, *Old Fort Crawford*, 183.

53. Jacob Van der Zee, "George Hunt's Narrative," *IJHP*, Vol. 11, 518-19.

54. W. E. Washburn, *The Indian and the Whiteman, Government Relations*, 360. 1964.

55. *ASP, IA*, Vol. 1, 799.

56. Jacob Van der Zee, "Fur Trade Operations in the Eastern Iowa Country," *IJHP*, Vol. 12, 521-22.

57. Bates to Stark, in Bates, *Life and Papers*, Vol. 2, 83-85.

58. *TP*, Vol. 14, 293-312.

59. Thomas McKenney and James Hall, *Indian Tribes of North America*, Vol. 1, 285.

60. Alanson A. Skinner, *Ethnology of the Ioway Indians*, Bull., Public Museum of the City of Milwaukee, Vol. 5, No. 4, 252.

61. McKenney and Hall, *op. cit.*, 285.

62. *Ibid.*, 286.

63. Skinner, *op. cit.*, 202.

64. *Ibid.*, 203.

65. *Ibid.*, 205.

66. *Ibid.*, 203.

67. Louis Houck, *History of Missouri,* Vol. 3, 98.

68. Stoddard, *op. cit.,* 396-97.

69. N. Boilvin to Secretary of War William Eustice, February 2, 1811, *TP,* Vol. 14, 439.

70. *Ibid.*

71. Van der Zee, "George Hunt's Narrative," *IJHP* Vol. 11, 518-19.

72. *TP,* Vol. 14, 439.

73. John Johnson to Governor Howard, July 3, 1812, TP, 14:578-579.

74. Van der Zee, "Fur Trade Operations in the Eastern Iowa Country," *IJHP,* Vol. 12, 509.

75. *TP,* Vol. 14, 508.

76. *Ibid.,* 654.

77. *Ibid.,* 674-75.

78. *Ibid.,* 670.

79. Governor Clark to Secretary of War, September 12, 1813, *TP,* Vol. 14, 697-98.

80. *WHC,* Vol. 11, 139.

81. *Ibid.,* 270.

82. M. Lisa to William Clark, November 23, 1815, *William Clark Papers,* MHS, St. Louis.

83. Edwin James, *An Account of an Expedition from Pittsburg to the Rocky Mountains,* Vol. 1, 80-81.

84. M. Lisa to William Clark, July 1, 1817, *Missouri Gazette* (July 5, 1817).

85. Kappler, *Treaties,* Vol. 1, 122.

86. "Treaties with the Twenty-one Tribes," *ASP, IA,* Vol. 1, 9.

87. *TP,* Vol. 15, 191.

88. *Ibid.,* Vol. 17, 473.

89. *Ibid.,* 540.

90. Houck, *op. cit.,* 156-58.

91. *TP,* Vol. 15, 379.

92. *MPP,* Vol. 2, 45-46.

93. Sibley to William Clark, February 3, 1819, *TP,* Vol. 15, 515.

94. *Ibid.*

95. *Ibid.,* Vol. 15, 516.

96. Hiram M. Crittenden, *A History of the American Fur Trade of the Far West,* Vol. 1, 12-16.

97. *TP,* Vol. 15, 562-64.

98. Edwin James, in *Early Western Travels,* R. G. Thwaites (ed.), Vol. 15, 230.

99. Thomas C. Donaldson, *The George Catlin Indian Gallery,* 149; George Catlin, *Notes on Eight Years Travel and Residence in Europe,* Vol. 2, 18.

100. James, *op. cit.,* 236.

101. *Ibid.,* 265.

102. *Ibid.,* 266.

103. Alanson Skinner, "Societies of the Iowa, Kansa and Ponca Indians," *Journal of the American Museum of Natural History,* Vol. 11, Pt. 9, 685; J. O. Dorsey, in BAE, *Annual Report* No. 15 (1893-1894), 238-40.

104. J. O. Dorsey, "Social Organization of the Siouan Tribes," *JAFL,* Vol. 4, 336-38.

105. Henry Lewis Morgan, *Ancient Society,* 156.

106. Skinner, *Ethnology of the Ioway Indians,* 193-95.

107. Alanson Skinner, "Traditions of the Iowa Indians," *JAFL,* Vol. 38, No. 160.

108. Dorsey, "Social Organization of the Siouan Tribes," *JAFL,* Vol. 4, 338-39.

109. Skinner, *Ethnology of the Ioway Indians,* 199.

110. James, *Early Western Travels,* Vol. 14, 273.

111. David Meriwether, *My Life in the Mountains and on the Plains,* Robert A. Griffin (ed.), 44-47.

112. *Ibid.,* 45-46.

113. *Ibid.,* 47.

114. *Ibid.*

115. *Ibid.,* 54.

116. *Ibid.,* 58-60.

117. Henry Atkinson to Secretary of War Calhoun, January 2, 1820, LR, OIA, NA.

118. Jedidiah Morse, *Report to the Secretary of War of the United States on Indian Affairs,* 203.

119. Thomas Forsyth, "Memoirs of the Sac and Fox," in *Indian Tribes of the Upper Mississippi Valley and Regions of the Great Lakes,* Vol. 2, 205. Emma H. Blair (ed.)

120. F. E. Stevens, *The Black Hawk War,* Chap. 10.

121. A. R. Fulton, *Red Men of Iowa,* 120.

122. A. H. Abel, "History of Indian Consolidation West of the Mississippi," *AHAAR,* Vol. 1, 288.

123. Morse, *Report on Indian Affairs,* 208.

124. *TP,* Vol. 15, 689.

125. *Ibid.,* Vol. 19, 208.

126. Meriwether, *My Life in the Mountains,* 103-04.

127. *Ibid.,* 104-13.

128. Thomas Forsyth to William Clark, August 27, 1821, *William Clark Papers,* MHS, St. Louis.

129. Thomas Forsyth to Secretary of War Calhoun, September 26, 1821, (RG 75 BIA SW LS, NA).

130. William Clark to Secretary of War Calhoun, January 8, 1822 (RG 75, SW, LR, NA).

131. Secretary of War Calhoun to Thomas Forsyth, July 26, 1822 (RG 75, LS, Office of Secretary of War, NA).

132. Duff Green to Secretary of War Calhoun, September 19, 1823 (RG 75, LR, Selected Letters, Vols. 16-18, Office of Secretary of War, NA).

133. Abstract of Licenses Granted to Trade with the Indian Tribes West of the Mississippi in the Superintendence of William Clark, October 3, 1822 (RG 75, Records of the Office of Secretary of War, LR, NA).

134. Duff Green to Secretary of War Calhoun, December 4, 1822, *Indian Papers,* Archives, MHS, St. Louis.

135. WHC, Vol. 20, 267.

136. *Council Proceedings,* William Clark to Secretary of War Calhoun, December 8, 1823 (RG 75, LR, Office of Secretary of War, OIA, NA).

Chapter 7

1. Duff Green to J. C. Calhoun, December 4, 1822, Indian Papers, MHS, St. Louis.

2. Chapman, Berlin, B., *The Otoes and the Missourias,* 1.

3. Duff Green to J. C. Calhoun, January 5, 1824, Records of the War Dept., Selected Letters, Vols. 16-18 (LR, NA).

4. Russell Farnham to Samuel Abbott, January, 1824, *Ayer Collection,* Newberry Library.

5. C. Kappler, *Treaties,* Vol. 2, 208, 215.

6. Record of BIA, (RG 75), Segregated Treaty File, Treaty of August 4, 1824, with Sac and Fox and Ioway, Remarks in Council, NA.

7. *Ibid.*

8. G. J. Garraghan, *The Jesuits of the Middle United States,* Vol. 1, 147-69.

9. Thomas McKenney and James Hall, "Moanahonga, or The Great Walker," *The Indian Tribes of North America,* Vol. 1.

10. Garraghan, *op. cit.,* 166-68.

11. William Clark to Ninian Edwards, January 25, 1825, St. Louis Superintendency (RG 75, M 234, R 747, NA).

12. Minutes of Council, Council House, St. Louis, January 6, 1825 (RG 75, M 234, R 747, NA).

13. *Journal of Proceedings* that took place under a Commission to Gen. William Clark and Gov. L. Cass (RG 75, Segregated Treaty File, 1825, BIA, NA).

14. Emma H. Blair, *Indian Tribes of the Upper Mississippi Valley and Great Lakes Regions,* Vol. 1, 356.

15. Journal of Proceedings, Commission to Gen. William Clark and Gov. L. Cass, August 5, 1825 (RG 75, Segregated Treaty Files, BIA, NA).

16. *Ibid.,* August 6, 1825.

17. *Ibid.,* August 9, 1825.

18. *Ibid.*

19. William Clark to Lewis Cass, Documents filed with Treaty of August 19, 1825, Segregated Treaty File (RG 75, NA).

20. William Clark to Secretary of War, March 1, 1826, St. Louis Superintendency (RG 75, M 234, R 747, NA).

21. William Clark to Agency Farmer, April, 1827, St. Louis Superintendency (RG 75, M 234, R 748, NA).

22. William Clark to Secretary of War, August 20 and October 27, 1827, St. Louis Superintendency (RG 75, M 234, R 748, NA).

23. William Clark to Secretary of War, November 25, 1826 (RG 75, M 234, R 747, NA).

24. John Dougherty to William Clark, November 1828, St. Louis Superintendency (RG 75, M 234, R 748, NA).

25. Kappler, *Treaties,* Vol. 1, 177-78.

26. Thomas Forsyth to William Clark, October 1, 1829, Forsyth Papers, Draper Collection, *WHC,* Vol. 6, 190.

27. Thomas G. Anderson to Colonel McKay, July 20, 1828, Drummond Island, *Michigan Pioneer History Collections,* Vol. 23, 149-50. William T. Hagan, *The Sac and Fox Indians,* 108, 112.

28. *MPP,* Vol. 2, 438.

29. Thomas L. McKenney, *Memoirs, Official and Personal with Sketches of Travel,* Vol. 1, 257-59.

30. *Ibid.*

31. McKenney, *Memoirs,* Vol. 1, 262.

32. Hughes to Clark, July 31, 1829; Clark to Secretary of War, St. Louis Superintendency (RG 75, M 234, R 749, NA).

33. Colonel Henry Atkinson to General Alexander Macomb, July 31, 1829, Department of the West, LS Letterbook 101, USAC; August 2, 1829, *ibid.*

34. Hughes to Clark, October 15, 1829, St. Louis Superintendency (RG 75, M 234, R 749, NA).

35. Clark to Secretary of War, December 8, 1829, St. Louis Superintendency (RG 75, M 234, R 749, NA).

36. Clark to Secretary of War, November 14, 1829, St. Louis Superintendency (RG 75, M 234, R 749, NA).

37. James Birch to Clark, November 13, 1829, St. Louis Superintendency (RG 75, M 234, R 749, NA).

38. Speech by Pumpkin (Pompakin), Records of BIA, LR, Ioway Agency, August 3, 1835, NA.

39. McKenney and Hall, *Indian Tribes of North America,* Vol. 1, 318-25.

40. Clark to Secretary of War, March 22, 1830, St. Louis Superintendency (RG 75, M 234, R 749, NA).

41. Clark to Secretary of War, February 9, 1830 (LR, OIA, ALS, NA).

42. Treaty of July 15, 1830, Extract from Minutes of Council, July 7, 1830, Segregated Treaty File, NA.

43. *Ibid.,* July 9, 1830.

44. Royce Cessions 151, 152, 153, in C. C. Royce, *Indian Land Cessions in the United States,* BAE, Vol. 18, Pt. 2.

45. Kappler, *Treaties*, Vol. 2; 1830 Treaty with Sauk and Foxes, etc. Article IV, 7 *Statutes*, 328.

46. 4 *Statutes*, 411.

47. Kappler, *Treaties*, Vol. 2, 306.

48. William Clark to E. Herring, May 21, 1834, St. Louis Superintendency (RG 75, M 234, R 750, NA).

49. E. Herring to William Clark, June 2, 1834, (RG 75, OIA, Letterbook 13, NA).

50. A. Hughes to William Clark, July 15, 1834, Ioway Sub Agency (RG 75, M 234, R 362, NA).

51. Memorial, July, 1835, St. Louis Superintendency (RG 75, M 234, R 750, NA).

52. 7 *Statutes*, 511.

53. Andrew Hughes to Henry Dodge, October 3, 1836, Ioway Sub Agency (RG 75, M 234, R 362, NA).

54. Andrew Hughes to William Clark, November 12, 1831, Iowa Sub Agency (RG 75, M 234, R 362, NA).

55. Records of BIA (RG 75) Letters Received (1837), GNA, Document A, NA.

56. William Clark to Commissioner, January 5, 1837, Ioway Agency (RG 75, M 234, R 362, and GNA, RG 75, M 234, M 307-0004, n.d., 1837, NA).

57. C. S. Stambaugh to Secretary of War, March 14, 1837, Sac and Fox File, NA.

58. Col. S. W. Kearny to Col. H. Atkinson, May 19 and May 26, 1837, Wisconsin Superintendency (RG 75, M 234, R 948, NA).

59. Journal of Proceedings of Council (RG 75, LR, B-402, Misc. File, 1837, NA).

60. 7 *Statutes*, 543.

61. Joshua Pilcher to C. A. Harris, November 23, 1837, Iowa Treaty File (C 471, NA).

62. William Clark to C. A. Harris, March 22, 1838, GNA (RG 75, M 234, R 307, NA).

63. J. Dougherty to William Clark, May 30, 1838, GNA (RG 75, M 234, R 307, NA).

64. *Ibid.*

65. John Dougherty to William Clark, April, 1838, Bellevue, GNA (RG 75, M 234, R 307-0137, NA).

66. A. Hughes to William Clark, Annual Report, 1835 (RG 75, M 234, R 362, NA).

67. A. Hughes to William Clark, January 23, 1835. GNA (RG 75, M 234, R 307, NA).

68. A. Hughes to William Clark, August 26, 1837 GNA (RG 75, M 234, R 307, NA).

69. McKenney and Hall, *Indian Tribes of North America*, Vols. 1 and 2 (Edinburg, 1933), and various earlier editions.

70. H. R. Schoolcraft, *HCPIT*, Vol. 3, 260.

71. Thwaites, *Early Western Travels*, Vol. 24, 313.

72. *Ibid.*, Vol. 22, 257-63.

73. *Ibid.*, 271-72.

74. George Catlin, *Portfolio of American Indian Painting*, Introduction.

75. T. Donaldson, *George Catlin Indian Gallery*, 151.

76. *Ibid.*

77. George Catlin, *Notes on Eight Years Travels and Residence in Europe with His North American Indian Collection*, Vol. 2, 31-32; T. Donaldson, *Catlin Indian Gallery*, 151.

78. Catlin. *Eight Years Travels*, 23, 227-28.

79. *Ibid.*, 23.

80. William N. Fenton and G. P. Kurath, *The Iroquois Eagle Dance, an Offshoot of the Calumet Dance*, BAE, Bull. 156, 277-78.

81. Donaldson, *op. cit.*, 149.

82. Catlin, *Eight Years Travels*, 227-28.

83. Donaldson, *op. cit.*, 151.

84. Catlin, *Eight Years Travels*, 152.

85. *Ibid.*, 201.

86. *Ibid.*, 171-72.

87. McKenney and Hall, *Indian Tribes of North America*, Vol. 2, 301.

88. *Ibid.*, 168.

89. *Ibid.*, Vol. 1, 291.

90. *Ibid.*, Vol. 2, 170.

91. Samuel Irvin, *Diary*, Manuscript Division, KSHS.

92. Pryor Plank, "The Ioway, Sac and Fox Indian Mission, and Its Missionaries, Rev. Samuel M. Irvin and Wife," *Transactions*, KSHS, Vol. 10, 312.

93. *Ibid.*

94. Schoolcraft, *HCPIT*, Vol. 3, 277, 356 ff.

95. *Ibid.*, 262.

96. *Ibid.*, 263.

97. *Ibid.*, 267,273.

98. J. O. Dorsey, *A Study of Siouan Cults*, BAE, Vol. 11, 423.

99. *Ibid.*, 426.

100. *Ibid.*, 426-28.

101. *Ibid.*, 429.

102. Pierre Chouteau to Andrew Hughes, December 25, 1830 (RG 75, M 234, R 362, NA).

103. Colin McLeod to William Clark, December 29, 1830 (RG 75, M 234, R 362, NA).

104. A. Hughes to William Clark, January 18, 1831, Ioway Agency (RG 75, M 234, R 362, NA).

105. *Ibid.*

106. *Ibid.*, February 18, 1831.

107. Hughes to Clark, February 15, 1831, Ioway Agency (RG 75, M 234, R 362, NA).

108. *Ibid.*, February 20, 1831.

109. John Ruland to William Clark, June 27, 1831, Ft. Leavenworth (RG 75, M 234, R 362, NA).

110. A. Hughes to William Clark, December 27, 1831 (RG 75, M 234, R 362, NA).

111. John Dougherty to Lewis Cass, November 19, 1831, Upper Missouri (RG 75, M 234, R 362, NA).

112. F. P. Prucha, "Laws of 1834," *American Indian Policy in the Formative Years, The Indian Trade and Intercourse Acts 1790-1834*, Chap. 10.

113. Capt. E. A. Hitchcock to C. A. Harris, May 1, 1838, GNA (RG 75, M 234, R 314, NA).

114. William Clark to Commissioner, October 22, 1831 (RG 75, M 234, R 362, NA).

115. Hughes to E. Herring, March 18, 1834, Ioway Agency (RG 75, M 234, R 362, NA).

116. Ioway and Omaha Treaty of 1835, October 20, 1835, Upper Missouri (RG 75, M 234, R 362, NA).

117. *Annual Report of the Commissioner of Indian Affairs* (1838), 4.

118. Father Pierre-Jean de Smet, *Life, Letters and Travels of Father Pierre-Jean De Smet, S. J., 1801-1873*, Vol. 1, 171.

119. William Clark to E. Herring, December 5, 1831, St. Louis Superintendency (RG 75, M 234, R 749, NA).

120. A. Hughes to E. Herring, January 24, 1834, Ioway Agency (RG 75, M 234, R 362, NA).

121. *Ibid.*

122. C. B. Creekmore to A. Hughes, July 29, 1832, Ioway Agency (RG 75, M 234, R 362, NA).

123. A. Hughes to Henry Dodge, May 21, 1837 GNA (RG 75, M 234, R 314, NA).

124. A. Hughes to William Clark, June 29, 1837, GNA (RG 75, M 234, R 314, NA).

125. Father De Smet, *op. cit.*, 150.

126. Major Bean to J. Pilcher, December 1, 1839, GNA (RG 75, M 234, R 307, NA).

1. McKenney and Hall, *History of the Indian Tribes of North America*, Vol. 1, 281.

2. Carolyn T. Foreman, "The Choctaw Academy," in *Chronicles of Oklahoma*, Vol. 9, 382-411; Vol. 10, 77-114.

3. Original in OHSIA, Section X, Iowa Indians.

4. J. Dougherty to William Clark, May 31, 1831, GNA (RG 75, M 234, R 307, NA).

5. *The Reverend E. McKinney Collection*, Vault 17-7 in Archives, KSHS.

6. Census of the Ioway Indians, September 5, 1842, GNA (RG 75, M 234, R 307, NA).

7. *The Journal of Rudolph Frederick Kurz*, edited by J. N. B. Hewitt, BAE Bull. 115.

8. *Ibid.*, 360.

9. *Ibid.*, 50-52.

10. *Ibid.*, 51-52.

11. Skinner, *Ethnology of the Ioway Indians*, Public Museum of the City of Milwaukee Bull., Vol. 5, No. 4, 250.

12. Skinner, *Ethnology of the Ioway Indians*, 251.

13. Samuel Irvin, *Diary*, KSHS.

14. Skinner, *Ethnology of the Ioway Indians*, 252.

15. Samuel Irvin, *Annual Report of the Commissioner of Indian Affairs*, 373.

16. Minutes of Council, September 21, 1841, GNA (RG 75, M 234, R 307, NA).

17. Minutes of Council, August 15, 1843, GNA (RG 75, M 234, R 307, NA).

18. Minutes of Council, October, 1843, GNA (RG 75, M 234, R 307, NA).

19. Irvin, *Annual Report*, 605.

20. Rev. William Hamilton and Rev. Samuel M. Irvin, *An Ioway Grammar*, Copy in Gilcrease Library, Tulsa.

21. Samuel Irvin, *Diary*, KSHS.

22. Skinner, *Ethnology of the Ioway Indians*, 206-207.

23. Alanson Skinner, *Anthropological Papers of the American Museum of Natural History*, Vol. 11, 684.

24. Irvin, *Diary*.

25. *Ibid.*

26. Skinner, *Ethnology of the Ioway Indians*, 264-71.

27. Irvin, *Diary*.

28. Skinner, *Ethnology of the Ioway Indians*, 223.

29. "Extracts from the unpublished Journals of Rev. William Hamilton, a missionary of the Presbyterian Board for twenty years among the Youas and Sac and Kansas and the Omahas of Nebraska," Henry Lewis Morgan Collection, University of Rochester Library, Box 25, Folder 94.

30. *Ibid.*

31. Irvin, *Diary*.

32. *Ibid.*

33. Schoolcraft, *HCPIT*, Vol. 1, 507.

34. Kurz, *Journal*, BAE Bull. 115, 45.

35. Skinner, *Ethnology of the Ioway Indians*, 201.

36. J. O. Dorsey, *JAFL*, Vol. 4, 340.

37. Henry Thoreau, from "Journal," in *People, Principles, and Politics*, Milton Meltzer (ed.), 60.

38. Hannah Worchester Hitchcock, "Cycle of Indian Territory — '40s," *S. A. Worchester Family*, Foreman Collection, OHSIA.

39. Angie Debo, *The Road to Disappearance*, 135-36.

40. D. C. Peattie (ed.), *Audubon's America, The Narratives and Experiences of John James Audubon*, 276.

41. *Ibid.*, 276-82.

42. George Catlin, *Notes on Eight Years Travel and Residence in Europe*, 2.

43. Catlin, *Eight Years Travel,* 40-42.

44. *Ibid.,* 152.

45. *Ibid.,* 211-12.

46. *Ibid.,* 222.

47. Supt. T. H. Harvey to Crawford, June 6, 1845, GNA (RG 75, M 234, R 307, NA).

48. Minutes of Council, April, 1846, GNA (RG 75, M 234, R 307, NA).

49. Council with Ioway, April 10, 1846, GNA (RG 75, M 234, R 307, NA).

50. *Ibid.*

51. A. Vaughn to Harvey, June 1, 1848, GNA (RG 75, M 234, R 308, NA).

52. Kurz, *Journal,* BAE Bull. 115, 31.

53. Richardson to Harvey, January 29, 1850, GNA (RG 75, M 234, R 308, NA).

54. *Annual Report of Commissioner of Indian Affairs* (1851), 361; Supt. D. C. Mitchell to Comm. L. Lea, September 11, 1852, GNA (RG 75, M 234, R 308, NA).

55. *Annual Report of Commissioner of Indian Affairs,* 1851, 363.

56. Richardson to Mitchell, January 10, 1852, Central Superintendency, LR, OIA, NA.

57. John Foreman to Commissioner of Indian Affairs, November 25, 1849, St. Louis, Roster of Superintendents and Agents, 1849-1878, NA.

58. D. Vanderslice to Commissioner, June 30, 1853, GNA (RG 75, M 234, R 308, NA).

59. A. M. Mitchell to Charles Mix, September 17, 1853, GNA (RG 75, M 234, R 308, NS).

60. Vanderslice to Manypenny, February 10, 1854, GNA (RG 75, M 234, R 308, NA).

61. Treaty with Iowas, May 17, 1854, 10 *Statutes,* 1069; Kappler, *Treaties,* Vol. 2, 466-69.

62. Vanderslice to A. Cummings, September 6, 1854, GNA (RG 75, M 234, R 308, NA).

63. *Annual Report of Commissioner of Indian Affairs* (1854), 307.

64. Vanderslice to Cummings, November 8, 1855, GNA (RG 75, M 234, R 308, NA).

65. Manypenny to Sharp, May 14, 1856 (Letter Book 54, OIA, NA), 224-27.

66. Berlin B. Chapman, "The Nemaha Half-breed Tract," *The Otoes and the Missourias,* Chap. 5.

67. Vanderslice to Commissioner, July 18, 1856, GNA (RG 75, M 234, R 308, NA).

68. *Annual Report of the Commissioner of Indian Affairs* (1859), GNA.

69. Vanderslice to Commissioner, June 25, 1857, GNA (RG 75, M 234, R 309, NA).

70. Leslie White (ed.), *Lewis Henry Morgan, The Indian Journals 1859-1862,* 139.

71. Noble Prentis, *History of Kansas,* 96.

72. J. Burbank to Commissioner, July 1, 1861, GNA (RG 75, M 234, R 310, NA).

73. Superintendent to Commissioner, March 7, 1862, Central Superintendency (RG 75, M 234, R 57, NA).

74. Canby to Burbank, December 14, 1863, GNA (RG 75, M 234, R 311, NA).

75. Burbank to Commissioner, January 12, 1866, GNA (RG 75, M 234, R 312, NA).

76. Doctor's Report, September 10, 1866, GNA (RG 75, M 234, R 312, NA).

77. Vanderslice to Superintendent Robinson, September 26, 1860, GNA (RG 75, M 234, R 310, NA).

78. White, *op. cit.,* 68.

79. *Ibid.,* 70.

80. *Ibid.,* 138.

81. *Ibid.*

82. *Annual Report of the Commissioner of Indian Affairs* (1857) (1862); "A Sketch of the Development of the Bureau of Indian Affairs and of Indian Policy," BIA, 61 (1969).

83. *Ibid.*

84. *MPP.* Vol. 6, 132.

85. *Ibid.,* 186.

86. 12 *Statutes,* 1171.

87. Kappler, *Treaties*, Vol. 2, 811.

88. Minutes of Council, October 22, 1861, GNA (RG 75, M 234, R 312, NA).

89. Secretary of Interior to Commissioner, July 31, 1863, Central Superintendency (RG 75, M 234, R 58, NA).

90. Burbank to Commissioner, January 9, 1864, GNA (RG 75, M 234, R 312, NA).

91. Minutes of Council, October 23, 1862, GNA (RG 75, M 234, R 310, NA).

92. Vanderslice to Burbank, October 8, 1862, GNA (RG 75, M 234, R 312, NA).

93. W. M. Albin to Commissioner, Report of October, 1864, Central Superintendency (RG 75, M 234, R 58, NA).

94. Albin to Commissioner, November 17, 1864, Central Superintendency (RG 75, M 234, R 58, NA).

95. White, *op. cit.*, 138-39.

96. *Ibid.*, 140.

97. Superintendent to Commissioner, August 22, 1865, GNA (RG 75, M 234, R 312, NA).

98. Burbank to Commissioner, September 9, 1865, GNA (RG 75, M 234, R 312, NA).

99. Burbank to Superintendent, December 18, 1865, GNA (RG 75, M 234, R 312, NA).

Chapter 9

1. *MPP*, Vol. 7, 8.

2. John Pope to Secretary of War, February 6, 1864, Northern Superintendency (RG 75, M 234, R 599, NA).

3. President Grant in *Daily Morning Chronicle*, September 9, 1869; reprinted in *MPP*, Vol. 7, 23.

4. *Annual Report of the Commissioner of Indian Affairs*, 1871.

5. T. Lightfoot to Superintendent, October 18, 1869, GNA (RG 75, M 234, R 313, NA).

6. B. Hallowell to Ely Parker, January 27, 1870, GNA (RG 75, M 234, R 313, NA).

7. *MPP*, Vol. 7, 47.

8. *Friends Committee Report* to Commissioner, E. P. Smith, February 14, 1875, GNA (RG 75, M 234, R 314, NA).

9. D. H. Holt to John Toffe, February 14, 1871, GNA (RG 75, M 234, R 313, NA).

10. S. W. Janney to Commissioner, March 1, 1871, GNA (RG 75, M 234, R 313, NA).

11. Secretary of the Interior, H. C. Clum, to Commissioner, July 14, 1871, GNA (RG 75, M 234, R 313, NA).

12. Ioway Chiefs and Head Men to the Commissioner, December 12, 1871, GNA (RG 75, M 234, R 313, NA).

13. S. W. Janney to Ely Parker, March 3, 1871, GNA (RG 75, M 234, R 313, NA).

14. E. S. Dundy to Commissioner, March 16, 1872, GNA (RG 75, M 234, R 313, NA).

15. Agent M. Kent to Commissioner, October 5, 1875, GNA (RG 75, M 234, R 314, NA).

16. Police Record Book, No. 13, Ao 13-Ao 15, Pottawatomie Agency, Federal Records Center, NA, Kansas City.

17. *Annual Report of Commissioner of Indian Affairs* (1877).

18. Agent Kent to Commissioner, September 10, 1878, Great Nemaha, Pottawatomie Agency, Federal Records Center, NA, Kansas City.

19. Miscellaneous File, A-85, n.d., Pottawatomie Agency, Federal Records Center, NA, Kansas City.

20. *MPP*, Vol. 7, 152.

21. Agent to Commissioner, December 27, 1875, GNA (RG 75, M 234, R 314, NA).

22. Opinion of U.S. District Attorney, in Nebraska, April 19, 1876, GNA (RG 75, M 234, R 314, NA).

23. Sac and Fox Agency, LS, Vol. 1, OHSIA, 244.
24. Commissioner to M. Kent, September 24, 1878, Great Nemaha Records, Pottawatomie Agency, OIA, Federal Records Center, NA, Kansas City.
25. *Ibid.*, October 4, 1878.
26. Agent to Commissioner, June 19, 1879, Sac and Fox, LS, Vol. 1, 60-62, OHSIA.
27. "Chiefs of the Ioway," Miscellaneous Records File, Box A-85, n.d., Pottawatomie Agency, Federal Records Center, NA, Kansas City. An abbreviated form of the above descriptions appeared in W. H. Jackson, *A Descriptive Catalogue of North American Indians*, 46-47.
28. *MPP,* Vol. 7, 475.
29. Executive Committee of the Society of Friends to the Commissioner, April 11, 1879, Central Superintendency (RG 75, M 234, R 70, NA).
30. Lawrie Tatum, *Our Red Brothers, and the Peace Policy of President U. S. Grant*, 285.

Chapter 10

1. John Shorb to Comm. H. E. Trowbridge, August 31, 1880, Sac and Fox Agency, LS, Vol. 8, OHSIA.
2. Acting Comm. E. M. Marble to J. S. Shorb, January 18, 1881, Sac and Fox Agency, LR, Federal Relations, OHSIA.
3. Commissioner to Agent, May 9, 1882, Sac and Fox Per Capita File, LR, OHSIA.
4. Carter to Price, June 30, 1882, Sac and Fox Agency, LS, Vol. 8, OHSIA, 476.
5. Carter to Price, July 18, 1883, *ibid.*, 356.
6. I. A. Taylor to Commissioner, June 13, 1884, Sac and Fox Agency, LS, Vol. 10, OHSIA, 153.
7. 23 *Statutes*, 351.
8. 51 Cong., 1 sess., *Sen. Exec. Docs.*, 171, 14.
9. *Annual Report of Commissioner of Indian Affairs* (1885), Lxv.
10. Commissioner to Agent Taylor, October 22, 1884, Sac and Fox Agency, LR, Tonkawa Indians File, OHSIA.
11. Taylor to Comm. Price, April 10, 1885, Sac and Fox Agency, LS, No. 466, Vol. 10, OHSIA.
12. Lawrie Tatum to Commissioner, April 18, 1885, Sac and Fox Agency, LS, Tonkawa Indians File, OHSIA.
13. "Indian Legislation," *Annual Report of Commissioner of Indian Affairs*, 49 Cong., 2 sess. (1887), 273.
14. *Ibid.*, 274.
15. 51 Cong., 1 sess., *Sen. Exec. Docs.*, 171, 14-16.
16. *Report of the Commissioner of Indian Affairs*, Pottawatomie and Great Nemaha Agents, September 5, 1887, 122.
17. Records of the Milwaukee Public Museum, collections dated 1922 and 1923.
18. Commissioner to Agent, September 29, 1884, Sac and Fox Agency, LR, Liquor Traffic, Peyote/Mescal Use and Gambling File, OHSIA.
19. *Annual Report of Commissioner of Indian Affairs*, 1888, Sac and Fox Agency.
20. Grant Foreman, *IPHC*, Vol. 93, 505, OHSIA.
21. *Ibid.*, Vol. 85, 427.
22. *Perkins Journal*, July 9, 1936, Newspaper Library, OHS.
23. Foreman, *op. cit.*, Vol. 83, 188.
24. *Ibid.*, Vol. 77, 177.
25. *Ibid.*, Vol. 42, 258.
26. *Ibid.*, Vol. 93, 505.
27. *Ibid.*, Vol. 85, 60.
28. *Ibid.*, Vol. 31, 414.
29. *The Edmund Sun-Democrat*, October 29, 1897, Newspaper Library, OHS.
30. Ioway Annuity Roll, 1883; Sac and Fox Agency, Census File, OHSIA.

31. Agent to Commissioner, December 21, 1882, Sac and Fox Agency, LS, Vol. 9, OHSIA, 183.

32. Agent John Shorb to Comm. H. E. Trowbridge, February 15, 1881, Sac and Fox Agency, LS, Vol. 9, OHSIA, 53.

33. Chief Hotchisee to Commissioner J. D. C. Atkins, December 6, 1886, Sac and Fox Agency, Ioway Indian, Traders File, OHSIA.

34. Commissioner to Agent Shorb, September 10, 1879, Sac and Fox Agency, LR, Intruders File, OHSIA.

35. Proclamation, February 12, 1880, *MPP*, Vol. 7, 598.

36. Commissioner to Agent M. B. Kent, September 27, 1882, GNA, Pottawatomie Agency, Book 4, Federal Records Center, NA, Kansas City.

37. Commissioner to Agent I. A. Taylor, August 11, 1884, Sac and Fox Agency, Trader Files, OHSIA.

38. Sac and Fox Agency, Council File, Ioway Indians, January 1, 1884, OHSIA.

39. *Ibid.,* June, 1885.

40. Commissioner to Agent, July 17, 1885 Sac and Fox Agency, Grazing Leases, OHSIA.

41. Commissioner Thomas J. Morgan to Agent S. L. Patrick, May 18, 1890, Sac and Fox Agency, LR, Vol. 15, OHSIA, 259.

Chapter 11

1. Jerome Commission to Ioway Tribe, Council Proceedings, May 8, 1890, Indian Office Document No. 4738, NA. Special microfilm order, Oklahoma Historical Society Research Library, Oklahoma City.

2. Act of February 13, 1891, 26 Stat. L 749. 51st Cong., 1 sess., Exec. Doc. 171, 2.

3. *Annual Report to the Commissioner, 1892*, 271; Agent's Report in Kansas: March 3, 1885, 23 Stat. 351; January 26, 1887, 24 Stat. 367; Assistant Commissioner A. C. Tonner, to A. C. Sharp, February 5, 1898, Pawnee Agency, *Federal Relations,* OHSIA; Charles Kappler to Commissioner of Indian Affairs, September 26, 1916, *ibid.,* (photostat copy).

4. Martha Royce Siegel, 1965, Field Notes, *Ioway.*

5. Grant Foreman (ed.), *Indian and Pioneer History,* Vol. 76, OHSIA, 498-99.

6. *Annual Report of Commissioner of Indian Affairs,* (1892), 405.

7. *Daily Oklahoma State Capitol,* November 15 and 17, 1894, Newspaper Library, OHS.

8. Memorial to the Commissioner of Indian Affairs and the Senate and House of Representatives of the United States, January 21, 1895. Copy in Gilcrease Library, Tulsa, Okla.

9. *Guthrie Times Record,* January 2, 1896, Newspaper Library, OHS.

10. *Indian Journal,* March 8, 1895.

11. Sac and Fox Agency, Agents Reports, August 31, 1898, OHSIA; Lee Patrick, *Annual Report of Commissioner of Indian Affairs (1893),* 263.

12. *33rd Annual Report of the Board of Indian Commissioners,* January 31, 1902, 781.

13. *Daily Oklahoman,* December 1, 1897, Newspaper Library, OHS.

14. Comm. R. V. Belt to Agent, November 22, 1890, Sac and Fox-Indian Dances, Ioway Indians, OHSIA.

15. Siegel, *op. cit.*

16. Sac and Fox Agency, Medical Reports, Physicians File, 1890-1899, OHSIA.

17. J. B. Shoenfelt to Lee Patrick, December 5, 1899, Sac and Fox Agency, Foreign Relations File, OHSIA.

18. Siegel, *op. cit.*

19. *El Reno News,* September 10, 1897, Newspaper Library, OHS.

20. E. L. Thomas to J. S. Tanksley, agency farmer, January 21, 1896, Sac and Fox-Shawnee Agency, LS, Vol. 23, OHSIA, 245.

21. D. M. Browning to E. L. Thomas, January 18, 1896, Sac and Fox Agency, Agents File, OHSIA.

22. *Annual Report of Commissioner of Indian Affairs* (1899), 36-37.

23. Traders Accounts, n.d., Shawnee Agency, OHSIA.

24. *Leases File,* 1897, Sac and Fox Agency, OHSIA.

25. Agents' Report, *Annual Report of the Secretary of the Interior* (1896), 165.

26. *Annual Report of the Commissioner of Indian Affairs,* 1899, 205.

27. Siegel, *op. cit.*

Bibliography

Manuscript Collections

Archives Nationales, Paris
    Archives de la Marine, Claude Delisle, *Memoires de Mr Le Sueur* (2JJ56-9:52, 54, 55, 82, 94). Copy in MS Div., Library of Congress.
Kansas State Historical Society. Archives and Manuscripts Division
    The Reverend E. McKinney Papers
    The Dairy of Reverend Samuel M. Irvin
Missouri Historical Society. St. Louis
    The Amos Stoddard Collection
    The Pierre Chouteau Papers
    The William Clark Papers
    Indian Papers
National Anthropology Archives (NAA). Smithsonian Institution, Washington
    Dorsey, J. Owen (NAA 4800)
        (293) *Tchiwere (and Winnebago) Folklore, Including Iowa Cults.* From the letters of Rev. William Hamilton. n.d.
        (294) *Origins of the Iowas, Otos and Missouri.* n.d.
        (296) Extracts from MSS. by William Hamilton concerning the Iowa and Oto. n.d.
        (297) Extracts from a series of letters concerning the Iowas and other Siouans, published approximately 1848 in a church newsletter by William Hamilton.
        (300) Notes on Iowa and Missouri social organization and marriage laws. n.d.
        (304) *Chiwere Texts,* Includes one Iowa fable. n.d.
        (305) *Chiwere Texts,* Legends. n.d.
        (306) Notes on verbs of saying in Chiwere. n.d.
        (308) Lists of Iowa personal names furnished by William Hamilton and Agent M. B. Kent, ca. 1880.
        (309) Iowa linguistics. *Iowa Grammar,* 73-88, plus 2 unnumbered pages, conjugations of Iowa verbs, 22 pp. Miscellaneous notes, 6 pp.
    Hamilton, William (NAA 1214-c, Iowa)
        Notes on Iowa gentes, names of months, and miscellaneous notes. n.d.
    Kent, M. B. (NAA 920, Iowa, 1881)
        List of 138 Iowa personal names with English translations. Notes by J. O. Dorsey in margins. English translations by William Hamilton.
    Gerard, W. R. (NAA 2842-c, Iowa)

Newberry Library, Ayer Collection. Chicago.
Oklahoma Historical Society, Indian Archives Division. Oklahoma City.
Section X, Iowa Indians; Grant Foreman (ed.) *Indian and Pioneer History Collection*, 112 Vols.; *Foreman Transcripts*, London Public Record Office, Colonial Affairs, 5, Vol. 67.; *The S. A. Worcester Family*, Grant Foreman Collection.
University of Rochester Library, New York
Henry Lewis Morgan Papers. "Extracts from the unpublished Journals of Rev. William Hamilton, a missionary of the Presbyterian Board for twenty years among the Youas and Sac and Kansas and the Omahas of Nebraska," Box 23, folder 94.

Printed Collections of Documents, Letters and Papers

Illinois Historical Collections. Illinois State Historical Library. Springfield.
Wisconsin Historical Collections. Wisconsin State Historical Society. Madison.

Federal and State Documents

A compilation of Messages and Papers of the Presidents, 1789-1902. Edited by James D. Richardson. 10 Vols. Washington, 1898.
American Archives. A Documentary History of the United States of America. Comp. by Peter Force. Ser. 4, Vols. 4, 5, 6; Ser. 5, Vols. 1, 2, 3. Washington, 1833, 1843, 1851.
American State Papers. Documents. Legislative and Executive of the United States, Vols. 1, 2, 7, 8, Indian Affairs; Vol. 5, Military Affairs. Washington, 1789, 1806, 1810.
Annual Reports of the Commissioner of Indian Affairs. Washington.
Bureau of Indian Affairs. *A Sketch of the Development of the Bureau of Indian Affairs, and of Indian Policy.* Washington, 1969.
Congress of the United States. Documents and Records:
    22 Cong., 1 sess., *Sen. Doc. 90.*
    48 Cong., 1 sess., *Sen. Report, No. 232.*
    51 Cong., 1 sess., *Sen. Exec. Doc. 171.*
    39 Cong., 2 sess., *Sen. Report, No. 156.*
Kappler, Charles J. *Indian Affairs: Laws and Treaties.*
    Vols. I, II, 1904, Vol. III, 1913, Vol. IV, 1919, Washington.
Royce, Charles C. *Indian Land Cessions in the United States, 1896-1897.* Bureau of American Ethnology, Vol. 18, Pt. 2. Washington, 1899.
Organic Acts for the Territories of the United States. Compiled from the *Statutes at Large of the United States.* 56 Cong., 1 sess., *Sen. Doc. 148.* Washington, Government Printing Office, 1900.
Reports of the Board of Indian Commissioners. Washington.
Reports of the Secretary of the Interior, including *Annual Report of the Commissioner of Indian Affairs.* Washington.
The Territorial Papers of the United States. Ed. by Clarence E. Carter, Vols. 1-27, and John P. Bloom, Vol. 27. Washington, 1934-1962.
Treaties and Other International Acts of the United States of America, 1776-1818. Vol. 2. Ed. by Hunter Miller. Washington, 1931.
U.S., Indian Claims Commission. The Ioway Tribe of the Iowa Reservation of Oklahoma and the Iowa Tribe of Kansas and Nebraska, *et al. v.* The United States. Dockets 135, 138, 153, 158, 209, 231, 79, 79-A.
U.S. *Statutes at Large.* Vols. 7, 10, 12, 23, 24, 26, 27, 28.
Ioway Tribe of Oklahoma. *Memorial to the President, the Commissioner of Indian*

Affairs and the Congress of the United States, 1895. Copy in Gilcrease Library,
Tulsa, Oklahoma.

National Archives, Washington

Records of the Bureau of Indian Affairs. Office of Indian Affairs.
    Agencies
        Ioway Agency. Record Group 75 (M 234, R 362), 1825-1837.
        Great Nemaha Agency. Record Group 75 (M 234, R 307-314), 1837-1876.
        Upper Missouri Agency. Record Group 75 (M 234, R 833).
        Pottawatomie and Great Nemaha Agency. Federal Records Center, Kansas City,
            Missouri.
    Superintendencies
        Central Superintendency. Record Group 75 (M 234, R 55-58), 1851-1880.
        Northern Superintendency. Record Group 75, (M 234, R 598-600), 1851-1876.
        St. Louis Superintendency. Record Group 75 (M 234, R 747-756), 1824-1851.
        Wisconsin Superintendency. Record Group 75 (M 234, R 948), 1824-1851.
    Inspectors' Files.
    Segregated Treaty Files.
    Treaty Files. Miscellaneous Records.
    Records of the Office of the Secretary of War.
    Roster of Superintendents and Agents, 1849-1878.
    Choteau, Auguste Rene. *Notes of 1816.* Record Group 75. *Ancient and Miscellaneous Surveys,* Vol. 4, No. 123.
    Cherokee Commission (Jerome Commission). *Council Proceedings at Ioway Village,* May 8-20, 1890. *Indian Office Document No. 4738.* Microfilm copy, Oklahoma Historical Society Library, Oklahoma City.
    Oklahoma Historical Society, Indian Archives Division.
        Records of the Sac and Fox and Shawnee Agency. Files: Agents, Census, Councils, Courts, Federal Relations, Foreign Relations, Leases, Ioway Indians, Intruders, Per Capita, Physicians, Tonkawa Indians, and Traders. LS and LR, Sac and Fox Agency.

Miscellaneous Sources

Brown, James A. "The Prairie Peninsula, an Interaction Area in the Eastern United States." Ph.D. dissertation, University of Chicago, 1965.
Folmer, Henri. "French Expansion Toward New Mexico in the Eighteenth Century." Master's thesis, University of Denver, 1939.
McKusick, Marshall. "Oneota Long Houses." Paper presented before the Society of American Archaeologists, Annual Meeting, Norman, Oklahoma, 1971.

Newspaper Collections

Oklahoma Historical Society Newspaper Library, Oklahoma City.
    Daily Oklahoman, Daily Oklahoma State Capitol, Edmund Sun-Democrat, El Reno News, Guthrie Times Record, Indian Journal, Lexington Leader, Norman Transcript, Perkins Journal, Cleveland City Leader
Missouri Historical Society, St. Louis
    Missouri Gazette

Books, Articles, Bulletins, Memoirs, and Other Printed Sources

Abel, Annie Heloise. "Indian Reservations in Kansas and the Extinguishment of Their Title," *Transactions of the Kansas State Historical Society,* Vol. 8, 72-109.

_____. "The History of Events Resulting in Indian Consolidation West of the Mississippi River," *American Historical Association,* Vol. 1 (1906), 241-75.

Anderson, Duane. *Ioway Ethnohistory: A Review.* Part 1. *Annals of Iowa,* Vol. 41, No. 8 (Spring, 1973), 1228-41. Part 2. *Annals of Iowa,* Vol. 42, No. 1 (Summer, 1973), 41-59.

Anderson, Thomas G. "Narrative," *Collections of the State Historical Society of Wisconsin,* Vol. 9 (1882), 137-206.

Bates, Frederick. *The Life and Papers of Frederick Bates,* Vols. 1 and 2. St. Louis, Missouri Historical Society, 1962.

Biddle, Nicholas, (ed.) *Journals of Expedition of Captains Lewis and Clark.* New York, 1922. Reprinted by the Heritage Press, New York, 1962.

Black Hawk: Life of Ma-Ka-Ka-Tai-Me-She-Kia-Kiak. An Autobiography. Ed. by J. B. Patterson. Boston, 1834; St. Louis, 1882.

Blair, Emma H., trans. *Indian Tribes of the Mississippi and Great Lakes Region,* as described by Nicolas Perrot, Bacqueville de la Potherie, Morrell Marston, and Thomas Forsyth. 2 Vols. Cleveland, Arthur H. Clark Co., 1911.

Bray, Robert T. "The Flynn Cemetery: An Orr Focus Oneota Burial Site in Allamakee County," *Journal of the Iowa Archeological Society,* Vol. 10, No. 4 (April, 1961), 15-25.

Bushnell, David I. *Villages of the Algonquian, Siouan and Caddoan Tribes West of the Mississippi.* Washington, Smithsonian Institution, Bureau of American Ethnology, Bull. No. 77 (1922).

Caldwell, Dorothy J. "The Big Neck Affair: Tragedy and Farce on the Missouri Frontier," *Missouri Historical Review,* Vol. 64, No. 4 (1970), 391-412.

Callender, Charles. *Social Organization of Central Algonkian Indians.* Milwaukee Public Museum Publications in Anthropology, No. 7 (1962).

Catlin, George. *Portfolio of American Indian Painting.* London, Published by Subscription by George Catlin, Egyptian Hall, Piccadilly, 1844.

_____. *Fourteen Ioway Indians.* W. S. Johnson, Naussau-Street, SOHO, London, 1844.

_____. *Notes on Eight Years' Travels and Residence in Europe: England, France and Belgium.* 2 Vols. Octavo, Vol. 2, with numerous illustrations. 2nd ed. published by the author at his Indian Collection. 6th ed., London, Waterloo Palace, 1848.

Chapman, Berlin B. *The Otoes and Missourias.* Oklahoma City, Times Journal Publishing Company, 1965.

_____. "Dissolution of the Iowa Reservation," *Chronicles of Oklahoma,* Vol. 14 (1936), 467-77.

_____. "Establishment of the Iowa Reservation," *Chronicles of Oklahoma,* Vol. 21 (1943), 366-77.

Charlevoix, Pierre Francois Xavier de, *Journal of a Voyage to North America Undertaken by Order of the French King....* 2 Vols. Ed. by L. P. Kellogg. Chicago, Caxton Club, 1923.

Chittenden, Hiram Martin. *American Fur Trade of the Far West.* 2 Vols. Palo Alto, Stanford University Press, 1954.

Debo, Angie. *The Road to Disappearance.* Norman, University of Oklahoma Press, 1941.

De Bougainville, Louis Antoine, *Relation et Memoirs Inedits,* Paris, 1867.

De Bougainville, L. A. *Adventure in the Wilderness: The American Journals of L. A. de Bougainville, 1756-60.* Ed. and trans. by E. P. Hamilton. Norman, University of Oklahoma Press, 1964.

Delanglez, Jean. "Tonti Letters," *Mid-America,* Vol. 21, No. 3 (July, 1939).

De Smet, Rev. Pierre-Jean, S. J. *Life, Letters and Travels of Father Pierre-Jean*

De Smet, S. J. 1801-1873. 4 Vols. Ed. by H. M. Chittenden and A. T. Richardson. *Bibliography*
New York, 1905.

Donaldson, Thomas C. *The George Catlin Indian Gallery.* Smithsonian Report for 1885.Washington, Government Printing Office, 1887.

Dorsey, J. O. *A Study of Siouan Cults.* Bureau of American Ethnology, *Eleventh Annual Report.* Washington, Smithsonian Institution, 1890.

————. *Omaha Sociology.* Bureau of American Ethnology, *Third Annual Report, 1881-1882.* Washington, Smithsonian Institution, 1884.

————. *Osage Traditions.* Bureau of American Ethnology, *Sixth Annual Report,* Washington, Smithsonian Institution. 1884-1885.

————. "Siouan Sociology." Bureau of American Ethnology, *Fifteeth Annual Report,* Washington, Smithsonian Institution, 1893-1894.

————. "The Sister and Brother, an Iowa Tradition," *American Antiquarian,* Vol. 4 (1881-2).

————. "Social Organization of the Siouan Tribes," *Journal of American Folk-Lore,* Vol. 4 (1891).

Driver, Harold E. *Indians of North America.* Chicago, University of Chicago Press, 1961.

Eggan, Fred, ed. *Social Anthropology of North American Tribes.* Chicago, 1937. Revised edition, 1955.

Ewers, John C. *The Horse in Blackfoot Indian Culture.* Bureau of American Ethnology, Bull. 159. Washington, 1955.

————. "Thomas M. Easterly's Pioneer Daguerretypes of Plains Indians," *Bulletin of the Missouri Historical Society,* Vol. 24, No. 4 (1968), 331-38.

————. "Chiefs from the Missouri and Mississippi: and Peale's Silhouettes of 1806," *Smithsonian Journal of History,* Vol. 1 (1966) 1-26.

————. "Charles Bird King, Painter of Indian Visitors to the Nation's Capital," *Smithsonian Report.* Washington, (1953), 463-73.

Fenton, William N., and G. P. Kurath, *Iroquois Eagle Dance, An Offshoot of the Calumet Dance.* Bureau of American Ethnology, Bull. 156. Washington, Smithsonian Institution, 1953.

Foreman, Carolyn T. "The Choctaw Academy," *Chronicles of Oklahoma,* Vol. 9 (1931), 382-411; Vol. 10 (1932), 77-114.

Fortier, Alcée. *A History of Louisiana.* 4 Vols. New York, 1904.

Fowler, M. L. "Northern Mississippi Valley, Notes and News." *American Antiquity,* Vol. 22, No. 4, Pt. 1, 440.

Fulton, A. R. *The Red Men of Iowa.* Des Moines, Mills and Company, 1888.

Garraghan, G. J., S. J., *The Jesuits of the Middle United States.* 3 Vols. New York, America Press, 1938.

Gayerré, Charles. *History of Louisiana.* 4 Vols. New Orleans, A. Hawkins, 1885.

Giraud, Marcel, "Étienne Véniard de Bourgmont's Exact Description of Louisiana," *Missouri Historical Society Bulletin,* Vol. 15, No. 1 (October, 1958), 3-19.

Griffin, James B. "A Hypothesis for the Prehistory of the Winnebago," *Culture in History, Essays in Honor of Paul Radin.* New York, 1960.

————. *Archaeology of the Eastern United States.* Chicago, University of Chicago Press, 1952.

Gunnerson, Dolores, *The Jicarilla Apache.* DeKalb, University of Northern Illinois Press, 1975.

Hagan, William T. *American Indians.* Chicago, University of Chicago Press, 1961.

————. *The Sac and Fox Indians.* Norman, University of Oklahoma Press, 1958.

Halpenny, Francess, and Andre Vachon (eds.), *Dictionary of Canadian Biography,* Vol. 1 (1966) Ed. by G. W. Brown and Marcel Trudeau. Vol. 2 (1969) Ed. by David Hayne and Andre Vachon. Toronto, University of Toronto Press.

Hamilton, William, "Autobiography of Rev. William Hamilton," *Transcriptions and Reports.* Nebraska State Historical Society, Vol. 1 (1885), 60-75.

Hamilton, William, and S. M. Irvin. *An Ioway Grammar.* Ioway and Sac Mission Press, Kansas, 1848.

343

Harmon, George Dewey. *Sixty Years of Indian Affairs.* Chapel Hill, University of North Carolina Press, 1941.

Henning, Dale. "Oneota Ceramics in Iowa," *Journal of the Iowa Archaeological Society,* No. 11 (1961).

————. "Oneota Culture in the Prairie Peninsula, *Development and Interrelationships of Oneota Culture in the Lower Missouri Valley,*" *Missouri Archaeologist,* No. 32 (1970), Chap. 7.

Hodge, Frederick Webb, ed. *Handbook of American Indians North of Mexico.* 2 Vols. Bureau of American Ethnology, Bull. No. 30. Washington, 1907.

Hoffhaus, Charles E. "Fort de Cavagnial, Imperial Fort in Kansas 1744-1764," *Kansas Historical Quarterly,* Vol. 30, No. 4 (Winter, 1964), 425-54.

Houck, Louis. *Spanish Regime in Missouri.* Vols. 1 and 2. Chicago, R. R. Donnelley & Sons, 1909.

Hyde, George E. *Indians of the Woodlands to 1725.* Norman, University of Oklahoma Press, 1962.

Irvin, Samuel M. The Waw-ru-haw-a, the Decline and Fall of Indian Superstitions," Philadelphia, Presbyterian Historical Society, 1871.

Jackson, Donald, ed. *The Journals of Zebulon Montgomery Pike.* Vols. 1 and 2. Norman, University of Oklahoma Press, 1966.

Jackson, William H. "Descriptive Catalogue of Photographs of North American Indians." *U.S. Geological Survey of the Territories,* Misc. Pub., No. 9 (1877).

James, Edwin, ed. *Account of an Expedition from Pittsburgh to the Rocky Mountains Performed in the Years 1819, 1820...* Vols. XIV-XVII, R. G. Thwaites Early Western Travels, Cleveland, Arthur H. Clark Co., 1904-1907.

Johnson, Sir William H. *The Papers of Sir William Johnson.* Vols. 1-12. Prepared by the Division of Archives and History, University of New York, Albany, 1921.

Kearny, Stephen Watts. "Journals." *Missouri Historical Society Collections,* Vol. 3, No. 1 (1908), 8-29; Vol. 35, No. 2, 99-131.

Kellogg, Louise Phelps. "The Fox Indians During the French Regime," *Proceedings of the State Historical Society of Wisconsin* (1908).

————. *The French Regime in Wisonsin and the Northwest.* Madison, State Historical Society of Wisconsin, 1925.

Keys, Charles R. "Iowa Prehistoric Cultures, *Palimpsest,* Vol. 32, No. 8 (1951), 323-45.

Kinnaird, Laurence. *Spain in the Mississippi Valley.* American Historical Association Annual Report, Vols. 1, 2, 3. Washington, 1945.

Kurz, Rudolph Frederick. *Journal of Rudolph Frederick Kurz, 1846-1852.* Ed. by J. N. B. Hewitt. Bureau of American Ethnology Bull. No. 115. Washington, 1937.

Bénard de La Harpe, Jean-Baptiste. *Journal Historique de l'Etablissement des Francais à la Louisiane.* Ed. by A.-L. Boimare. New Orleans and Paris, Hector Bossange, 1831.

Le Page du Pratz, Antoine M. *The History of Louisiana.* London, Beckett, 1744. Reprint, New Orleans, J. S. W. Harmanson, 1947.

Lewis, Meriwether, and William Clark. *History of the Expedition under the Command of Lewis and Clark.* 4 Vols. Ed. by Elliot Coues. New York, 1893.

————. *Original Journals of the Lewis and Clark Expedition 1804-1806.* 8 Vols. Ed. by Reuben Gold Thwaites. New York, 1904.

Loomis, N. M. and A. P. Nasatir, ed. and trans. *Pedro Vial and the Roads to Santa Fe.* Norman, University of Oklahoma Press, 1967.

Lowie, Robert H. *Indians of the Plains.* American Museum of Natural History, Anthropology Handbook No. 1. New York, McGraw-Hill, 1954.

Long, Stephen H. *James Account of Long's Expedition in Early Western Travels, 1904-1907.* Vol. 15. Ed. by R. G. Thwaites. Cleveland, Arthur H. Clark & Co.

Lyon, E. Wilson. *Louisiana in French Diplomacy, 1759-1804.* Norman, University of Oklahoma Press, 1934.

McCracken, Harold. *George Catlin and the Old Frontier.* New York, Dial Press, 1959.

McKenney, Thomas L. *Memoirs, Official and Personal: With Sketches of Travels*

Among the Northern and Southern Indians Embracing a War Excursion and Descriptions of Scenes Along the Western Borders. Vols. 1 and 2. New York, Paine & Burgess, 1846.

McKenney, Thomas L., and James Hall. *The Indian Tribes of North America.* 3 Vols. Edinburgh, John Grant, 31 George IV Bridge, 1933-4.

McKusick, Marshall. *The Grant Oneota Village.* Report 4. Iowa City, Office of State Archeologist, University of Iowa, 1971.

Mahan, Bruce E. *Old Fort Crawford and the Frontier.* Iowa City, University of Iowa Press, 1926.

Margry, Pierre. *Découvertes et établissements des Francais dans l'Ouest et dans le sud de l'Amérique Septentrionale (1614-1754). Mémoires et documents originaux.* 6 Vols. Paris, Imprimerie D. Jonast, 1886.

Maximillian, Prince of Wied. *Travels in the Interior of North America, 1832-1834.* Vols. 22, 23, and 24. R. G. Thwaites ed., *Early Western Travels 1748-1846.* Cleveland, Arthur H. Clark Co., 1904-1907.

Meriwether, David. *My Life in the Mountains and the Plains.* Norman, University of Oklahoma Press, 1965.

Meyer, W. Roy. "The Iowa Indians, 1836-1885," *Kansas Historical Quarterly,* Vol. 28, No. 3 (1962), 273-300.

Miner, W. H. *The Iowa.* Cedar Rapids, The Torch Press, 1911.

Morgan, Henry Lewis. *Ancient Society.* Chicago, Charles H. Kerr & Co., 1909.

————. *The League of the Iroquois.* Rochester, 1851; New York, 1862; New York, Corinth Books, 1962.

————. *Systems of Consanguinity and Affinity.* Smithsonian Contributions to Knowledge. Vol. 17. Washington, Smithsonian Institution, 1871.

Morse, Jedidiah, Rev. *A Report to the Secretary of War of the United States on Indian Affairs.* New Haven, S. Converse, 1822.

Mott, Frank Luther, "The Pronunciation of the Word Iowa," *Iowa Journal of History and Politics,* Vol. 23, No. 3 (1925), 353-62.

Mott, Mildred. "The Relation of Historic Indian Tribes to Archaeological Manifestations in Iowa." *Iowa Journal of History and Politics,* Vol. 36, No. 3 (1938), 227-314.

Murdock, George P. "Ethnograpic Atlas," *Ethnology,* Vol. 1, No. 1 (1962); Vol. 2, No. 2 (1963); Vol. 4, No. 2 (1965); Vol. 6, No. 2 (1967), Pittsburgh.

Nasatir, A. P. *Before Lewis and Clark.* 2 Vols. St. Louis, St. Louis Historical Documents Foundation, 1952.

————. "Ducharme's Invasion of Missouri," *Missouri Historical Review,* Vol. 24, No. 1 (1929), 3-25; Vol. 24, No. 2 (1930), 238-60.

————. "Anglo Spanish Frontier on the Upper Mississippi," *Iowa Journal of History and Politics,* Vol. 29, No. 2 (1931), 155-232.

————. "Anglo Spanish Rivalry in the Iowa Country," *Iowa Journal of History and Politics,* Vol. 28, No. 3 (1930), 337-89.

————. "The Anglo Spanish Frontier in the Illinois Country During the American Revolution 1779-1783," *Journal of the Illinois Historical Society,* Vol. 21, No. 3 (1928-1929), 291-358.

Nute, Grace Lee. "Posts in the Minnesota Fur Trading Area, 1660-1855," *Minnesota History,* Vol. 11, No. 4 (1930).

O'Callaghan, E. B. (ed.). *Documents Relative to the Colonial History of the State of New York: Procured in Holland, England and France.* 15 Vols. Albany, 1856-1877.

Oglesby, Richard E. *Manuel Lisa and the Opening of the Missouri Fur Trade.* Norman, University of Oklahoma Press, 1963.

Oliver, Symmes C. "Ecology and Cultural Continuity as Contributing Factors in the Social Organization of the Plains Indians." *American Archaeology and Ethnology,* University of California, Vol. 48, No. 1 (1962).

Peattie, D. C. (ed.). *Audubon's American, the Narratives and Experiences of John James Audubon.* Boston, Houghton Mifflin Co., 1940.

Perrin du Lac, M. Francois Marie. *Traveles Through the Two Louisianas, and Among the Savage Nations of the Missouri.* Vol. 6 of *A Collection of Modern and Contem-*

porary Voyages and Travels. London, 1807.

Perrot, Nicolas. *Memoire sur les moeurs, Coutumes et Religion des Sauvages de l'Amérique Septentrionale.* Ed. by Father Jules Tailhan. Paris, 1864.

Peterson, William J. "Ioways Bid Farewell," *Palimpsest,* Vol. 19, No. 10 (1938), 397-400.

Phillips, Paul Chrisler, and J. W. Smurr, *The Fur Trade.* 2 Vols. Norman, University of Oklahoma Press, 1961.

Pike, Zebulon Montgomery. *The Expedition of Zebulon Montgomery Pike to Headwaters of the Mississippi River, Through Louisiana Territory, and in New Spain, During the Years 1805-6-7.* 3 Vols. Ed. by Elliot Coues. New York, Francis P. Harper, 1895.

_____. *The Journals of Zebulon Montgomery Pike.* Ed. by Donald Jackson. Norman, University of Oklahoma Press, 1966.

Plank, Pryor. "The Iowas and Sac and Fox Mission and Its Missionaries, Rev. Samuel M. Irvin and Wife." *Transactions of the Kansas State Historical Society,* Vol. 10 (1908), 312-25.

Prucha, Francis P. *American Indian Policy in the Formative Years. The Indian Trade and Intercourse Acts, 1790-1834.* Cambridge, Harvard University Press, 1962.

Quaife, Milo Milton (ed.). *The Western Country in the 17th Century.* Memoirs of Antoine Lamothe Cadillac and Pierre Liette. Citadel Press, New York, 1962.

Radin, Paul. *The Winnebago Tribe,* Bureau of American Ethnology, 37th Annual Report 1915-1916 (1923), 35-550.

Ragland, Hobart D. "Missions of the Society of Friends Among the Tribes of the Sac and Fox Agency," *The Chronicles of Oklahoma,* Vol. 33, 169-82.

Richman, Irving Berdine. *Ioway to Iowa.* Iowa City, State Historical Society of Iowa, 1931.

Schoolcraft, H. R. *History and Statistical Information Respecting the History, Condition and Prospects of the Indian Tribes of the United States.* 6 Vols. Philadelphia, J. B. Lippincott & Co., 1851-1857.

_____. *Report of Rev. S. M. Irvin on Indians of Iowa and Sac Mission.* 28 Cong., 2 sess. Sen. Ex. Doc., Vol. 1 (Ser. 449).

Secoy, Frank R. *Changing Military Patterns of the Great Plains, 17th Century through Early 19th Century.* Monographs of the American Ethnological Society, Vol. 21 (1953).

Shea, John Gilmary. *Discovery and Exploration of the Mississippi Valley with the Original Narratives of Marquette, Allouez, Membre, Hennepin and Anastase Douay.* New York, Redfield, Clinton Hall, 1852.

Shea, John Gilmary (ed.). *Early Voyages Up and Down the Mississippi by Cavelier, St. Cosmo, Le Sueur, Gravier and Guignas.* Albany, Joel Munsell, 1861.

Sibley, H. H. "Memoir of Jean B. Faribault," *Minnesota Historical Society Collections,* Vol. 3 (1880), 168-79.

Skinner, Alanson A. "A Summer Among the Sac and Iowa Indians," *Yearbook of the Public Museum of Milwaukee,* Vol. 2 (1922), 116-22.

_____. *Ethnology of the Ioway Indians.* Public Museum of the City of Milwaukee, Bull. No. 4, Vol. 5 (1926).

_____. *Medicine Ceremonies of the Menominees, Iowas and Wahpeton Dakota.* Indian Notes and Monographs, Museum of the American Indian, Heye Foundation, Vol. 4 (1920).

_____. "Societies of the Iowa, Kansa, and Ponca Indians," *Journal of Anthropology Papers,* American Museum of Natural History, Vol. 11 (1915), Pt. 9.

_____. "Traditions of the Iowa Indians," *Journal of American Folk-Lore,* Vol. 38 (1925), 160.

Stevens, F. E. *The Blackhawk War, Including a Review of Black Hawk's Life.* Chicago, F. E. Stevens, 1903.

Stoddard, Amos. *Sketches, Historical and Descriptive of Louisiana.* Philadelphia, M. Carey, 1812.

Surrey, N. M. M. *The Commerce of Louisiana During the French Regime, 1699-1763.*

Studies in History, Economics and Public Law, Vol. 53, No. 1. New York, Columbia University Press, 1916.

Tatum, Lawrie. *Our Red Brothers and the Peace Policy of President Ulysses S. Grant.* Philadelphia, 1899; Reprinted, Lincoln, University of Nebraska Press, 1970.

Thomas, Alfred Barnaby (ed. and trans.). *After Coronado, Spanish Exploration Northeast of New Mexico, 1697-1727.* Norman, University of Oklahoma Press, 1935.

Thoreau, Henry. *People, Principles, and Politics.* Ed. by Milton Meltzer. New York, Hill and Wang, 1963.

Thwaites, Reuben Gold (ed.). *Early Western Travels, 1748-1846.* 32 Vols. Cleveland, Arthur H. Clark Co., 1904-1907.

_____. *Jesuit Relations and Allied Documents, Travels and Explorations of the Jesuit Missionaries in New France, 1610-1791.* 73 Vols. New York, Pagent Book Co., 1959.

Tucker, Sara Jones. *Indian Villages of the Illinois Country,* Vol. 2, Pt. 1. Scientific Papers, Illinois State Museum. Springfield, Atlas, 1942.

Van der Zee, Jacob. "Forts in the Iowa Country," *Iowa Journal of History and Politics,* Vol. 12, No. 2 (1914).

_____. "The French Discovery and Exploration of the Eastern Iowa Country before 1763," *Iowa Journal of History and Politics,* Vol. 12, No. 3 (1914).

_____. "French Expedition Against the Sac and Fox Indians in the Iowa Country, 1734-1735," *Iowa Journal of History and Politics,* Vol. 12, No. 2 (1914).

_____. "Fur Trade Operations in the Eastern Ioway Country from 1800 to 1833," *Iowa Journal of History and Politics,* Vol. 12, No. 4 (1914), 496.

_____. "Fur Trade Operations in the Eastern Iowa Country under the Spanish Regime." *Iowa Journal of History and Politics,* Vol. 12, No. 3 (1914).

_____. "George Hunt's Narrative, in Old Fort Madison: Some Source Materials," *Iowa Journal of History and Politics,* Vol. 11 (1913), 517-45.

Villiers, Baron Marc de. *Le Découverte de Missouri et L'Histoire du Fort D'Orleans 1673-1728.* Paris, Librairie Ancienne Honoré Champion, 1925.

Washburn, Wilcomb E. *The Indian and the Whiteman, Government Relations.* Garden City, Documents in American Civilization Series, 1964.

Wedel, Mildred Mott. "Oneota Sites on the Upper Iowa River," *The Missouri Archaeologist,* Vol. 21 (December, 1959).

_____. "Indian Villages on the Upper Iowa River," *Palimpsest,* Vol. 47, No. 12 (1961), 561-92.

_____. "The Iowa Indians," *Handbook of North American Indians, Indians of the Plains,* rev. ed. Washington, Smithsonian Institution, in press.

_____. "Le Sueur and the Dakota Sioux," *Aspects of Upper Great Lakes Anthropology.* Ed. by Elden Johnson. St. Paul, Minnesota Historical Society, 1974.

_____. "Ethnohistory: Its Payoffs and Pitfalls for Iowa Archeologists," *Journal of the Iowa Archeological Society,* Vol. 23 (1976), 1-44.

_____. "A Synonymy of Names for the Ioway Indians," *Journal of the Iowa Archeological Society,* Vol. 25 (1978), 49-77.

Wedel, Waldo R. *An Introduction to Kansas Archeology.* Bureau of American Ethnology, Bull. 174. Washington, 1959.

_____. *Prehistoric Man on the Great Plains.* Norman, University of Oklahoma Press, 1961.

Wharton, Clifton, "The Expedition of Major Clifton Wharton in 1844," *Collections of the Kansas State Historical Society,* Vol. 16 (1923-1925), 272-305.

White, Leslie A. (ed.). *Lewis Henry Morgan: The Indian Journals, 1859-62.* Ann Arbor, University of Michigan Press, 1959.

White, R. H. (ed.). *Messages of the Governors of Tennessee.* 4 Vols. Nashville, Tennessee Historical Commission, 1952.

Whitman, William. "Origin Legends of the Oto," *Journal of American Folk-Lore,* Vol. 51 (1938), 173, 205.

_____. *The Oto.* New York, Columbia University Press, 1937.

————. "Descriptive Grammar of Ioway-Oto," *International Journal of American Linguistics,* Vol. 13 (1947), 233-48.

Wistrand-Robinson, Lila *et al. Otoe and Iowa Indian Language.* 2 Vols. Park Hill, Oklahoma, Christian Chrildren's Fund American Indian Project, 1978.

Wright, Muriel. *A Guide to the Indian Tribes of Oklahoma.* Norman, University of Oklahoma Press, 1951.

Index

Abnaki Indians: at Fort St. Louis, 19; at San Luis, 81

Accault, Michel (French trader to Ioways): 18, 23

Agencies, of the Ioways: Ioway Sub Agency, 149-50, 195; Great Nemaha Agency, 168, 171, 188, 199, 200, 202, 241, 288; Sac and Fox Agency, Indian Territory, 287; Otoe Agency, Indian Territory, 307

Agents, Indian: 62, 96, 111, 117, 119-20, 130, 131, 133, 143, 145, 149-50, 195, 215-16, 245, 248-49, 260, 266, 287-89, 291-92, 299-300, 304-306, 308, 313, 314; trader-agent collusion, 195, 196, 313-14; new laws on agent-trader relationship, 198; power extended, 198, 262; fraud and swindles of, 250, 260-63, 271; and Thomas Lightfoot, 270-72

Agent-trader-Indian relationship in 1830s: 194-99

Agriculture, Ioway: 10-12, 26, 57, 114, 118, 133-34, 148-49, 154, 171, 188, 248-51, 275, 292, 306; and new techniques, 226-27; and land sales, 250; failure of experimental farms, 250-51

Aguilar, Alonso Rael de: 30

Aiaouese: *see* Ioway Indians

Aiauways: *see* Ioway Indians

Aiouas: *see* Ioway Indians

Albin, W. M. (Superintendent of Indian Affairs): 260-63

Alcohol, Indian use of: 56, 112, 118-20, 126, 195, 197-98, 202-4, 215, 233, 242, 247-48, 291, 310

Allotment of land to individual Indians: 130-31, 279, 298, 305

Allotments: 304-6; and problems of Ioways, 306-17; in Kansas and Nebraska, 314; *see also* severalty

American colonies in late 1700's: 58, 61-63, 69

American Fur Company: 119-20, 134, 139, 151, 167, 175, 195-97, 199; complaint of, 167; charges of making spirits to trade to Indians, 203

American Revolution: 64, 69

Anderson, Thomas G. (trader): 79

André, Father Louis: 17-18

Annuities: 118, 142, 144, 148, 170, 194, 196, 204, 213-15, 237, 239-40, 242, 244-46, 248, 259, 264, 282-83, 287-89; compromise for, 216, traders' claims on, 314; spent at Guthrie, 295

Aouas: *see* Ioway Indians

349

74,; law and maintenance of order, 185-86, 193, 219, 227, 255; in 1840's, 190; chief's responsibilities, 213-14; transfers of power in, 256, 259-60, 277; under Indian Reorganization Act of 1934, 296; under Oklahoma Indian Welfare Act of 1936, 298

Tribal relations (Ioway): with Chippewas (Ojibways) 23; with Foxes, 23, 29, 33, 36, 168; with Illinois, 21-22; with Kansas (Kaws), 58, 72, 255, 307; Kickapoos, 36, 210, 276; Mascoutins, 21-22; Miamis, 23; Missourias, 58, 118; Omahas, 49, 114, 126, 130, 131, 139, 187, 188, 200-2, 239n; Osages, 58, 71, 72, 101, 103, 109, 111, 118, 141, 307; Otoes, 3, 10, 25-26, 31, 33, 37, 49, 68, 70-71, 114, 120, 126, 128, 130, 139, 187, 221, 273, 295, 307, 312; Ottawas, 23; Pawnees, 37, 92, 187, 188, 202, 221, 242, 243, 309; Peorias, 48; Piankashaws, 26; Pottawatomies, 168, 237; Poncas, 114; Sacs, 81, 103, 130, 134, 147, 151, 167, 168, 194, 201, 255; Sac and Fox, 81-82, 117, 119, 133-35, 140, 152, 159, 200, 201, 221-27; Sioux, 23-27, 31, 37, 41, 49, 114, 130, 159, 167, 187, 188, 200; Tonkawas, 289, 290

Trudeau, Lt. Gov. Don Zenon: 72-74

Ulloa, Antonio de: 49

United States government: councils with Ioways, 92, 93, 119-28, 144-49, 159; tribal delegations to Washington, 93, 141-42, 168, 246, 266, 299, 307; chiefs appointed by, 125, 202; requests denied to visit, 163, 250, 270; reduction of Ioway power, 239, 240, 242; treaty obligations, 134, 149, 163, 170, 258, 308; civilization, or acculturation, policies and procedures, 96, 154, 171, 176, 204, 226, 247-48, 250, 253-54, 275, 292; Dawes Act, 303ff. *See also* petitions of Ioways

Upper Iowa River: 7, 9, 14, 17, 21, 26, 28

Usher, J. P. (Secretary of the Interior): 258

Vanderslice, Daniel (agent): 245, 247, 249-51, 260, 263

Vanderslice, G. (Ioway): 249

Van Quackenbourne, Father, of St. Regis school: 143-44

Vasques, Gabriel Baron (agent): 143, 145

Vaudreuil, Pierre F. Rigaud de Cavagnial, Marquis de: 38, 43

Vaughn, Alfred J. (agent): 216, 245

Vetter, Joseph (Ioway): 274, 301, 304, 307

Villages (Ioway): 8, 10, 20-21, 26, 28, 33, 36, 46, 48, 49, 57, 60, 64, 83, 87, 112, 113, 117, 119, 129-30, 133, 134, 137, 149, 154-55, 158, 164, 168, 174, 176, 188-91, 241, 247, 254, 294, 305, 306

Villasur, Pedro de, expedition of 1720: 30, 34

Villiers, Nicolas Coulonde: 36

Visits (Ioway): 17-18, 143, 172, 189, 190, 200, 221, 255, 276, 293, 295, 312, 315; to La Baye, 18; to Fort San Carlos, 51; to Cahokia, 64; to George R. Clark, 65; to San Luis, 65; to and from Sacs, 185, 255; to Europe, 229ff; to and from Winnebagos, 244, 255; *see also* United States

Voi-ri-gran (Ioway chief): 92

Wachamonga (Ioway chief): 214, 221

Waiakida (Ioway soldiers and police): duties and privileges of, 219; tatooing, 220-21

Wakantas (sacred spirits of the Ioways): 192, 220, 244

Walking Rain (Ioway): 168, 215, 229

Wapacahona (Ioway chief): 240

War belts: 67

War ceremonies (Ioway): 106, 178-79, 181, 193, 242

Ward, Robert (Ioway): 273

War of 1812: 110-16, 129, 136, 202;

UNIVERSITY OF OKLAHOMA PRESS FIFTIETH ANNIVERSARY

OKLAHOMA

50

1929
1979